IELTS
READING

刘洪波 编著

雅思阅读真经

5

（机考笔试综合版）

中国人民大学出版社
· 北京 ·

编辑寄语

真的是令人难以置信，《雅思阅读真经5》在短短一个多月的时间里，就完成了书稿审读、复杂的版式和封面设计，即将付印了。这来自责任编辑每天审稿到深夜，来自作者与策划人不分昼夜的细节讨论，来自出版社对于作者和书稿质量的信任。

说到刘洪波老师，脑海里立即浮现出来的是一张曾经广泛张贴于各大高校的雅思培训海报。海报上，刘洪波老师身着白色对襟衫，剃着光头，手握长箫，神态潇洒不羁，颇有道骨仙风。如今的刘洪波老师蓄起了头发，有时也穿起了西装，更多了一份儒雅与淡定。

还记得自己当年刚刚涉足雅思备考图书策划领域，到各大书店调研时，在醒目位置总能看到《雅思阅读真经》的身影。这套图书从2004年出版《雅思阅读真经1》到2009年出版《雅思阅读真经4》，至今畅销不衰，也引来了无数的模仿者，各类雅思圣经、雅思胜经，层出不穷。然而真正能够自己出雅思阅读文章的又有几人呢？这不仅要求作者要有扎实的英文功底，博览国外经典著作，特别是学术类杂志，而且要有来自十数年雅思培训，对真题了如指掌的自信。

在沉寂数年之后，刘洪波老师终于推出了《雅思阅读真经5》。全书60多篇阅读文章，篇篇直指真题。或者是对真题追本溯源，找到文章出处进行缩编；或者是针对真题，寻找多篇满足其内容主旨的文章进行汇编，以至于我们在最后为保证一个读者能接受的、性价比最高的定价，想要删减一些内容时，60多篇文章，竟然是一篇也舍不得删。

《雅思阅读真经5》回归了《真经1》按题型编排、集中练习的形式，不仅使考生能够按题型进行强化训练，而且有效地扩大了考生的阅读量。在《雅思阅读真经5》创作的过程中，刘洪波老师更是迸发出了极大的热情和创意：所有题目都是亲自命题，以保证所有题目的命题思路和考点设计都和真实的考试高度一致；每篇文章前都有精彩导读，以激发读者的阅读兴趣；每篇文章后都有核心词汇，帮助考生理解和记忆；每篇文章后还有同义词考点，以强化考生对雅思考试核心——同义替换的学习。是的，从这本书的每一个细节里，我们都能感受到作者的良苦用心。

亲爱的读者，如果您再细心一些，注意到这本书的版式设计的话，你就会发现：60多篇文章竟然用了60多种不同的设计，字体、字号、版面都各不相同。而所有这些繁复、细致的工作，目的只有一个，那就是对雅思考试阅读真题从内容到形式最大程度上的仿真，使您对真实的雅思考试有最直观的感受。当然，也希望您能喜欢书中专门为刘洪波老师设计的卡通形象哦，呵呵。

"宝剑锋从磨砺出，梅花香自苦寒来"。《雅思阅读真经5》是作者多年集大成之作，相信也能成为读者的挚爱珍藏。刘洪波老师还专门为封面题写了书名，细观封面，您是否也感受到了一股冷月清风的江湖侠义之气？愿您手持刘洪波老师倾心打造的《真经》、《总纲》、《考点词》这三把名剑，在雅思的"江湖"中披荆斩棘，获得成功。

和和

取 经 路 上

　　教育国际化势不可挡。这种国际化的意义在于能够让更多的人汲取最先进的知识和理念，能够让更多的人开阔视野和增长见闻。无数人为此奋力奔波，希望求取真经，到达理想的彼岸。在这个过程中，语言关是最基本也是最重要的环节。

　　语言是一种载体，承载着文化交流与传承的功能。语言具有突出的民族性，因而在语言学习的过程中，最大的障碍也源自文化差异。了解和掌握每种文化的精髓所在，是语言学习中的乐趣和收获。

　　测试是一种形式。测试的内容是由应用场景提取的模型。测试的特点是科学和有效。测试的目的是为了推广和传播更多的文化概念。这就是测试文化，这就是测试科学。

　　雅思考试是一种描述性、开放式测试。每个参加考试的人均能找到对应的成绩。雅思考试分为A类和G类。A类和G类的区别在于阅读和写作。这样的测试风向标说明，出题方强调学术阅读和写作明显区别于生活文字。这样的测试风向标也说明，读写测试虽然分别进行，但是能力并进。读是输入，写是输出，正确把握，相得益彰。

　　留学生活中的阅读内容和习惯，与我们原有的阅读方式有一定差异，这是一种快节奏的学习方式，也是跨文化交流的重要内容之一。这一点非常鲜明地体现在雅思阅读考试和写作考试中。因此，在A类阅读中，会有大量科普文章，在G类阅读中会强调实用文字。A类写作强调学术写作模式，G类写作更侧重语言实用场景。

　　刘洪波老师被誉为雅思教父，用他多方面的才华，用他丰富的人生阅历，用他对教育的热情和对事业的不倦追求，对雅思培训作出了三大卓越贡献：

　　（1）开创了真经流派。这是一种革命性流派。这种流派强调要使用有针对性的素材，进行有针对性的训练，要让分数和学习能力并进。雅思考试追求一种公平性。真经流派，通过阅读有效素材，可以减少背景差异所产生的起跑不公平，使得雅思考试对语言的测试更为准确和公平。这对雅思考试本身是一种推进。真经流派营造了读写并进的大环境，对整个英语学习也是重要推动。

　　（2）开创了说文解字法。这是一种强调语言综合能力的学习方法。讲文章、讲文化、解记忆、解用法，降低"母语"和"非母语"学习者之间的文化差异，提高单词的记忆效果和使用水平。让输入型学习直接促进输出型考试，是读写并进的基础。有助于考试英语底蕴的整体提升。

　　（3）精解、浓缩、简化雅思写作真经。这是一种快速提升写作能力的方法，是国内第一套基于官方评分标准研发的写作理论，完全符合A、G类不同的测试方向和评判标准，也是读写并进理念的科学成果。

　　我在2000年参加雅思考试，2001年接触雅思图书出版，2004年认识刘洪波老师。那个时候，已经知道他在澳洲的神奇经历（11次雅思考试，无数个案辅导案例，上百种工作体验，几经波澜的求学和求职经历，见即将出版的《留学super之路》）。8年后，与刘老师首次合作，受益良多，对事业的理解，对教育的感受都有实质性的提高和变化。"取经"，也是实践人生理想，求取事业真经。我对他的阅历概括成三个形象，分别是benben，harvey和bobo。

为学业——
生活而奋斗！

BEN

代表当年在澳大利亚的刘洪波。那个时候，他跟现在的所有考生一样，从备考，到留学，要适应海外生活。青春，是一种独一无二的资本，才华源于勤奋和天赋。就他个人而言，他真心支持所有的留学生。勇于求学，是一种热情真实的人生态度。

我要——
做一名好老师！

HARVEY

代表刚刚出版《雅思阅读真经》的他。作为国内第一本阅读的真题还原，书中展示了他的天赋和阅历，展示了他对雅思的深刻理解和对教学的无比自信。此后，他不断修缮这个概念，不断沉淀，不断积累，让他的"真经流派"更为扎实和深厚。

我要——
让每一个学生考高分！

BOBO

是开始涉足网络教育的他。开微博，讲网课，远程辐射，全球推广。零距离贴近考生，也真实展现自我。师者，传道、授业、解惑也。一路伴随考生，工作和生活都平添无限自豪。

　　这套书共3本，《雅思阅读真经5（机考笔试综合版）》中的60篇主体文章采用了60种视觉处理方式，囊括剑桥所有的阅读展现形式；《剑桥雅思阅读考点词真经（机考笔试综合版）》设置"一书多用"的方式，在分项讲解词汇之后，设置"九宫格"总表，可以分纵横两种顺序进行记忆，避免出现位置记忆。精雕细琢，煞费苦心。《雅思阅读真经总纲（机考笔试综合版）》凝练精华，文采飞扬。谁站在文化的最前沿，谁就能引领教育的方向；谁站在科技的最前沿，谁就能开启学习之光。

　　就整个《雅思阅读真经5》而言，迄今为止包括三个版本：

　　版本1：《雅思阅读真经5》，这是最初的版本，强调分题型训练，问世之后，在各大书城排行榜雄踞榜首。

　　版本2：《雅思阅读真经5（剑10版）》，后出版的《剑10》选用了跟"真经5"同题材的文章，所以不得已改版。加入新题库中文章，进一步完善考点设计。

　　版本3：《雅思阅读真经5（机考笔试综合版）》，是学为贵教育在广泛汲取全球考试经验的基础上，对考点设计和考试形式的完善和发展。

磨剑三尺雪，前途怎可寻？但得真经在，一战定乾坤。

雅思真经群号：284587791（本群提供关于真经系列图书的相关答疑）

雅思真经1：283347399（满）

雅思真经2：137869797

吕蕾公众微信号：lvlei1973

吕蕾微博：http://weibo.com/lvlei1973

吕蕾博客：http://blog.sina.com.cn/wonderfullei

喜马拉雅电台：吕蕾1973

心藏三剑，笑谈雅思

十多年磨了三名剑，希望能帮你轻松征服雅思阅读。

三名剑

▲ 太阿剑——《雅思阅读真经总纲》

王道威严之剑，相传为秦皇佩剑，秉天意而扫六合八荒。《雅思阅读真经总纲》精论阅读方法、各题型技巧和官方命题思路总结，堂皇应对天下所有剑桥雅思真题。本书包含了剑桥雅思真题答案的概率统计列表，提出了"首题不蒙NG，末题不蒙False"的口号；公开了Heading题的三份简化图解；总结了"天下间所有的阅读题只有一种命题思路"；传授了独孤九剑的总纲："无招胜有招"。这是我个人的雅思阅读方法论和课堂讲义笔记精华所在。

▲ 鱼肠剑——《剑桥雅思阅读考点词真经》

刺客精准之剑，刺客专诸闻吴王有鱼炙之好，往太湖边习烤鱼之术，藏剑于鱼，鱼美而刃锋，成功击杀吴王僚，一剑改乾坤。《剑桥雅思阅读考点词真经》很神奇，列出了《剑桥雅思》每道阅读题和原文的考点同义词设计。你可以看到resemble这个词被《剑4》、《剑7》、《剑8》同时考到；fertiliser一词在《剑7》中就考了两次。这本词汇书让你透过命题者华丽的外衣直视最原始的考点隐藏设计。这本书的考点清单部分考生能一天看完一遍，相当于做完了《剑桥雅思4—8》这5本书的所有阅读题目，是雅思考前图穷匕见之必备斩首利器。

▲ 赤霄剑——《雅思阅读真经5》

宏志定鼎之剑。汉高祖使之斩白蛇，出身微末而身登大宝。望诸君提三尺赤霄立不世之基业，心想而事成。

《雅思阅读真经》的历史

公元2004年5月，中国第一本以雅思考试真题题库机经为素材研发的教材《雅思阅读真经》出版，接连命中考题。一石千浪，跟风者众，从此开创了真题题库和考试机经的教材流派。

其作者被媒体誉为雅思教父。

2005年，《雅思阅读真经2》出版。

2007年，《雅思阅读真经3》出版。

2009年，《雅思阅读真经4》出版。

2011年，作者应邀赴英国剑桥大学雅思命题机构考察交流。

2012年，《雅思阅读真经5》出版。

2015年，《剑桥雅思全真模拟试题集10》出版，因与《雅思阅读真经5》考点相同，《雅思阅读真经5》升级为《雅思阅读真经5（剑10版）》。

《雅思阅读真经5》的特点

1. 题库背景

雅思阅读考试的文章来自国外的学术类杂志。我们通过考试机经回忆尽可能找到考试文章的出处。比如"选择与幸福"一文，我确定考试文章改编自2004年4月 *Scientific American* 中 "The Tyranny of Choice" 一文。原文12 000字左右，雅思命题者将其缩编为1 000字左右。在2008年8月13日和2011年7月30日考到。我根据考试回忆确定重点，也缩编至1 000字上下。

有的直接出处找不到，就找到多篇满足机经重点的文章进行融合汇编。

也有的来源比较神秘。比如本书最后一套题，正好对应2010年9月4日考试。

最花时间的就是找文章和汇编了。经常要读十几篇才能选出一篇或两篇中意的。好处是自己的英文阅读能力再次大大提升，了解众多百科知识。有时甚至爱上了查找阅读资料，觉得昨天的自己是多么孤陋寡闻啊！居然不知道巧克力的历史，不知道大名鼎鼎的伏尼契手稿，不知道厄尔尼诺的起因。曾一度感悟"一日不读书，面目可憎"的心境。接着好奇为什么考生讨厌雅思阅读。

2. 题型集训

为叙述方便，《雅思阅读真经》下简称《真经》。

《真经5》回归到《真经1》的题型集训。

其实我喜欢《真经1》的题型集中练习，事实也证明学习效果很好。《真经2—4》为了弥补当时真题的不足，我按真实考试中的3篇一套题安排，以便考生模考。时至2013年剑桥雅思已经出版了《剑4—9》，2015年出版《剑10》。考生其实已经不缺整套题的真题模考，反而按题型编排的强化训练教材是市场空白。

《真经5》因此而生。

今天的升级也是为了让这一理念更完美。

3. 真题考点

如果说上面两点还可以被模仿的话，下面这个特点却很难被复制——《真经5》中单项题型训练的题目全部由我自己命题，没有任何外教参与。这样我可以承诺本书命题思路和考点设计和剑桥雅思高度一致。举例证明。

例1：《真经5》【管理学之父】

题目：A term Drucker <u>first used</u> to represent future workers

原文：He saw the need for a new name for workers and so he <u>coined</u> one himself that is in common usage today. The word is "knowledge worker" and...

《剑桥雅思7》第21页第13题

题目：The word "echolocation" was <u>first used</u> by someone working as a _____.

原文：The American zoologist Donald Griffin, who was largely responsible for the discovery of sonar in bats, <u>coined</u> the term "echolocation" to...

《剑桥雅思5》第73页第31题

题目：where the expression AI was <u>first used</u>

原文：The field was launched, and the term "artificial intelligence" <u>coined</u>, at a conference in 1956...

考点为coin作动词指"造词，创造"，同义表达为first use。

这属于考点词设计一致。

例2：《真经5》【莫尔斯电码】

True/False/Not Given判断

Mose donated his money to the school he once attended.

《剑桥雅思8》第25页第24题

True/False/Not Given判断

Class F airspace is airspace which is below 365m and not near airports.

这两道题看似没有关联，其实命题思路完全一致。你做一做，再对比一下就明白了。这是雅思考试中True题命题思路中最难的一种。每本《剑桥雅思》只出一题，意味着考四次雅思才会碰到一个这种命题，属于区分8分和9分水平的题。

这属于命题思路设计一致。

所以《真经5》远远超越了我以前编著的《真经1—4》。毕竟，那时候剑桥公开的真题太少，不易对比、归纳、总结。而且那时的我还年轻，没有把《剑桥雅思》每本讲个几十遍。某一天我忽然恍然大悟，发现了它最本质的东西。（比如后来我才开始统计所有剑桥真题答案的概率，提出了True/False/Not Given中"首题少选NG，末题少选False"的口号，并首次应用在《真经5》里。）

《真经5》中还有很多暗合剑桥真题的特点，留待考生慢慢去发现，就像寻找达·芬奇密码，会很有意思的。

亲爱的考生，当你某一天能把《真经5》中的大部分题目和《剑桥雅思》系列题目从命题思路上一一对应的时候，就说明你已把握了雅思阅读最本质的秘密。上考场拿高分，易如反掌观纹。

4. 词汇注释

但我担心你们发现这些重要的东西太慢，就在每篇文章后直接把雅思阅读考点词给你们列出来了；我担心你们背单词没兴趣，就注解了一些有趣的单词；我担心你们阅读长篇英语文章没兴趣，又在每篇文章前加了一个小小的中文导读，希望能引起你的好奇。

好多创意都是第一次出现在英语教材中的，不知效果如何。如好，我会坚持，也欢迎今后其他阅读教材效仿。

《雅思阅读真经5》使用建议

最初写这本书的目的是给贵学教育作雅思基础段内部教材用的，不准备公开出版，因为盗版抄袭太厉害。

所以，《真经5》适合基础薄弱的雅思考生。从每一种题型学起，结合文章记忆单词，熟悉同义考点词等，为将来做整套《剑桥雅思》真题打基础。

同时，由于《真经5》收录文章的特点，它又适合那些已经做完《剑桥雅思》系列、期待预测押题的考生。建议考生选择重点练习自己的薄弱题型，然后认真记忆每篇文章后面附的考点词。

随便聊聊

回首数数，我磨过的剑有很多。就雅思阅读和词汇来说，我能记得出版过的有：《雅思阅读真经》、《雅思阅读真经2》、《雅思阅读真经1&2》、《雅思阅读真经3》、《雅思阅读真经4》、《雅思阅读经典教程》、《雅思阅读基础教程》、《雅思词汇6.5+》、《雅思词汇5.5+》、《剑桥雅思阅读单词速记》、《雅思G类阅读教程》等等。所以，不是随便磨一剑就叫"名剑"的。你看我磨了这十几剑之后，现在才敢小心翼翼地吆喝一句："工欲善其事，必先利其器。客官，想看名剑么？"

如果你已拥有《真经5》，我不建议再购买《真经1—4》。我从《真经1—4》中抽调了部分近年活跃度很高的文章重新命题后，收录到了《真经5》里。

至今，我最得意的书是《英文字根词源精讲》，超神器。可惜能欣赏的人不多。《真经5》的单词注释中，字根、词源、有趣的故事等，都抽调自该书。那些年拼命看拉丁文，如今注解轻松了。

《真经5》中如有难题疑问和建议请在微博上与我交流。

我有雅思听说读写四节免费的公开课在网上流传，考生也称为雅思教父四大讲座，"考鸭"必修课。要听，这是我送给全国考生们的礼物。（请登录school.guixue.com听课）

很多城市有培训机构用我的名字和北京雅思品牌开设培训班，低劣的教学质量浪费了学员的精力和时间，深感抱歉。因为"刘洪波"没注册，而"北京雅思"是特殊名词，也注册不了，所以我创立了贵学教育，北京雅思和北京托福都成为贵学教育的子品牌。请登录贵学教育官网：www.guixue.com核实该培训机构是否隶属于贵学教育旗下真正的北京雅思分校。

致谢

感谢我的学生和读者。本书的面世要重点感谢吕蕾女士。感谢她的不断敦促和鼓励，让我以前所未有的热情和执著完成本书。

在本书的编写过程中，赵小锐、刘畅、谭乐、刘娟、付晓楠、田杨、冯涛、成岩、程玲、李慧芳、刘素良、焦磊、柏立明、焦鸿、曹爱丽、张靖娴、袁伟、李海静、刘伟、杨志、贾玉梅、李悦、张璐、焦丽娜、尚莉、袁乐、邓素娟、殷博、戚旗、史策、范欣南、张儒雅、胡瑞青、沈小燕、张强、董哲羽、何运娟、陈星樵、高尚勇、冯鑫、李前领也参与了资料收集及部分编写工作，在此一并感谢。

刘洪波公众微信号：liuhongbo-guixue

刘洪波微博：http://weibo.com/lhbgx

刘洪波博客：http://blog.sina.com.cn/lhbgx

刘洪波

2015年5月于北京

《真经5》与历年真题配对统计表

序号	题型	文章名称	考试时间
Reading Passage 1		The Refrigerator 冰箱的发明	2012-09-22……
Reading Passage 2		Alfred Nobel 诺贝尔奖	2011-04-30，2012-08-04 ……
Reading Passage 3		Lost Giant: Mammoth 猛犸象	2011-08-13，2012-08-04， 2014-05-10……
Reading Passage 4		Tasmanian Tigers 塔斯马尼亚虎	2011-03-05，2013-03-09 ……
Reading Passage 5		The Lost Continent 柏拉图与亚特兰蒂斯	……
Reading Passage 6		Clarence Saunders 超市起源	2009-12-03，2012-02-25 ……
Reading Passage 7	Summary 单词填写题	Fraud in Science 学术欺骗	2012-01-12……
Reading Passage 8		Graffiti: Street Art or Crime 涂鸦争议	2011-09-15，2011-12-17， 2012-08-25，2014-12-06……
Reading Passage 9		Ancient Money 古代钱币	2012-05-10，2014-01-18 ……
Reading Passage 10		Talc Powder 滑石粉	2010-03-06，2013-01-05 ……
Reading Passage 11		Soviet's New Working Week 苏联工作制	2009-02-07，2012-07-21 ……
Reading Passage 12		Spectacular Saturn 土星	2010-01-14……
Reading Passage 13		Thomas Young 托马斯·杨	2010-11-20……
Reading Passage 14		Yawn 哈欠研究	2010-10-09，2012-09-22 ……
Reading Passage 15		A Brief History of Chocolate 巧克力的历史	2012-08-25……
Reading Passage 16	True/False/Not Given 句子理解判断题	Morse Code 莫尔斯电码	2009-12-03，2012-06-09 ……
Reading Passage 17		Torch Relay 奥运火炬传递	2009-03-07，2010-02-27， 2012-02-04……
Reading Passage 18		The Voynich Manuscript 伏尼契手稿	2009-06-27，2012-05-19 ……

续前表

序号	题型	文章名称	考试时间
Reading Passage 19	True/False/Not Given 句子理解判断题	Bondi Beach 悉尼邦戴海滩	2011-02-19，2012-10-20 ……
Reading Passage 20		The Dutch Tulip Mania 荷兰郁金香危机	2010-04-24，2011-07-30 ……
Reading Passage 21		The Benefits of Bamboo 竹子的好处	2009-04-25，2010-03-06， 2011-07-09，2013-09-12……
Reading Passage 22		Chinese Yellow Citrus Ant for Biological Control 蚂蚁防虫	2007-09-01，2011-06-23 ……
Reading Passage 23		Animal Self-medication 动物自疗	2009-09-12，2011-01-15， 2012-01-07，2014-03-13……
Reading Passage 24		Rapid, Urban and Flexible RUF 双模交通	2010-12-18……
Reading Passage 25		Self-esteem Myth 谈自尊	2009-03-05……
Reading Passage 26		William Gilbert and Magnetism 吉尔伯特与磁场	2010-08-05，2012-09-06 ……
Reading Passage 27	Paragraph Heading 段落中心思想题	Pearls 珍珠	2009-08-22，2014-02-15 ……
Reading Passage 28		Temperaments and Communication Styles 性格与人际关系	2010-04-10……
Reading Passage 29		E-book 电子书	2009-04-04，2010-09-11 ……
Reading Passage 30		Self-marketing 自我营销	……
Reading Passage 31		Maps and Atlas 地图册	2010-11-06，2012-04-14 ……
Reading Passage 32		Dyes and Pigments 染料和颜料	……
Reading Passage 33		TV Addiction 电视瘾	2009-04-25，2010-09-25 ……
Reading Passage 34		Medieval Toys and Childhood 中世纪玩具	……

续前表

序号	题型	文章名称	考试时间
Reading Passage 35	Matching 信息匹配题	Orientation of Birds 鸟类定向	2010-07-31，2012-05-10 ……
Reading Passage 36		Liar Detector 测谎仪	2009-03-21，2010-01-30， 2012-01-12，2013-08-29， 2014-01-25……
Reading Passage 37	Matching 信息匹配题	Left-handed 左撇子	2010-01-30，2011-09-17 ……
Reading Passage 38		Choice and Happiness 选择与幸福	2008-08-13，2011-07-30， 2013-05-18 ……
Reading Passage 39		The Father of Modern Management 管理学之父	2010-02-20，2012-01-07， 2013-03-09……
Reading Passage 40		Ambergris 龙涎香	2010-07-10……
Reading Passage 41		Interpretation 口译	2010-11-27，2011-03-19 ……
Reading Passage 42		Barristers and Solicitors 法律顾问	……
Reading Passage 43		An Exploration of Alchemy 炼金术	……
Reading Passage 44		Isambard Kingdom Brunel 工程师布鲁内尔	2010-06-05，2014-02-22 ……
Reading Passage 45		Artist Fingerprints 艺术家指纹	2010-03-20，2011-11-26 ……
Reading Passage 46		Mental Gymnastics 大脑体操	2005-06-25，2011-03-19 ……
Reading Passage 47	Multiple Choice 选择题	Koala 考拉	2010-06-26，2013-04-13 ……
Reading Passage 48		Violin Making 小提琴制作	2010-02-27，2012-05-19， 2014-06-28 ……
Reading Passage 49		El Niño 厄尔尼诺	2010-02-06，2012-08-11， 2013-04-06 ……
Reading Passage 50		Booming Bittern 麻鸦回归	2010-01-09，2012-03-08， 2013-03-09 ……

续前表

序号	题型	文章名称	考试时间
Reading Passage 51		Jethro Tull and Seed Drill 播种机的发明	2012-05-19……
Reading Passage 52	Diagram 图表题	The Oceanographer's Dream Ship 深海奇船	2010-10-14……
Reading Passage 53		Travelers' Accounts 旅行游记	2011-01-08……
Reading Passage 54		Perfume 香水制造	2009-05-16 ……
Reading Passage 55	Diagram 图表题	From Novices to Experts 从新手到专家	2009-02-28，2010-10-23， 2013-02-16……
Reading Passage 56		Two Wings and a Kit-box 乌鸦制造工具	2009-02-07，2009-05-09 ……

目 录

CHAPTER 3　Paragraph Heading段落中心思想题　/163

CHAPTER 6　Diagram图表题　/311

CHAPTER 7　Real Test真题模考　/347

APPENDIX附录　/373

Introduction
介绍

这是一篇955字的雅思学术类阅读文章。通过它我们可以了解：

1. 雅思阅读真实考试的每篇文章是由2~4种不同题型组合而成的。

2. 如何在不牺牲理解力的前提下提高阅读速度。

下篇导读： 【如何提高阅读速度】

考试时间： ……

　　留学生要阅读大量的英语文献。一个好的阅读者的定义是每分钟阅读1 000个单词。这意味着一篇雅思阅读文章1分钟就可读完。雅思阅读考生半小时就可搞定，还剩半小时可小睡一会儿。你也能做到。如何做到，请读下文。☺

Reading Passage

*You should spend about 20 minutes on **Questions 1–13** which are based on Reading Passage 1 below.*

Improving Reading Speed

It is safe to say that almost anyone can double his speed of reading while maintaining equal or even higher comprehension. In other words, anyone can improve the speed with which he gets what he wants from his reading.

The average college student reads between 250 and 350 words per minute on fiction and non-technical materials. A "good" reading speed is around 500 to 700 words per minute, but some people can read 1,000 words per minute or even faster on these materials. What makes the difference? There are three main factors involved in improving reading speed: (1) the desire to improve, (2) the willingness to try new techniques and (3) the motivation to practice.

Learning to read rapidly and well presupposes that you have the necessary vocabulary and comprehension skills. When you have advanced on the reading comprehension materials to a level at which you can understand college-level materials, you will be ready to begin speed reading practice in earnest.

Understanding the role of speed in the reading process is essential. Research has shown a close relation between speed and understanding. For example, in checking progress charts of thousands of individuals taking reading training, it has been found in most cases that an increase in rate has been paralleled by an increase in comprehension, and that where rate has gone down, comprehension has also decreased. Most adults are able to increase their rate of reading considerably and rather quickly without lowering comprehension.

Some of the facts which reduce reading rate:

(a) limited perceptual span i.e., word-by-word reading;

(b) slow perceptual reaction time, i.e., slowness of recognition and response to the material;

(c) vocalisation, including the need to vocalise in order to achieve comprehension;

(d) faulty eye movements, including inaccuracy in placement of the page, in return sweep, in rhythm and regularity of movement, etc.;

(e) regression, both habitual and as associated with habits of concentration

(f) lack of practice in reading, due simply to the fact that the person has read very little and has limited reading interests so that very little reading is practiced in the daily or weekly schedule.

Since these conditions act also to reduce comprehension, increasing the reading rate through eliminating them is likely to result in increased comprehension as well. This is an entirely different matter from simply speeding up the rate of reading without reference to the conditions responsible for the slow rate. In fact, simply speeding the rate, especially through forced acceleration, may actually result, and often does, in making the real reading problem more severe. In addition, forced acceleration may even destroy confidence in ability to read. The obvious solution, then is to increase rate as a part of a total improvement of the whole reading process.

A well planned program prepares for maximum increase in rate by establishing the necessary conditions. Three basic conditions include:

(a) Eliminate the habit of pronouncing words as you read. If you sound out words in your throat or whisper them, you can read slightly only as fast as you can read aloud. You should be able to read most materials at least two or three times faster silently than orally.

(b) Avoid regressing (rereading). The average student reading at 250 words per minute regresses or rereads about 20 times per page. Rereading words and phrases is a habit which will slow your reading speed down to a snail's pace. Furthermore, the slowest reader usually regresses most frequently. Because he reads slowly, his mind has time to wander and his rereading reflects both his inability to concentrate and his lack of confidence in his comprehension skills.

(c) Develop a wider eye-span. This will help you read more than one word at a glance. Since written material is less meaningful if read word by word, this will help you learn to read by phrases or thought units.

Poor results are inevitable if the reader attempts to use the same rate indiscriminately for all types of material and for all reading purposes. He must learn to adjust his rate to his purpose in reading and to the difficulty of the material he is reading. This ranges from a maximum rate on easy, familiar, interesting material or in reading to gather information on a particular point, to minimal rate on material which is unfamiliar in content and language structure or which must be thoroughly digested. The effective reader adjusts his rate; the ineffective reader uses the same rate for all types of material.

Rate adjustment may be overall adjustment to the article as a whole, or internal adjustment within the article. Overall adjustment establishes the basic rate at which the total article is read; internal adjustment involves the necessary variations in rate for each varied part of the material. As an analogy, you plan to take a 100-mile mountain trip. Since this will be a relatively hard drive with hills, curves, and a mountain pass, you decide to take three hours for the total trip, averaging about 35 miles an hour. This is your overall rate adjustment. However, in actual driving you may slow down to no more than 15 miles per hour on some curves and hills, while speeding up to 50 miles per hour or more on relatively straight and level sections. This is your internal rate adjustment. There is no set rate, therefore, which the good reader follows inflexibly in reading a particular selection, even though he has set himself an overall rate for the total job.

In keeping your reading attack flexible, adjust your rate sensitivity from article to article. It is equally important to adjust your rate within a given article. Practice these techniques until a flexible reading rate becomes second nature to you.

Questions 1–4

Choose the appropriate letters A–D and write them in boxes 1–4 on your answer sheet.

1 Which of the following is not a factor in improving your reading speed?

  A willing to try new skills

  B motivation to improve

  C desire to practice

  D hesitate to try new techniques

2 Understanding college level materials is a prerequisite for

  A learning to comprehend rapidly.

  B having the necessary vocabulary.

  C beginning speed reading.

  D practicing comprehension skills.

3 For most people

  A a decrease in comprehension leads to a decrease in rate.

  B a decrease in rate leads to an increase in comprehension.

  C an increase in rate leads to an increase in comprehension.

  D an increase in rate leads to a decrease in comprehension.

4 Speeding up your reading rate through forced acceleration often results in

  A reducing comprehension.

  B increasing comprehension.

  C increasing your reading problem.

  D reducing your reading problem.

Questions 5–9

Complete the table below.

Choose NO MORE THAN THREE WORDS *from the passage for each answer.*

Factors	Effects	Reduces rate	Increases rate
Wider eye span	(5)		YES
(6)	Word-by-word reading	YES	
Slow perceptual reaction	(7)	YES	

| (8) | Return sweep inaccuracy | YES | |
| (9) | Concentrate and be confident | · | YES |

Questions 10–13

Do the following statements agree with the information given in the Reading Passage?

In boxes 10–13 on your answer sheet write

>   **TRUE**   *if the statement is true*
>
>   **FALSE**   *if the statement is false*
>
>   **NOT GIVEN**   *if the information is not given in the passage*

10   In gathering material on a topic a reader must maximise his reading rate.

11   Overall adjustment means different reading speeds for different parts of the passage.

12   The rate of 35 miles per hour is rather low when climbing mountain.

13   A good reader never establishes a set rate for reading an article.

CHAPTER 1

Summary
单词填写题

介绍：可细分为1. 原文选词填空完成摘要；2. 从题目后面的单词列表中
选词填空完成摘要；3. 从原文选词填空完成句子；4. 从原文选词
回答问题。

概率：真实考试40个题目中平均10个题

难度：前3种：★★★☆☆

第4种（从原文选词回答问题）：★★☆☆☆

单词填写题

雅思机考 (IELTS Computer Based) 界面及说明：

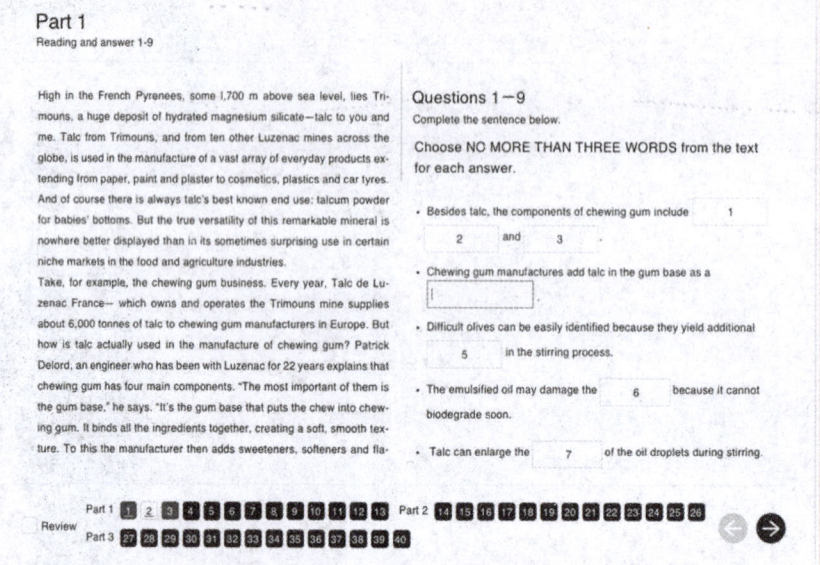

单词填写题题目显示在界面的右侧。输入内容无限制，大小写均可。内容自动保存。

如何答题：将答案填入右侧题目的空白方框处。

如何修改：鼠标定位入方框，直接修改，内容会自动保存。

www.ieltscb.com 提供免费机考练习。

下篇导读： 【冰箱的发明】

考试时间： 2012-09-22……

　　古人制冷的方法；冰箱的发明和改良；冰箱和制冷技术促进了许多行业的发展，改变了人们的饮食习惯和生活方式，促进了健康；家里可以没有电视，但不能没有冰箱；冰箱还可应对雅思口语和写作话题——"谈谈生活中的一种电器产品"；"上世纪伟大的发明之一"；"考鸭"爱冰箱。

Reading Passage 1

The Refrigerator

Many of the conveniences we enjoy in our homes are the result of years of innovation by dedicated inventors. Though we take many of them for granted, some—like the refrigerator—have hugely affected the way we live our lives. Who invented the refrigerator, and how has it evolved over time?

Early Refrigeration

Preserving food has not always been easy. Centuries ago, people gathered ice from streams and ponds and did their best to store it year-round in icehouses and cellars, so they had a ready supply to keep their food cold. Even with ice, people were often limited to eating locally grown foods that had to be purchased fresh and used daily. The Egyptians, Chinese and Indians were some of the early people to use ice in food preservation. In 1626, Sir Francis Bacon was also testing the idea that cold could be used to preserve meat; his chilly experiment caused him to develop pneumonia, from which he died on Easter Day, April 9, 1626.

Even Peter Mark Roget, compiler of Roget's Thesaurus, studied refrigeration, suggesting a design for a "frigidarium." Progress took time, however, and snow and ice served as the primary means of refrigeration until the beginning of the 20th century.

Iceboxes

According to the Association of Home Appliance Manufacturers, one of the next steps between storing ice underground and modern refrigeration was the icebox. Introduced in 19th century England, wooden iceboxes were lined with tin or zinc, and filled with sawdust, seaweed and other materials to keep the ice from melting. Drip pans caught the water that melted and had to be emptied daily.

In the United States, warm winters in 1889 and 1890 caused ice shortages that fueled the need to create a better refrigeration system. An *Encyclopedia Britannica* entry attributes the beginning of commercial refrigeration to Alexander C. Twinning, an American businessman, in 1856. Later, an Australian named James Harrison reviewed the refrigerator used by Twinning, and another made by physician John Gorrie, and developed vapor-compression refrigeration for the brewing and meatpacking industries.

In 1859, France's Ferdinand Carré created a more advanced system that used ammonia as a coolant; the earlier vapor-compression machines used air. The ammonia worked well, but was toxic if it leaked. Engineers worked until the 1920s to come up with better alternatives, one of which was Freon.

Electric Refrigeration

According to a paper published by Wright State University, Fred W. Wolf invented the first commercially viable electric refrigerator in the United States. Sold for the first time in 1913, the DOMELRE, an air-cooled refrigeration unit, was mounted on top of an icebox.

In 1915, Alfred Mellowes designed an electric refrigeration unit that differed from other refrigerators because it was self-contained; the compressor was in the bottom of the cabinet. Guardian Refrigerator Company started manufacturing and selling Mellowes' version of the refrigerator in 1916. Despite offering a high-quality product, the company struggled, producing fewer than 40 appliances in two years.

W.C. Durant, who was president of General Motors, eventually purchased the Guardian Refrigerator Company privately, and the business was renamed Frigidaire. Appliances were mass produced much like cars, and the first Frigidaire refrigerator was completed in September 1918 in Detroit.

Continued improvements in how the refrigerator was produced, along with organisational changes in the company resulted in a better product and a reduced price. Frigidaire eventually added ice cream cabinets to models in 1923, soda fountain equipment in 1924, and water and milk coolers in 1927. By 1929, 1 million refrigerators had been produced, a marked improvement from the early years.

Greener Refrigeration

Albert Einstein is remembered for many scientific achievements, but, as *Time* magazine notes, it's often overlooked that he also made great contributions to eco-friendly refrigeration. In 1930, Einstein and a colleague patented a refrigerator that cools with ammonia, butane and water instead of Freon, a contributor to global warming.

Although Einstein's original refrigerator was not very energy efficient, researchers from Oxford have adjusted his plans and believe they have a version that could be competitive in the marketplace in the future.

Questions 1–6

Complete the summary below.

Use **ONE WORD ONLY** *from the passage for each answer.*

refrigeration

In ancient time, people mainly used ice and snow as the means of 1 *refriga* to store food. Then icebox was introduced during 19th century and commercial refrigeration was applied to 2 *brewing* as well as 3 *bakery* *meatpacking* industries. In 1859, 4 *ammon* replaced air as a coolant, but it was poisonous. The safer 5 *freon* took over it in 1920s. Electric refrigerator came on stage during that time and was continually upgraded. Even Einstein made contributions by inventing 6 *greener* refrigerator.

ecofriendly

4.25

▶ 核心词汇

词汇	释义
convenience	[kən'viːnɪəns] *n.* 便利，方便（形容词形式：convenient）
innovation	[ˌɪnə'veɪʃn] *n.* 创新，革新（字根nov来源于拉丁文novus，指 "new"。如：novel *adj.* 新奇的；*n.* 小说；novelist小说家；novice新手）
dedicated	['dedɪkeɪtɪd] *adj.* 专注的；献身的，富有献身精神的（动词形式：dedicate；名词形式：dedication）
take sth. for granted	认为……是理所当然
evolve	[ɪ'vɒlv] *v.* 进化，发展（拉丁文volvere是 "滚，转" 的意思，英语单词中包含volve和volut的字母组合即有to roll的含义。evolve滚动着向上→发展，进化；evolution进化，演变；involve滚在里边→包含，牵涉；revolve重新滚动→旋转，考虑；revolution革命。沃尔沃Volvo是瑞典著名的汽车品牌，拉丁文意思是 "我在旋转"）
preserve	[prɪ'zɜːv] *v.* 保存（同义词：conserve）
pneumonia	[njuː'məʊnɪə] *n.* 肺炎
refrigeration	[rɪˌfrɪdʒə'reɪʃn] *n.* 制冷，冷藏
melt	[melt] *v.* 熔化，溶解，融化（同义词：thaw）
brewing	[bruːɪŋ] *n.* 酿造
meatpacking	[miːt'pækɪŋ] *n.* 肉类加工
vapor	['veɪpə(r)] *n.* 水汽，水蒸气（动词：evaporate 蒸发，挥发）
compression	[kəm'preʃn] *n.* 压缩
toxic	['tɒksɪk] *adj.* 有毒的，中毒的（来源于希腊文里的toxon，意为弓箭。荷马史诗《伊利亚特》Iliad中还能寻到踪迹。后来战争中人们普遍在箭头上涂上毒药，以提高弓箭的杀伤力，字根tox就有了 "毒" 的含义。如：toxicant 毒物，毒药；detoxify 解毒；toxicologist毒物学家，欧阳锋；intoxicate心里中毒→使陶醉）
leak	[liːk] *v.* 漏出，泄漏（同义词：ooze）
commercially	[kə'mɜːʃəlɪ] *adv.* 商业上
viable	['vaɪəbl] *adj.* 可行的（同义词：feasible）
mount	[maʊnt] *v.* 安装，安置
version	['vɜːʃn] *n.* 版本
purchase	['pɜːtʃəs] *v.* 购买（同义词：buy）
overlook	[ˌəʊvə'lʊk] *v.* 忽略，忽视（同义词：ignore；反义词：exaggerate，overstate）
eco-friendly	['iːkəʊfrendlɪ] *adj.* 环保的，对生态环境友好的
patent	['pætnt] *v.* 申请专利；*n.* 专利
original	[ə'rɪdʒənl] *adj.* 最初的（名词形式：origin 起源；动词形式：originate）
adjust	[ə'dʒʌst] *v.* 调整，调节（名词形式：adjustment）

competitive	[kəm'petətɪv] *adj.* 有竞争力的，竞争的（名词形式：competition 竞争；competitor 竞争者；动词形式：compete）

▶ 雅思阅读真题同义词考点

evolve	—develop, upgrade, progress, advance, grow
toxic	—poisonous, noxious, venomous
viable	—feasible, possible, workable, practical
overlook	—ignore, neglect, underestimate
eco-friendly	—environmental-friendly, green, low-carbon
competition	—rivalry, contest, battle, combat

*并列结构考点：and, or, as well as, both…and, not only…but also…, other than, in addition, besides, on the one hand…on the other hand…, neither… nor…

下篇导读：【诺贝尔奖】

考试时间：2011-04-30，2012-08-04……

　　诺贝尔的一生；炸药的发明过程；危险的实验；他的遗嘱；历史上第一位诺贝尔和平奖获得者是他的秘书？ ☺

Reading Passage 2

Alfred Nobel

The man behind the Nobel Prize

Part 1

Since 1901, the Nobel Prize has been honouring men and women from all corners of the globe for outstanding achievements in physics, chemistry, medicine, literature, and for work in peace. The foundations for the prize were laid in 1895 when Alfred Nobel wrote his last will, leaving much of his wealth to the establishment of the Nobel Prize.

Alfred Nobel was born in Stockholm on October 21, 1833. His father Immanuel Nobel was an engineer and inventor who built bridges and buildings in Stockholm. In connection with his construction work Immanuel Nobel also experimented with different techniques for blasting rocks. Successful in his industrial and business ventures, Immanuel Nobel was able, in 1842, to bring his family to St. Petersburg. There, his sons were given a first class education by private teachers. The training included natural sciences, languages and literature. By the age of 17 Alfred Nobel was fluent in Swedish, Russian, French, English and German. His primary interests were in English literature and poetry, as well as in chemistry and physics. Alfred's father, who wanted his sons to join his enterprise as engineers, disliked Alfred's interest in poetry and found his son rather introverted.

In order to widen Alfred's horizons his father sent him abroad for further training in chemical engineering. During a two-year period Alfred Nobel visited Sweden, Germany, France and the United States. In Paris, the city he came to like best, he worked in the private laboratory of Professor T. J. Pelouze, a famous chemist. There he met the young Italian chemist Ascanio Sobrero who, three years earlier, had invented nitroglycerine, a highly explosive liquid. But it was considered too dangerous to be of any practical use. Although its explosive power greatly exceeded that of gunpowder, the liquid would explode in a very unpredictable manner if subjected to heat and pressure. Alfred Nobel became very interested in nitroglycerine and how it could be put to practical use in construction work. He also realised that the safety problems had to be solved and a method had to be developed for the controlled detonation of nitroglycerine.

Part 2

After his return to Sweden in 1863, Alfred Nobel concentrated on developing nitroglycerine as an explosive. Several explosions, including one (1864) in which his brother Emil and several other persons were killed, convinced the authorities that nitroglycerine production was exceedingly dangerous. They forbade further experimentation with nitroglycerine within the Stockholm city limits and Alfred Nobel had to move his experimentation to a barge anchored on Lake Malaren. Alfred was not discouraged and in 1864 he was able to start mass production of nitroglycerine. To make the handling of nitroglycerine safer Alfred Nobel experimented with different additives. He soon found that mixing nitroglycerine with kieselguhr would turn the liquid into a paste which could be shaped into rods of a size and form suitable for insertion into drilling holes. In 1867 he patented this material under the name of dynamite. To be able to detonate the dynamite rods he also invented a detonator (blasting cap) which could be ignited by lighting a fuse. These inventions were made at the same time as the pneumatic drill came into general use. Together these inventions drastically reduced the cost of blasting rock, drilling tunnels, building canals and many other forms of construction work.

The market for dynamite and detonating caps grew very rapidly and Alfred Nobel also proved himself to be a very skillful entrepreneur and businessman. Over the years he founded factories and laboratories in some 90 different places in more than 20 countries. Although he lived in Paris much of his life he was constantly traveling. When he was not traveling or engaging in business activities Nobel himself worked intensively in his various laboratories, first in Stockholm and later in other places. He focused on the development of explosives technology as well as other chemical inventions, including such materials as synthetic rubber and leather, artificial silk, etc. By the time of his death in 1896 he had 355 patents.

Part 3

Intensive work and travel did not leave much time for a private life. At the age of 43 he was feeling like an old man. At this time he advertised in a newspaper "Wealthy, highly-educated elderly gentleman seeks lady of mature age, versed in languages, as secretary and supervisor of household." The most qualified applicant turned out to be an Austrian woman, Countess Bertha Kinsky. After working a very short time for Nobel she decided to return to Austria to marry Count Arthur von Suttner. In spite of this Alfred Nobel and Bertha von Suttner remained friends and kept writing letters to each other for decades. Over the years Bertha von Suttner became increasingly critical of the arms race. She wrote a famous book, *Lay Down Your Arms* and became a prominent figure in the peace movement. No doubt this influenced Alfred Nobel when he wrote his final will which was to include a Prize for persons or organisations who promoted peace. Several years after the death of Alfred Nobel, the Norwegian Storting (Parliament) decided to award the 1905 Nobel Peace Prize to Bertha von Suttner.

Alfred Nobel died in San Remo, Italy, on December 10, 1896. When his will was opened it came as a surprise that his fortune was to be used for Prizes in Physics, Chemistry, Physiology or Medicine, Literature and Peace. The executors of his will were two young engineers, Ragnar Sohlman and Rudolf Lilljequist. They set about forming the Nobel Foundation as an organisation to take care of the financial assets left by Nobel for this purpose and to coordinate the work of the Prize-Awarding Institutions. This was not without its difficulties since the will was contested by relatives and questioned by authorities in various countries.

Alfred Nobel's greatness lay in his ability to combine the penetrating mind of the scientist and inventor with the forward-looking dynamism of the industrialist. Nobel was very interested in social and peace-related issues and held what were considered radical views in his era. He had a great interest in literature and wrote his own poetry and dramatic works. The Nobel Prizes became an extension and a fulfillment of his lifetime interests.

Questions 1–4

The summary below is based on Part 1.

*Choose **NO MORE THAN THREE WORDS** from the passage for each answer.*

Immanuel Nobel was an engineer who developed various techniques for **1** ~~blasting rocks~~ for his construction work. He sent his son, Alfred Nobel, abroad to receive training in **2** ~~chemical engineering~~ Paris, Alfred Nobel worked in a private laboratory, and met the inventor of nitroglycerine, which was considered highly unpractical due to its **3** ~~practical~~ risk. Alfred Nobel became interested in how to apply this explosive liquid in **4** ....

Questions 5–8

The summary below is based on Part 2.

*Choose **NO MORE THAN THREE WORDS** from the passage for each answer.*

After his return to Sweden, Alfred Nobel focused on developing nitroglycerine. Since the experiments were too dangerous and were **5** ~~forbade~~ within the city area by the government of the Stockholm city, Nobel had to move his experiments to a lake. Finally, he discovered **6** ~~kieselguhr~~ that could be combined with nitroglycerine to convert liquid into a paste. He called this material **7** ~~dynamite~~ and patented it. His inventions came into general use and made great contributions to construction work by lowering the **8** ~~cost~~ .

Questions 9–10

The summary below is based on Part 3. Choose no more than three words from the passage for each answer.

Although Nobel proved himself to be a great inventor and businessman, his private life was not that successful. His secretary left him and eventually became a famous protestor against the **9** ~~arms race~~ That was part of the reason why Noble included **10** ~~Nobel~~ in his final will.

▶ 核心词汇

词汇	释义
construction	[kən'strʌkʃn] *n.* 建筑物，建造
blast	[blɑːst] *v.* （用炸药）炸毁
venture	['ventʃə(r)] *n.* 冒险事业，冒险（风险投资VC，就是venture capital的缩写）
poetry	['pəʊətrɪ] *n.* 诗，诗歌【总称】（区别：a poem 一首诗；poet *n.*诗人）
enterprise	['entəpraɪz] *n.* 事业，企业
introverted	['ɪntrəvɜːtɪd] *adj.* 内向的，含蓄的（反义词：extroverted）
nitroglycerine	[ˌnaɪtrəʊ'glɪsəriːn] *n.* 硝化甘油，炸药
explosive	[ɪk'spləʊsɪv] *adj.* 爆炸的，易爆炸的　*n.*爆炸物，炸药
exceed	[ɪk'siːd] *v.* 超过，超越，（在数量和质量等方面）胜过（同义词：excel）
be subject to	使受到，使遭遇；易于……的（subject作名词含义很多，常考的是：实验对象；学科）
barge	[bɑːdʒ] *n.* 驳船，游艇
anchor	['æŋkə(r)] *v.* 抛锚
additive	['ædətɪv] *n.* 添加剂（区分：in addition）
kieselguhr	['kɪzəlˌgʊ(r)] *n.* 硅藻土
paste	[peɪst] *n.* 面团，糨糊
insertion	[ɪn'sɜːʃn] *n.* 插入（物）
patent	['pætnt] *v.* 获得……专利，给予……专利权，取得专利权；*n.* 专利（区分：patient *n.* 病人；patron *n.* 赞助人；potent *adj.* 有力的）
dynamite	['daɪnəmaɪt] *n.* 炸药，具有爆炸性的事物；有潜在危险的人（dyn-指power力量。比如有力量的玩意就是dynamite炸药；我们形容一个精力充沛的人是dynamic person；如果一个家庭或一个团队长期保持他们的powerful position，我们可以称作dynasty王朝。品一品中国名牌王朝干红葡萄酒Dynasty，相信有助于该字根记忆。）
detonate	['detəneɪt] *v.* （使）爆炸，引爆，触发（一连串事件）
ignite	[ɪg'naɪt] *v.* 点燃，引发
pneumatic	[njuː'mætɪk] *adj.* 充气的，气动的，装满空气的
entrepreneur	[ˌɒntrəprə'nɜː(r)] *n.* 企业家
synthetic	[sɪn'θetɪk] *adj.* 合成的，人造的（同义词：artificial）
verse	[vɜːs] *v.* 使熟练或者精通；作诗
prominent	['prɒmɪnənt] *adj.* 杰出的，著名的
executor	[ɪg'zekjətə(r)] *n.* 遗嘱执行人
asset	['æset] *n.* 资产，财产

penetrating	['penɪtreɪtɪŋ] *adj.* 敏锐的，有洞察力的，聪明的；响亮的（动词形式：penetrate *v.* 穿透，洞察）
dynamism	['daɪnəmɪzəm] *n.*（人的）活力，精力；魄力，劲头
radical	['rædɪkl] *adj.* 根本的，基本的；激进的；彻底的（radi=root根，来源于拉丁文 radix。如：radical指从根儿上就变了，彻底的→激进的，激进分子；e-出 + radic 根 + -ate动词后缀→把根拨出→eradicate根除，消灭；我们吃萝卜是吃它的根，所以萝卜叫radish。）

▶ **雅思阅读真题同义词考点**

various	—a variety of, different, versatile, many, diversified
forbid	—ban, prohibit, deter, prevent, do not allow, do not permit
discover	—find, uncover, figure out, work out, detect
lower	—reduce, decrease, drop
protestor	—opponent, objector, go against

　　*转折关系考点：but, yet, however, whereas, nonetheless, nevertheless, notwithstanding, although, though, instead

下篇导读：【猛犸象】

考试时间： 2011-08-13，2012-08-04，2014-05-10……

　　2007年科学家在俄罗斯发现了一只被冰冻了4万年的小猛犸象。小象只有一个月大，完好无损。科学家如获至宝，掀起了对这种冰河巨象的研究热情。下文将带你回到冰河世纪，走近猛犸象。 ☺

Reading Passage 3

Lost Giant: Mammoth

In 1643, workers unearthed some huge bones in a Belgian field. The naturalists who studied them were convinced they had come from a humanlike giant. Their length, after all, tallied with a biblical reference to Og, a giant king supposedly killed by Moses.

In 1728, British anatomist Hans Sloane identified similar remains from Siberia as belonging to elephants. But what were hot-climate animals doing in Siberia? Only at the end of the 18th century did French zoologist Georges Cuvier conclude that giant bones like these were from an elephant relative that died out long ago: the mammoth.

So where did these mysterious giants come from? What were they like? And what drove them to extinction? Biologists have been arguing over these questions ever since Cuvier's time. In the past few years, however, a wealth of new information has emerged, thanks in part to DNA studies.

The mammoth has one of the best fossil records, offering an incredible insight into the evolution of this lineage. "You can trace how the anatomy has changed from a general, elephant-like animal to this very specialised creature that is the woolly mammoth," says Adrian Lister of the Natural History Museum in London.

By themselves, though, bones can tell us only so much. Luckily, the freezer-like conditions in which woolly mammoths lived and died have preserved not only bones but also flesh and hair. Sometimes entire animals have been found frozen, such as Lubya, a 1-month-old mammoth discovered in 2007. Thanks to hairs from two frozen specimens, around half the woolly mammoth genome has now been sequenced.

It has long been clear that mammoths arose in Africa, says Lister, because fossils of ancestral mammoths dating back as far as 5 million years ago have been found there. In 2006, three groups sequenced the woolly mammoth's mitochondrial DNA, revealing the structure of the elephant family tree. The studies show that the lineage leading to African elephants split off from the common ancestor first, around 6 million years ago. Not too long after that, the mammoths forked away from what would become the Asian elephant.

There is little evidence of adaptation to cold in these individuals, which makes sense because the climate was still relatively mild. But times were changing. Around 2.5 million years ago, an epoch of ice ages began. Many forests, which had provided trees and bushes for nourishment, were replaced by open grassland.

These dramatic changes led to the evolution of a new kind of mammoth, the steppe mammoth, which adapted to life in a colder world and to the changing vegetation. "The steppe mammoth's teeth had more enamel ridges to deal with a more grassy diet, and a higher crown to tolerate greater wear," says Lister.

Fossils recently unearthed in China show that the steppe mammoth evolved there about 1.7 million years ago and gradually spread out across the Northern Hemisphere, replacing earlier forms. It was around this time that some mammoths crossed a land bridge joining Siberia to North America. There, mammoths evolved into distinctive North American forms and some eventually spread as far south as Central America. Meanwhile, some steppe mammoths were becoming ever more specialised for cold climates and open grassland, giving rise to the woolly mammoth, the most famous of its kind.

The woolly mammoth's most distinctive feature was its long, shaggy coat. Preserved specimens have a wide range of hair colour: blond, red, brown, even black. Besides its long hair, the woolly mammoth had a thick layer of fat to insulate against the cold. It also had smaller ears and a shorter tail than its forebears, which would minimise heat loss. Its huge tusks may have been used like a snowplow to expose vegetation to eat or to break up ice.

So woolly mammoths were built for the cold, and they thrived during a series of ever deeper ice ages. The species spread west and east to occupy much of the Northern Hemisphere, including North America, while other mammoth species died out. Studies of mitochondrial DNA from 40 woolly mammoth specimens show its population and range expanded as the world entered the last ice age around 100,000 years ago and remained stable during that ice age. And then, as the ice age ended, it went extinct.

What happened? Some biologists think that the extinction took place very rapidly, triggered by a sudden, dramatic event around 12,000 years ago. One suggestion is that some kind of mega-disease wiped out the species. Another is that a meteorite impact in North America triggered catastrophic change. And then there's the "blitzkrieg hypothesis," which blames the mammoth's demise on the spread of spear-wielding human hunters.

Hunting clearly did happen, as cave paintings and the occasional spearhead lodged in bone testify. But there's growing evidence that woolly mammoths didn't die out as suddenly as such cataclysmic visions would have us believe.

Dating of mammoth remains by Lister and others suggests that the woolly mammoth's range had been in decline for several thousand years before they disappeared. And genetic studies show a loss of genetic diversity, a sign of a shrinking population. This was probably a result of trees' replacing grassland as the world began to warm up again. By 12,000 years ago, woolly mammoths were restricted to the steppes of Siberia.

But climate change seems unlikely to be the whole story, either, as mammoths had survived previous warm periods. "It's possible that you only get extinction if you get a combination of factors coming together," says Lister.

The last stand of the mammoths appears to have taken place on Wrangel Island, in the Arctic Ocean off the coast of Siberia. Here a population of mammoths was cut off from the Siberian mainland 9,000 years ago as ice sheets melted and sea level rose. However, the climate and vegetation remained suitable for them, and they survived for 5,000 years before dying out around 4,000 years ago—around the time humans arrived.

Nobody knows what caused the extinction of the Wrangel mammoths. There is no direct evidence that humans killed them, so it is possible that the island was simply too small to support a mammoth population. However, ancient DNA collected from the remains of some of these last mammoths paints a picture of a stable population that thrived for 5,000 years and then suddenly died out, rather than a population in terminal decline, suggesting that humans had a hand in it.

Questions 1–7

Complete the summary below.

*Choose **NO MORE THAN THREE WORDS** or numbers from the passage for each answer.*

The chronology of mammoths

Fossil evidences show that about 5 million years ago mammoths originated from 1 ...Africa... . Then some mammoths split off from the ancestor of 2 ...African elephant... . In order to cope with the climate change that occurred around 2.5 million years ago, mammoths evolved into a new species, called the 3 ...steppe mammoth... . About 1.7 millions years ago, these animals gradually spread out from China across the Northern Hemisphere, and travelled via land bridge into 4 ...North America... . Some of them went further south to 5 ...Central America..., where they evolved to the well-known kind, named the 6 ...woolly... . Eventually, the mammoths went extinct around 7 ...4000... years ago.

Questions 8–12

Complete the summary below.

*Choose **ONE WORD ONLY** from the passage for each answer.*

The features of the woolly mammoths

The woolly mammoths were built for the cold and thrived during the ice age. Their skin was covered with long 8 ...hair..., and their 9 ...fat... helped isolate from the cold. The woolly mammoths had smaller ears and shorter tails which consumed less 10 ...that heat... Their ivories were rather huge and may have been used to smash 11 ...ice... and discover 12 ...vegetation...

▶ 核心词汇

词汇	释义
unearth	[ʌn'ɜːθ] *v.* 发掘；破获（同义词：uncover；discover；excavate）
tally	['tælɪ] *v.* 记录（原意为小木条，符木；古人在其上刻划计数）
biblical	['bɪblɪkl] *adj.* 圣经的，依据圣经的（Bible圣经）
extinction	[ɪk'stɪŋkʃn] *n.* 灭绝（动词和形容词形式：extinct）
fossil	['fɒsl] *n.* 化石　*adj.* 化石的
lineage	['lɪnɪɪdʒ] *n.* 血统，家系（line指"线形，排队"；-age指"关系，出身"）
trace	[treɪs] *v.* 追踪，查探（同义词：find；detect）
anatomy	[ə'nætəmɪ] *n.* 解剖，解剖学
woolly	['wʊlɪ] *adj.* 长毛的，毛茸茸的；羊毛的，似羊毛的
genome	['dʒiːnəʊm] *n.* 基因组，染色体组（gene *n.*基因。中文翻译为音译）
sequence	['siːkwəns] *v.* 按顺序排好（派生词：subsequently *adv.*后来；随后。consequence *n.*结果）
ancestral	[æn'sestrəl] *adj.* 祖先的，祖传的（名词形式：ancestor）
split off	分离；分裂
adaptation	[ˌædæp'teɪʃn] *n.* 适应；改编（动词形式：adapt）
ridge	[rɪdʒ] *n.* 山脊，山脉
diet	['daɪət] *n.* 饮食，食物
tolerate	['tɒləreɪt] *v.* 忍受，容忍
wear	[weə(r)] *n.* 磨损（常用词组：wear and tear 磨损）
distinctive	[dɪ'stɪŋktɪv] *adj.* 有特色的，与众不同的
shaggy	['ʃægɪ] *adj.* 毛发粗浓杂乱的，蓬松的；表面粗糙的
insulate	['ɪnsjʊleɪt] *v.* 隔离，使孤立
tusk	[tʌsk] *n.* 长牙，獠牙
thrive	[θraɪv] *v.* 茁壮成长（同义词：prosper）
meteorite	['miːtɪəraɪt] *n.* 陨星，陨石；流星（区分：comet彗星）
hypothesis	[haɪ'pɒθəsɪs] *n.* 假设（区分：hypnosis 催眠）
spearhead	['spɪəhed] *n.* 矛头；先锋（spear 标枪；矛。那么反义词"盾"怎么说？shield）
cataclysmic	[ˌkætə'klɪzmɪk] *adj.* 大变动的；洪水的（区分：catastrophe *n.* 大灾难，大祸）
terminal	['tɜːmɪnl] *adj.* 末端的，终点的（terminal作名词指"终点站"，首都机场的T3航站楼就是Terminal 3；电影《终结者》*Terminator*）
migrate	[maɪ'greɪt] *v.* 移动，移居
via	['vaɪə] *prep.* 经过，通过

isolate	['aɪsəleɪt] v. 使隔离；使孤立（名词形式：isolation。字根sol指"单独的"，如：solo独奏。后面《小提琴制作》一文会再次学习）
ivory	['aɪvərɪ] n. 象牙（ivory tower象牙塔。语出圣经。指与世隔绝的梦幻境地、逃避现实生活的世外桃源、隐居之地。）
smash	[smæʃ] v. 打碎

▶ 雅思阅读真题同义词考点

extinct	—die out, vanish, perish, exterminate, eradicate, wipe off
originate from	—come from, result from, stem from, derive from, begin with，root in
trace	—find, detect, discover
famous	—well-known, household, prominent, outstanding
isolate	—separate, insulate, inaccessible, unreachable
catastrophe	—disaster, calamity, tragedy
via	—by, through, by way of, by means of

下篇导读： 【塔斯马尼亚虎】

考试时间： 2011-03-05，2013-03-09……

　　长得像老虎，其实我是一匹来自塔斯马尼亚的袋狼；我很丑可是我很温柔；人类使我灭绝，现在又开始怀念我。☺

Reading Passage 4

Tasmanian Tigers

Scientists and researchers from across the globe have devoted much of their time and research to find whether the Tasmanian Tigers still exist or not. The Tasmanian tiger, also known as the Thylacine, has been declared extinct 23 years back but was wiped off from the Australian mainland even much before in the 1940's.

Researchers like Dr Austin from the Australian Centre for Ancient DNA collected animal droppings that were found around Tasmania in the late 1950's and even in the 60's and conserved them in the Art Gallery and Tasmanian Museum. Dr Austin, who took special interest to collect evidences and reports on the Tasmanian Tigers, also extracted DNA from bones of both the Tasmanian Tiger and Tasmanian Devil that were once found on mainland Australia. Many scientists believe that they would be able to reproduce a clone from the available DNA of a 136-year-old Thylacine specimen conserved in ethanol since 1866. The geneticists of the Australian museum believe they would be able to replicate bits of this wonderful creature from its century-old ancestor.

The evidences from the ancient Aboriginal rock paintings and fossils reveal that the major population of the Thylacine was based mainly throughout Australia and Papua New Guinea. In 1803, when the European settlers arrived in Australia, there was a healthy population of Tasmanian Tigers. They almost looked like large dogs with stripes on their back. They had heavy stiff tails, large heads and were the world's largest marsupial carnivore. Owing to the tiger's unusual structure and shape, the Europeans compared it with the Hyena. Its yellow-brown coat comprises of more than 15 clear dark stripes that ran across its back and base of its tail. This gave it the nickname of a Tiger. The female Tasmanian tiger had a pouch with four teats but unlike other marsupials, the pouch opened at the back.

According to analysis of the skeleton of the Tasmanian Tigers, it has been found that these carnivores mainly relied on stamina than speed in the chase. The stomach of the tigers was muscular and had an ability to distend for allowing the animal to eat huge amount of food at one time. The stomachs were adapted in a way for compensating longer period without eating when the tigers failed to hunt and during food scarcity.

The analysis of the skeletal frame of the tigers reveals that they preferred to single out their preys and exhaust them before killing. Other studies on these extinct animals showed that the animals used to hunt in small family groups. They were nocturnal ambush predators.

The food list of the Tasmanian Tiger included kangaroos, wombats, birds, wallabies and small animals like potoroos and possums. Apart from these animals, the Tasmanian emu formed a favourite meal of the Tasmanian Tiger. However, these tigers were considered a blood drinker in the twentieth century because these carnivores mainly ate the sheep and poultry of the farmers. Their bad reputation led to mass killing of Tigers by humans.

These creatures were shy and mute animals but barked huskily at the time when it was excited and restless. The Tasmanian Tiger loved to stay away from human contacts, which made the early settlers believe that they were timid creatures. It had a nervous personality compared to other marsupials. When they were captured, they used to die out of fear and shock. They hardly used to put up some resistance before their enemies. They had a high sense of smell that helped them to track their preys and eventually kill them down. They were not very swift in reaction and rather looked lazy and they ran briskly and awkwardly when chased.

It is believed that the fierce and wild hunters of Australia, Dingo is somewhat responsible for the extinction of the Tasmanian tigers. These wild dogs may have competed for food and shelter with the Thylacine resulting in the death of the tigers from areas like Papua New Guinea and Australian mainland.

In the early 18th century, after the European settlers started inhabiting most of the lands in the Australian mainland and in Tasmania, much of the forests and grasslands were cleared so that they could be converted to farmlands. This movement led to a huge clash between the settlers and the native animals who could not cope with the environmental situation, which resulted in the extermination of these fine creatures.

Evidences have been collected which suggest that almost 2000 Tasmanian tigers were killed when a large portal company announced a handsome reward for killing a tiger on its properties. Another possibility is that the Tasmanian tigers could not deal with the significant change in the climate and their living area. Shortage of water and food could be another primary reason of their extinction.

The last Tasmanian tiger was captured in 1933 and was kept in the Hobart Zoo but it died three years later in 1936 making an end to this species. The Australian media became so anxious about the Tasmanian Tigers that they even offered a reward of 1 million dollars for anyone who would find or could prove that they are still alive somewhere in Australia. Many still believe that these tigers can be seen in the ancient forests of Tasmania where this mysterious animal swirls like smoke in its usual habitat. Until now, there have been hundreds of reported sightings of Tasmanian tigers but none has been confirmed. It was concluded by the researchers that only half of the sightings and reports needed investigation and the rest were fake.

Questions 1–11

Complete the summary below.

Choose NO MORE THAN THREE WORDS from the passage for each answer.

The Tasmanian tiger, also known as the Thylacine, has been announced extinct many years ago. Now many geneticists assert that they are capable of recreating a **1** ...*clone*... from DNA extracted from its bone specimen.

Tasmanian tigers belong to marsupials that have a **2** ...*pouch*... in common. They looked like big dogs with over 15 dark stripes on the body. When chasing their preys, these animals primarily depended on **3** ...*stamina*... to prevail. Their stomach could inflate so they could eat large amount of food each time to **4** ...*compensate*... period lack of food.

The diet of the Tasmanian tiger included the **5** ...*sheep*... and **6** ...*poultry*... and this resulted in mass killing of the tigers by people in the twentieth century. Indeed, these creatures were shy and timid. They seldom set up some **7** ...*resistance*... in front of the foes and used to die out of fear when captured.

There were several factors contributing to the extinction of the Tasmanian tiger. Another kind of wild animal called **8** ...*wild dingo*... was its rival for habitats and food sources. The **9** *European*... destroyed the forests and grassland where the tigers lived, and these native animals could not cope with this change.

The last Tasmanian tiger perished in the Hobart Zoo in **10** ...*1963*... and this marked the termination to this species. But many still believe that they are alive. So far lots of **11** ...*sightings*... of the tigers have been reported, but none of them has been proven.

sighting

▶ **核心词汇**

词汇	释义
evidence	['evɪdəns] *n.* 证据；迹象
extract	['ekstrækt] *v.* 提取，拔出（ex-表示"向外"，tract表示"拖，拉"，比如tractor *n.*拖拉机）
clone	[kləʊn] *n.* 克隆，复制（1963年英国基因学家 J.B.S. 哈尔丹制造了"克隆"一词，来源于希腊单词klon，意为"嫩枝"）
specimen	['spesɪmən] *n.* 标本
geneticist	[dʒə'netɪsɪst] *n.* 基因学家，遗传学者（gen-表示"产生"，比如gene *n.* 基因；generate *v.* 产生；generation *n.* 一代人；那么hydrogen是什么呢？因为hydro指"水"，比如hydropower水力发电，所以hydrogen就是"产生水的"氢元素H）
replicate	['replɪkeɪt] *v.* 复制
ancestor	['ænsestə(r)] *n.* 祖先
ancient	['eɪnʃənt] *adj.* 古代的（看看这三个词：ancestor, ancient, antique *n.*古董，它们中的an-/anti-都指时间向以前推移，"过去"之意，可一起记忆）
aboriginal	[ˌæbə'rɪdʒənl] *adj.* 土著的（可做名词，指"土著居民"）
reveal	[rɪ'viːl] *v.* 揭示
stripe	[straɪp] *n.* 斑纹，条纹（喜欢打台球的同学注意：花色球叫stripe ball，全色球是solid ball，白球叫cue ball）
carnivore	['kɑːnɪvɔː(r)] *n.* 食肉动物（carn表示"肉"，vore表示"吃"，所以反义词是herbivore 食草动物）
owing to	由于（因果关系是雅思阅读的重要考点，被考了无数遍）
skeleton	['skelɪtn] *n.* 骨架，骨骼（游戏中的骷髅兵）
stamina	['stæmɪnə] *n.* 耐力，持久力
stomach	['stʌmək] *n.* 胃（认认这些词：lung, liver, kidney, intestine, vein）
compensate	['kɒmpenseɪt] *v.* 补偿，赔偿（名词形式：compensation）
scarcity	['skeəsəti] *n.* 缺乏，不足（形容词形式：scarce）
prey	[preɪ] *n.* 猎物，被捕食者
exhaust	[ɪɡ'zɔːst] *v.* 使筋疲力尽
nocturnal	[nɒk'tɜːnl] *n.* 夜间的
predator	['predətə(r)] *n.* 掠食者（反义词：prey）
mute	[mjuːt] *adj.* 哑的，沉默的（同义词：dumb）
timid	['tɪmɪd] *adj.* 胆小的
resistance	[rɪ'zɪstəns] *n.* 反抗，抵抗（动词形式：resist）
be converted to	被转变成

extermination	[ɪkˌstɜːmɪˈneɪʃn] *n.* 消灭，根绝
property	[ˈprɒpəti] *n.* 地产（该词另一个含义是"特点，特性"，也被雅思真题考到）
fake	[feɪk] *adj.* 假的，伪造的

▶ 雅思阅读真题同义词考点

ancient	— early, in the past, old
replicate	— copy, duplicate, imitate
mainly	— primarily, principally
eventually	— finally, at last, in the end
rely on	— depend on, account on, be based on

*因果关系考点：owing to, thanks to, due to, according to, be based on, because of, on account of, as a result of, leading to, because, since, for, in that, as, therefore, hence

下篇导读： 【柏拉图与亚特兰蒂斯】

考试时间： ……

　　千古传说大西国，哲学之王柏拉图在著名《对话录》中称其为亚特兰蒂斯。古文明为何突然神秘消失，它和百慕大三角又有什么联系？ ☺

Reading Passage 5

The Lost Continent

A continent the size of Europe, boasting beautiful cities, advanced technology and utopian government... subjected to a great cataclysm *and reduced to rubble that sank beneath the sea, lost forever. The legend of Atlantis has been around for thousands of years, and whatever its factual validity may be, it can truthfully claim a noble heritage: its earliest proponent was Plato.

The Greek philosopher wrote of Atlantis in two of his dialogues, "Timaeus" and "Critias," around 370 B.C. Plato explained that this story, which he claimed to be true, came from then-200-year-old records of the Greek ruler Solon, who heard of Atlantis from an Egyptian priest. Plato said that the continent lay in the Atlantic Ocean near the Straits of Gibraltar until its destruction 10,000 years previous.

In "Timaeus," Plato described Atlantis as a prosperous nation out to expand its domain: "Now in this island of Atlantis there was a great and wonderful empire which had rule over the whole island and several others, and over parts of the continent," he wrote, "and, furthermore, the men of Atlantis had subjected the parts of Libya within the columns of Heracles as far as Egypt, and of Europe as far as Tyrrhenia."

Plato went on to tell how the Atlanteans made a grave mistake by seeking to conquer Greece. They could not withstand the Greeks' military might, and following their defeat, a natural disaster sealed their fate. "Timaeus" continued: "But afterwards there occurred violent earthquakes and floods; and in a single day and night of misfortune all your warlike men in a body sank into the earth, and the island of Atlantis in like manner disappeared in the depths of the sea."

Interestingly, Plato told a more metaphysical* version of the Atlantis story in "Critias." There he described the lost continent as the kingdom of Poseidon, the god of the sea. This Atlantis was a noble, sophisticated society that reigned in peace for centuries, until its people became complacent and greedy. Angered by their fall from grace, Zeus chose to punish them by destroying Atlantis.

Although Plato was the first to use the term "Atlantis," there are antecedents to the legend. There is an Egyptian legend which Solon probably heard while traveling in Egypt, and was passed down to Plato years later. The island nation of Keftiu, home of one of the four pillars that held up the sky, was said to be a glorious advanced civilisation which was destroyed and sank beneath the ocean.

More significantly, there is another Atlantis-like story that was closer to Plato's world, in terms of time and geography... and it is based in fact. The Minoan Civilisation was a great and peaceful culture based on the island of Crete, which reigned as long ago as 2200 B.C. The Minoan island of Santorini, later known as Thera, was home to a huge volcano. In 1470 B.C., it erupted with a force estimated to be greater than Krakatoa, obliterating everything on Santorini's surface. The resulting earthquakes and tsunamis devastated the rest of the Minoan Civilisation, whose remnants were easily conquered by Greek forces.

Perhaps Santorini was the "real" Atlantis. Some have argued against this idea, noting Plato specified that Atlantis sank 10,000 years ago, but the Minoan disaster had taken place only 1,000 years earlier. Still, it could be that translation errors over the centuries altered what Plato really wrote, or maybe he was intentionally blurring the historical facts to suit his purposes. And there exists yet another strong possibility: that Plato entirely made Atlantis up himself.

Regardless, his story of the sunken continent went on to captivate the generations that followed. Other Greek thinkers, such as Aristotle and Pliny, disputed the existence of Atlantis, while Plutarch and Herodotus wrote of it as historical fact. Atlantis became entrenched in folklore all around the world, charted on ocean maps and sought by explorers.

In 1882, Ignatius Donnelly, a U.S. congressman from Minnesota, brought the legend into the American consciousness with his book, Atlantis: The Antediluvian World. In more recent years, the psychic Edgar Cayce (1877-1945) became the U.S.'s most prominent advocate of a factual Atlantis. Widely known as "The Sleeping Prophet," Cayce claimed the ability to see the future and to communicate with long-dead spirits from the past. He identified hundreds of people—including himself—as reincarnated* Atlanteans.

Cayce said that Atlantis had been situated near the Bermuda island of Bimini. He believed that Atlanteans possessed remarkable technologies, including supremely powerful "fire-

crystals" which they harnessed for energy. A disaster in which the fire-crystals went out of control was responsible for Atlantis's sinking, he said, in what sounds very much like a cautionary fable on the dangers of nuclear power. Remaining active beneath the ocean waves, damaged fire-crystals send out energy fields that interfere with passing ships and aircraft—which is how Cayce accounted for the Bermuda Triangle.

Cayce prophesied that part of Atlantis would rise again to the surface in "1968 or 1969." It didn't, and no one has yet found hard evidence that it was ever there. With sonar tracing and modern knowledge of plate tectonics, it appears impossible that a mid-Atlantic continent could have once existed. Still, many argue that there must have been an Atlantis, because of the many cultural similarities on either side of the ocean which could not have developed independently, making Atlantis quite literally a "missing link"—the topographical* equivalent of Bigfoot.

Glossary

metaphysical: Highly abstract or theoretical; abstruse

reincarnated: be born anew in another body after death

topographical: Graphic representation of the surface features of a place or region on a map

Questions 1–10

Complete the summary below.

*Choose **NO MORE THAN THREE WORDS** from the passage for each answer.*

The story of Atlantis originated from **1** ...., and then passed down to the **2** ...., from whom the Greek philosopher, Plato, procured the records and described them in two of his dialogues. In "Timaeus", Plato depicted Atlantis as a great empire, to which the parts of Libya and Tyrrhenia had been **3** .... But the Greek army defeated Atlanteans, and some **4** .... such as violent earthquakes and floods, followed. The island finally vanished in the sea. However, "Critias" has another version. Plato ascribed the destruction of the continent to Atlanteans' **5** .... and **6** ...., which incurred punishment from the Greek God. No matter what the truth is, the sunken Atlantis kept mesmerising people generation after generation. More recently, Edgar Cayce, a psychic of the US, even claimed that Atlanteans **7** .... high technologies, including **8** .... the powerful energy source, much like today's **9** .... But there is no hard evidence. Still, many believed the existence of the lost continent, on the basis of the **10** .... on both sides of the ocean.

▶ 核心词汇

词汇	释义
boast	[bəʊst] *v.* 有……可以夸耀
cataclysm	['kætəklɪzəm] *n.* 灾难，大洪水
legend	['ledʒənd] *n.* 传说，传奇（形容词形式：legendary）
validity	[və'lɪdəti] *n.* 有效性，正确性（相应词形变化：valid *adj.*，validate *v.*）
proponent	[prə'pəʊnənt] *n.* 支持者、倡导者（前三个字母 "pro" 表示 "支持"，反义词是 "op-ponent"——opponent。）
philosopher	[fə'lɒsəfə(r)] *n.* 哲学家（相应词形变化：philosophy *n.* 哲学　philosophical *adj.* 哲学的）
priest	[priːst] *n.* 牧师
prosperous	['prɒspərəs] *adj.* 繁荣的（相应词形变化：prosper *v.*，prosperity *n.*）
grave	[greɪv] *adj.* 严重的，重大的（名词形式：gravity）
withstand	[wɪð'stænd] *vt.* 抵挡，经受住
might	[maɪt] *n.* 力量，威力（形容词形式：mighty）
disaster	[dɪ'zɑːstə(r)] *n.* 灾难，灾祸（ "dis-aster" 表示 "否定意义＋星星"，古罗马人相信人的生活受天上的星星的位置影响，这个单词字面意思为 "星位不正"，那么必然有 "灾祸、灾难" 降临。）
seal	[siːl] *vt.* 结束（原意：密封，加封条）
sophisticated	[sə'fɪstɪkeɪtɪd] *adj.* 高度发展的，成熟完善的
greedy	['griːdɪ] *adj.* 贪婪的（名词形式：greed。Greed属于 "七宗罪" Seven Deadly Sins 之一，其他六个为Pride/Vanity, Envy, Gluttony, Lust, Anger/Wrath, and Sloth。）
antecedent	[ˌæntɪ'siːdnt] *n.* 先前的事情，前面的事件（ "ante" 表示 "先" 或者 "前"。）
pillar	['pɪlə(r)] *n.* 柱子，栋梁，重要的支持者
glorious	['glɔːrɪəs] *adj.* 显赫的；光荣的（名词形式：glory）
obliterate	[ə'blɪtəreɪt] *v.* 删除；使淹没（名词形式：obliteration）
devastate	['devəsteɪt] *v.* 毁坏（形容词形式：devastating；所谓devastating beauty，其字面意思是 "具有毁灭性的美丽"，其实说的就是某人的美貌 "倾国倾城"。）
remnant	['remnənt] *n.* 剩余，残余
blur	[blɜː(r)] *v.* 把……弄模糊，使界限不清
captivate	['kæptɪveɪt] *v.* （以某种感染力）吸引，迷住（名词形式：captivation）
prophet	['prɒfɪt] *n.* 先知，预言者
supremely	[suː'priːmlɪ] *adv.* 极度地；至高地（形容词形式：supreme）
harness	['hɑːnɪs] *v.* 利用……使产生动力

nuclear	[ˈnjuːklɪə(r)] *adj.* 核的，原子能的（几个具体搭配：核弹nuclear bomb；核能 nuclear energy；核燃料nuclear fuel；核反应堆nuclear reactor。）

▶ 雅思阅读真题同义词考点

boast	—have, possess, pride oneself on, lay claim to
proponent	—advocate, supporter, champion
withstand	—endure, survive, tolerate, weather
might	—power, force, potency
devastate	—ruin, wreck, ravage, destroy
captivate	—attract, charm, fascinate, enchant, draw
harness	—use, utilise, employ, exploit

下篇导读：【超市起源】

考试时间：2009-12-03，2012-02-25……

　　探寻现代超市的起源；看克拉伦斯·桑德斯打破传统，设计并不断升级顾客自选售货方式；他的创新和思想超前于他的时代。☺

Reading Passage 6

Clarence Saunders

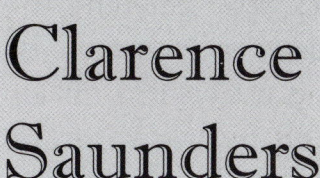

Clarence Saunders was an American grocer who first developed the modern retail sales model of self service. His ideas have had a massive influence on the development of the modern supermarket. Clarence Saunders worked for most of his life trying to develop a truly automated store, developing Piggly Wiggly, Keedoozle, and Foodelectric store concepts.

Born in Virginia, Saunders left school at 14 to clerk in a general store. Later he worked in an Alabama coke plant and in a Tennessee sawmill before he returned to the grocery business. By 1900, when he was nineteen years old, he was earning $30 a month as a salesman for a wholesale grocer. In 1902 he moved to Memphis where he formed a grocery wholesale cooperative. Through his experiences he became convinced that many small grocers failed because of heavy credit losses and high overhead. Consequently in 1915 he organised the Saunders-Blackburn Co., a grocery wholesaler which sold for cash only and encouraged its retail customers to do the same.

After leaving Clarksville, Tennessee, on September 6, 1916, Saunders launched the self-service revolution in the USA by opening the first self-service Piggly Wiggly store, at 79 Jefferson Street in Memphis, Tennessee, with its characteristic turnstile at the entrance. Customers paid cash and selected their own goods from the shelves.

The store incorporated shopping baskets, self-service branded products, and checkouts at the front. Removing unnecessary clerks, creating elaborate aisle displays, and rearranging the store to force customers to view all of the merchandise were just some of the characteristics of the early Piggly Wiggly stores. The concept of the "Self-Serving Store" was patented by Saunders in 1917.

Though this format of grocery market was drastically different from its competitors, the style became the standard for the modern grocery store and later supermarket. By 1922, six years after opening the first store, Piggly Wiggly had grown into 1,200 stores in 29 states. By 1932, the chain had grown to 2,660 stores doing over $180 million annually. Piggly Wiggly stores were both owned by the firm and franchised.

The success of Piggly Wiggly encouraged a raft of imitators, including Handy Andy stores, Helpy Selfy stores, Mick-or-Mack stores and Jitney Jungle, all of which operated under patented systems. Saunders then listed Piggly Wiggly on the New York Stock Exchange.

In the early 1920s Saunders began construction of a pink marble mansion in Memphis. Then, in early 1923, a group of franchised outlets in New York failed. Because of this financial reversal, Saunders was forced to sell his partly completed Memphis mansion to the city. The mansion, nicknamed the Pink Palace, eventually became the city's historical and natural history museum. Today, the Pink Palace includes a walk-through model of the first Piggly-Wiggly store, complete with 2¢ packets of Kellogg's Cornflakes and 8¢ cans of Campbell's Soup. Some of the grounds of the mansion were sold off to developers who built an upscale residential development, Chickasaw Gardens.

Saunders went on to create the "Clarence Saunders Sole Owner of My Name Stores" chain in 1928. The chain, which was known by the public as "Sole Owner" stores, initially flourished, with 675 stores operating and annual sales of $60 million in 1929. However the chain went into bankruptcy in 1930 at the start of the Great Depression.

During the war, Saunders designed and sold wooden toys. In the late 1920s, to promote his newest grocery venture, Saunders founded a professional football team. The full name of the team was the *Clarence Saunders Sole Owner of My Name Tigers*, but it was usually just called *The Tigers*. *The Tigers* played professional teams from around the country, including the *Chicago Bears* and the *Green Bay Packers*. In 1929, the *Tigers* beat the *Green Bay Packers* 20–6. In 1930 the National Football League invited *The Tigers* to join their organisation, but Saunders refused their offer. It is claimed that Saunders disbanded his football team because he did not like to travel to other cities for away games.

Then, in 1937, Saunders designed and constructed a prototype of an automated store, which he called the "Keedoozle" (for "Key Does All"). The Keedoozle was a completely automated store, similar to very large vending machine, based on modern supply chain principles.

Merchandise was displayed as single units each within a glass cabinet under which was a keyhole. Customers entering the store were handed a small pistol-like key that they placed in the keyhole below the goods they wished to buy, the quantity being determined by the number of times they pulled the key's trigger. This action, recorded on punched tape, activated back office machinery to assemble the order, which was then dispatched to the checkout on a conveyor belt. On reaching the checkout, the customer's tape was run through a reader to produce the bill, their groceries being assembled, boxed and waiting for collection. This system eliminated the need for shopping carts; and it increased savings in space, in the labor needed to stock the shelves, and in the time customers spent queuing at the checkout.

Saunders developed two versions of the Keedoozle. The first was developed in 1937, the development of which was abandoned when the United States entered World War II. Saunders returned to the idea in 1948, opening an improved version. Saunders sold twelve franchises to the revised concept. In 1949 he predicted: "In five years there will be a thousand Keedoozles throughout the U.S., selling $5 billion worth of goods."

Unfortunately the machinery, much of which Saunders built himself, proved unreliable, particularly at busy times and the resulting delays coupled with a heavy maintenance bill killed the Keedoozle in 1949.

Until the time of his death in October 1953, Saunders was developing plans for another automatic store system called the "Foodelectric." The Foodelectric concept is a clear predecessor to self checkout. Saunders described it as follows:

"The store operates so automatically that the customer can collect her groceries herself, wrap them and act as her own cashier. It eliminates the checkout crush, cuts overhead expenses and enables a small staff to handle a tremendous volume... I can handle a $2 million volume with only eight employees."

The central invention was a primitive computer, or "shopping brain" which was loaned the shopper, who then roams among the store's glass-enclosed items. To get a box of noodles, she slips the computer into a slot. The price registers in the computer and the noodle box slides down a chute. When she reaches the cashier, there is no need to wait while the prices of individual items are rung up. She simply pays the total displayed on the computer's windowed forehead.

Saunders had a reputation for brilliance, contrariness, and eccentricity. Sadly, his death came just as the full impact of his "better idea" for grocery merchandising was becoming apparent; his creative genius was decades ahead of his time.

Questions 1–5

Complete the summary using the list of words below.

NB *There are more words than spaces so you will not use them all.*

Clarence Saunders spent his life time developing automated store. In 1915, he opened a grocery wholesaler which sold for cash only because he believed many grocers became bankruptcy due to 1 .... and 2 .... His first self-serving store called 3 .... employed shopping baskets, checkouts at the front, elaborate aisle displays and less 4 .... This style was the benchmark for the 5 ....

List of Words

Handy Andy	Piggly Wiggly	franchises	competitors
supermarket	high price	heavy credit losses	clerks
Foodelectric	high cost		

Questions 6–11

Complete the summary using the list of words below.

NB *There are more words than spaces so you will not use them all.*

In 1937, Saunders designed a completely automated store called the Keedoozle. The 6 .... were placed within a glass cabinet and customers used a key to decide what and how many goods they wished to buy. This information then passed to 7 .... which could assemble the order and dispatch it to the checkout. This store saved both consumers' waiting time and the 8 .... needed to stock the shelves, and 9 .... were no longer necessary. However, because of the 10 ...., the Keedoozle ended in 1949.

List of Words

keyhole	sample goods	trigger	back office machinery	busy time
staff	shopping carts	unreliable machinery	space	customer

▶ 核心词汇

词汇	释义
automated	['ɔːtəmeɪtɪd] *adj.* 自动化的（auto-表示"自己"。automobile *n.* 汽车；automatic *adj.* 自动的；autonomous *adj.* 自治的；autonomy *n.* 自治；autobiography，autocracy）
sawmill	['sɔːmɪl] *n.* 锯木厂
overhead	[ˌəʊvə'hed] *n.* 管理费用，经常费用
launch	[lɔːntʃ] *v.* 发动，开展（活动、计划等）
turnstile	['tɜːnstaɪl] *n.* （入口处等的）旋转式栅门，旋杆
incorporate	[ɪn'kɔːpəreɪt] *v.* 包含，混合（名词形式：incorporation公司。区分cooperate *v.* 合作，协作）
elaborate	[ɪ'læbərət] *adj.* 精心制作的
merchandise	['mɜːtʃəndaɪs] *n.* 商品，货物（同义词：goods, commodity）
franchise	['fræntʃaɪz] *v.* 给……以特许权，出售特许权（franchiser *n.* 经销商，代销商）
a raft of	大量的
imitator	['ɪmɪteɪtə(r)] *n.* 模仿者（动词形式：imitate；名词形式：imitation）
mansion	['mænʃn] *n.* 大厦
outlet	['aʊtlet] *n.* 经销店；出口（喜欢shopping的同学不用背这个词啦，燕莎奥特莱斯outlets，赛特奥特莱斯outlets；指品牌直销购物中心）
reversal	[rɪ'vɜːsl] *n.* 倒转，颠倒
upscale	[ˌʌp'skeɪl] *adj.* 高档的
The Great Depression	经济大萧条（指1929至1933年间全球性的经济大衰退，推荐了解该事件背景）
disband	[dɪs'bænd] *v.* （使）解散，散伙，解体
prototype	['prəʊtətaɪp] *n.* 原型，雏形，蓝本
vending machine	自动贩卖机
pistol-like	['pɪstllaɪk] *adj.* 类似手枪的
assemble	[ə'sembl] *v.* 集合，收集
eliminate	[ɪ'lɪmɪneɪt] *v.* 排除，淘汰
maintenance	['meɪntənəns] *n.* 维持，保持；保养（动词形式：maintain）
predecessor	['priːdɪsesə(r)] *n.* 前任，前辈；原有事物，前身
crush	[krʌʃ] *n.* 拥挤的人群
volume	['vɒljuːm] *n.* 量，大量（该词还指"体积，容积"。area指"面积"）
roam	[rəʊm] *v.* 随便走；眼睛或手（缓慢地）扫遍，摸遍
slot	[slɒt] *n.* 位置；狭槽
chute	[ʃuːt] *n.* 斜槽；滑道

| contrariness | ['kɑntreərɪnɪs] *n.* 矛盾；乖张 |
| eccentricity | [ˌeksen'trɪsətɪ] *n.* 古怪，反常，怪癖（形容词形式：eccentric） |

▶ 雅思阅读真题同义词考点

launch	—introduce, start, spring
overhead	—expense, expenditure, cost
a raft of	—a lot of, massive, many
imitate	—copy, emulate, replicate, duplicate
staff	—clerk, employee, worker, crew, personnel
eccentric	—strange, odd, weird, peculiar, bizarre, abnormal, unusual

下篇导读： 【学术欺骗】

考试时间： 2012-01-12……

　　编造实验结论，抄袭学术论文，中外皆有。看一位学术造假者差一点儿获得诺贝尔奖！呼唤科学界的学术道德。 ☺

Reading Passage **Ⅰ**

Fraud in Science

A For many years physicists lagged way behind biologists in the perpetration of scientific fraud. But in 2002 they have caught up in spectacular style with the ambitious opus of Jan Henrik Schon of Bell Labs, who placed seven of his fictive works in *Nature* and nine in *Science*. Schon was even talked about as a possible Nobel Prize winner. But other researchers grew more and more suspicious until finally someone pointed out that he had published identical graphs in separate papers, supposedly on different phenomena. The laboratory convened an external investigation panel and Schon was found guilty of misconduct and sacked.

B Fraud in science is a minor irritant from one perspective, a serious problem from another. Most instances of fraud concern work of little importance and are quickly forgotten. Some practitioners forsake the safety of mundane fabrication and concoct spectacular experiments about matters at the cutting edge of their fields. But one can argue that the more ambitious the fraud, the more quickly it will be discovered.

C The Schon case does not strongly support this contention. His fraud remained undetected for two years. He was detected because of an insider's tip, not by the usual checking mechanisms of science: refereeing and replication. Had he had the good sense to stop in time, his oeuvre might have gained him a professorship from which he could have directed the work of an army of honest PhDs and laid a firmer basis for his scientific standing.

D Science is a cumulative process, however, and in the long run each brick must bear the load of those placed above it. So there is much force to the argument that incorrect results of any kind—whether obtained by fraud, self-deception, or other regrettable human frailties—cannot last indefinitely.

E But they can last a long time, breezing past the conventional checkpoints of scientific quality without the slightest difficulty. This is the sense in which fraud is a serious problem, both of methodology and of public relations. Scientists point to the refereeing system as a guarantor of quality, but in the next breath will assert that referees cannot be expected to detect fraud. In fact, a referee, who after all is just doing an unpaid paper review, cannot test for much more than plausibility. That's a useful function, but it's not very effective as a screen against fraud.

F Replication is central to scientific methodology, but in practice it's almost never an exact duplication of the kind necessary to support an accusation of fraud. There are plenty of honest reasons why two researchers may get different results from the same experiment. A claim that cannot be replicated is generally ignored, not publicly repudiated. Like refereeing, replication plays a useful purpose in science, but it is not designed to detect fraud and rarely does so.

G Many, perhaps most, cases of fraud come to light because someone in the perpetrator's laboratory, someone in a position to observe his behaviour and see the raw data, gets uncomfortable enough to blow the whistle. The front line of defense against fraud is not methodological but personal. The lab chief is in the best position to detect fraud. Only he can demand to see the lab notebooks, evidence that is beyond the reach of outsiders.

H Science, by this analysis, is institutionally vulnerable to fraud. Its quality control mechanisms do not prevent fraud, yet as each new case bursts into public view, scientists find themselves put in the generally false position of declaring that there is no need to worry, because the quality control mechanisms of science infallibly detect fraud.

I A more direct answer would be that research is not a process that can be made efficient. There is an inevitable degree of waste in the system, and fraud is generally not a serious enough problem to justify any measure that would cost significant time or money. However, it has not proved to be a popular response to go before Congress or the news cameras and declare, "Fraud happens— forget about it."

J There's a strong case for viewing the prevention of fraud as the direct responsibility of the lab chief. If the people he or she has hired are disturbed enough to cook data, the lab chief should get to know about it. If the lab chief puts his name on the concoction, intending to draw credit for it, he deserves a big share of the blowback. But at present every fraud case seems to end the same way. The perpetrator disappears from view, slinking off to become a pathologist in a Midwestern hospital. And the lab chief receives the commiseration of his pals for the unfortunate occurrence that fate visited on him.

Questions 1–5

Complete the summary below.

Choose your answers from the list below the summary.

NB *There are more words than spaces, so you will not use them all.*

Scientific fraud has been brought to the spotlight recently, as some practitioners **1** .... *abandon* the standard research methodology and forge experiment results. These **2** .... *concoctive* results cannot last forever because science is **3** .... *a cumulative process*, in which the later experiments are built on the results of the former ones. To prevent fraud, refereeing and replication, as the usual checking mechanisms of science, **4** .... *function* usefully, but not effectively. But **5** .... *the lab chief* can play an important role in the front line of defense against fraud.

List of Words		
the lab chief	function	working
accurate	concoctive	use
perpetrators	a cumulative process	abandon
design		

▶ 核心词汇

词汇	释义
fraud	[frɔːd] *n.* 欺骗（行为）
perpetration	[ˌpɜːpəˈtreɪʃn] *n.* 犯（罪行、错误等），施行（欺骗、谋杀等）（相关词形变化 perpetrate *v.*，perpetrator *n.*）
opus	[ˈəʊpəs] *n.* 大作，杰作，主要作品
suspicious	[səˈspɪʃəs] *adj.* 怀疑的，可疑的（动词形式：suspect）
identical	[aɪˈdentɪkl] *adj.* 同样的，完全相同的
convene	[kənˈviːn] *v.* 集合，召集（组织人员等）开会
panel	[ˈpænl] *n.* （由选定人员组成的）专门小组，评定小组
misconduct	[ˌmɪsˈkɒndʌkt] *n.* 不端行为，不法行为（很明显mis-conduct指的是"行为conduct"上的错误举动。）
sack	[sæk] *vt.* 解雇
perspective	[pəˈspektɪv] *n.* （观察问题的）视角，观点
forsake	[fəˈseɪk] *v.* 放弃，抛弃
fabrication	[ˌfæbrɪˈkeɪʃn] *n.* 捏造，伪造（动词形式：fabricate）
referee	[ˌrefəˈriː] *v.* 审阅，坚定
throng	[θrɒŋ] *v.* 在……群集，使拥塞
frailty	[ˈfreɪltɪ] *n.* 脆弱，品德上的弱点（形容词形式：frail。英国大文豪莎士比亚Shakespeare名言："弱者，你的名字是女人！"其英语原文为"Frailty, thy name is woman." "thy"相当于现代英语中的代词"your"。）
indefinitely	[ɪnˈdefɪnətlɪ] *adv.* 无定限地，无限期地（相关单词：indefinite *adj.*，definite *adj.*）
duplication	[ˌdjuːplɪˈkeɪʃn] *n.* 复制，重复（动词形式：duplicate）
repudiate	[rɪˈpjuːdɪeɪt] *v.* 驳斥，批驳（名词形式：repudiation）
vulnerable	[ˈvʌlnərəbl] *adj.* 易受诱惑的，易受……影响的（名词形式：vulnerability）
infallibly	[ɪnˈfæləblɪ] *adv.* 绝对无误地（相关单词：infallible *adj.*，fallible *adj.*，fallibility *n.*）
inevitable	[ɪnˈevɪtəbl] *adj.* 不可避免的，必然的
justify	[ˈdʒʌstɪfaɪ] *v.* 证明……正当/正确（"just"是形容词，表示"正义的、正直的"，后边加上"ify"变成动词。体会下边一句话的含义："Ends justify means."——只要能达成目的，一切手段都是正确的。即"为达到目的可以不择手段"。）
Congress	[ˈkɒŋgres] *n.* （美国等国的）国会、议会（"con-gress"表示"共同/一起＋行走"，一群人走到一起去开会、去吵架，这样构成了国会。为什么"progress"表示"进步"？"pro-gress"，字面意思就是"往前走"。还有几个典型的表示国会的单词，Parliament 英国等国，Knesset 以色列等，Diet 日本、瑞士等。）
cook	[kʊk] *v.* 篡改（数据、账目等）

commiseration	[kəˌmɪzəˈreɪʃn] *n.* 同情，怜悯；慰问（动词形式：commiserate）

▶ 雅思阅读真题同义词考点

fraud	—deceit, deception, dishonesty, cheating
misconduct	—misbehaviour, delinquency, wrongdoing
sack	—fire, dismiss, discharge
forsake	—abandon, desert, discard, throw away
fabrication	—forgery, fiction, falsehood, invention
inevitable	—unavoidable, foreseeable, predictable, inescapable

下篇导读：　【涂鸦争议】

考试时间：　2011-09-15，2011-12-17，2012-08-25，2014-12-06……

　　涂鸦起源于美国黑帮在街头墙壁涂画记号，如今已演变成一种另类艺术。但许多国家对此有不同的看法和立法。有的涂鸦艺人举办个人艺术展览，有的却被判入狱思过。😊

Reading Passage 8

Graffiti: Street Art or Crime

On the face of it, as a society, we seem to be a little mixed-up when it comes to "graffiti", as you call it if you work in the local council's cleansing department, or "street art" as you say if you're the man—and they do mainly seem to be male—wielding the spray can.

But the confusion now runs deeper than those who spray and those who remove the paint. Great British institutions have been polarised. Last week the might of English law delivered its verdict at Southwark Crown Court in London where five members of the DPM Graffiti Crew were jailed—one, And rev. Gillman, for two years—after admitting conspiracy to cause criminal damage, costing the taxpayer at least £1 m.

By contrast, just down the road from the Court, the riverside facade of Tate Modern had been covered in giant murals by six urban artists with international reputations, including Blu from Bologna, Faile from New York, and Sixeart from Barcelona, in the first display of street art at a major museum.

The courtroom and the museum were so close that supporters of the men on trial popped down to the Tate to do a bit of retouching during one lunchtime break at the court. "There is a huge irony in the juxtaposition of the two events," said one of the artists.

The man to credit for bringing street art into established gallery spaces is Banksy. A few years ago he was sneaking his work into galleries such as the Louvre and Tate Britain. Now Tate Modern is selling his book in its gift shop. His works sell for hundreds of thousands of pounds and he was recently featured in a retrospective exhibition alongside Andy Warhol. He, more than anyone else, has legitimised the genre and spawned a new generation of young imitators—much to the displeasure of those who want to clean up behind them.

Bob has been involved in graffiti since 1982 when he was a punk. He now works, by day, for a London art gallery and describes himself as an upstanding taxpayer. "London is to street art, at the start of the 21st century, what Paris was for Impressionism at the start of the 20th," he says with genuine immodesty. "And yet we hate graffiti more than anywhere else in the world. England is by far and away the most draconian for punishments for what are only economic crimes."

A gallery in New York in the United States launches an exhibition next week based on the work of those convicted at Southwark. "DPM—Exhibit A", at the Anonymous Gallery Project in Soho, will display large photographs of the convicts' work alongside copies of their charge sheets to ask whether the men are criminals or artists.

It is a question which prompts different answers in different parts of the world, says Cedar Lewinsohn, the curator of the exhibition at Tate Modern. "Brazil for instance is more relaxed about it," he says. "In parts of Australia, they are like the UK and people really hate graffiti and tags on vans and trains, but in Melbourne drivers compete with each other as to whose van is more decorated."

They have similarly schizophrenic responses in other nations too. In Toronto, police have just hired a street artist to paint walls to help find the man who murdered the street artist's brother. Elsewhere in Canada, a court has ruled that, after a police crackdown on graffiti artists, a 28-year-old man is only allowed to venture into town if he is accompanied by his mother. One internet blogger wrote: "In their twenties and still vandalising other people's property—shouldn't they have moved on to drug dealing, or perhaps become real estate agents by that age?"

Street art, you see, is a highly polarising phenomenon. On the one hand there are those like the American artist Elura Emerald, who is also involved in next week's New York exhibition, who insist that "artists who paint on the street are merely expressing themselves, not hurting anyone" and should not be punished "but appreciated and celebrated." Then there are those like Judge Christopher Hardy who, in court in Southwark, described the activities of the DPM Crew as "a wholesale self-indulgent campaign to damage property on an industrial scale." How is such a dichotomy to be resolved? How, the Independent asked the street artist Bob, can artistic expression be reconciled with the fear and loathing that graffiti inspires in many citizens who see it as a symbol of lawlessness and the deterioration of their neighbourhood? "Well, not by sending them to jail," he says. Greenwich and Tower Hamlets councils in London agree. They commissioned members of the DPM to lead summer workshops as street art tutors for young and vulnerable people. The two councils sent references to court vouching that the DPM men were "positive" and "inspirational" in working with "young people who aren't able to do reading or writing." But it was not enough to save them from prison.

Questions 1–9

Complete the summary using the list of words, A–R, below.

The debate as to whether graffiti constitutes art is **1** .... D .... the establishment in

Great Britain. While one group of "graffiti artists" were being sent to prison, in an art gallery

not far from the court the work of several major street artists was being **2** .... J ...... G

on the side of the gallery facing the river. The street artist Bansky is responsible for

3 ...... L .... street art, leading to **4** .... L .... by the younger generation. London

has been described as the centre of street art in the world, but ironically at the same time the

5 .... H ...... there are greater.

Whether graffiti artists are considered as **6** ...... O ... C .... to be imprisoned or not

depends on which country they are in. For instance people in Brazil are **7** ...... R .... about

street art. So the question is whether street artists should be **8** .... F ...... as wrongdoers or

9 ...... Q .... as artists.

A	cleaned	**B**	uniting	**C**	criticising
D	dividing	**E**	destroying	**F**	punished
G	exhibited	**H**	penalties	**I**	displeasure
J	criminals	**K**	pleasure	**L**	promoting
M	avoided	**N**	painters	**O**	rewards
P	imitations	**Q**	appreciated	**R**	easygoing

▶ **核心词汇**

词汇	释义
graffiti	[grə'fiːtɪ] *n.* 涂鸦，在墙上的乱涂乱写（是graffito的复数形式。另一个词doodle也指涂鸦，特别指通过装饰公司的logo来纪念特定的节日或事件。比如百度和谷歌在某个节日时首页logo的变化）
wield	[wiːld] *v.* 手持着使用（武器、工具等）
spray	[spreɪ] *n.* 喷雾，喷雾器
institution	[ˌɪnstɪ'tjuːʃn] *n.* 机构
polarise	['pəʊləraɪz] *v.* 极化，两极分化（polar *n.*极，两极；*adj.* 两极的；polar bear 北极熊）
verdict	['vɜːdɪkt] *n.* （陪审团的）裁决，裁定
conspiracy	[kən'spɪrəsɪ] *n.* 阴谋，反叛，共谋（spir=to breathe，呼吸，来源于拉丁文spirare。如：spirit呼吸，生命的根源→精神，灵魂；aspire 对着某物呼吸→渴望；inspiration里面的呼吸，精神的启示→灵感。conspiracy字面意思就是"一同呼吸"→"共谋，共同促成"。民国时期著名的法学家、翻译家吴经雄在*Beyond West and East*《超越东西方》一书中说：A man respires, aspires, perspires, inspires, and finally expires.一个人先是呼吸，接着立志，然后出汗，然后奋发，最后断气。）
facade	[fə'sɑːd] *n.* 建筑物的正面；外表
mural	['mjʊərəl] *n.* （通常指大型的）壁画
retouch	[ˌriː'tʌtʃ] *v.* 润色，修描
juxtaposition	[ˌdʒʌkstəpə'zɪʃn] *n.* 并列，毗邻
sneak into	潜入，混进，混入
retrospective	[ˌretrə'spektɪv] *adj.* 回顾的，怀旧的（spec=to see, to look看见；如：spectacle用来看的东西→景象，眼镜；prospect 向前看→前途，期望；inspect往里看→检查，视察；respect再一次看，一再注视→重视，尊敬；suspect向下看，像看到外表现象以下的东西→怀疑；retrospect 往回看→回顾，反省；spectrum看得到的→光谱。）
legitimise	[lɪ'dʒɪtəmaɪz] *v.* 使合法，给……以合法地位
genre	['ʒɒnrə] *n.* 类型，种类，样式
spawn	[spɔːn] *v.* 引起，酿成（该词另一动词词义为：产卵。）
immodesty	[ɪ'mɒdɪstɪ] *n.* 无礼
draconian	[drə'kəʊnɪən] *adj.* 严厉的，苛刻的
curator	[kjʊə'reɪtə(r)] *n.* （图书馆等的）馆长
tag	[tæg] *n.* 标签（同义词：label）
vandalise	['vændəlaɪz] *v.* 肆意破坏（尤指公共财产）

self-indulgent	[selfɪn'dʌldʒənt] *adj.* 放纵自己的
campaign	[kæm'peɪn] *n.* 运动
dichotomy	[daɪ'kɒtəmɪ] *n.* 一分成二，对分
reconcile	['rekənsaɪl] *v.* 使和好，使和解；调停，排解（争端等）
loath	[ləʊθ] *adj.* 不愿意的，不喜欢的
deterioration	[dɪˌtɪərɪə'reɪʃn] *n.* 恶化，变坏
vulnerable	['vʌlnərəbl] *adj.* 易受伤的；易受批评的（同义词：subject，fragile）
vouch	[vaʊtʃ] *v.* 保证，担保；确定

▶ 雅思阅读真题同义词考点

polarise　　　　—divide, category, classify, group

criminal　　　　—convict, in jail, in prison, imprisoned

legitimate　　　—legal, lawful, justified

promote　　　　—improve, develop, boost

imitate　　　　—copy, duplicate, replicate *reprduce*

relaxing　　　　—easygoing, comfortable, not rigid, not nervous

下篇导读：【古代钱币】

考试时间： 2012-05-10，2014-01-18……

　　钱币是怎样在人类的历史中应运而生的；各国古代的钱币发展和艺术；中国孔方兄的出现，是因为古人衣服没有口袋，要用绳子串起钱币中间的方孔，方便携带保存。☺

Reading Passage 9

Ancient Money

Money as a medium of exchange in barter and trade has always in all times found expression in some form or other from necessity thereof. In the remotest periods, before gold or silver were generally in use, it took the form of animals, oxen, sheep, lambs, shells, etc. Thus people find used cattle in Germany, leather in Rome, sugar in the West Indies, shells in Siam, lead in Burma, platinum in Russia, tin in Great Britain, iron and nails in Scotland, brass in China, and finally copper, silver and gold the world over.

Gold and silver were originally in lumps, nuggets and bars, and in this manner weighed out in the making of payments for commercial transactions. Because there was no certainty of the purity of the metal no convenience in size necessity arose for smaller amounts and divisions, which were gradually made, vouched for, and a die stamp invented which was punched by hand on one side of the smaller lumps of gold and silver, thereby attesting to its purity and value, and so originated the first acts of coinage, which is generally attributed far back in ancient history to Lydia, a country in Asia Minor, celebrated for its mineral wealth and gold, where probably the first gold states were thus stamped with the symbol of a lion pressed on one side of the coin. Silver was first coined in these crude lumps on the island of Aegina, where the ancient Greeks stamped a turtle on their first silver coins over 700 years before the Christian era.

When the actual coinage of money was an accomplished and accepted fact, it was furthered along by the Greek nations, who, after stamping thereon turtles, owls, images and other objects of their divinity, finally with Alexander the Great, began to impress upon their coins crude portraits or heads of living persons and rulers. This method was kept up and improved upon by the Romans, who became proficient in the art, in consequence of which today an immense number of Roman coins and silver Denarii, were preserved for centuries.

After the decline and fall of the Roman empire, the coinage of money from an artistic standpoint began to deteriorate, and from the Byzantine period, money became crude in form and expression, unequal in shape or value, lacking design and execution. The early English Kings coined pennies, but they were crude and uncertain. William the Conqueror, in 1066, issued fair specimens of pennies, and Edward I, in 1280, issued a new coinage of pennies, half pence and farthings, but it remained for Queen Elizabeth of England to set a step forward when she introduced the first experiment of milling money, instead of hammering, and also the establishment in 1600 of a Colonial silver currency for use of the East Indian Company. After this period coins began to get more of an even roundness and shape, and all the large pieces, such as silver dollars or crowns, show again the gradual improvement and symmetry in the artistic work of coinage.

The Chinese asserted a coinage forty centuries ago, and seemed to have an organisation all of their own. It was different from those of all other countries, yet created through the same necessity of having some metal of a certain value to use as a medium of exchange in trade. This metal, mostly of bronze, finally developed into the familiar round brass coin, with a square hole in the centre called cash, which has been in use for centuries, the peculiar hieroglyphics thereon being generally the emperor's name, authority, and the value, which no doubt enabled a Chinese scholar to trace back their rulers by this method as one did on the Roman and other coins. They also made use of porcelain and small seashells. The coins of Japan issued some of copper, and Korea an alloy of both. The holes in these Chinese coins and in almost all coins of Asiatic countries came from the need of stringing them like beads for preservation, as the Chinese and Hindu had no pockets in the clothes they wore at that time.

The first money used in America was furnished chiefly by Great Britain and Spain, but the limited amount, scarcity, and need of it tempted the colony of Massachusetts to create a small mint in this country, in 1652, where they struck some silver pieces which are known as Oak or Pine Tree money, and are quite rare.

During and after the American war for independence, various coins were struck by private individuals and by orders of Congress. The state coinage of copper cents began with New Hampshire, 1776; Vermont and Connecticut, 1785; New Jersey, 1786; New York, 1787; followed by others until April 2nd, 1792, when President Washington signed a law to establish a United States mint, which went into effect at once. On September 1st the first six pounds of copper were bought for coinage. On September 21st, three coinage presses arrived from Europe and early in October 1792, the first half dimes and a few copper cents patterns were struck by the new United States mint. In 1793 the regular issue of copper cents began, which first appeared in a number of different styles, such as wreath, link, liberty cap, etc.. In 1794 the first dollar, half dollar and half dime were struck, in 1796 the first quarter and dime, in 1873 the first trade dollar. Gold coins were also issued by private parties as early as 1834. The study of ancient coins is one of the most interesting historic as well as artistic subjects. Some coins are today the only record extant of important events in the world's history and the existence of cities and nations long since gone forever.

Questions 1–8

Complete the summary using the list of words, A–P, below.

In the beginning of money usage, people 1 .... crude lumps of gold and silver to make payments in trade transactions. Later, 2 .... amounts and portions were made and a die stamp was used to 3 .... to the purity and value. That is how coinage originated. It is generally believed that gold was first coined in 4 ...., and silver on the island of Aegina. The techniques of coinage were promoted by 5 ...., and then Roman. But as the Roman Empire fell, the coin lost its 6 .... value and became crude again. Until Queen Elizabeth of England introduced the first experiment of milling money, the 7 .... and 8 .... of coinage work revived. In ancient China, people used 9 .... to store coins with holes because there were no pockets in their clothes. The study of ancient coins has a 10 .... meaning since some are the only record of ancient civilisation.

A	historic	**B**	strings	**C**	beads	**D**	artistic
E	Great Britain	**F**	punched	**G**	attest	**H**	the Greek nations
I	Lydia	**J**	sold	**K**	smaller	**L**	gradual improvement
M	large	**N**	symmetry	**O**	furnished	**P**	weighed out

▶ 核心词汇

词汇	释义
exchange	[ɪksˈtʃeɪndʒ] *n.* 交换，交易
barter	[ˈbɑːtə(r)] *n.* 交换，以物易物的交换
oxen	[ˈɒksən] *n.* （ox的复数）牛，公牛
originally	[əˈrɪdʒənəlɪ] *adv.* 最初，原先（相应词形变化：origin *n.*，originate *v.*）
lump	[lʌmp] *n.* 块、团形状，不规则的块或团
transaction	[trænˈzækʃn] *n.* 交易，业务
vouch for	担保，保证
punch	[pʌntʃ] *v.* 用力打进（除此之外，"punch"还有一个含义使用频率很高，作动词表示"用拳猛击"，例如"You should have punched him!""你就应该给他一拳！"）
attest to	证明，证实
coinage	[ˈkɔɪnɪdʒ] *n.* 铸币，造币
celebrated	[ˈselɪbreɪtɪd] *adj.* 著名的（"celebrate"作动词表示"祝贺，赞美"，无论走到哪里都受到人们的祝贺，听到别人的赞美之辞，此人必定了得，名气不小！）
crude	[kruːd] *adj.* 天然的，未经加工的（名词形式：crudity；典型搭配"crude oil"表示"原油"。）
owl	[aʊl] *n.* 猫头鹰（晚上特别能熬夜的人中文里把他们称为"夜猫子"，对应的英语也差不多是这个意思——night owl，那与之相反，晚上不熬夜，早晨起来精神饱满的人一般被形容为"fresh daisy"，来自短语"as fresh as a daisy in the morning"。）
divinity	[dɪˈvɪnətɪ] *n.* 神，神威（形容词形式：divine）
proficient	[prəˈfɪʃnt] *adj.* 熟练的，精通的（名词形式：proficiency）
in consequence of	由于……的缘故
immense	[ɪˈmens] *adj.* 巨大的，无边的（名词形式：immensity）
decline	[dɪˈklaɪn] *n.* 下倾，下降，衰败，衰落（这个单词的第一个释义就是它的基本含义，即"de-cline"对应"下＋倾"。）
deteriorate	[dɪˈtɪərɪəreɪt] *v.* 恶化，变糟（名词形式：deterioration）
specimen	[ˈspesɪmən] *n.* 样品，样本
issue	[ˈɪʃuː] *v.* 发行（钞票等）
hammer	[ˈhæmə(r)] *v.* 用锤敲打（作名词表示"锤子"，这里活用作动词。）
colonial	[kəˈləʊnɪəl] *adj.* 殖民（地）的（相应词形变化：colony *n.*，colonise *v.*，colonisation *n.*）
symmetry	[ˈsɪmətrɪ] *n.* 对称，相称（形容词形式：symmetrical）

porcelain	['pɔːsəlɪn] *n.* 瓷器，瓷
alloy	['ælɔɪ] *n.* 合金
string	[strɪŋ] *v.* 串起……（作名词表示"一串儿……"，例如"a string of beads"。）
bead	[biːd] *n.* 珠子[形容词形式：beady，经常用来形容人的眼睛，那么什么样的眼睛才是"beady eyes"呢？第一，不大；第二，圆；第三、闪亮（动人）。]
scarcity	['skeəsətɪ] *n.* 缺乏，不足（形容词形式：scarce）

▶ **雅思阅读真题同义词考点**

exchange	—trade, swap, barter
originally	—initially, primarily, at the outset
celebrated	—famous, renowned, eminent, distinguished
crude	—raw, unrefined, unpolished, unprocessed
proficient	—capable, skilled, adept, competent
immense	—vast, enormous, gigantic, colossal, immeasurable
symmetry	—balance, evenness, equilibrium, regularity
scarcity	—lack, shortage, paucity, insufficiency

下篇导读： 【滑石粉】

考试时间： 2010-03-06，2013-01-05……

　　无处不在的滑石粉；从纸张、化妆品、爽身粉到口香糖；滑石粉在口香糖中的作用；滑石粉提高橄榄油的产量；滑石粉作为水果的防晒霜？ ☺

Reading Passage 10

Talc Powder

How talc found its way into food and agricultural products—from chewing gum to olive oil.

High in the French Pyrenees, some 1,700 m above sea level, lies Trimouns, a huge deposit of hydrated magnesium silicate—talc to you and me. Talc from Trimouns, and from ten other Luzenac mines across the globe, is used in the manufacture of a vast array of everyday products extending from paper, paint and plaster to cosmetics, plastics and car tyres. And of course there is always talc's best known end use: talcum powder for babies' bottoms. But the true versatility of this remarkable mineral is nowhere better displayed than in its sometimes surprising use in certain niche markets in the food and agriculture industries.

Take, for example, the chewing gum business. Every year, Talc de Luzenac France—which owns and operates the Trimouns mine supplies about 6,000 tonnes of talc to chewing gum manufacturers in Europe. But how is talc actually used in the manufacture of chewing gum? Patrick Delord, an engineer who has been with Luzenac for 22 years explains that chewing gum has four main components. "The most important of them is the gum base," he says. "It's the gum base that puts the chew into chewing gum. It binds all the ingredients together, creating a soft, smooth texture. To this the manufacturer then adds sweeteners, softeners and flavourings. Our talc is used as a filler in the gum base. The amount varies between, say, 10 and 35 per cent, depending on the type of gum. Fruit flavoured chewing gum, for example, is slightly acidic and would react with the calcium carbonate that the manufacturer might otherwise use as a filler. Talc, on the other hand, makes an ideal filler because it's non-reactive chemically. In the factory, talc is also used to dust the gum base pellets and to stop the chewing gum sticking during the lamination and packing processes." Delord adds.

The chewing gum business is, however, just one example of talc's use in the food sector. For the past 20 years or so, olive oil processors in Spain have been taking advantage of talc's unique characteristics to help them boost the amount of oil they extract from crushed olives. According to Patrick Delord, talc is especially useful for treating what he calls "difficult" olives. After the olives are harvested—preferably early in the morning because their taste is better if they are gathered in the cool of the day—they are taken to the processing plant. There they are crushed and then stirred for 30–45 minutes. In the old days, the resulting paste was passed through an olive press but nowadays it's more common to add water and centrifuge the mixture to separate the water and oil from the solid matter. The oil and water are then allowed to settle so that the olive oil layer can be decanted off and bottled. "Difficult" olives are those that are more reluctant than the norm to yield up their full oil content. This may be attributable to the particular species of olive, or to its water content and the time of year the olives are collected—at the beginning and the end of the season their water content is often either too high or too low. These olives are easy to recognise because they produce a lot of extra foam during the stirring process, a consequence of an excess of a fine solid that acts as a natural emulsifier. The oil in this emulsion is lost when the water is disposed of. Not only that, if the waste water is disposed of directly into local fields—often the case in many smaller processing operations—the emulsified oil may take some time to biodegrade and so be harmful to the environment.

"If you add between a half and two per cent of talc by weight during the stirring process, it absorbs the natural emulsifier in the olives and so boosts the amount of oil you can extract," says Delord. "In addition, talc's flat, 'platey' structure helps increase the size of the oil droplets liberated during stirring, which again improves the yield. However, because talc is chemically inert, it doesn't affect the colour, taste, appearance or composition of the resulting olive oil."

If the use of talc in olive oil processing and in chewing gum is long established, new applications in the food and agriculture industries are also constantly being sought by Luzenac. One such promising new market is fruit crop protection, being pioneered in the US. Just like people, fruit can get sunburned. In fact, in very sunny regions up to 45 percent of a typical crop can be affected by heat stress and sunburn. However, in the case of fruit, it's not so much the ultra violet rays which harm the crop as the high surface temperature that the sun's rays create.

To combat this, farmers normally use either chemicals or spray a continuous fine canopy of mist above the fruit trees or bushes. The trouble is, this uses a lot of water—normally a precious commodity in hot, sunny areas—and it is therefore expensive. What's more, the ground can quickly become waterlogged. "So our idea was to coat the fruit with talc to protect it from the sun," says Greg Hunter, a marketing specialist who has been with

Luzenac for ten years. "But to do this, several technical challenges had first to be overcome. Talc is very hydrophobic: it doesn't like water. So in order to have a viable product we needed a wet table powder—something that would go readily into suspension so that it could be sprayed onto the fruit. It also had to break the surface tension of the cut in (the natural waxy, waterproof layer on the fruit) and of course it had to wash off easily when the fruit was harvested. No-one's going to want an apple that's covered in talc."

Initial trials in the State of Washington in 2003 showed that when the product was sprayed onto Granny Smith apples, it reduced their surface temperature and lowered the incidence of sunburn by up to 60 per cent. Today the new product, known as Invelop Maximum SPF, is in its second commercial year on the US market. Apple growers are the primary target although Hunter believes grape growers represent another sector with long term potential.

Questions 1–9

Complete the sentence below.

*Choose **NO MORE THAN THREE WORDS** from the text for each answer.*

1   Besides talc, the components of chewing gum include ...sweethers..., ...softeners.. and
    ....f.o.l.var.fing

2   Chewing gum manufactures add talc in the gum base as a ....filler...... .

3   Difficult olives can be easily identified because they yield additional ...tt........ in
    the stirring process.

4   The emulsified oil may damage the ...environment... because it cannot biodegrade soon.

5   Talc can enlarge the ...size........... of the oil droplets during stirring.

6   Since it is ...chemically..., talc doesn't change the traits of the olive oil.

7   The new application of talc is to protect ...fruit..... crop

8   Spraying talc powder onto apples can lower their ...surface........ and reduce sunburn.

9   Today, ...product....... are the major customers of Invelop Maximum SPF.

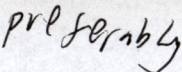

▶ **核心词汇**

词汇	释义
talc	[tælk] *n.* 滑石，云母
hydrated	['haɪdreɪtɪd] *adj.* 含水的，与水结合的
magnesium	[mæg'niːzɪəm] *n.*【化】镁（金属元素）
silicate	['sɪlɪkeɪt] *n.* 硅酸盐
array	[ə'reɪ] *n.* 数组；一大批
cosmetic	[kɒz'metɪk] *n.* 美容品，化妆品（常用单词：moisturiser保湿；sun screen 防晒霜；hand lotion/moisturiser护手霜；night cream晚霜；skin care护肤；whitening美白；facial cleanser洗面奶；facial mask/masque面膜；lipstick 口红）
versatility	[ˌvɜːsə'tɪlətɪ] *n.* 多用途（形容词形式：versatile）
niche	[niːʃ] *n.* 有利可图的缺口，商机
component	[kəm'pəʊnənt] *n.*成分（同义词：ingredient）
texture	['tekstʃə(r)] *n.* 质地；结构
acidic	[ə'sɪdɪk] *adj.*（味）酸的；[化]酸的，酸性的
calcium	['kælsɪəm] *n.*【化】钙（calc=lime 石灰/stone 石头。古代商人用小圆石头来计算得失损益，古罗马的算盘也是用calculus作为算珠。calculate "计算" 一词即源于此。所以calculus既有 "计算→微积分" 的含义，又有 "小圆石→结石" 的含义）
carbonate	['kɑːbəneɪt] *n.* 碳酸盐
pellet	['pelɪt] *n.* 小球
lamination	[ˌlæmɪ'neɪʃən] *n.* 叠层，层压
boost	[buːst] *v.* 促进，提高；增加（同义词：improve，increase）
centrifuge	['sentrɪfjuːdʒ] *v.* 使离心，以离心机分离
attributable	[ə'trɪbjətəbl] *adj.* 可归因于……的；由……引起的
foam	[fəʊm] *n.* 泡沫
stir	[stɜː(r)] *v.* 搅拌
be disposed of	处理，去掉，清除
inert	[ɪ'nɜːt] *adj.*【化】惰性的
combat	['kɒmbæt] *v.* 与……战斗；防止；减轻
canopy	['kænəpɪ] *n.*【建】顶篷，顶盖
mist	[mɪst] *n.* 薄雾（fog 雾；frost 霜；hail 冰雹）
incidence	['ɪnsɪdəns] *n.* 发生率（incident *n.* 事件）

▶ **雅思阅读真题同义词考点**

component	—ingredient, element, factor, part
versatile	—all-around, diversified, many-sided
yield	—produce, provide, create
inert	—unchangeable, stable, inactive, stagnant, sluggish
major	—main, primary, chief, principal, dominant, leading

下篇导读： 【苏联工作制】

考试时间： 2009-02-07，2012-07-21……

　　苏联的五年计划在做什么？为什么要改变工作时间？三班倒的来历？
新工作时间的优势？工人阶级最终战胜了斯大林？ :)

Reading Passage 11

Soviet's New Working Week

A historian investigates how Stalin changed the calendar to keep the Soviet people continually work.

A "There are no fortresses that Bolsheviks cannot storm." With these words, Stalin expressed the dynamic self-confidence of the Soviet Union's Five Year Plan: weak and backward Russia was to turn overnight into a powerful modern industrial country. Between 1928 and 1932, production of coal, iron and steel increased at a fantastic rate, and new industrial cities sprang up, along with the world's biggest dam. Everyone's life was affected, as collectivised farming drove millions from the land to swell the industrial proletariat. Private enterprise disappeared in city and country, leaving the State supreme under the dictatorship of Stalin. Unlimited enthusiasm was the mood of the day, with the Communists believing that hard-working manpower alone would bring about a new world.

B Enthusiasm spread to time itself, in the desire to make the state a huge efficient machine, where not a moment would be wasted, especially in the workplace. Lenin had already been intrigued by the ideas of the American Frederick Winslow Taylor (1856-1915), whose time-motion studies had discovered ways of stream-lining effort so that every worker could produce the maximum. The Bolsheviks were also great admirers of Henry Ford's assembly line mass production and of his Fordson tractors that were imported by the thousands. The engineers who came with them to train their users helped spread what became a real cult of Ford. Emulating and surpassing such capitalist models formed part of the training of the new Soviet Man, a heroic figure whose unlimited capacity for work would benefit everyone in the dynamic new society. All this culminated in the Plan, which has been characterised as the triumph of the machine, where workers would become supremely efficient robot-like creatures.

C Yet this was Communism whose goals had always included improving the lives of the proletariat. One major step in that direction was the sudden announcement in 1927 that reduced the working day from eight to seven hours. In January

67

1929, all industries were ordered to adopt the shorter day by the end of the Plan. Workers also had an extra hour off on the eve of Sundays and holidays. Typically though, the state took away more than it gave, for this was part of a scheme to increase production by establishing a three-shift system. This meant that the factories were open day and night and that many had to work at highly undesirable hours.

D Hardly had that policy been announced, though, than Yuri Larin, who had been a close associate of Lenin and architect of his radical economic policy, came up with an idea for even greater efficiency. Workers were free and plants were closed on Sundays. Why not abolish that wasted day by instituting a continuous work week so that the machines could operate to their full capacity every day of the week? When Larin presented his idea to the Congress of Soviets in May 1929, no one paid much attention. Soon after, though, he got the ear of Stalin, who approved. Suddenly, in June, the Soviet press was filled with articles praising the new scheme. In August, the Council of Peoples' Commissars ordered that the continuous work week be brought into immediate effect, during the height of enthusiasm for the Plan, whose goals the new schedule seemed guaranteed to forward.

E The idea seemed simple enough, but turned out to be very complicated in practice. Obviously, the workers couldn't be made to work seven days a week, nor should their total work hours be increased. The solution was ingenious: a new five-day week would have the workers on the job for four days, with the fifth day free; holidays would be reduced from ten to five, and the extra hour off on the eve of rest days would be abolished. Staggering the rest-days between groups of workers meant that each worker would spend the same number of hours on the job, but the factories would be working a full 360 days a year instead of 300. The 360 divided neatly into 72 five-day weeks. Workers in each establishment (at first factories, then stores and offices) were divided into five groups, each assigned a colour (which appeared on the new Uninterrupted Work Week calendars distributed all over the country) Colour-coding was a valuable mnemonic device, since worker might have trouble remembering what their day off was going to be, for it would change every week. A glance at the colour on the calendar would reveal the free day, and allow workers to plan their activities. This system, however, did not apply to construction or seasonal occupations, which followed a six-day week, or to factories or mines which had to close regularly for maintenance: they also had a six-day week, whether interrupted (with the same day off for everyone) or continuous. In all cases, though, Sunday was treated like any other day.

F Official propaganda touted the material and cultural benefits of the new scheme. Workers would get more rest; production and employment would increase (for more workers would be needed to keep the factories running continuously); the standard of living would improve. Leisure time would be more rationally employed, for cultural activities (theatre, clubs, sports) would no longer have to be crammed into a weekend, but could flourish every day, with their facilities far less crowded. Shopping would be easier for the same reasons. Ignorance and superstition, as represented by organised religion, would suffer a mortal blow, since 80 per cent of the workers would be on the job on any given Sunday. The only objection concerned the family, where normally more than one member was working: well, the Soviets insisted, the narrow family was far less important than the vast common good and besides, arrangements could be made for husband and wife to share a common schedule. In fact, the regime had long wanted to weaken or sideline the two greatest potential threats to its total dominance: organised religion and the nuclear family. Religion succumbed, but the family, as even Stalin finally had to admit, proved much more resistant.

G The continuous work week, hailed as a Utopia where time itself was conquered and the sluggish Sunday abolished forever, spread like an epidemic. According to official figures, 63 per cent of industrial workers were so employed by April 1930; in June, all industry was ordered to convert during the next year. The fad reached its peak in October when it affected 73 per cent of workers. In fact, many managers simply claimed that their factories had gone over to the new week, without actually applying it. By then, though, problems were becoming obvious. Most serious (though never officially admitted), the workers hated it. Coordination of family schedules was virtually impossible and usually ignored, so husbands and wives only saw each other before or after work; rest days were empty without any loved ones to share them—even friends were likely to be on a different schedule. Confusion reigned: the new plan was introduced haphazardly, with some factories operating five-, six- and seven-day weeks at the same time, and the workers often not getting their rest days at all.

H The Soviet government might have ignored all that, but the new week was far from having the vaunted effect on production. With the complicated rotation system, the work teams necessarily found themselves doing different kinds of work in successive weeks. Machines, no longer consistently in the hands of people who knew how to tend them, were often poorly maintained or even broken. Workers lost a sense of responsibility for the special tasks they had normally performed.

I As a result, the new week started to lose ground. Stalin's speech of June 1931, which criticised the "depersonalised labour" its too hasty application had brought, marked the beginning of the end. In November, the government ordered the widespread adoption of the six-day week, which had its own calendar, with regular breaks on the 6th, 12th, 18th, 24th, and 30th, with Sunday usually as a working day. By July 1935, only 26 per cent of workers still followed the continuous schedule, and the six-day week was soon on its way out. Finally, in 1940, as part of the general reversion to more traditional methods, both the continuous five-day week and the novel six-day week were abandoned, and Sunday returned as the universal day of rest. A bold but typically ill-conceived experiment was at an end.

Questions 1–10

Complete the sentence below.

*Choose **NO MORE THAN THREE WORDS** from the text for **EACH BLANK**.*

1   Between 1928 and 1932, only State supreme controlled by Stalin remained and *private enterprise* vanished.

2   To maximise workers' productivity, Frederick Winslow Taylor had invented approaches of *steam-lining*.

3   A *three-shift system* could enable factories open day and night.

4   *Yuri Larin* proposed a plan to keep the machines operating every day.

5   *Color-coding* was used to help workers to remember the rotation of their free days.

6   Authority acclaimed that the new scheme would *benefit* production and employment.

7   *organised religon* and *the nuclear family* were the biggest risks to the Soviet regime.

8   *workers* were the most resistant force to the new work week.

9   Workers had to do unfamiliar job and sometimes caused failure of *machines*.

10 In 1931, Stalin described the outcome of new work scheme as the *depersonalised labour*

▶ 核心词汇

词汇	释义
fortress	['fɔːtrəs] *n.* 堡垒，要塞
dynamic	[daɪ'næmɪk] *adj.* 充满活力的，精力充沛的
collectivise	[kə'lektɪvaɪz] *v.* 使公有化，使集体化
swell	[swel] *v.* 增强；肿胀
proletariat	[ˌprəʊlə'teəriət] *n.* 工人阶级
supreme	[suː'priːm] *adj.* 最高的，至高的，无上的（supreme court 最高法院）
dictatorship	[dɪk'teɪtəʃɪp] *n.* 独裁，专政；独裁权 [dic=to say说。如：in-朝、向 + dic说 + -ate（动词后缀）→向……说，宣告，通知→indicate指出，显示；dictation说出来的东西→听写，笔录；dictionary说话方式集合的地方（-ary）→字典；pre-提前 + dict说→predict预言；contra-反着 + dict说→contradict反驳，顶嘴。那么不靠法律，而是靠一个人讲话治国来就是dictatorship独裁]
intrigue	[ɪn'triːg] *v.* 激起……的好奇心
cult	[kʌlt] *n.* 狂热的崇拜，礼拜
emulate	['emjʊleɪt] *v.* 努力赶上；模仿（同义词：imitate）
capitalist	['kæpɪtəlɪst] *adj.* 资本主义的（作名词指资本家）
culminate	['kʌlmɪneɪt] *v.* 达到极点
triumph	['traɪʌmf] *n.* 胜利；（成功的）典范
adopt	[ə'dɒpt] *v.* 采用，采纳（区别单词adapt）
undesirable	[ˌʌndɪ'zaɪərəbl] *adj.* 不受欢迎的；不方便的
stagger	['stægə(r)] *v.* 错开时间
mnemonic	[nɪ'mɒnɪk] *adj.* 记忆的，记忆术的
propaganda	[ˌprɒpə'gændə] *n.* 宣传，宣传运动
tout	[taʊt] *v.* 兜售
superstition	[ˌsuːpə'stɪʃn] *n.* 迷信，迷信行为
regime	[reɪ'ʒiːm] *n.* 政治制度，政权，政体
succumb	[sə'kʌm] *v.* 屈服
hail	[heɪl] *v.* 赞扬（或称颂）……为
sluggish	['slʌgɪʃ] *adj.* 懒散的，无精打采的
epidemic	[ˌepɪ'demɪk] *n.* 流行病，风尚等的流行
reign	[reɪn] *v.* （情感或氛围）盛行
haphazardly	[hæp'hæzədli] *adv.* 偶然地，随意地，杂乱地（同义词：randomly）
vaunted	['vɔːntɪd] *adj.* 被自我吹嘘的
rotation	[rəʊ'teɪʃn] *n.* 轮流，循环（动词形式：rotate）

hasty	['heɪstɪ] *adj.* 仓促完成的；草率的；轻率的

▶ 雅思阅读真题同义词考点

vanish	—disappear, fade out, go way
approach	—way, method
propose	—come up with, provide
authority	—government, official
resist	—counteract, object, oppose

下篇导读：【土星】

考试时间：2010-01-14……

　　土星介绍；名字来历；美丽的环；它的卫星；引力；自转公转；人类对土星的探索。☺

Reading Passage 12

Spectacular Saturn

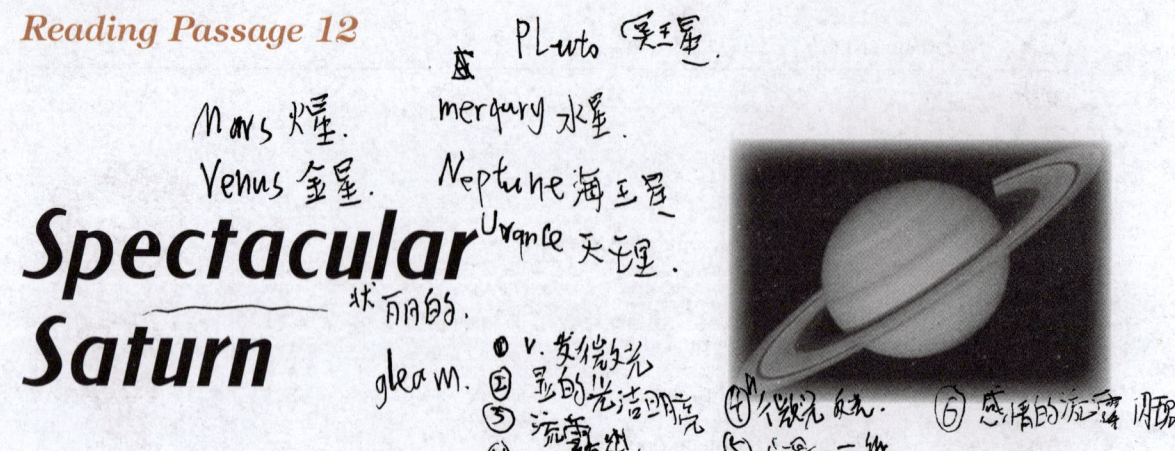

Saturn is the second largest planet. Only Jupiter is larger. Saturn has seven thin, flat rings around it. The rings consist of numerous narrow ringlets, which are made up of ice particles that travel around the planet. The gleaming rings make Saturn one of the most beautiful objects in the solar system. Jupiter, Neptune, and Uranus are the only other planets known to have rings. Their rings are much fainter than those around Saturn.

Saturn's diameter at its equator is about 74,900 miles, almost 10 times that of Earth. The planet can be seen from Earth with the unaided eye, but its rings cannot. Saturn was the farthest planet from Earth that the ancient astronomers knew about. They named it for the Roman god of agriculture.

Saturn travels around the Sun in an elliptical (oval-shaped) orbit, The planet takes about 10,759 Earth days, or about 29 1/2 Earth years, to go around the Sun, compared with 365 days, or one year, for Earth.

Rotation

As Saturn travels around the Sun, it spins on its axis, an imaginary line drawn through its centre. Saturn's axis is not perpendicular (at an angle of 90 degrees) to the planet's path around the Sun. The axis tilts at an angle of about 27 degrees from the perpendicular position. Saturn rotates faster than any other planet except Jupiter. Saturn spins around once in only 10 hours 39 minutes, compared to about 24 hours, or one day, for Earth.

Surface and atmosphere

Most scientists believe Saturn is a giant ball of gas that has no solid surface.

However, the planet seems to have a hot solid inner core of iron and rocky material. Around this dense central part is an outer core that probably consists of ammonia, methane, and water. A layer of highly compressed liquid metallic hydrogen surrounds the outer core. Above this layer lies a region composed of hydrogen and helium in a viscous form.

A dense layer of clouds covers Saturn. Photographs of the planet show a series of belts and zones of varied colours on the cloud tops. This banded appearance seems to be caused by differences in the temperature and altitude of atmospheric gas masses. The plants and animals that live on Earth could not live on Saturn. Scientists doubt that any form of life exists on the planet.

Temperature

The tilt of Saturn's axis causes the Sun to heat the planet's northern and southern halves unequally, resulting in seasons and temperature changes. Each season lasts about 7 $\frac{1}{2}$ Earth years, because Saturn takes about 29 times as long to go around the Sun as Earth does. Saturn's temperature is always much colder than Earth's, because Saturn is so far from the Sun. The temperature at the top of Saturn's clouds averages-285 degrees F (-175 degrees C).

Density and mass

Saturn has a lower density than any other planet. It is only about one-tenth as dense as Earth, and about two-thirds as dense as water. That is, a portion of Saturn would weigh much less than an equal portion of Earth, and would float in water.

Although Saturn has a low density, it has a greater mass than any other planet except Jupiter. Saturn is about 95 times as massive as Earth. The force of gravity is a little higher on Saturn than on Earth.

Rings

The rings of Saturn surround the planet at its equator. They do not touch Saturn. The seven rings of Saturn consist of thousands of narrow ringlets. Saturn's major rings are extremely wide. The outermost ring, for example, may measure as much as 180,000 miles across. However, the rings of Saturn are so thin that they cannot be seen when they are in direct line with Earth. They vary in thickness from about 660 to 9,800 feet (200 to 3,000 metres). A space separates the rings from one another.

Saturn's rings were discovered in the early 1600's by the Italian astronomer Galileo. Galileo could not see the rings clearly with his small telescope, and thought they were large satellites. In 1656, after using a more powerful telescope, Christiaan Huygens, a Dutch astronomer, described a "thin, flat" ring around Saturn. In 1675, Giovanni Domenico Cassini, an Italian-born French astronomer, announced the discovery of two separate rings made up of swarms of satellites.

Satellites

In addition to its rings, Saturn has 25 satellites that measure at least 6 miles (10 kilometres) in diameter, and several smaller satellites. The largest of Saturn's satellites, Titan, has a diameter of about 3,200 miles—larger than the planets Mercury and Pluto. Titan is one of the few satellites in the solar system known to have an atmosphere. Its atmosphere consists largely of nitrogen. Many of Saturn's satellites have large craters. For example, Mimas has a crater that covers about one-third the diameter of the satellite.

Flights to Saturn

In 1973, the United States launched a space probe to study both Saturn and Jupiter. This craft, called Pioneer-Saturn, sped by Jupiter in 1974 and flew within 13,000 miles of Saturn on Sept. 1, 1979. The probe sent back scientific data and close-up photographs of Saturn. The data and photographs led to the discovery of two of the planet's outer rings.

Pioneer-Saturn also found that the planet has a magnetic field, which is 1,000 times as strong as that of Earth. This field produces a large magnetosphere (zone of strong magnetic forces) around Saturn. In addition, data from the probe indicated the presence of radiation belts inside the planet's magnetosphere. The belts consist of high-energy electrons and protons, and are comparable to Earth's Van Allen belts.

In 1977, the United States launched two space probes—Voyager 1 and Voyager 2—to study Saturn and other planets. Voyager 1 flew within 78,000 miles of Saturn on Nov. 12, 1980. On Aug. 25, 1981, Voyager 2 flew within 63,000 miles of the planet.

The Voyager probes confirmed the existence of Saturn's seventh ring. They also found that the planet's rings are made up of ringlets. In addition, the probes sent back data and photographs that led to the discovery or confirmation of the existence of nine satellites. In 1997, the United States launched the Cassini probe to study Saturn, its rings, and its satellites. The probe began orbiting Saturn in 2004.

Questions 1–10

*Answer the questions below using **NO MORE THAN THREE WORDS** from the passage for each answer.*

1   Which is the biggest planet in the solar system?   ~~Saturn~~ Jupiter.

2   How many Earth years does Saturn take to travel around the Sun? $29\frac{1}{2}$

3   How many minutes does Saturn take to rotate around each time?   639.

4   What view probably results from the varied temperature and altitude of atmospheric gas?   different

5   What determines the force of gravity on a planet?   mass   band of appearance.

6   How many rings does Saturn have?   7

7   What are ringlets made up of?

8   Who first stated the ring around Saturn?

9   Why is one of Saturn's satellites, Titan, so special except for its large size?

10   What helped scientist discover the magnetic field of Saturn?

▶ 核心词汇

词汇	释义
numerous	['njuːmərəs] *adj.* 许多的，数量庞大的
ringlet	['rɪŋlət] *n.* 小环（"let"放在一些名词的后边表示"小、在……上佩带的小饰物"，所以droplet表示"小滴"，bracelet表示"手镯"，piglet是"小猪"。进一步想想，anklet不就是"脚链、脚镯"吗！）
particle	['pɑːtɪkl] *n.* 微粒，颗粒；【物】粒子
diameter	[daɪ'æmɪtə(r)] *n.* 直径，直径长（"dia-"表示"穿过，通过"，"-meter"表示"测量，计量"。穿过圆的圆心并且可以利用其测量与圆相关的一些数据，指"直径"。"半径"可以用"semi-diameter"，表示"直径的一半"，前缀"semi-"表示"一半"。）
equator	[ɪ'kweɪtə(r)] *n.* 赤道（longitude 经度；latitude 纬度）
unaided	[ʌn'eɪdɪd] *adj.* 无外援的，独立的
astronomer	[ə'strɒnəmə(r)] *n.* 天文学者，天文学家
elliptical	[ɪ'lɪptɪkl] *adj.* 椭圆的
orbit	['ɔːbɪt] *n.* 轨道；*v.* 在……轨道上运行
spin	[spɪn] *v.* 快速旋转，自转
axis	['æksɪs] *n.* 轴，轴线
perpendicular	[ˌpɜːpən'dɪkjələ(r)] *adj.* 垂直的，成直角的
tilt	[tɪlt] *v.* 倾斜
core	[kɔː(r)] *n.*【地质学】地核（mantle 地幔；crust 地壳）
dense	[dens] *adj.* 密集的，稠密的（density 密度）
ammonia	[ə'məʊnɪə] *n.*【化】氨，氨水
methane	['miːθeɪn] *n.*【化】甲烷，沼气
metallic	[mə'tælɪk] *adj.* 金属的，金属性的（metal *n.* 金属）
helium	['hiːlɪəm] *n.*【化】氦
viscous	['vɪskəs] *adj.* 黏的，黏性的
gravity	['grævətɪ] *n.* 重力
swarms of	成群的
nitrogen	['naɪtrədʒən] *n.*【化】氮，氮气
crater	['kreɪtə(r)] *n.* 火山口，环形山（magma 岩浆；lava 熔岩）
probe	[prəʊb] *n.* 探测器，探测仪
radiation	[ˌreɪdɪ'eɪʃn] *n.* 辐射，放射物
electron	[ɪ'lektrɒn] *n.* 电子（proton 质子；neutron 中子；atom 原子；quanta 量子）

▶ **雅思阅读真题同义词考点**

numerous	—abundant, considerable, many
consist	—comprise, include, make up
altitude	—high, height, elevation
spin	—rotate, turn, swirl
describe	—state, tell, depict, portray

下篇导读：【托马斯·杨】

考试时间： 2010-11-20……

　　托马斯·杨，无所不会的英国神仙？精通医学、力学、数学、光学、声学、语言学、动物学、埃及学、音乐、杂技等。建立三原色原理有木有？翻译罗塞塔石碑有木有？中学物理课本杨氏双缝干涉实验有木有？他没有虚度生命中的每一天。 ☺

Reading Passage 13

Thomas Young

Thomas Young was a famous English polymath whose scientific investigations helped unravel the mysteries of sight, light, mechanics, energy, physiology and Egyptology.

In his recent biography, Andrew Robinson described Thomas Young as "the last man who knew everything" and this is certainly no outlandish claim. Although a modest man who cared more about learning than about gaining fame through his discoveries, Thomas Young was arguably the great ever English polymath (a person with encyclopaedic, broad or varied knowledge), a man who, as Robinson says, proved Newton wrong, explained how we see, cured the sick and deciphered the Rosetta Stone, among other feats of genius.

The Early Years of Thomas Young

Thomas Young was into a Quaker family in Milverton, Somerset in 1773. The youngest of ten children, Young was a precocious and exceptionally quick-witted child who was fluent in Greek and Latin by the age of fourteen and had also made strides into learning French, Italian, Hebrew, Chaldean, Syriac, Samaritan, Arabic, Persian, Turkish and Amharic. Having initially been educated at exclusive boarding schools, in 1786 Young was removed from school so that he might continue his phenomenal studies privately with friends of his father.

A Career in Medicine

In 1793 Young began to study medicine at St. Bartholomew's Hospital in London although he was to leave in 1794 to continue his medical studies in Edinburgh. It was during this time that Young began to distance himself from his Quaker roots. After completing his studies in Edinburgh in 1795, Young travelled to Göttingen in Germany where he was awarded a Doctor of Physics degree in 1796. After obtaining his doctorate, Young moved to Emmanuel College, Cambridge where he taught and also began to research scientific matters outside the scope of medicine.

Having received a substantial inheritance on the death of his uncle, Young moved to London in 1799 and established himself as a physician at 48 Welbeck Street. Although his medical practice was never particularly successful, Young maintained that medicine was his primary occupation and so often published his academic articles anonymously to avoid damaging his reputation as a physician.

An Extraordinary Breadth of Knowledge

Despite the important impact on medical scholarship of his work on haemodynamics and his Young's Rule for determining drug dosages for children, Thomas Young is perhaps best known for his groundbreaking work in numerous other fields:

Eyesight and colour

Young's first submissions to the Royal Society consisted of studies on eyesight. He was able to determine that the ability of the eye to focus on images both near and far was due to muscles surrounding the lens of the eye that changed its shape and therefore its focal length. He also developed a theory, later taken up by the physicist Hermann Von Helmholtz, that ascribed colour vision to three types of receptors in the eye, each with a sensitivity to only one of the three primary colours. It was not until the twentieth century that this theory was confirmed.

Wave Theory of Light

In Young's own estimation, his discovery that light travelled in waves (thereby disproving Newton's light particle theory) was his greatest achievement.

Young's first paper on light, read to the Royal Society in 1800, focused primarily on the difficulties in explaining various phenomena from the viewpoint of the particle theory.

Young's idea was simple. If light propagates like a wave, such as a wave in water, or a sound wave, then when two of the waves meet so as to reinforce each other, the light will be brighter. But if, as in other waves, they meet when the low point of one and the high point of the other coincide, the waves will interfere with each other and blot each other out.

Young did various experiments to show that this was indeed the case with light, the most famous of which was the passing of light through an opaque surface with a double slit to allow two beams of light to pass. Young argued that the resulting pattern of light and shadow produced by the two combined light sources demonstrated that light was a wave. He also explained the colours found at the fringes of shadows by the interference of waves, which blot out some colours of the white light, leaving other colours of the spectrum intact. In the same way he explained the colours produced when two glass plates come into contact, and many other situations that produce coloured fringes, including the rainbow, as due to the wave character of light.

Young's modulus

Young was interested in other fields of physics, including the motion of bodies and the properties of materials. He developed a measure, now called "Young's modulus", which helps engineers and scientists measure the elasticity of materials.

Egyptology

Towards the end of his life, Young turned his attention back to languages and became one of the first people to try and decipher hieroglyphics. Although the final translation is often credited to Jean Francois Champollion, Young made significant advances towards the translation of the Rosetta Stone.

Languages

Young was interested in the evolution of language groups, and divided the world's languages into five major families: The Monosyllabic, the Indo-European, the Tataric, the African, and the American. His thoughts on this subject were published in an article for the *Quarterly Review* in 1813.

Based on work by German philologist Johann Christoph Adelung, Young made a comparison of the words for "heaven," "sky," and "earth" in more than 400 different languages believing that these words would exist in all languages and would be the least likely to experience change. Young was not the first to promote the study of language families, although he did coin the name "Indo-European" to refer to the major European language group.

Although he was certainly not immune to mistakes, Thomas Young was a great scientist, linguist and innovator and, without his considerable discoveries, many distinct disciplines would have been disadvantaged.

Questions 1–10

Answer the questions below using NO MORE THAN THREE WORDS from the passage for each answer.

1　When was English polymath Thomas Young born? *1773*

2　What was Thomas Young's major profession in London? *Mindine*

3　When was Young's eyesight and colour theory proved true? *twentieth century.*

4　What was contradicted by Young's theory of light? *Newton's light particle theory.*

5　Which feature of light can explain the production of colourful rainbow? *wave character of light,*

6　What can be calculated by "Young's modulus"? *elasticity of materials*

7　What object helped people understand hieroglyphics? *final translation.*

8　How many categories did Young classify the languages? *5.*

9　Who first used the term "Indo-European"? *Young*

10　List three terms which might be most stable during language evolution, according to Young.

heaven sky earth.

▶ 核心词汇

词汇	释义
polymath	['pɒlɪmæθ] *n.* 博学者，博识者（poly指"多"，字根math来自manthanein，指"学习"。所以polymath指"多学"）
unravel	[ʌn'rævl] *v.* 解开；阐明
physiology	[ˌfɪzɪ'ɒlədʒɪ] *n.* 生理学
Egyptology	[ˌiːdʒɪp'tɒlədʒɪ] *n.* 埃及古物学
encyclopaedic	[enˌsaɪkləʊ'piːdɪk] *adj.* 如百科辞典的，百科全书式的（源于希腊词enkyklios paideia: en-=in; kykilos=circle; paideia=education; 包罗整个教育以及知识领域的事物。字根circ=ring环。如：circle圆圈；周期；circulate循环；circumstance周围一圈的，周遭的→环境；cyclist 骑自行车的人；bicycle 两个圆环→自行车；cyclone旋风；recycle再循环，再生。）
decipher	[dɪ'saɪfə(r)] *v.* 破译（密码）
stride	[straɪd] *n.* 步幅；进展
substantial	[səb'stænʃl] *adj.* 有实力的；有财产的
anonymously	[ə'nɒnɪməslɪ] *adv.* 不具名地，化名地（anonym *n.* 匿名者；anonymous *adj.* 匿名的）
haemodynamics	['hiːməʊdaɪ'næmɪks] *n.* 血流动力学
dosage	['dəʊsɪdʒ] *n.* （按剂量的）给药，剂量（a dose of liquid medicine一次服量的药水）
submission	[səb'mɪʃn] *n.* 提交，呈递
lens	[lenz] *n.* 眼睛中的水晶体；透镜
ascribe	[ə'skraɪb] *v.* 把……归于
estimation	[ˌestɪ'meɪʃn] *n.* 估计，评价
propagate	['prɒpəgeɪt] *v.* 扩散，使蔓延
blot out	覆盖，遮住
opaque	[əʊ'peɪk] *adj.* 不透明的；无光泽的（反义词：transparent）
fringe	[frɪndʒ] *n.* 边缘（同义词：edge, rim）
spectrum	['spektrəm] *n.* 【物理学】谱，光谱
modulus	['mɒdjʊləs] *n.* 系数，模数
elasticity	[ˌiːlæ'stɪsətɪ] *n.* 弹性，弹力（形容词形式：elastic；但是"弹簧"是spring）
hieroglyphics	[ˌhaɪərə'glɪfɪks] *n.* 象形文字
evolution	[ˌiːvə'luːʃn] *n.* 演变，发生
philologist	[fɪ'lɒlədʒɪst] *n.* 语言学者，文献学者
immune	[ɪ'mjuːn] *adj.* 不受影响的；免除……的（immune system免疫系统；immunity免疫力）

► 雅思阅读真题同义词考点

profession	—occupation, job, work, vocation
prove	—confirm, certify, verify
contradict	—disprove, deny, dispute, oppose
calculate	—measure, compute, count
feature	—trait, attribute, character, characteristic, property, quality
stable	—unchangeable, steady, settled

CHAPTER 2

True/False/Not Given
句子理解判断题

介绍：分成True/False/Not Given和Yes/No/Not Given两种，对考生无区别。真实考试中选True的概率大于False大于Not Given。

概率：真实考试40个题目中平均12个题，多分布于2篇文章中，平均每篇6题。

难度：★★★★☆

句子理解判断题

雅思机考（IELTS Computer Based）界面及说明：

Part 1
Reading and answer 1-10

A

When most of us hear the word chocolate, we picture a bar, a box of bon-bons, or a bunny. The verb that comes to mind is probably "eat," not "drink," and the most apt adjective would seem to be "sweet." But for about 90 percent of chocolate's long history, it was strictly a beverage, and sugar didn't have anything to do with it. "I often call chocolate the best-known food that nobody knows anything about," said Alexandra Leaf, a self- described "chocolate educator" who runs a business called Chocolate Tours of New York City.

B

The terminology can be a little confusing, but most experts these days use the term "cacao" to refer to the plant or its beans before processing, while the term "chocolate" refers to anything made from the beans, she explained. "Cocoa" generally refers to chocolate in a powdered form, although it can also be a British form of "cacao." Etymologists trace the origin of the word "chocolate" to the Aztec word "xocoatl," which referred to a bitter drink brewed from cacao beans. The Latin name for the cacao tree, Theobroma cacao, means "food of the gods."Many modern histori-ans have estimated that chocolaty has been around for about 2000 years,

Questions 1—10
Choose the correct answer.

1. Chocolate used to be a bitter drink in the past.
   - ◉ TRUE
   - ○ FALSE
   - ○ NOT GIVEN

2. Chocolate has been consumed by human beings for more than 3,000 years.
3. Before chocolate was made, cacao beans had been worthless.
4. Chocolate had been considered as a medicine and used in hospitals.
5. Chocolate was confined to the rich because people believed it was nutritious.
6. The first modern chocolate bar was made by a Dutchman.
7. Nestle was the brand name of the first milk chocolate.

句子理解判断题左侧是文章，右侧是题目，点击题目会展开候选项。

如何答题：点击正确答案。

修改答案：点击所选择的新答案。

www.ieltscb.com 提供免费机考练习。

下篇导读： 【哈欠研究】

考试时间： 2010-10-09，2012-09-22……

我们为什么打哈欠？是因为犯困还是感到无聊？为什么打哈欠会传染？打哈欠在生理上对人体有什么作用？ ☺

Reading Passage 14

Yawn

All humans yawn. So do most vertebrate animals. Surely it serves some useful function. But what that might be has puzzled scientists throughout the ages.

Now a series of experiments suggests a surprising reason for yawning. It cools the brain, says Andrew C. Gallup, PhD, a postdoctoral research associate at Princeton University.

"We have collected data on rats, parakeets, and humans. All the data supports the brain-cooling hypothesis," Gallup says.

Here's the basic idea:

When you start to yawn, powerful stretching of the jaw increases blood flow in the neck, face, and head.

The deep intake of breath during a yawn forces downward flow of spinal fluid and blood from the brain.

Cool air breathed into the mouth cools these fluids.

"Together these processes may act like a radiator, removing too hot blood from the brain while introducing cooler blood from the lungs and extremities, thereby cooling

brain surfaces," Gallup says.

To answer skeptics, Gallup has laid out a more detailed anatomical description of the process in the medical literature.

We Yawn More When It's Cool

Gallup's theory predicts that colder outside air should cool the brain better than hot air. The body should therefore yawn more when the air is cool, and yawn less when the air is hot.

Nowhere is better to test this than in Tucson, Arizona. Gallup's team went there twice: Once in the winter, when it was a cool 71.6 degrees F outside, and once in early summer, when it was 98.6 degrees F.

The researchers asked 80 pedestrians to look at pictures of people yawning. It's well known that people often yawn when they see others yawn.

Sure enough, in the cooler weather 45% of people yawned when they looked at the pictures. But in hotter weather, only 24% of people yawned. Moreover, people yawned more if they'd been outside longer in the cool weather, and yawned less if they'd been outside longer in the hot weather.

These results mimicked an earlier study in which Gallup's team showed that budgie parakeets yawned more in cool temperatures than they did in hot temperatures. And it supported a rat study in which rat brains cooled a bit when the animals yawned.

What We Say When We Yawn

Gallup says his brain cooling theory of yawning is the only theory that explains all these experimental results. But he has not yet convinced those who prefer another theory.

Physician Adrian G. Guggisberg agrees with Gallup that changes in room temperature can trigger yawning. But he's wary of the brain cooling theory. And he offers an alternative interpretation of Gallup's Tucson study.

"The fact that yawning is suppressed during high temperatures suggest that it fails precisely when we need it," Guggisberg tells. "There are other ways to regulate body temperature, such as sweating, and it is unclear why we would need another regulator which fails when it matters." Yawn theorists split into two camps. Like Gallup, one side says yawning must have a physiological cause, and a physical benefit. The other side says yawning is a form of communication that offers various social benefits.

Guggisberg prefers the social theory of yawning. He sees the physiological effects

of yawning as too small to account for their persistence through evolution. But he sees the contagious effect of yawning as a key clue.

"The more people are susceptible to contagious yawning, the better their social competence and empathy," Guggisberg says. "In humans it is clear that yawning has a social effect. It is probably an unconscious behaviour. It is not clear what yawning communicates or what it achieves. But clearly it transmits some information that has some effect on brain networks or behaviour."

Across cultures, Guggisberg says, the yawn is understood as a sign of sleepiness and boredom. The yawn thus communicates to others that one is experiencing a moderately unpleasant experience but not an immediate threat.

"We might have to get used to the idea that yawns have a primarily social rather than primarily physiological effect," Guggisberg and colleagues wrote in a recent article.

Gallup argues that whatever message yawning communicates, it is far too ambiguous and subtle to be so well-conserved throughout evolutionary history.

"It is not that I don't think there is any social function to yawning, because clearly it is contagious," Gallup says. "But we have to think of it as a process driven by physiological triggers we are unable to control. If it happens in a meeting, it should not be a sign of disrespect or insult."

Questions 1–10

Do the following statements agree with the information given in the Reading Passage?

In boxes 1–10 on your answer sheet, write

TRUE	*if the statement agrees with the information*
FALSE	*if the statement contradicts the information*
NOT GIVEN	*if there is no information on this*

1 All vertebrate animals yawn.

2 Yawning can encourage blood circulation in some parts of the body.

3 Yawning can keep your mind clear and active.

4 Yawning can infect even through watching pictures of people yawning.

5 The results of the study in animals are consistent with that of Gallup's Tucson study.

6 Sweating is more effective than yawning in cooling the brain.

7 The contagious effect of yawning indicates that it plays a physiological role.

8 It is a widespread idea that people yawn when they are bored or sleepy.

9 Gallup doesn't accept Guggisberg's idea at all.

10 According to Gallup, yawning in a meeting is an impolite behaviour.

▶ 核心词汇

词汇	释义
yawn	[jɔːn] *v.* 打呵欠（区别：sneeze打喷嚏；hiccup打嗝）
vertebrate	['vɜːtɪbrət] *adj.* 脊椎动物的
puzzle	['pʌzl] *v.* 使……困惑；使……为难（同义词：confuse）
postdoctoral	[ˌpəʊst'dɒktərəl] *adj.* 博士后的
stretch	[stretʃ] *v.* 伸展
jaw	[dʒɔː] *n.* 下巴，下颚
spinal	['spaɪnl] *adj.* 脊髓的，脊柱的
radiator	['reɪdɪeɪtə(r)] *n.* 散热器，暖气片
pedestrian	[pə'destrɪən] *n.* 行人，步行者（ped=foot足。如：pedal脚的→脚踏板；expedition 使脚向外→远征，探险；impede脚不行了，双脚被缠住了→妨碍。pedicab脚踩 的计程车→三轮车。）
mimic	['mɪmɪk] *v.* 效仿；模仿（该动词过去式和过去分词为：mimicked）
alternative	[ɔːl'tɜːnətɪv] *adj.* 供选择的，选择性的
interpretation	[ɪnˌtɜːprɪ'teɪʃn] *n.* 解释，翻译
suppress	[sə'pres] *v.* 抑制，压制
precisely	[prɪ'saɪslɪ] *adv.* 精确地，恰恰
physiological	[ˌfɪzɪə'lɒdʒɪkl] *adj.* 生理学的
contagious	[kən'teɪdʒəs] *adj.* 感染性的；会蔓延的
be susceptible to	易受（同义词：be vulnerable to）
competence	['kɒmpɪtəns] *n.* 能力，胜任
empathy	['empəθɪ] *n.* 同感，共鸣（path=suffering 受苦的，来源于希腊文pathos，直接进入 英语，指演说、作品、音乐中引起的怜悯或悲怆情绪。sym-共同 + pathy受苦→ 让我们共同受苦→sympathy同情，体谅；em-进入 + pathy受苦→empathy同感， 共鸣）
unconscious	[ʌn'kɒnʃəs] *adj.* 无意识的，不省人事的（反义词：conscious）
boredom	['bɔːdəm] *n.* 厌倦
moderately	['mɒdərətlɪ] *adv.* 适度地
threat	[θret] *n.* 威胁（动词形式：threaten）
rather than	而非（反义词组：other than）
ambiguous	[æm'bɪgjʊəs] *adj.* 模糊不清的，引起歧义的
subtle	['sʌtl] *adj.* 微妙的
insult	['ɪnsʌlt] *n.* 侮辱，凌辱
be consistent with	和……一致

▶ 雅思阅读真题同义词考点

encourage	—increase, boost, improve
contagious	—infective, infectious, catching, epidemic, spreading
alternative	—choice, replacement, substitute
threat	—danger, risk, hazard
rather than	—instead of, not…but…

下篇导读：　【巧克力的历史】

考试时间：　2012-08-25……

　　巧克力的千年历史；神的食物？古代货币？魔力豆？春药？美国大兵的工资？雀巢的来历？让你眼花缭乱的巧克力。☺

Reading Passage 15

A Brief History of
<u>Chocolate</u>

A When most of us hear the word chocolate, we picture a bar, a box of bonbons, or a bunny. The verb that comes to mind is probably "eat," not "drink," and the most apt adjective would seem to be "sweet." But for about 90 percent of chocolate's long history, it was strictly a beverage, and sugar didn't have anything to do with it. "I often call chocolate the best-known food that nobody knows anything about," said Alexandra Leaf, a self-described "chocolate educator" who runs a business called Chocolate Tours of New York City.

B The terminology can be a little confusing, but most experts these days use the term "cacao" to refer to the plant or its beans before processing, while the term "chocolate" refers to anything made from the beans, she explained. "Cocoa" generally refers to chocolate in a powdered form, although it can also be a British form of "cacao." Etymologists trace the origin of the word "chocolate" to the Aztec word "xocoatl," which referred to a bitter drink brewed from cacao beans. The Latin name for the cacao tree, *Theobroma cacao*, means "food of the gods."

C Many modern historians have estimated that chocolate has been around for about 2000 years, but recent research suggests that it may be even older. In the book *The True History of Chocolate*, authors Sophie and Michael Coe make a case that the earliest linguistic evidence of chocolate consumption stretches back three or even four millennia, to pre-Columbian cultures of Mesoamerica such as the Olmec. Last November, anthropologists from the University of Pennsylvania announced the discovery of cacao residue on pottery excavated in Honduras that could date back as far as 1400 B.C. It appears that the sweet pulp of the cacao fruit, which surrounds the beans, was fermented into an alcoholic beverage of the time.

D It's hard to pin down exactly when chocolate was born, but it's clear that it was cherished from the start. For several centuries in pre-modern Latin America, cacao beans were considered valuable enough to use as currency. One bean could be traded for a tamale, while 100 beans could purchase a good turkey hen, according to a 16th-century Aztec document.

E Both the Mayans and Aztecs believed the cacao bean had magical, or even divine, properties, suitable for use in the most sacred rituals of birth, marriage and death. According to the book *The Chocolate Connoisseur*, Aztec sacrifice victims who felt too melancholy to join in ritual dancing before their death were often given a gourd of chocolate (tinged with the blood of previous victims) to cheer them up.

F Sweetened chocolate didn't appear until Europeans discovered the Americas and sampled the native cuisine. Legend has it that the Aztec king Montezuma welcomed the Spanish explorer Hernando Cortes with a banquet that included drinking chocolate, having tragically mistaken him for a reincarnated deity instead of a conquering invader. Chocolate didn't suit the foreigners' taste buds at first—one described it in his writings as "a bitter drink for pigs"—but once mixed with honey or cane sugar, it quickly became popular throughout Spain.

G By the 17th century, chocolate was a fashionable drink throughout Europe, believed to have nutritious, medicinal and even aphrodisiac properties. But it remained largely a privilege of the rich until the invention of the steam engine made mass production possible in the late 1700s.

H In 1828, a Dutch chemist found a way to make powdered chocolate by removing about half the natural fat (cacao butter) from chocolate liquor, pulverising what remained and treating the mixture with alkaline salts to cut the bitter taste. His product became known as "Dutch cocoa," and it soon led to the creation of solid chocolate. The creation of the first modern chocolate bar is credited to Joseph Fry, who in 1847 discovered that he could make a moldable chocolate paste by adding melted cacao butter back into Dutch cocoa. By 1868, a little company called Cadbury was marketing boxes of chocolate candies in England. Milk chocolate hit the market a few years later, pioneered by another name that may ring a bell—Nestle.

I   In America, chocolate was so valued during the Revolutionary War that it was included in soldiers' rations and used in lieu of wages. While most of us probably wouldn't settle for a chocolate paycheck these days, statistics show that the humble cacao bean is still a powerful economic force. Chocolate manufacturing is a more than 4-billion-dollar industry in the United States, and the average American eats at least half a pound of the stuff per month.

J   In the 20th century, the word "chocolate" expanded to include a range of affordable treats with more sugar and additives than actual cacao in them, often made from the hardiest but least flavourful of the bean varieties. But more recently, there's been a "chocolate revolution," Leaf said, marked by an increasing interest in high-quality, handmade chocolates and sustainable, effective cacao farming and harvesting methods. "I see more and more American artisans doing incredible things with chocolate," Leaf said. "Although, I admit that I tend to look at the world through cocoa-tinted glasses."

Questions 1–10

Do the following statements agree with the information given in the Reading Passage?

In boxes 1–10 on your answer sheet, write

TRUE   *if the statement agrees with the information*

FALSE   *if the statement contradicts the information*

NOT GIVEN   *if there is no information on this*

1   Chocolate used to be a bitter drink in the past.

2   Chocolate has been consumed by human beings for more than 3,000 years.

3   Before chocolate was made, cacao beans had been worthless.

4   Chocolate had been considered as a medicine and used in hospitals.

5   Chocolate was confined to the rich because people believed it was nutritious.

6   The first modern chocolate bar was made by a Dutchman.

7   Nestle was the brand name of the first milk chocolate.

8   During the Revolutionary War, chocolate was used to pay the wages of American soldiers.

9   On average, an American consumed over a pound of chocolate per day.

10   Handmade chocolates are much more expensive.

▶ 核心词汇

词汇	释义
bonbon	['bɒnbɒn] *n.*【法语】小糖果
apt	[æpt] *adj.* 恰当的，适当的
beverage	['bevərɪdʒ] *n.* 饮料（同义词：drink）
terminology	[ˌtɜːmɪ'nɒlədʒɪ] *n.* 专门名词，术语学（term *n.* 术语）
etymologist	[ˌetɪ'mɒlədʒɪst] *n.* 语源学家
brew	[bruː] *v.* 调制，酝酿，酿造
consumption	[kən'sʌmpʃn] *n.* 消费（动词形式：consume；相关名词：consumer 消费者，customer 顾客）
anthropologist	[ˌænθrə'pɒlədʒɪst] *n.* 人类学家（anthropology 人类学；philanthropist 慈善家；phi- 指"爱"）
residue	['rezɪdjuː] *n.* 残余，残渣
excavate	['ekskəveɪt] *v.* 挖掘
pulp	[pʌlp] *n.* 果肉
ferment	[fə'ment] *v.* 使发酵
tamale	[tə'mɑːleɪ] *n.*（墨西哥的）玉米面团包馅卷
divine	[dɪ'vaɪn] *adj.* 神圣的
ritual	['rɪtʃʊəl] *n.*（宗教等的）仪式
sacrifice	['sækrɪfaɪs] *v.* 牺牲（sacr=sacred神圣的。sacrifice使成为神圣的东西→牺牲，献祭。人们相信为信仰奉献生命之后，灵魂和精神将成为神圣的；古代以活人献祭神灵，是最原始的牺牲。）
victim	['vɪktɪm] *n.*受害人，牺牲者，牺牲品
gourd	[gʊəd] *n.* 葫芦
banquet	['bæŋkwɪt] *n.* 宴会，盛宴
deity	['deɪətɪ] *n.* 神，上帝
nutritious	[njʊ'trɪʃəs] *adj.* 营养的（名词形式：nutrient 营养物质，nutrilite营养物。安利"纽崔莱"就是nutrilite的英译）
alkaline	['ælkəlaɪn] *adj.* 碱性的，碱的（反义词：acid）
ration	['ræʃn] *n.* 定量，配给量；口粮
in lieu of	代替

▶ 雅思阅读真题同义词考点

apt	—appropriate, proper, suitable
worthless	—unvalued, useless
divine	—holy, sacred, hallowed, heavenly
ritual	—ceremony, exercise
in lieu of	—exchange, substitute, replace

下篇导读：【莫尔斯电码】

考试时间：2009-12-03，2012-06-09······

　　我们都知道SOS，这是最著名的莫尔斯电码。莫尔斯电码的产生与重大意义，世界上第一份莫尔斯电报电文："上帝创造了何等的奇迹！"莫尔斯的一生，推动了电报在全球的迅猛发展。小心，雅思阅读真题还另有一篇考电报发明。🙂

Reading Passage 16

Morse Code

Samuel Finley Breese Morse, inventor of several improvements to the telegraph, was born in Charlestown, Mass. on April 27, 1791. As a student at Yale College, Morse became interested in both painting and in the developing subject of electricity. After his graduation in 1810, he first concentrated on painting, which he studied in England. He would later become a well-known portrait artist.

After moving to New York in 1825, he became a founder and the first president of the National Academy of Design. He also ran for office, but was defeated in both his campaigns to become New York mayor. Meanwhile, Morse maintained a steady interest in invention, taking out three patents for pumps in 1817 with his brother Sidney Edwards Morse. It wasn't until 1832 that he first became interested in telegraphy.

That year, Morse was traveling to the United States from Europe on a ship, when he overheard a conversation about electromagnetism that inspired his idea for an electric telegraph. Though he had little training in electricity, he realised that pulses of electrical current could convey information over wires. The telegraph, a device first proposed in 1753 and first built in 1774, was an impractical machine up until that point, requiring 26 separate wires, one for each letter of the alphabet. Around that time two German engineers had invented a five-wire model, but Morse wanted to be the first to reduce the number of wires to one.

Between 1832 and 1837 he developed a working model of an electric telegraph, using crude materials such as a home-made battery and old clock-work gears. He also acquired two partners to help him develop his telegraph: Leonard Gale, a professor of science at New York University, and Alfred Vail, who made available his mechanical skills and his family's New Jersey iron works to help construct better telegraph models.

Morse's first telegraph device, unveiled in 1837, did use a one-wire system, which produced an EKG-like line on tickertape. The dips in the line had to be de-coded into letters and numbers using a dictionary composed by Morse, this assuming that the pen or pencil wrote clearly, which did not always happen. By the following year he had developed an improved system, having created a dot-and-dash code that used different numbers to represent the letters of the English alphabet and the ten digits. (His assistant Vail has been credited by Franklin T. Pope—later a partner of Thomas Edison—with inventing this "dots and dashes" version). This coding system was significantly better, as it did not require printing or decoding, but could be "sound read" by operators. In 1838, at an exhibition of his telegraph in New York, Morse transmitted ten words per minute using the Morse code that would become a standard throughout the world.

In 1842, Morse convinced Congress to provide $30,000 in support of his plan to "wire" the United States. Meanwhile, Morse also solicited and received advice from a number of American and European telegraphy experts, including Joseph Henry of Princeton, who had invented a working telegraph in 1831, and Louis Breguet of Paris. In 1844, Morse filed for a patent (granted 1849) of the printing telegraph. He had already proved that his device worked over short distances, and the Federal funds he raised had allowed him to string a wire from Baltimore to Washington. On May 11, 1844, Morse sent the first inter-city message. Soon thereafter, he gave the first public demonstration, in which he sent a message from the chamber of the Supreme Court to the Mount Clair train depot in Baltimore. The message itself was borrowed from the Bible by the daughter of the Commissioner of Patents and said, "What hath God wrought?" By 1846, private companies, using Morse's patent, had built telegraph lines from Washington to Boston and Buffalo, and were pushing further. The telegraph spread across the US more quickly than had the railroads, whose routes the wires often followed. By 1854, there were 23,000 miles of telegraph wire in operation. Western Union was founded in 1851, and in 1868, the first successful trans-Atlantic cable link was established. Though Morse didn't invent the telegraph and did not single-handedly create Morse Code, he may have been telegraphy's greatest promoter, and undoubtedly contributed to its rapid development and adoption throughout the world.

Morse died of pneumonia in New York on April 2, 1872. Late in his life, he shared his considerable wealth through grants to colleges such as Yale and Vassar, in addition to charities and artists.

Questions 1–10

Do the following statements agree with the information given in the Reading Passage?

In boxes 1–10 on your answer sheet, write

YES	*if the statement agrees with the claims of the writer*
NO	*if the statement contradicts the claims of the writer*
NOT GIVEN	*if it is impossible to say what the writer thinks about this*

1   The telegraph was invented by Morse.

2   Morse preferred painting to electricity subject when he was a student.

3   Too many separated wires of the telegraph prototype made it unfeasible.

4   The alphabet contains 26 letters.

5   Franklin T. Pope believed that Morse created "dots and dashes" coding system.

6   It is unnecessary for operators to decipher Morse code.

7   Morse invented the printing telegraph in 1844.

8   The wires sometimes followed the railroad routes in US.

9   Morse took part in setting up trans-Atlantic cable link.

10   Morse donated his money to the school he once attended.

▶ 核心词汇

词汇	释义
telegraph	['telɪgrɑːf] *n.* 电报（机）（"tele-graph"表示"远+写"，传递"远处写来的信息"。）
academy	[ə'kædəmɪ] *n.* 学院，研究院（英语中这个单词最初专门指Plato柏拉图的哲学学派。到英联邦国家留学的学生要参加雅思A类考试，这里的A代表"academic"，即academy的形容词形式。）
steady	['stedɪ] *adj.* 稳定的，稳固的（田径赛场上听到发令员喊："预备……跑！"，同样场景在英语国家人们常听到"Ready, steady, go!"）
take out a patent for...	取得一项……的专利
overhear	[ˌəʊvə'hɪə(r)] *vt.* 无意中听到
impractical	[ɪm'præktɪkl] *adj.* 不切实际的，无用的（相关单词：practical *adj.*，practice *n.*，practise *v.*）
alphabet	['ælfəbet] *n.* 字母表（希腊Greek字母表里共有二十四个字母，不同于英文的二十六个字母。它的第一个字母是alpha，第二个是beta，英文单词里对应"字母表"这个概念的单词就是由这两个单词共同构成的。）
unveil	[ˌʌn'veɪl] *vt.* 向公众透露，揭示（"veil"这个单词是名词，表示"面罩，面纱"，那么"unveil"的基本含义就是"揭掉面罩，揭掉面纱"，进而引申为"揭示，揭露，透露"。）
decode	[ˌdiː'kəʊd] *vt.* 解码，译（密码文电等）（"code"是"密码，编码"的意思，加上前缀"de-"就得到现在的"解码，破译"的含义。）
dot	[dɒt] *n.* （莫尔斯电码中的）点（很多现代人认为比较舒服的朋友与朋友之间的关系是在交往过程中，人与人之间很有默契，双方都不必"dot every i and cross every t"，字面含义是"不用给每个字母i都加点，也不用在每个字母t上都写下它的最后一笔"。意即"即便一方没有把自己的意思百分之百地表达出来，对方也充分明白了他或她的意图，这样生活中的很多细节就变得简单得多"。）
digit	['dɪdʒɪt] *n.* （0到9中的任何一个）数字，数位（形容词形式：digital，"digital camera"就是"数码相机"。）
transmit	[træns'mɪt] *vt.* 传送，输送（名词形式：transmission）
convince	[kən'vɪns] *vt.* 使确信，使信服（形容词形式：convincing）
solicit	[sə'lɪsɪt] *vt.* 征求，请求
file	[faɪl] *vi.* （~ for）提出申请（作名词"file"表示"文件，文档"，用作动词表示"提出书面申请"。）
Supreme Court	最高法院
depot	['depəʊ] *n.* （美）火车站

commissioner	[kə'mɪʃənə(r)] *n.* 长官，专员
charity	['tʃærətɪ] *n.* 慈善，施舍行为

▶ 雅思阅读真题同义词考点

academy	—school, college, conservatoire
steady	—stable, constant, perpetual, ceaseless, unchanging, unvarying
unveil	—reveal, disclose, uncover, unwrap
convince	—persuade, sway, win over, prevail upon
commissioner	—official, officer, administrator
charity	—donations, contributions, offerings, alms

下篇导读：【奥运火炬传递】

考试时间：2009-03-07，2010-02-27，2012-02-04……

　　奥运火炬接力传递的起源、历史与发展。历届奥运会点火仪式的特色。2008北京奥运会祥云火炬的特点。 ☺

Reading Passage

Torch ▼
▲ Relay

A Fire is a sacred symbol dating back to prehistoric times. In ancient Greece it symbolised the creation of the world, renewal and light. It was also the sacred symbol of Hephaestus, and a gift to the human race from Prometheus, who stole it from Zeus. At the centre of every city-state in ancient Greece there was an altar with an ever-burning fire and in every home the sacred Flame burned, dedicated to Hestia, goddess of the family.

B Torch Relay races started in ancient Greece as religious rituals held at night. Soon they turned into a team athletic event, initially among adolescents, and further developed to become one of the most popular ancient sports. The enchanting power of fire was a source of inspiration. Sacred flames lit by the rays of the sun always burned in Olympia, in an altar dedicated to Hestia. Fire was ignited with the help of a concave mirror, which has the ability to concentrate the rays of the sun on a single spot. When the head priestess touched that point with the Torch, the Flame was lit.

C The Ancient Greeks held a "lampadedromia" (the Greek word for Torch Relay), where athletes competed by passing on the Flame in a relay race to the finish line. In ancient Athens the ritual was performed during the Panathenaia fest, held every four years in honour of the goddess Athena. The strength and purity of the sacred Flame was preserved through its transportation by the quickest means; in this case a relay of Torchbearers. The Torch Relay carried the Flame from the altar of Prometheus to the altar of goddess Athena on the Acropolis. Forty youths from the ten Athenian tribes had to run a distance of 2.5 kilometres in total.

D For the modern Olympic Games the sacred Flame is lit in Olympia by the head priestess, in the same way as in antiquity, and the ritual includes the athletes' oath. The Flame is then transmitted to the Torch of the first runner, and the journey of the Torch Relay begins. The modern Torch Relay is a non-competitive replication of the ancient Flame relay and a symbolic celebration of the Olympic Games. In a prophetic speech at the end of the Stockholm Games, on June 27, 1912, Baron Pierre de Coubertin said: "And now great people have received the Torch and have thereby undertaken to preserve and quicken its precious Flame. Lest our youth temporarily let the Olympic Torch fall from their hands other young people on the other side of the world are prepared to pick it up again."

E The Torch Relay, as the opening of the Olympic celebration, was revived in the Berlin Olympiad in 1936 and since then the Torch Relay has preceded every Olympic Summer Games. Starting from Olympia and carried by the first runner, the young athlete Konstantinos Kondylis, the Flame travelled for the first time hand to hand until it reached the Berlin Olympic Stadium. Since, the Flame's magic has marked and has been identified with the beginning of the Games. In Olympiads that followed, the Torch Relay continued to play an important role, having been enriched with the characteristics and cultures of the host countries. The choice of the athlete who lights the Flame in the Olympic stadium is always symbolic to the host country.

F For the 1960 Olympic Games in Rome, the Flame followed a route in homage to the Greek and Roman civilisations. It was carried from Piraeus to Rome on the ship "Americo Vespucci" and passed through some of the best-known or important historical monuments of the two countries. It was the first time that the event was covered by television. In the Mexico Olympiad in 1968, the Flame followed the route taken by Christopher Columbus, and the athletics champion Enriqueta Basilio was the first woman to light the Flame in the Olympic stadium. For the Montreal Games in 1976, the Flame travelled by satellite from Athens to Ottawa, and in the 1992 Games in Barcelona, a Paralympics archery medalist Antonio Rebollo lit the Flame in the stadium with a burning arrow. In Sydney 2000, the Flame made its journey underwater in the Great Barrier Reef. And the Beijing 2008 Olympic Torch Relay will traverse the longest distance, cover the greatest area and include the largest number of people.

G The design of the Beijing 2008 Olympic Torch takes advantage of Chinese artistic heritage and technological expertise. The design of the aluminum torch features traditional scrolls and "Lucky Cloud". It stands 72 centimetres high and weighs 985 grams. The Torch incorporates technological innovations to be able to remain lit in winds of up to 65 kilometres-an-hour and lit in rain of up to 50 millimetres-an-hour. And the torch can keep burning for 15 minutes. Other technological advancements prevent colour discolouration and corrosion around the cone from which the Flame burns. The Torch construction is also environmentally-conscious. The materials are recyclable, and the propane fuel meets environmental requirements. "The Beijing Olympic Torch boasts both distinctive Chinese cultural features, and technical excellence and sophisticated materials. It will carry the friendship that Chinese people extend to the world and the Olympic spirit to the five continents and to the peak of Mt. Qomolangma," said BOCOG President Liu Qi. "The torch and the Olympic Flame are symbols which embody the Olympic Values of excellence, respect and friendship. They inspire us to be the best we can be in all that we do," added IOC President Jacques Rogge. "The magnificent design of the torch for the Beijing 2008 Olympic Torch Relay will also add a very unique Chinese flavour to the relay, as the 'Clouds of Promise' carry the Beijing Games' message to the world."

Questions 1–10

Do the following statements agree with the information given in the Reading Passage?

In boxes 1–10 on your answer sheet, write

TRUE	*if the statement agrees with the information*
FALSE	*if the statement contradicts the information*
NOT GIVEN	*if there is no information on this*

~~TRUE~~ **1** Altars had been built in every ancient Greece city.

NOT GIVEN **2** Torch Relay races originated from ancient Greece as rituals dedicated to Prometheus.

FALSE **3** There are only ten tribes living in Ancient Greek.

FALSE **4** The ancient and modern Olympic Games obtained the sacred Flame in Olympia in different ways.

TRUE **5** The Torch Relay was restarted at the Berlin Games as the opening of Olympic celebration.

FALSE **6** The opening ceremony had been suspended temporarily before the Berlin Olympiad. NG

NOT GIVE **7** Host countries choose well-known national athlete to light flames. T

TRUE **8** In the Mexico Olympiad in 1968, the Flame was lit by Christopher Columbus. F

TRUE **9** The Beijing 2008 Olympic Torch can keep burning in the light rain.

NOT GIVEN **10** The design of the torch for the Beijing 2008 Olympics is the best so far.

▶ **核心词汇**

词汇	释义
torch	[tɔ:tʃ] *n.* 火把，火炬（electric torch 手电筒）
relay	['ri:leɪ] *n.* 接力
sacred	['seɪkrɪd] *adj.* 宗教的，神圣的（同义词：holy）
symbolise	['sɪmbəlaɪz] *v.* 象征，作为……的象征（名词形式：symbol）
altar	[ˈɔːltə(r)] *n.* 祭坛（alt = high 高的，来源于拉丁文 altus，"high"。altar 高的地方→祭坛。特洛伊战争中希腊联军的统帅阿伽门侬为了联军的胜利而把女儿送到了 the altar of gods 的上面。ex-向上 + alt 高的→exalt 提升，晋升，赞扬。alt 高的 + -itude 抽象名词词尾→altitude 高度；海拔。）
concave mirror	凹透镜
priestess	['pri:stɪs] *n.* 女祭司（priest 牧师；missionary 传教士；sister 修女；bishop 主教）
antiquity	[æn'tɪkwəti] *n.* 古代
preserve	[prɪ'zɜːv] *v.* 保护，维持
host country	主办国；东道主（host 主持人）
homage	['hɒmɪdʒ] *n.* （向伟人表示的）崇敬，致敬
monument	['mɒnjʊmənt] *n.* 遗迹，遗址，名胜古迹
archery	['ɑːtʃərɪ] *n.* 箭术
traverse	[trə'vɜːs] *v.* 穿越
heritage	['herɪtɪdʒ] *n.* 传统，遗产（动词形式：inherit 继承）
expertise	[ˌekspɜː'tiːz] *n.* 专门知识或技能
flavour	['fleɪvə(r)] *n.* 特色
suspend	[sə'spend] *v.* 延缓
temporarily	['temprərəlɪ] *adv.* 临时（形容词形式：temporary 暂时的，临时性的）
corrosion	[kə'rəʊʒn] *n.* 侵蚀（动词形式：corrode）

▶ 雅思阅读真题同义词考点

symbolise	—illustrate, represent, stand for
heritage	—tradition, convention
expertise	—know-how, specialty
suspend	—defer, delay, halt, hang, hold over, interrupt, postpone
dedicate	—assign, devote, inscribe

下篇导读：【伏尼契手稿】

考试时间：2009-06-27，2012-05-19……

神秘的伏尼契手稿静静躺在耶鲁大学的图书馆里。精美的插图，流畅的文字，却无人认识；是古代炼金术士的记录，是占星家的谜语，还是外星人遗失的画册？随着专家的分析，答案正在揭晓…… ☺

Reading Passage 18

The Voynich Manuscript

It is the most famous undeciphered text of all time—a medieval book of science, full of beautiful illustrations and strange wisdom, and containing not a single word that anyone's been able to make heads or tails of—the Voynich manuscript. The Voynich manuscript is an unsolved mystery, at least so far. According to the best information we have now, we still don't know who wrote it, what it says, or what its purpose was.

Somewhere in Europe, probably northern Italy, sometime in the early 1400s, animals were slaughtered (either sheep, calves, or goats) and their skin turned into parchment. Probably very soon thereafter, someone, most likely two people, took a quill pen in hand and wrote a 38,000-word book using common ink, beginning to end, using an alphabet and language that have defied all identification. It's not a huge book, measuring about 16 cm by 23 cm, and about 5cm thick, about 240 pages.

The book has six sections, delineated by the types of illustrations. Section 1 is the largest at 130 pages, and contains detailed drawings of 113 plants and flowers that nobody has been able to identify. It's called the Botanical section. Section 2 is 26 pages of Astrological drawings; lots of circular and concentric diagrams, and some signs of the zodiac. The third section is called the Biological section and contains mainly drawings of nude women frolicking in intricately plumbed pools. Section 4 is the Cosmological section, featuring the most impressive foldouts that appear to be circular diagrams of some cosmic nature. The fifth section is Pharmaceutical, with over 100 drawings of herbs, roots, powders, tinctures, and potions of undecipherable contents or use. The last section, called Stars, is the most mysterious: it's 23 solid pages of text only, in short paragraphs. Some of the illustrations show Eastern influence, including a probable map of the circular city of Baghdad, the centre of Eastern knowledge.

A few hundred years later, a cover was added, but unfortunately it's blank. Also at some later date, the illustrations were coloured, by someone less careful than the original artist.

The book was owned by the English astrologer John Dee during the 16th century, who wrote his own page numbers in the upper right corner of each leaf. Dee sold it to Emperor Rudolph II of Germany, with the understanding that it was the original work of Roger Bacon, a 13th century friar widely regarded as one of the fathers of the scientific method. From there the book passed to one or two other owners, who wrote their names in it, and at one point it was presented to the scholar Athanasius Kircher in Rome along with a signed letter from a Johannes Marcus Marci expressing a hope that Kircher could translate it, in 1666. Marci's letter is still preserved with the book. The manuscript's history becomes unclear at that point, until it was discovered by antique book dealer Wilfrid Voynich in 1912 at the Jesuit college at Villa Mondragone in Italy. Voynich brought it to the attention of the world. After several owners, the book was eventually donated to its current home, the Beinecke Library at Yale University, under its official name of MS 408.

Since its discovery, hypotheses have abounded as to what the Voynich manuscript means. Many believe it's written in a type of code, but all efforts to find decodable patterns have failed. Some believe it may be what's called a constructed language, which is a language that's deliberately planned and invented rather than naturally evolved. Some have speculated that it's to be used with a Cardan Grille, a paper with holes in it that you lay on top of the page and read only the revealed letters. Perhaps the most popular theory is that it's a hoax, written at practically any time since the parchment was made, and for just about any purpose ranging from financial gain to scholarly fraud to someone's weekend lark.

Let's look at the book's properties to see what we can learn. Here's an important one. There are no corrections in the book. There are also no places where the text has been squeezed to fit onto the page. This would be highly improbable if it were an original manuscript; we would absolutely expect there to be such minor errors in a first edition. So how do we explain this? There are a number of possible explanations, but two of them are most likely.

The first is that the book is a copy, perhaps even of something written by Roger Bacon. If a scribe has an original to work from, he can see how many words there are and properly plan everything to fit onto the page. And if he copies carefully, there will be no corrections. The copy theory is also consistent with other characteristics, such as its appearance of having been written straight through by only one or two people. If it is a copy, this alone doesn't tell us much that's useful in trying to decipher it. But it does leave us wondering why anyone would go to the trouble of making a nice copy of a book that doesn't say anything.

The second theory to explain the book's neat appearance is perhaps more revealing. The text could be complete nonsense, made up as the scribe went. There would be no need for corrections. There would be no need to compress the writing as space ran out.

So here comes a favourite hypothesis: In the early 1400s, some professional, perhaps a physician or an astrologer or an alchemist, wanted to create some marketing material that demonstrated he had rare knowledge from the East. He engaged a monk or other scribe to produce a book filled with wondrous and curious illustrations from multiple sciences, and a text that nobody could read, which he could tell his customers was the source of whatever great Eastern wisdom he wanted. The monk had a colleague assist, and the two devised an alphabet and used their own multilingual familiarity with written language to devise a convincing nonsense text. It was well done enough that its owner could even use it to impress his colleagues. Thus, this anonymous professional ended up with impressive marketing collateral that's conceptually identical to the labcoat worn by a naturopath, the energy diagram on the wall of a yoga guru, and the purchased-online title of "doctor" sported by alternative practitioners of every variety.

Questions 1–12

Do the following statements agree with the information given in the Reading Passage?

In boxes 1–12 on your answer sheet, write

TRUE	*if the statement agrees with the information*
FALSE	*if the statement contradicts the information*
NOT GIVEN	*if there is no information on this*

1 No one can recognise a single word in the Voynich manuscript. T

2 Someone wrote this book in a language that was popular in the early 1400s. T

3 Section 2 of the Voynich manuscript contains illustrations of some stars. F

4 Section 5 of the Voynich manuscript describes medical contents. T

5 There is no drawing at all in Section 6. F

6 Several hundred years later a blank cover was added to protect the manuscript. N

7 Roger Bacon once owned this book and wrote his name in it. T

8 Finally, it was the book dealer Voynich who donated this book to Yale University. T

9 Some believe that this mysterious book was made by extraterrestrial intelligence. N

10 It is almost impossible for an original manuscript to have no mistakes and revisions. F

11 The copy theory implies that the text of this book could have no meaning. T

12 This book could be a promotional maneuver or a selling trick in the past. F

▶ 核心词汇

词汇	释义
manuscript	['mænjʊskrɪpt] *n.* 手稿，原稿（man/manu=hand手。如：management用手控制，经操作和控制达到目标→管理；manager经理；manual手册，手工的；manu手 + script写→manuscript手抄本，原稿；man手 + -cle表"小东西"的名词词尾→手上的小东西→manacle手铐）
decipher	[dɪ'saɪfə(r)] *v.* 解密，破解
medieval	[ˌmedi'iːvl] *adj.* 中世纪的；原始的
illustration	[ˌɪlə'streɪʃn] *n.* 插图，插画（该词还指"说明，例证"）
parchment	['pɑːtʃmənt] *n.* 羊皮纸，羊皮纸文稿
alphabet	['ælfəbet] *n.* 字母表，字母系统（希腊Greek字母表里共有二十四个字母，不同于英文的二十六个字母。它的第一个字母是alpha，第二个是beta，英文单词里对应"字母表"这个概念的单词就是由这两个单词共同构成的。）
defy	[dɪ'faɪ] *v.* 违抗
delineate	[dɪ'lɪnieɪt] *v.* 描绘，描写
botanical	[bə'tænɪkl] *adj.* 植物学的（botanical garden 植物园）
zodiac	['zəʊdiæk] *n.* 黄道带，十二宫图
cosmological	[kɒz'mɒlədʒɪkl] *adj.* 宇宙论的，宇宙哲学的
pharmaceutical	[ˌfɑːmə'suːtɪkl] *adj.* 制药的
astrologer	[ə'strɒlədʒə(r)] *n.* 占星家
antique	[æn'tiːk] *adj.* 古老的，年代久远的
donate	[dəʊ'neɪt] *v.* 捐赠（名词形式：donation）
hypotheses	[haɪ'pɒθəsɪs] *n.* 假定，臆测
hoax	[həʊks] *n.* 骗局；恶作剧
fraud	[frɔːd] *n.* 骗子，欺骗，诡计
property	['prɒpəti] *n.* 性能；道具，内容
scribe	[skraɪb] *n.* 抄写员；作家
characteristics	[ˌkærəktə'rɪstɪks] *n.* 特性，特征
neat	[niːt] *adj.* 灵巧的；整洁的；优雅的
revealing	[rɪ'viːlɪŋ] *adj.* 透露真情的；有启迪作用的
physician	[fɪ'zɪʃn] *n.* 【医】医师，内科医师
alchemist	['ælkəmɪst] *n.* 炼金术士（后来该词发展为：chemist化学家）
familiarity	[fəˌmɪli'ærəti] *n.* 熟悉，精通（词组：be familiar with）
anonymous	[ə'nɒnɪməs] *adj.* 匿名的，无名的
collateral	[kə'lætərəl] *adj.* 并行的；旁系的，附属的

yoga	['jəʊɡə] *n.* 瑜伽
guru	['ɡʊruː] *n.* 大师
extraterrestrial	[ˌekstrətə'restrɪəl] *adj.* 地球外的（terrestrial *adj.* 陆地的，地球上的。ET就是extraterrestrial的缩写，该词名词意思为"外星人"）
maneuver	[mə'nuːvə] *n.* 策略；花招

▶ 雅思阅读真题同义词考点

decipher	—decode, interpret, translate, explain
medical	— pharmaceutical, surgical
hoax	—deceive, fool, fraud, cheat
maneuver	—trick, intrigue, ploy, tactic, scheme, operation, exercise
revise	—alter, amend, change, correct, improve, rewrite, adjust

下篇导读：【悉尼邦戴海滩】

考试时间：2011-02-19，2012-10-20……

　　迷人的悉尼邦戴海滩，Beach goers的梦想之地；邦戴海滩的历史与发展；伟大的海滩救生员；防鲨网的功能；澳大利亚留学必去必读。☺

Bondi Beach

In the early 1800s swimming at Sydney's beaches was a controversial pastime. Convicts were forbidden from bathing in Sydney Harbour because of "the dangers of sharks and stingrays, and for reasons of decorum." By the 1830's sea bathing was a popular activity despite being officially banned between 9.00am and 8.00pm.

During the 1900s these restrictive attitudes began to relax and the beach became associated with health, leisure and democracy—a playground everyone could enjoy equally.

A popular spot

There is clear evidence—in the form of significant Aboriginal rock carvings in particular—that Aboriginal people occupied sites in the area now known as Waverley in the period before European settlement. An important type of tool was first found in the region and is still known as the Bondi point. A number of place names within Waverley, most famously Bondi, have been based on words derived from Aboriginal languages of the Sydney region.

The beginnings of the suburb go back to 1809, when the early road builder, William Roberts, received from Governor Bligh a grant of 81 hectares of what is now most of the business and residential area of Bondi Beach.

In 1851, Edward Smith Hall and Francis O'Brien purchased 200 acres of the Bondi area that embraced almost the whole frontage of Bondi Beach, and it was named the "The Bondi Estate." Between 1855 and 1877 O'Brien purchased Hall's share of the land, renamed the land the "O'Brien Estate," and made the beach and the surrounding land available to the public as a picnic ground and amusement resort.

As the beach became increasingly popular, O'Brien threatened to stop public beach access. However, the Municipal Council believed that the Government needed to intervene to make the beach a public reserve. It was not until June 9, 1882, that the Government acted and Bondi Beach finally became a public beach.

Waverley Council built the first surf bathing sheds in about 1903 and by 1929 an average of 60,000 people were visiting the beach on a summer weekend day. The opening of the pavilion that year attracted an estimated crowd of up to 200 000.

By the 1930s Bondi was drawing not only local visitors but also people from elsewhere in Australia and overseas. Advertising at the time referred to Bondi Beach as the "Playground of the Pacific."

Bondi Beach hosted the beach volleyball competition at the 2000 Summer Olympics. A temporary 10,000-seat stadium, a much smaller stadium, 2 warm-up courts, and 3 training courts were set up to host the tournament.

Bondi Beach is the end point of the City to Surf Fun Run, the largest running event in the world, which is held each year in August. The race attracts over 63,000 entrants who complete the 14 km run from the central business district of Sydney to Bondi Beach. Other annual activities at Bondi Beach include Flickerfest, Australia's premier international short film festival in January, World Environment Day in June, and Sculpture By The Sea in November. In addition to many activities, the Bondi Beach Markets are open every Sunday.

The surf lifesaving movement

The increasing popularity of sea bathing during the late 1800s and early 1900s raised concerns about public safety and how to prevent people from drowning. In response, the world's first formally documented surf lifesaving club, the Bondi Surf Bathers' Life Saving Club, was formed in 1907. Surf patrol members wearing their distinctive red and yellow quartered caps first appeared at Bondi that summer. Many key features of surf rescue were established in those early years, including several Australian inventions.

From Bondi, the surf lifesaving movement spread initially through New South Wales and then to the rest of Australia and the world. With the reassuring presence of surf lifesavers on duty, beaches became places of exhilarating swimming and surfing rather than potential tragedy.

Along with the digger and the bushman, the surf lifesaver held an iconic place in Australia's cultural imagery. The lifesaver grew to become an accepted feature of the beach and a symbol of what was seen to be good about being Australian.

This was powerfully reinforced by the dramatic events of "Black Sunday" at Bondi in 1938. Some 35,000 people were on the beach and a large group of lifesavers were about to start a surf race when three freak waves hit the beach, sweeping hundreds of people out to sea. Lifesavers rescued 300 people. The largest mass rescue in the history of surf bathing confirmed the place of the lifesaver in the national imagination.

Today, Surf Life Saving Australia is one of the largest and most successful nationwide associations of volunteers dedicated to protecting the safety of beach goers. Surf lifesavers have rescued over 520,000 people in the 80 years since records have been kept.

Sharks and shark nets

Since 1937, not one person has died from a shark attack at Bondi. However there are still regular shark sightings at Bondi. Swimmers are alerted to the presence of sharks when they are detected, but the first line of defence for many decades has been shark nets.

Shark nets are used on open ocean beaches in QLD and NSW. They are simply a straight, rectangular piece of net suspended in the water between buoys. They are anchored at either end, usually about 200 metres from shore, in about 10 metres of water. Most shark nets stretch about 200 metres along the beach and down to a depth of 6 metres. Floats at the top and sinkers at the bottom keep the net upright in the water. The mesh holes are 50cm wide; small enough to entangle sharks, and other large marine species, but big enough to leave smaller fish alone. The nets, however, are not intended to form a complete barrier, and sharks can still get through. The nets act as a deterrent by interrupting the territorial swimming patterns of sharks. In a typical 20km stretch of coastal surf beach, a strip of net will be set up every couple of kilometres along the beach.

Questions 1–10

Do the following statements agree with the information given in the Reading Passage?

In boxes 1–10 on your answer sheet, write

> **YES**   *if the statement agrees with the claims of the writer*
>
> **NO**   *if the statement contradicts the claims of the writer*
>
> **NOT GIVEN** *if it is impossible to say what the writer thinks about this*

1 Not many people liked to swim at Sydney's beaches in the early 1800s.   N

2 Criminals were prohibited from bathing in Sydney Harbour because they were Y dangerous to public.

3 The Government bought back Bondi beach from O'Brien to make it open to public. Y

4 Bondi Beach is a popular place in sports world.   NOT

5 Bondi Beach is the most famous beach in Australia.   Y

6 The official surf lifesaving movement originated from Bondi.   N

7 The digger and the bushman also work at the beach to rescue surfers.   NOT

8 Thanks to lifesavers no one drowned on "Black Sunday".   Y

9 Shark nets are very effective in protecting swimmers.   Y

10 No shark can pass through the shark nets.   N

► 核心词汇

词汇	释义
controversial	[ˌkɒntrəˈvɜːʃl] *adj.* 有争议的，有争论的
decorum	[dɪˈkɔːrəm] *n.* 礼仪，礼貌
officially	[əˈfɪʃəli] *adv.* 正式地，官方地
restrictive	[rɪˈstrɪktɪv] *adj.* 限制的，限制性的（同义词：limitative）
be associated with	与……有关系，与……相联系
democracy	[dɪˈmɒkrəsi] *n.* 民主，民主主义（dem=people 民众，如：demo人民，国民 + cracy 统治→人民统治→democracy民主；epi-在……中间 + demic人民→在国民中扩散、流行→epidemic流行的，传染的，传染病。）
aboriginal	[ˌæbəˈrɪdʒənl] *adj.* 土著的，原始的（作名词指"原住民，土著居民"）
settlement	[ˈsetlmənt] *n.* 定居，殖民
derive from	来源于
suburb	[ˈsʌbɜːb] *n.* 郊区；边缘（形容词形式：suburban；"sub-"表示"次于，低于"，"urban"表示"城市的，都市的"，因此"suburban"表达"郊区的"。）
residential	[ˌrezɪˈdenʃl] *adj.* 住宅的，与居住有关的
embrace	[ɪmˈbreɪs] *v.* 环抱
frontage	[ˈfrʌntɪdʒ] *n.* 前方；临街
available	[əˈveɪləbl] *adj.* 有效的，可利用的
intervene	[ˌɪntəˈviːn] *v.* 干涉，调停，插入
estimated	[ˈestɪmətɪd] *adj.* 估计的，预计的
tournament	[ˈtʊənəmənt] *n.* 锦标赛，联赛
premier	[ˈpremɪə(r)] *adj.* 第一的；最初的
drowning	[draʊn] *n.* 溺死（动词形式：drown）
exhilarating	[ɪgˈzɪləreɪtɪŋ] *adj.* 使人愉快的，令人喜欢的
iconic	[aɪˈkɒnɪk] *adj.* 图标的，形象的（名词形式：icon）
imagery	[ˈɪmɪdʒəri] *n.* 像；意象；比喻
rescue	[ˈreskjuː] *v.* 营救，援救（同义词：save）
alert	[əˈlɜːt] *adj.* 警惕的，警觉的（作动词指"警告"）
anchor	[ˈæŋkə(r)] *v.* 抛锚，使固定
entangle	[ɪnˈtæŋgl] *v.* 使纠缠，卷入

▶ 雅思阅读真题同义词考点

suburban	—peripheral, outlying, out-of-town
associate	—connect, link, join, combine
derive from	—originate from, come from, stem from, result from
intervene	—insert, interfere, interrupt
rescue	—save, recover, release, free
alert	—warn, caution, precaution

下篇导读：【荷兰郁金香危机】

考试时间：2010-04-24，2011-07-30……

　　我为花狂！郁金香在荷兰的历史；哪种花最贵？郁金香交易诞生期货市场？郁金香股市交易？从郁金香狂热到经济泡沫；粗心水手把昂贵的郁金香当作洋葱吃？ ☺

Reading Passage 20

The Dutch Tulip Mania

A Tulips have long held a significant role in Dutch history and culture ever since they were introduced to the Netherlands from the Ottoman Empire in the mid-1500s. So strong was the Dutch love affair with tulips during the Dutch Golden Age of the mid-1600s that a tulip bulb bubble or "Tulip Mania" even occurred. Generally considered to be the first recorded financial bubble, the Tulip Mania of 1636—1637 was an episode in which tulip bulb prices were propelled by speculators to incredible heights before collapsing and plunging the Dutch economy into a severe crisis that lasted for many years.

B The Golden Century is the name of the period in Dutch history between 1600 and 1700 when the port city of Amsterdam was one of the richest of all cities in Western Europe due to its strong role in international trade. Trading companies became dominant players in the Netherlands' trade with Indonesia and other far-away lands. Amsterdam's booming economy led to a flourishing of the arts and architecture, as well as trade in blue glass, china and other luxury goods.

C Dutch trade with foreign lands led to the importation of exotic goods that were never seen before by Europeans. Tulips were first introduced to Europe from Turkey when a sultan sent bulbs and seeds to Vienna. Shortly after 1554, these seeds were sent to Amsterdam, where their popularity began to rise. A university study in 1593 led to the discovery that tulips could withstand the harsh northern-European climate, which further boosted their desirability in the Netherlands. With their intensely colourful petals, tulips were unlike any other flower popular in Europe at that time and having tulips growing in one's garden became an important status symbol.

D Tulip plants originate in the form of tulip bulbs which do not flower until seven to twelve years later. Between April and May, tulips bloom for about one week, with bulbs appearing between June and September, thus confining Dutch sales to that season. A rudimentary derivatives market, similar to modern-day options and futures contracts, eventually arose so that traders could conduct trade in tulips all year round. Traders entered into tulip contracts by signing contracts for future tulip purchases before a notary. The very active tulip contract market eventually became an integral part of the overall booming Dutch tulip industry.

E As the Dutch tulip market became increasingly sophisticated, tulips were classified into groups and priced according to their rarity. In general, solid-coloured tulips were worth less than those with multiple colours. *Couleren* was the classification for solid-coloured red, white, or yellow tulips, *rosen* referred to multi-coloured tulips, often red, pink, or white and *violetten* described the white tulips with purple or lilac on them. *Bizarden* were the most popular tulips, with a yellow background and red, brown, or purple colouration. Tulips that were infected with the benign mosaic virus, which caused "flames" of colour to appear upon the petals, sold at a premium due to their unique beauty and rarity.

F Tulip prices steadily rose with their growing popularity and bulbs were purchased at higher and higher prices by speculators who planned to turn around and sell them for a profit, similar to modern-day house "flippers." From 1634 to 1637, an index of Dutch tulip prices soared from approximately one guilder per bulb to a lofty sixty guilders per bulb. Traders who sold their bulbs for a profit began to reinvest all of their profit into new tulip bulb contracts or new bulbs to sell to other Dutch citizens or to take with them on trips around the world to sell alongside with spices from the Dutch East India Company. Many merchants sold all of their belongings to purchase a few tulip bulbs for the purpose of cultivating and selling them for more profit than they could have ever made in a lifetime as a merchant. As the tulip bulb bubble crescendoed, already pricey tulip bulbs experienced a twentyfold price explosion in just a single month. By the peak of tulip mania in February of 1637, a single tulip bulb was worth about ten times a craftsman's annual income.

G Successful Dutch tulip bulb traders, the archaic counterparts to the day traders of the late 1990s Dot-com bubble and the house flippers of the mid-2000s U.S. housing bubble, could earn up to 60,000 florins in a month—approximately $61,710 in current U.S. dollars. Tulip bulb speculation became so widespread by

1636 that they were traded on Amsterdam's Stock Exchange and in Rotterdam, Haarlem, Leyden, Alkmar, Hoorn, and other towns. Around the same time, tulip speculation even spread to Paris and England, where tulips were traded on the London Stock Exchange. In both cities, traders strove to push tulip prices up to the lofty levels seen in Amsterdam but were only moderately successful in their attempt.

H Astronomically-high tulip bulb prices resulted in some equally astonishing anecdotes such as the sailor who mistakenly ate an extremely rare *Semper Augustus* tulip bulb thinking it was an onion. This "onion" was so valuable that it could have fed his whole ship's crew for an entire year. The helpless sailor was jailed for several months for his innocent but costly mistake. Another similar anecdote is of a traveling English botanist who was unaware of the Dutch tulip mania of the time, who peeled and dissected a wealthy Dutchman's four thousand florin *Admiral Von der Eyk* tulip bulb mistaking it for an unusual species of onion. The bewildered English traveller was quickly led through the streets, followed by a mob, to be brought before a judge who sentenced him to prison until he could pay for the damage.

I Like all bubbles, the Dutch tulip bulb bubble continued to inflate beyond people's wildest expectations until it abruptly "popped" in the winter of 1636-37. A default on a tulip bulb contract by a buyer in Haarlem was the main bubble-popping catalyst and caused the tulip bulb market to violently implode as sellers overwhelmed the market and buyers virtually disappeared altogether. Some traders attempted to support prices, to no avail. Within just a few days, tulip bulbs were worth only a hundredth of their former prices, resulting in a full-blown panic throughout Holland. Dealers refused to honour contracts, further damaging confidence in the tulip bulb market. Eventually, the government attempted to stem the tulip market meltdown by offering to honour contracts at 10% of their face value, which only caused the market to plunge even further. The brutal popping of the tulip bulb bubble ended the Dutch Golden Age and hurled the country into a mild economic depression that lasted for several years. The traumatic tulip bulb crash resulted in a suspicion toward speculative investments in Dutch culture for a very long time after.

Questions 1–10

Do the following statements agree with the information given in the Reading Passage?

In boxes 1–10 on your answer sheet, write

TRUE	*if the statement agrees with the information*
FALSE	*if the statement contradicts the information*
NOT GIVEN	*if there is no information on this*

1　It is perceived that the first written account of economic bubble was Tulip Mania.　T

2　A research found that tulips could well adapt to the demanding environment in Dutch.　T

3　An advanced futures market developed to help tulip trade all year round.　F

4　Violetten was more expensive than Couleren.　T

5　The highest price belonged to tulips with "flames" of colour caused by some virus.　N

6　The CEOs of Dot-com in late 1990s could earn about $61,710 each month.　T N

7　Amsterdam's Stock Exchange and London Stock Exchange were set up at the same time.　N

8　One sailor ate a tulip bulb because he considered it was nutritious.　F

9　Finally, The Dutch tulip bubble burst into an economic depression.　T

10　The government took steps to save the tulip market but failed.　T

▶ 核心词汇

词汇	释义
mania	['meɪnɪə] *n.* 癫狂，狂热
bulb	[bʌlb] *n.* 球茎，块茎植物
episode	['epɪsəʊd] *n.* 插曲，片断
propel	[prə'pel] *v.* 推进
speculator	['spekjʊleɪtə(r)] *n.* 投机倒把者，投机商人（动词形式：speculate）
collapse	[kə'læps] *v.* 倒塌，崩溃
plunge	[plʌndʒ] *v.* 暴跌，骤降，突降
exotic	[ɪg'zɒtɪk] *adj.* 异国的，外来的
petal	['petl] *n.* 花瓣
status	['steɪtəs] *n.* 地位，身份（sta, st=to stand站立，如：station车站；constitute站在一起→组成，设立；institute从内部站立→创立；prostitute以站在众人之前来维持生计的人→妓女；substitute在下面站着的→替代品，候补队员；superstition在上面站着的→迷信，偶像崇拜；statue站着的东西→雕像；status站着的状态→地位。）
confine	[kən'faɪn] *n./v.* 限制，局限于
rudimentary	[ˌruːdɪ'mentrɪ] *adj.* 基本的，初步的（同义词：fundamental）
derivative	[dɪ'rɪvətɪv] *n.* 衍生性金融商品
notary	['nəʊtərɪ] *n.* 公证人，公证员
sophisticated	[sə'fɪstɪkeɪtɪd] *adj.* 复杂的；精致的（同义词：complicated）
benign	[bɪ'naɪn] *adj.* 温和的；有利于健康的
mosaic	[məʊ'zeɪɪk] *adj.* 拼花的（音译"马赛克"。指"镶嵌，镶嵌图案，镶嵌工艺"。早期希腊人的大理石马赛克最常用黑色与白色来相互搭配。只有权威的统治者及有钱的富人才请得起工匠、购得起材料来表现此奢侈艺术。）
virus	['vaɪrəs] *n.* 病毒
premium	['priːmɪəm] *n.* 费用，额外费用，加价
lofty	['lɒftɪ] *adj.* 极高的
crescendo	[krə'ʃendəʊ] *v.* 渐强（反义词：decrescendo）
archaic	[ɑː'keɪk] *adj.* 古体的，古色古香的
anecdote	['ænɪkdəʊt] *n.* 掌故，趣闻，轶事
botanist	['bɒtənɪst] *n.* 植物学家
dissect	[dɪ'sekt] *v.* 切开，解剖（动物等）；仔细分析或研究（sect=to cut 切割。如：sect宗教教派，流派；bisect平分，一分为二；insect躯体分割成一节一节的→昆虫；intersection相互切割，纵横切割→交叉，十字路口；dis- = apart；dissect切割开来。）

bewildered	[bɪ'wɪldə(r)] *adj.* 困惑的；不知所措的（同义词：puzzled）
abruptly	[ə'brʌptlɪ] *adv.* 突然地；意外地（同义词：suddenly）
catalyst	['kætəlɪst] *n.*【化】催化剂；【比喻】触发因素；促进因素
hurl	[hɜːl] *v.* 猛投，用力掷
traumatic	[trɔː'mætɪk] *adj.* 创伤的（名词形式：trauma）
demanding	[dɪ'mɑːndɪŋ] *adj.* 过分要求的，苛求的

▶ 雅思阅读真题同义词考点

account   —record, evidence, register

plunge   —decrease, dive, drop, fall, plummet

exotic   —foreign, strange

rudimentary —fundamental, basic, preliminary, infrastructural

demanding   —burdensome, arduous, rigorous, exacting

burst   —explode, break

下篇导读： 【竹子的好处】

考试时间： 2009-04-25，2010-03-06，2011-07-09，2013-09-12……

　　非洲国家现在流行种竹子，但不是为了养熊猫。竹子的好处太多啦，简直是"罄竹难书"啊。做人要学竹子高风亮节，雅思考生要做竹子真题，才能胸有成竹。 ☺

Reading Passage 21

The <u>Benefits</u> of <u>Bamboo</u>

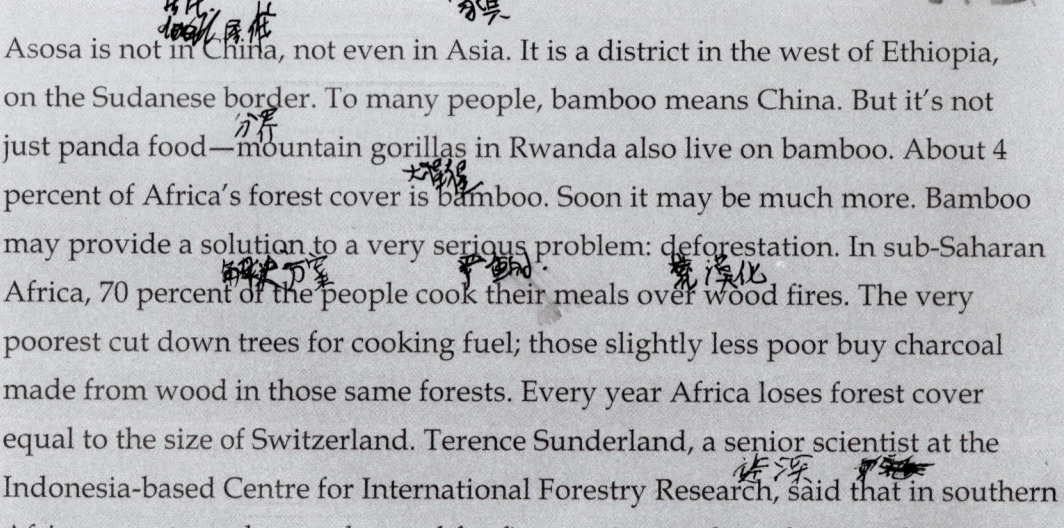

In the district of Asosa, the land is thick with bamboo. People plant it and manage the forests. They rely on its soil-grabbing roots to stabilise steep slopes and riverbanks, cutting erosion. They harvest it to burn for fuel, to make into charcoal sticks to sell to city dwellers and to build furniture.

Asosa is not in China, not even in Asia. It is a district in the west of Ethiopia, on the Sudanese border. To many people, bamboo means China. But it's not just panda food—mountain gorillas in Rwanda also live on bamboo. About 4 percent of Africa's forest cover is bamboo. Soon it may be much more. Bamboo may provide a solution to a very serious problem: deforestation. In sub-Saharan Africa, 70 percent of the people cook their meals over wood fires. The very poorest cut down trees for cooking fuel; those slightly less poor buy charcoal made from wood in those same forests. Every year Africa loses forest cover equal to the size of Switzerland. Terence Sunderland, a senior scientist at the Indonesia-based Centre for International Forestry Research, said that in southern Africa, even trees that can be used for fine carving, such as ebony and rosewood, are being cut down and made into charcoal.

Deforestation starts a vicious circle of drought and environmental decline. Burning wood releases the carbon stored inside. And deforestation accounts for at least a fifth of all carbon emissions globally. As tree cover vanishes, the land dries out and the soil erodes and becomes barren—a major reason for Ethiopia's periodic famines.

Reliance on hardwood fuel poses more present dangers as well. It's a woman's job to collect firewood, and when trees are scarce, women must walk farther and farther to find it, an often dangerous journey. Much cooking, moreover, is done indoors. The resulting air pollution kills some two million people a year. Almost half the deaths are from pneumonia in children under 5. Bamboo and charcoal made from bamboo burn more efficiently and cleanly than wood and wood charcoal.

Sunderland is talking to several southern African governments about bamboo. Farther north, the International Network for Bamboo and Rattan, a membership organisation of 38 countries based in Beijing, is providing technical support for growing and using bamboo in Ghana and Ethiopia.

How does bamboo improve on hardwood? Cut down a hardwood tree and it's gone. It will take several decades for another to grow in its place; it can take a century for a forest to grow back after cutting. But bamboo is a grass, not a tree. Under the right conditions, it can grow a full metre a day—you can literally watch it grow. It is also fast maturing. A new bamboo plant is mature enough to harvest after three to six years, depending on the species. Most important, bamboo is renewable. Unlike hardwood trees, bamboo regrows after harvesting, just as grass regrows after cutting. After it is mature, bamboo can be harvested every single year for the life of the plant.

Bamboo has other advantages. Its roots grab onto soil and hold it fast. Plant bamboo on a steep slope or riverbank and it prevents mudslides and erosion. And bamboo is parsimonious with Africa's most precious resource: water. "In Africa you want everything," said Dr. Chin Ong, a retired professor of environmental science at the University of Nottingham in England. "You want firewood, you want to reduce erosion, to maintain the water supply, generate cash and employment. Bamboo comes the closest—it gives you the most things."

Bamboo is not the perfect plant. Although the kinds of bamboo that grow in Africa are not invasive—some varieties that grow in cooler climates are—it can be very difficult to get rid of the networks of roots when the plant is no longer wanted. While bamboo can tolerate dry conditions, like any plant it will grow more slowly with less water, and it cannot grow in desert climates—exactly where it is needed most. And most bamboo is hollow, which means it burns more quickly than hardwood. Fortunately, bamboo that grows in Africa's lowlands is one of the few solid bamboo species.

Because bamboo requires few nutrients, it can grow in soil inhospitable to other plants—not only does it thrive there, it can reclaim the land so other plants can thrive, too. Its roots leach heavy metals from the soil, hold the soil together and draw water closer to the surface. One example is a project in Allahabad, India, to reclaim land whose topsoil had been depleted by the brick industry. In 1996, an INBAR project planted the land with bamboo. Five years later, villagers could farm the land again. Dust storms—a local scourge—were greatly reduced. The bamboo also helped raise the water table by seven metres. In 2007, the project won the global Alcan Prize for Sustainability.

Charcoal, of course, is not the only thing that can be made of bamboo. Its tensile strength makes it a good construction material, and it is also used for furniture, flooring and textiles, among other things. Paradoxically, harvesting bamboo to make durable goods is greener than not harvesting bamboo. Here's why: bamboo culms—the poles—do not live as long as hardwood trees, usually up to a decade. When an old culm decays, it releases carbon into the atmosphere. (The root system, which hold 30 to 40 percent of its carbon, last much longer.) This means that an untouched bamboo forest is a poor carbon sink. Fortunately, the best way to turn bamboo into an excellent carbon sink is to make money with it—harvest the bamboo to make durable products before it starts its decay. Treated bamboo flooring or furniture will last as long as wood, storing its carbon the whole time.

Questions 1–10

Do the following statements agree with the information given in the Reading Passage?

In boxes 1–10 on your answer sheet, write

TRUE	*if the statement agrees with the information*
FALSE	*if the statement contradicts the information*
NOT GIVEN	*if there is no information on this*

1 Only giant pandas feed on bamboo. F

2 Giant pandas eat bamboo only. N

3 No less than 20% of carbon emission in this world is caused by deforestation. F

4 Replacing hardwood with bamboo as fuel can reduce the mortality of children under 5. F

5 Bamboo is a kind of renewable, fast-growing tree. T

6 One benefit of bamboo is that it needs less water to grow. T

7 Bamboo can grow in the extremely dry environment. T

8 Hollow bamboo grows faster than solid species in Africa's lowlands. N

9 Planting bamboo can gradually improve the soil fertility. F

10 Cutting down bamboo forest to produce durable goods before its decay is beneficial to the environment. T

▶ 核心词汇

词汇	释义
stabilise	['steɪbəlaɪz] *v.* 稳定，安定
erosion	[ɪ'rəʊʒn] *n.* 侵蚀，腐蚀（动词形式：erode）
dweller	['dwelə(r)] *n.* 居民，居住者（同义词：settler，inhabitant）
deforestation	[ˌdiːˌfɒrɪ'steɪʃn] *n.* 采伐森林
carving	['kɑːvɪŋ] *n.* 雕刻
vicious circle	恶性循环（反义词：beneficial circle）
barren	['bærən] *adj.* 贫瘠的；不生育的（反义词：fertile）
periodic	[ˌpɪəri'ɒdɪk] *adj.* 周期的，定期的
famine	['fæmɪn] *n.* 饥荒
pneumonia	[njuː'məʊniə] *n.* 肺炎
literally	['lɪtərəlɪ] *adv.* 照字面地，逐字地（liter=letter 文字，如：literal文字的；illiteracy 不认字的→文盲；literature文字的集合体→文学，文献。）
maturing	[mə'tʃʊərɪŋ] *n.* 成熟（动词和形容词形式：mature；反义词：immature）
invasive	[ɪn'veɪsɪv] *adj.* 侵略性的，攻击性的（动词形式：invade）
tolerate	['tɒləreɪt] *v.* 忍受，默许
hollow	['hɒləʊ] *adj.* 空的，中空的（区别hallow）
inhospitable	[ˌɪnhɒ'spɪtəbl] *adj.* 荒凉的；冷淡的（反义词：hospitable *adj.*热情好客的）
thrive	[θraɪv] *v.* 繁荣，兴旺（同义词：prosper，boom）
deplete	[dɪ'pliːt] *v.* 使减少，弄空，耗尽……的资源
textile	['tekstaɪl] *n.* 纺织品，织物
paradoxically	['pærədɒksɪklɪ] *adv.* 自相矛盾地，似非而是地
durable	['djʊərəbl] *adj.* 耐用的，持久的
decay	[dɪ'keɪ] *n.* 衰退，腐烂
mortality	[mɔː'tæləti] *n.* 死亡数，死亡率 [形容词形式：mortal；反义词：immortal不朽的。mort来源于拉丁文mors，mori，"to die"。拉丁格言：memento mori（Remember that you must die）人皆有死。Amor【罗神】埃莫即爱神丘比特，该词本身就包含了mors死亡。人们期望爱amor能超越死亡而永恒，但爱情总会消亡的，因为爱是凡人mortal之事，必有一死。]
fertility	[fə'tɪləti] *n.* 多产，肥沃（fertile *adj.*富饶的，肥沃的；fertiliser *n.* 化肥）

▶ 雅思阅读真题同义词考点

mature	—adult, full-grown, ready
deplete	—drain, exhaust, impoverish, use up
tolerate	—put up with, endure, bear, withstand
mortal	—fatal, lethal, vital
fertile	—abundant, fruitful, productive

下篇导读： 【蚂蚁防虫】

考试时间： 2007-09-01，2011-06-23……

　　"蚂蚁蚂蚁，蝗虫的大腿；蚂蚁蚂蚁，蜻蜓的眼睛；蚂蚁蚂蚁，防虫没问题！"中国黄皮肤蚂蚁能否征服全世界的害虫？ ☺

Reading Passage 22

Chinese Yellow Citrus Ant for Biological Control

A In 1476, the farmers of Berne in Switzerland decided that, according to this story, there was only one way to rid their fields of the cutworms attacking their crops. They took the pests to court. The worms were tried, found guilty and excommunicated by the archbishop. In China, farmers had a more practical approach to pest control. Rather than rely on divine intervention, they put their faith in frogs, ducks and ants. Frogs and ducks were encouraged to snap up the pests in the paddies and the occasional plague of locusts. But the notion of biological control began with an ant. More specifically, the story says, it started with the predatory yellow citrus ant Oecophylla smaragdina, which has been polishing off pests in the orange groves of southern China for at least 1700 years. The yellow citrus ant is a type of weaver ant, which binds leaves and twigs with silk to form a neat, tent-like nest. In the beginning, farmers made do with the odd ants' nest here and there. But it wasn't long before growing demand led to the development of a thriving trade in nests and a new type of agriculture—ant farming.

B For an insect that bites, the yellow citrus ant is remarkably popular. Even by any standards, Oecophylla smaragdina is a fearsome predator. It's big, runs fast and has a powerful nip—painful to humans but lethal to many of the insects that plague the orange groves of Guangdong and Guangxi in southern China. And for at least 17 centuries, Chinese orange growers have harnessed these six-legged killing machines to keep their fruit groves healthy and productive. The story explains that citrus fruits evolved in the Far East and the Chinese discovered the delights of their flesh early on. As the ancestral home of oranges, lemons and pommels, China also has the greatest diversity of citrus pests. And the trees that produce the sweetest fruits, the mandarins—or kan—attract a host of plant—eating insects, from black ants and sap-sucking mealy bugs to leaf-devouring caterpillars. With so many enemies, fruit growers clearly had to have some way of protecting their orchards.

C The West did not discover the Chinese orange growers' secret weapon until the early 20th century. At the time, Florida was suffering an epidemic of citrus canker and in 1915 Walter Swingle, a plant physiologist working for the US Department of Agriculture, was, the story says, sent to China in search of varieties of orange that were resistant to the disease. Swingle spent some time studying the citrus orchards around Guangzhou, and there he came across the story of the cultivated ant. These ants, he was told, were "grown" by the people of a small village nearby who sold them to the orange growers.

D The earliest report of citrus ants at work among the orange trees appears in a book on tropical and subtropical botany written by His Han in AD 304. The people of Chiao-Chih sell in their markets ants in bags of rush matting. The nests are like silk. The bags are all attached to twigs and leaves which, with the ants inside the nests, are for sale. The ants are reddish-yellow in colour, bigger than ordinary ants. In the south if the kin trees do not have this kind of ant, the fruits will all be damaged by many harmful insects, and not a single fruit will be perfect.

E Initially, famers relied on nests that they collected from the wild or bought in the market—where trade in nests was brisk. It is said that in the South Orange trees, which are free of ants, will have wormy fruits. Therefore

the people race to buy nests for their orange trees, wrote Liu Hsun in *Strange Things Noted in the Soutti* about AD 890. The business quickly became more sophisticated. From the 10th century, country people began to trap ants in artificial nests baited with fat. "Fruit growing families buy these ants from vendors who make a business of collecting and selling such creatures", wrote Chuang Chi-Yu in 1130. They trap them by filling hogs or sheep's bladders and placing them with the cavities open next to the ant nests. They wait until the ants have migrated into the bladders and take them away. This is known as "rearing orange ants". Farmers attached the bladders to their trees, and in time the ants spread to other trees and built new nests. By the 17th century, growers were building bamboo walkways between their trees to speed the colonisation of their orchards. The ants ran along these narrow bridges from one tree to another and established nests "by the hundreds of thousands".

F Did it work? The orange growers thought so. One authority, Chi Ta Chun, writing in 1700, stressed how important it was to keep the fruit trees free of insect pests, especially caterpillars. "It is essential to eliminate them so that the trees are not injured. But hand labour is not nearly as efficient as ant power..."

Swingle was just as impressed. Yet despite this reports, many Western biologists were skeptical. In the West, the idea of using one insect to destroy another was new and highly controversial. The first breakthrough had come in 1888, when the infant orange industry in California had been saved from extinction by the Australian Vidalia beetle. This beetle was the only thing that had made any inroad into the explosion of cottony cushion scale that was threatening to destroy the state's citrus crops. But, as Swingle now knew, California's "first" was nothing of the sort. The Chinese had been expert in bio-control for many centuries.

G The story goes on to say that the long tradition of ants in the Chinese orchards only began to waver in the 1950s and 1960s with the introduction of powerful organic. Although most fruit growers switched to chemicals, a few hung onto their ants. Those who abandoned ants in favour of chemicals quickly became disillusioned. As costs soared and pests began to develop resistance to the chemicals, growers began to revive the old ant patrols. They had good reason to have faith in their insect workforce. Research in the early 1960s showed that as long as there were enough ants in the trees, they did an excellent job of dispatching some pests—mainly

the larger insects—and had modest success against others. Trees with yellow ants produced almost 20 per cent more healthy leaves than those without. More recent trials have shown that these trees yield just as big a crop as those protected by expensive chemical sprays.

H One apparent drawback of using ants and one of the main reasons for the early skepticism by Western scientists was that citrus ants do nothing to control mealy bugs, waxy-coated scale insects which can do considerable damage to fruit trees. In fact, the ants protect mealy bugs in exchange for the sweet honeydew they secrete. The orange growers always denied this was a problem but Western scientists thought they knew better. Research in the 1980s suggests that the growers were right all along. Where mealy bugs proliferate under the ants' protection they are usually heavily parasitised and this limits the harm they can do. Orange growers who rely on carnivorous ants rather than poisonous chemicals maintain a better balance of species in their orchards. While the ants deal with the bigger insect pests, other predatory species keep down the numbers of smaller pests such as scale insects and aphids. In the long run, ants do a lot less damage than chemicals—and they're certainly more effective than excommunication.

Questions 1–10

Do the following statements agree with the information given in the Reading Passage?

In boxes 1–10 on your answer sheet, write

TRUE	*if the statement agrees with the information*
FALSE	*if the statement contradicts the information*
NOT GIVEN	*if there is no information on this*

1　Chinese farmers had depended on divine intervention to control pests such as locusts. F

2　The shape of the nest made by the yellow citrus ant resembles a tent. T

3　China has the most citrus pests counted in types in the world. T

4　Swingle came to China in order to search an insect for the US government. F

5　With the growing demand, some people started to build synthetic nests to collect ants from the 10th century. T

6　Western people were initially impressed by Swingle's theory of pest prevention. F

7　Chinese farmers realised that price of pesticides became expensive. N

8　Trees without ants had grown more unhealthy leaves than those with. F

9　Citrus ants can control all kinds of pests which are harmful to fruit trees. T

10　Chinese orange farmers proposed that ant protection doesn't work out of China. T

▶ 核心词汇

词汇	释义
citrus	['sɪtrəs] *adj.* 柑橘属植物的
cutworm	['kʌtwɜ:m] *n.* 糖蛾，切根虫
pest	[pest] *n.* 害虫（pesticide 杀虫剂；字根cide=kill 杀）
try	[traɪ] *v.* 审判
guilty	['gɪltɪ] *adj.* 有罪的
excommunicate	[ˌekskə'mju:nɪkeɪt] *v.* 驱逐
archbishop	[ˌɑ:tʃ'bɪʃəp] *n.* 大主教，总教主（bishop主教，国际象棋中的"相"就是"主教"，也是这个单词）
approach	[ə'prəʊtʃ] *n.* 方法，途径
faith	[feɪθ] *n.* 信念，信仰
plague	[pleɪg] *n.* 瘟疫，灾祸
predatory	['predətrɪ] *adj.* 掠夺的
thriving	[θraɪvɪŋ] *adj.* 繁荣的，蒸蒸日上的（动词形式：thrive）
insect	['ɪnsekt] *n.* 昆虫
lethal	['li:θl] *adj.* 致命的
diversity	[daɪ'vɜ:sətɪ] *n.* 多样性，差异
caterpillar	['kætəpɪlə(r)] *n.* 毛毛虫（也指"履带式拖拉机"，美国某著名工程机械公司以此命名）
physiologist	[ˌfɪzɪ'ɒlədʒɪst] *n.* 生理学家
tropical	['trɒpɪkl] *adj.* 热带的
botany	['bɒtənɪ] *n.* 植物学（botanic garden植物园）
twig	[twɪg] *n.* 小枝，嫩枝，末梢
sophisticated	[sə'fɪstɪkeɪtɪd] *adj.* 复杂的
artificial	[ˌɑ:tɪ'fɪʃl] *adj.* 人造的，仿造的，假的
vendor	['vendə(r)] *n.* 小贩，供应商
creature	['kri:tʃə(r)] *n.* 生物
colonisation	[ˌkɒlənaɪ'zeɪʃn] *n.* 殖民，定居
controversial	[ˌkɒntrə'vɜ:ʃl] *adj.* 有争议的，有争论的
breakthrough	['breɪkθru:] *n.* 突破
resistance	[rɪ'zɪstəns] *n.* 抵抗
workforce	['wɜ:kfɔ:s] *n.* 劳动力
dispatch	[dɪ'spætʃ] *v.* 杀死，消灭
trial	['traɪəl] *n.* 试验

skepticism	['skeptɪsɪzəm] *n.* 怀疑论（形容词形式：skeptic）
honeydew	[ˌhʌnɪdjuː] *n.* 蜜汁，甘汁
proliferate	[prə'lɪfəreɪt] *v.* 激增，增值；扩散
poisonous	['pɔɪzənəs] *adj.* 有毒的

▶ 雅思阅读真题同义词考点

resemble	—be similar to, look like
artificial	—synthetic, man-made
descend	—decline, drop, fall, plunge
cope with	—deal with, dispose, handle
worship	—pray, appeal, beg, petition
decorate	—adorn, beautify, fix up, ornament, embellish

下篇导读：　【动物自疗】

考试时间：　2009-09-12，2011-01-15，2012-01-07，2014-03-13······

猩猩吃有毒的草治疗自己的疾病（以毒攻毒，欧阳锋？）

中国古代老马通灵为士兵衔来草药（真的假的？）

老鼠、鹦鹉为什么要吃黏土？（饿极了？）

家猫在死亡前为何会孤独地离家出走？（避免主人悲伤？）😊

Reading Passage 23

Animal Self-medication

Chausiki, a wild chimpanzee in the Mahale Mountains of Tanzania, was sick. She dozed lethargically while those around her fed. Her urine was dark, her stools were loose, her back was visibly stiff, and she ignored her whimpering young son. She then sought out a little shrub, the "bitter-leaf" or "goat-killer". Chausiki stripped away the highly toxic outer layers of its shoots. For twenty minutes she chewed and sucked the more mildly poisonous inner pith. The son tried to copy his mother, but he spat out the bitter plant in obvious disgust. A day later, Chausiki was cured. She travelled swiftly ahead of her group, and fed as usual.

Two scientists were watching her: Mohamedi Seifu Kalunde, a Tanzanian traditional herbalist, and Michael Huffman, an American biologist. The herbalist informed his companion that the bitter-leaf plant is a strong, broad-spectrum medicine used against malaria, schistosomiasis, amoebic dysentery and intestinal worms. Later chemical analysis showed that bitter-leaf pith contains at least ten different compounds active against parasites.

Huffman and Seifu's account of Chausiki's cure was one of the first scientific reports of animal self-medication. Cindy Engel tells the story well in Wild Health, a wonderful collection of tales about the ways in which animals prevent and cure ill-health. A general in Han Dynasty China noticed that sick horses gained vigour from eating Plantago asiatica, and fed it with good effect to his sick soldiers. Modern laboratory studies have found that poisoned rats turn to eating clay, and rats in pain will choose food laced with painkillers. Engel develops the argument that wild animals maximise their chances of good health when they live in rich natural environments where they are free to direct their own behaviour.

Engel is not a sentimentalist. She notes the widespread belief that wild creatures— and house cats—go off to die in stoic solitude, but points out that if an animal is sick and weak, the safest thing it can do is to hide from predators and pushy rivals of its own species. It goes off alone not to die, but to give itself the best chance of living. Similarly, she doesn't believe that animals have a mystic ability to identify specific cures for specifically diagnosed diseases. They choose foods that cure the symptoms of disease. Our folk feeling that medicine has to be bitter to do any good may derive from the fact that natural cures often taste of tannins or alkaloids. A chimp with a stomach ache may seek out a broad-spectrum antidote like the bitter-leaf. Or it may swallow whole leaves from several different kinds of hairy plants: leaves with "Velcro" hooks help clear out intestinal worms. Bears before hibernation and snow geese before migration also turn to Velcro plants. Domestic dogs and cats chew grass, which has the same scouring effect. Many wild animals, and some people, develop "pica" when ill, a craving to eat earth—particularly clay, which assuages diarrhea and binds to many plant poisons. Among the most famous clay-eaters are the parrots of the Amazon. Scarlet macaws, blue and gold macaws, and hosts of smaller birds perch together in their hundreds to excavate the best clay layer along a riverbank. Parrots' regular diet is tree seeds, which the trees defend with toxic chemicals, and clay is an essential buffer to the toxins.

Plants and animals have evolved myriad strategies for defending themselves against the continuous onslaught. Those that cannot do so efficiently become extinct. Animals have coherent, self-repairing skin, closing, mucus-lined orifices, complex immune systems, and behavioural dodges to avoid being eaten alive. Plants have bark and hairs and, above all, toxins. Fungal toxins range from antibiotics that repel and kill predatory bacteria, to poisons strong enough to kill off mushroom-collecting gourmets. No surprise, then, that small doses of some of these bio-active substances are effective as medicines. If plants use them against their own micro and macro-parasites, animals can borrow the effects to medicate themselves.

Engel's suggestion is that we would have much to gain from studying animals' health-related behaviour. Animals occasionally indulge in recreational drugs—they get drunk, sedate themselves into a stupor, and eagerly consume stimulants. Nature's pharmacy provides many intoxicants. They work by mimicking the action of neurological chemicals, and plants produce them because they defend against herbivorous predators. Getting high ought to reduce an animal's adaptive fitness; falling out of trees and stumbling away from predators is not the best way to get your genes into the next generation. One proposed explanation is that animal alcoholics are after the high calorie nourishment of ethanol.

A better theory is that drugs are a short circuit to the pleasure centres. Pleasure is usually a reward for behaviour patterns that are good for survival and reproduction. By taking a psychoactive drug, animals (and people) skip the hard work of getting food, getting resources or getting laid, and get the pleasure pay-off directly. Because psychoactive chemicals are rare in the wild and come in small doses, the casualty rate in spaced-out animals hasn't been high enough for it to be a factor in selection. Human technology has given us artificially purified drugs, often attractively packaged and marketed for anyone who wants them. "The social brake of legislation seems powerless against the unhealthy combination of natural desire and technological know-how," Engel remarks, ruefully.

Animals don't always do the healthy thing. There are wild bears in the Yosemite National Park that scavenge waste dumps and become obese, often twice their normal weight. Baboons, too, jump (or rather don't) at the opportunity to become couch potatoes. In the Serengeti reserve they can lie about all morning till the waste trucks from the hotels arrive, binge on high-sugar, high-fat, high-protein leftovers, and relax all afternoon. Over the years the baboons have got fatter, reached puberty earlier and acquired higher levels of cholesterol and insulin. The lesson is, of course, that when an animal is removed from the environment in which it evolved, drives and desires that were once adaptive can become highly maladaptive—a lesson it has taken people a long time to understand.

Questions 1–10

Do the following statements agree with the information given in the Reading Passage?

In boxes 1–10 on your answer sheet, write

YES	*if the statement agrees with the claims of the writer*
NO	*if the statement contradicts the claims of the writer*
NOT GIVEN	*if it is impossible to say what the writer thinks about this*

1 Two scientists observed that a female chimpanzee taught her son how to use the bitter-leaf to cure stomach ache.   *N*

2 In ancient China, horses found Plantago asiatica and fed sick soldiers.   *NOT — Y*

3 When sick or weak, some wild animals depart from the group in order to survive.

4 According to our folk feeling, the bitter the medicine tastes, the better healing effect it has.   *N*

5 Dogs and cats eat grass to clean their intestines.   *Y*

6 Parrots eat clay because it helps them digest tree seeds.   *N*

7 Toxin is one of the plants' self-defense mechanisms against their natural enemies.   *N*

8 Animals sometimes prefer recreational drugs which in fact shorten the odds of survival.   *Y*

9 Wild bears occasionally take psychoactive drugs to get pleasure.   *NOT*

10 People should not always keep animals in zoos.   *Y*

▶ 核心词汇

词汇	释义
chimpanzee	[ˌtʃɪmpænˈziː] *n.* 黑猩猩
lethargically	[ləˈθɑːdʒɪklɪ] *adv.* 昏昏沉沉地
urine	[ˈjʊərɪn] *n.* 尿，小便
stiff	[stɪf] *adj.* 僵硬的，呆板的（同义词：rigid）
shrub	[ʃrʌb] *n.* 灌木，灌木丛
strip away	去掉表面的薄覆盖物
toxic	[ˈtɒksɪk] *adj.* 有毒的（同义词：poisonous）
malaria	[məˈleərɪə] *n.*【医】疟疾
vigour	[ˈvɪɡə(r)] *n.* 精力，活力
clay	[kleɪ] *n.* 黏土，泥土
stoic	[ˈstəʊɪk] *adj.* 坚忍的，苦修的
solitude	[ˈsɒlɪtjuːd] *n.* 单独，孤独；偏僻处（sol=alone单独的，如：sole单个的；solely单独地；solo独唱，独奏，单独表演；solid完全结合成一个整体→固体，可靠的，一致的。）
diagnose	[ˈdaɪəɡnəʊz] *v.* 诊断
antidote	[ˈæntɪdəʊt] *n.* 解药，解毒剂
intestinal	[ɪnˈtestɪnl] *adj.* 肠的
domestic	[dəˈmestɪk] *adj.* 家养的，国内的
scouring	[ˈskaʊərɪŋ] *n.* 洗净，冲刷，洗涤
assuage	[əˈsweɪdʒ] *v.* 减轻，缓和（同义词：alleviate）
diarrhea	[ˌdaɪəˈrɪə] *n.* 腹泻
myriad	[ˈmɪrɪəd] *adj.* 无数的，多种的，各式各样的
orifice	[ˈɒrɪfɪs] *n.* 孔，洞口
indulge in	任凭自己沉溺于……
sedate	[sɪˈdeɪt] *v.* 使昏昏入睡，使镇静
stupor	[ˈstjuːpə(r)] *n.* 恍惚，昏迷
pharmacy	[ˈfɑːməsɪ] *n.* 药房，配药学，药学
ethanol	[ˈeθənɒl] *n.* 乙醇
legislation	[ˌledʒɪsˈleɪʃn] *n.* 立法，制定法律
scavenge	[ˈskævɪndʒ] *v.* （在废物中）寻觅
obese	[əʊˈbiːs] *adj.* 极为肥胖的，肥大的（名词形式：obesity肥胖症）

maladaptive	[ˌmæləˈdæptɪv] *adj.* （个体、物种等）不适应的，适应不良的（前缀mal-=badly, ill 不好的；与bene-相反。比如malnourished营养失调的，营养不良的）

▶ 雅思阅读真题同义词考点

cure	—treat, heal, remedy, restore
depart	—go off, exit, leave
shorten	—reduce, lessen, cut, decrease
diagnose	—analyse, deduce, interpret
indulge	—spoil, impair, pamper
domestic	—home, local, national, civil

下篇导读：【RUF双模交通】

考试时间： 2010-12-18……

　　BRT、购车摇号、尾号限行都是浮云；将来我们可以驾车以时速120千米在首都市区飞驰；这要依靠双模交通系统：公路和轨道结合。☺

Reading Passage 24

√ Rapid, Urban and Flexible

The car is so popular that it is about to strangle itself in success. On the other hand, traditional bus/train transit systems are so unattractive that they will never be able to become a real alternative to the car in a society where there is freedom of choice. Something new has to be invented. Something which is as flexible as the car, but as efficient as the train regarding capacity and environmental impact. A Dual Mode system is able to offer this new combination.

Modern cities are very low in density. People prefer to have space around them. It is good for the children and you have more privacy than in high-rise buildings. The consequence is that travel patterns are very diffuse both in time and in space. People are traveling from everywhere to everywhere and at the time they choose to travel. This makes it extremely difficult to transport people with traditional transit. Normally people are not willing to walk more than 400m to a station, so a Light Rail system will only appeal to a minor part of the travelers. A Dual Mode system like RUF (Rapid, Urban and Flexible) is able to cover widespread cities. For that reason it is a better alternative to the car than traditional transit.

The vehicles drive manually a few kilometres on ordinary roads in order to get to the rail system. The driver programs the RUF to know its destination and this information is transferred to the system when the vehicle gets near to the monorail. The system guides the vehicle to enter the guide way without waiting and at 30 km/h. From there on the driver can relax until he gets close to his destination where he takes over control again and drives manually to his destination. The main part of the trip is automated and the system knows when to turn right or left and when to get off. The automated part is very safe and energy efficient. The travel speed is typically 120 km/h on average. Travel times are short and predictable.

The RUF system will be implemented as a network of guide ways. A typical mesh size will be 5 km x 5 km, so a typical commuter will use 3 sections of the rail. At every junction, the speed is reduced to 30 km/h. The top speed between junctions can reach 200 km/h, but typically it will be 150 km/h when the mesh size is 5 km x 5 km. The reason for this speed reduction during switching is partly that the safety has to be extremely high in an automated system, partly that if the speed was any higher, and the radius of curvature would be much higher (it goes with the square of the speed). In an existing city it will not be possible to find room for soft curves. At 30 km/h the comfort criteria will allow for a 26 m radius of curvature.

The vehicles in the RUF system are coupled to form trains when they use the guide way. The length of the train depends on the demand. During night everybody will be allowed to travel alone. During rush hour 1 RUF per second can enter the guide way system. This means that a train of 10 RUFs can be created in approximately 10 seconds. This train creation can be made before merging onto the main rail. This way a very high capacity can be obtained. Capacity is more than just a number. The quality of capacity depends on the frequency. It is much better to have a capacity of 20,000 passengers per hour per direction with many small units than the same capacity obtained by squeezing people into large trains.

The RUF system can reduce the energy consumption from individual traffic. The main factor is the reduction of air resistance due to close coupling of vehicles. The energy consumption per RUF can be reduced to less than 1/3 at 100 km/h. Since RUF is an electric system, renewable sources can be used without problems. A combination of windmills and a RUF rail could be used over water. Solar cells can also be integrated into the system and ensure completely sustainable transportation.

The RUF system uses the space very efficiently. Only 2.5 m x 2.5 m is required for the rail. This means that it will often be possible to place a guide way along existing traffic corridors. A tunnel solution can be created that one tube can contain 3 rails. This means that the cost will be much lower than that of a train system requiring 2 tubes. The third rail can be used to supply more capacity for rush hour traffic in one direction or to help in an emergency.

The vehicles in a RUF system "rides" very safely on top of a triangular monorail. This means that derailments are impossible and that the users will feel safe because it is easy to understand that when the rail is actually inside the vehicle it is absolutely stable. The special rail brake ensures that braking power is always available even during bad weather. The brake can squeeze as hard against the rail as required in order to bring the vehicle to a safe stop. If a vehicle has to be evacuated, a walkway between the two rails can be used.

Personal Rapid Transit (PRT) is a beautiful system where small vehicles drive on demand on a guide way system. It is much better than traditional transit. Unfortunately it has never been fully implemented. Part of the reason is that it is not a Dual Mode system. It cannot leave the guide way. RUF can work as a PRT system where it is relevant (in dense parts of a town), but is also a Dual Mode system. In this respect it can be seen as a PRT+ system.

It will be impossible to start the RUF system as a system with privately owned RUFs from the start. Nobody would invest in a new infrastructure without knowing if anybody would like to buy the vehicles for it. For that reason, it is the intention to start it as a Public Transport system. Since the guide way is very slender and relatively inexpensive, such a system will be less costly than traditional public transport. It would also be a success compared to traditional transit because of the very high level of service offered in RUF.

Questions 1–10

Do the following statements agree with the information given in the Reading Passage?

In boxes 1–10 on your answer sheet, write

TRUE	*if the statement agrees with the information*
FALSE	*if the statement contradicts the information*
NOT GIVEN	*if there is no information on this*

1 Traditional transit systems are unappealing and cannot displace cars because they are not flexible.

2 Low density of cities has caused uncertainty of people's travel pattern.

3 A Dual Mode system like RUF is free of charge.

4 The main part of the trip needs drivers to control the vehicle in the RUF system.

5 Low speed during switching can reduce the radius of curvature.

6 Many individual RUFs achieve higher quality than large trains with the same capacity.

7 Over-water RUF rail uses a combination of windmills and solar cells.

8 During bad weather, RUF systems must be shut down.

9 PRT is an improved version of RUF system.

10 It is the government who should invest in RUF system.

▶ 核心词汇

词汇	释义
strangle	['stræŋgl] *v.* 扼死
alternative	[ɔːl'tɜːnətɪv] *n.* 二中择一，可供选择的办法
flexible	['fleksəbl] *adj.* 易曲的，灵活的，柔软的
efficient	[ɪ'fɪʃnt] *adj.* 有效率的（区别：effective）
diffuse	[dɪ'fjuːs] *v.* 散播，传播，漫射，扩散（同义词：spread）
dual	['djuːəl] *adj.* 双的，二重的，双重
widespread	['waɪdspred] *adj.* 分布广泛的，普遍的
manual	['mænjuəl] *n.* 手册，指南
monorail	['mɒnəʊreɪl] *n.* 单轨铁路（mono-指"单独，一个"，如：monologue独白；monopoly独占，垄断。）
guideway	['gaɪdweɪ] *n.* 导轨，导沟，导槽
predictable	[prɪ'dɪktəbl] *adj.* 可预言的
mesh	[meʃ] *n.* 网孔，网丝，网眼，圈套
commuter	[kə'mjuːtə(r)] *n.* 通勤者，经常往返者
junction	['dʒʌŋkʃn] *n.* 连接，接合，交叉点，汇合处
radius	['reɪdɪəs] *n.* 半径，范围，辐射光线，有效航程，范围，界限
curvature	['kɜːvətʃə(r)] *n.* 弯曲，曲率
consumption	[kən'sʌmpʃn] *n.* 消费，消费量
renewable	[rɪ'njuːəbl] *adj.* 可更新的，可恢复的
windmill	['wɪndmɪl] *n.* 风车（区别：treadmill 跑步机）
tunnel	['tʌnl] *n.* 隧道，地道
triangular	[traɪ'æŋgjələ(r)] *adj.* 三角形的，三人间的（triangle 三角形；circle 圆形；square 正方形；rectangle长方形；ellipse椭圆形；sector扇形）
derailment	[dɪ'reɪlmənt] *n.* （火车等）出轨
brake	[breɪk] *n.* 闸，刹车
evacuate	[ɪ'vækjʊeɪt] *v.* 疏散（vac, van, void=empty空的，如：vacuum真空；e-出 + vac空 + -uate动词词尾→空出去→evacuate疏散，撤离；a-加强 + void空→空出来→avoid回避，消除。）
implement	['ɪmplɪment] *v.* 贯彻，实施
infrastructure	['ɪnfrəstrʌktʃə(r)] *n.* 基础设施
slender	['slendə(r)] *adj.* 苗条的；微薄的，微弱的

▶ **雅思阅读真题同义词考点**

flexible	—elastic, not rigid
dual	—two, double, both…and…
commute	—exchange, travel
evacuate	—leave, quit, depart
implement	—carry out, bring about, complete

下篇导读：【谈自尊】

考试时间： 2009-03-05……

　　自尊的人交税多？自尊让你学习进步？自尊让人职业成功？自尊的人不抽烟不喝酒不打架？自尊给你雅思高分？自尊能给你快乐。☺

Reading Passage 25

Self-esteem Myth

People intuitively recognise the importance of self-esteem to their psychological health, so it isn't particularly remarkable that most of us try to protect and enhance it in ourselves whenever possible. What is remarkable is that attention to self-esteem has become a communal concern, at least for Americans, who see a favourable opinion of oneself as the central psychological source from which all manner of positive outcomes spring. The corollary, that low self-esteem lies at the root of individual and thus societal problems and dysfunctions, has sustained an ambitious social agenda for decades. Indeed, campaigns to raise people's sense of self-worth abound.

Consider what transpired in California in the late 1980s. Prodded by State Assemblyman John Vasconcellos, Governor George Deukmejian set up a task force on self-esteem and personal and social responsibility. Vasconcellos argued that raising self-esteem in young people would reduce crime, teen pregnancy, drug abuse, school underachievement and pollution. At one point, he even expressed the hope that these efforts would one day help balance the state budget, a prospect predicated on the observation that people with high self-regard earn more than others and thus pay more in taxes. Along with its other activities, the task force assembled a team of scholars to survey the relevant literature. The results appeared in a 1989 volume entitled The Social Importance of Self-Esteem, which stated that "many, if not most, of the major problems plaguing society have roots in the low self-esteem of many of the people who make up society." In reality, the report contained little to support that assertion.

Gauging the value of self-esteem requires, first of all, a sensible way to measure it. Most investigators just ask people what they think of themselves. Naturally enough, the answers are often coloured by the common tendency to want to make oneself look good. Unfortunately, psychologists lack any better method to judge self-esteem, which is worrisome because similar self-ratings of other attributes often prove to be way off. Consider, for instance, research on the relation between self-esteem and physical attractiveness.

It seems plausible that physically attractive people would end up with high self-esteem because they are treated more favourably than unattractive ones—being more popular, more sought after, more valued by lovers and friends, and so forth. But it could just as well be that those who score highly on self-esteem scales by claiming to be wonderful people all around also boast of being physically attractive.

At the outset, we had every reason to hope that boosting self-esteem would be a potent tool for helping students. Logic suggests that having a good dollop of self-esteem would enhance striving and persistence in school, while making a student less likely to succumb to paralysing feelings of incompetence or self-doubt. Early work showed positive correlations between self-esteem and academic performance, lending credence to this notion. Modern efforts have, however, cast doubt on the idea that higher self-esteem actually induces students to do better.

Even if raising self-esteem does not foster academic progress, might it serve some purpose later, say, on the job? Apparently not. Studies of possible links between workers' self-regard and job performance echo what has been found with schoolwork: the simple search for correlations yields some suggestive results, but these do not show whether a good self-image leads to occupational success, or vice versa. In any case, the link is not particularly strong.

Further researches show that high self-esteem does not lessen a tendency toward violence, that it does not deter adolescents from turning to alcohol, tobacco, drugs and sex, and that it fails to improve academic or job performance. Then we got a boost when we looked into how self-esteem relates to happiness. The consistent finding is that people with high self-esteem are significantly happier than others. They are also less likely to be depressed.

One especially compelling study was published in 1995, after psychologists at the University of Utah, surveyed more than 13,000 college students, and high self-esteem emerged as the strongest factor in overall life satisfaction.

Robin Di Matteo of the University of California at Riverside reported data from more than 600 adults ranging in age from 51 to 95. Once again, happiness and self-esteem proved to be closely tied. Before it is safe to conclude that high self-esteem leads to happiness, however, further research must address the shortcomings of the work that has been done so far.

What then should we do? Should parents, teachers and therapists seek to boost self-esteem wherever possible? In the course of our literature review, we found some indications that self-esteem is a helpful attribute. It improves persistence in the face of failure. And individuals with high self-esteem sometimes perform better in groups than do those with low self-esteem. Also, a poor self-image is a risk factor for certain eating disorders, especially bulimia. Other effects are harder to demonstrate with objective evidence, although we are inclined to accept the subjective evidence that self-esteem goes hand in hand with happiness.

So we can certainly understand how an injection of self-esteem might be valuable to the individual. But imagine if a heightened sense of self-worth prompted some people to demand preferential treatment or to exploit their fellows. Such tendencies would entail considerable social costs. And we have found little to indicate that indiscriminately promoting self-esteem in today's children or adults, just for being themselves, offers society any compensatory benefits beyond the seductive pleasure it brings to those engaged in the exercise.

Questions 1–10

Do the following statements agree with the information given in the Reading Passage?

In boxes 1–10 on your answer sheet, write

> **YES**   *if the statement agrees with the claims of the writer*
>
> **NO**   *if the statement contradicts the claims of the writer*
>
> **NOT GIVEN**   *if it is impossible to say what the writer thinks about this*

1   John Vasconcellos claimed that higher self-esteem would benefit government's revenue.

2   The report asserted that many social problems stemmed from the low self-esteem of people.

3   Good looking is a reliable attribute to measure self-esteem.

4   High self-esteem helps students achieve better scores.

5   Students with better academic performance are likely to achieve later occupational success.

6   People with high self-regard are less likely to smoke.

7   There is positive correlation between happiness and self-esteem.

8   Adults generally feel much happier than college students do.

9   Low self-esteem may cause ill-health.

10   People's self-esteem can be boosted by taking a training course.

▶ **核心词汇**

词汇	释义
intuitively	[ɪn'tjuːɪtɪvlɪ] *adv.* 直觉地，直观地（名词形式：intuition；区别：tuition *n.*学费）
communal	[kə'mjuːnl] *adj.* 公民的，公共的（community *n.*社会，社区；communist *n.* 共产主义者）
corollary	[kə'rɒlərɪ] *n.* 必然的结果，推论
dysfunction	[dɪs'fʌŋkʃn] *n.* 机能障碍，机能失调（前缀dys-表示"困难的，有病的"。如：dysbiosis 生态失调）
abound	[ə'baʊnd] *v.* 丰富，非常多，充满
transpire	[træn'spaɪə(r)] *v.* 发生
prod	[prɒd] *v.* 刺激，促使
relevant	['reləvənt] *adj.* 有关的，相关联的（反义词：irrelevant）
plague	[pleɪg] *v.* 使染瘟疫；使痛苦，造成麻烦
assertion	[ə's3ːʃn] *n.* 主张；明确肯定（动词形式：assert）
revenue	['revənjuː] *n.* （国家的）岁入，税收
gauge	[geɪdʒ] *v.* 测量，测定
plausible	['plɔːzəbl] *adj.* 貌似真实的，貌似有理的
sought after	很吃香的，广受欢迎的（动词原形：seek）
potent	['pəʊtnt] *adj.* 有效的，强有力的
strive	[straɪv] *v.* 努力奋斗，力求
succumb	[sə'kʌm] *v.* 屈服
credence	['kriːdns] *n.* 相信，凭证
foster	['fɒstə(r)] *v.* 培养，促进（同义词：cultivate）
vice versa	反之亦然
deter	[dɪ't3ː(r)] *v.* 阻止，制止
adolescent	[ˌædə'lesnt] *n.* 青春期，青少年
attribute	[ə'trɪbjuːt] *n.* 属性，（人或物的）特征；价值
exploit	[ɪk'splɔɪt] *v.* 利用（……为自己谋利）
compensatory	[ˌkɒmpen'seɪtərɪ] *adj.* 补偿性的，代偿（动词形式：compensate）
seductive	[sɪ'dʌktɪv] *adj.* 诱惑的，引诱的 [duc=to lead引导，如：deduce往下引导→推论，推导；induce往里引导→归纳，引诱；seduce 向旁边引导→引诱；educe向外(e-=ex-)引导→引出，唤起；education教育。所以education不是给予，而是引导出学习的兴趣和天性，引导正确的学习方法。]

▶ 雅思阅读真题同义词考点

revenue	—earnings, income, proceeds, gain
attribute	—feature, trait, characteristic, quality
correlation	—relation, relationship, connection, association
plague	—trouble, harass, worry
compensate	—balance, make up for, offset

下篇导读： 【吉尔伯特与磁场】

考试时间： 2010-08-05，2012-09-06……

　　古希腊人困惑于磁石现象，中国人也早已发明了罗盘，但英国人吉尔伯特用了20年的时间研究磁铁，最后著书立说《论磁石》，成为电磁学的奠基人、实验科学研究的开拓者。 😊

Reading Passage 26

William Gilbert
and
Magnetism

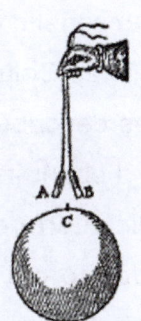

The accredited father of the science of electricity and magnetism was the English scientist, William Gilbert, who was a physician and man of learning at the court of Elizabeth. Prior to him, all that was known of electricity and magnetism was what the ancients knew, that the lodestone possessed magnetic properties and that amber and jet, when rubbed, would attract bits of paper or other substances of small specific gravity. William Gilbert's great treatise *On the Magnet*, printed in Latin in 1600, containing the fruits of his researches and experiments for many years, indeed provided the basis for a new science.

William Gilbert was born in Colchester, Suffolk, on May 24, 1544. He studied medicine at St. John's College, Cambridge, graduating in 1573. He was prominent in the College of Physicians and became its president in 1599. The following year he was appointed physician to Queen Elizabeth I, and a few months before his death on Dec. 10, 1603, physician to James I.

The ancient Greeks knew about lodestones, strange minerals with the power to attract iron. Some were found near the city of Magnesia in Asia Minor (now Turkey), and that city lent its name to all things magnetic. The early Chinese also knew about lodestones and about iron magnetised by them. Around the year 1000 they discovered that when a lodestone or an iron magnet was placed on a float in a bowl of water, it always pointed south. From this developed the magnetic compass, which quickly spread to the Arabs and from them to Europe.

Britain was a major seafaring nation in 1588 when the Spanish Armada was defeated, opening the way to British settlement of America. British ships depended on the magnetic compass, yet no one understood why it worked. Did the pole star attract it, as Columbus once speculated; or was there a magnetic mountain at the pole, as described in Odyssey, which ships should never approach, because the sailors thought its pull would yank out all their iron nails and fittings. Did the smell of garlic interfere with the action of the compass, which is why helmsmen were forbidden to eat it near a ship's compass? For nearly 20 years William Gilbert conducted ingenious experiments to understand magnetism.

"William Gilbert was fascinated by magnets," as Dr. David P. Stern of NASA notes. Given two magnets, Gilbert knew that magnetic poles can attract or repel, depending on polarity. In addition, however, ordinary iron is always attracted to a magnet. Gilbert guessed, correctly, that near a permanent magnet iron became a temporary magnet, of a polarity suitable for attraction. That is, the end of an iron bar stuck to an S pole of a magnet (south-seeking pole) temporarily becomes an N-pole. Because magnetic poles always come in matched pairs, the other end of the bar temporarily becomes an S-pole, and can in its turn attract more iron. Gilbert confirmed his guess of temporary ("induced") magnetism by an original experiment. Using strings, he hung two parallel iron bars above the pole of a terrella, a model earth he designed for this experiment, and noted that they repelled each other. Under the influence of the terrella, each became a temporary magnet with the same polarities, and the temporary poles of each bar repelled those of the other one.

In 1600 Gilbert published *De Magnete* in Latin. Very quickly it became the standard work throughout Europe on electrical and magnetic phenomena. In this work he describes many of his experiments with his model earth terrella. From his experiments, he concluded that the Earth was itself magnetic and that this was the reason compasses pointed north. In his book, he also studied static electricity using amber. Gilbert strongly argued that electricity and magnetism was not the same thing. For evidence, he (incorrectly) pointed out that electrical attraction disappeared with heat, magnetic attraction did not. By keeping clarity, Gilbert's strong distinction advanced science for nearly 250 years. It took James Clerk Maxwell to show electromagnetism is, in fact, two sides of the same coin.

De Magnete is not only a comprehensive review of what was known about the nature of magnetism, Gilbert added much knowledge through his own experiments. He likened the polarity of the magnet to the polarity of the Earth and built an entire magnetic philosophy on this analogy. In Gilbert's animistic explanation, magnetism was the soul of the Earth and a perfectly spherical lodestone, when aligned with the Earth's poles, would spin on its axis, just as the Earth spins on its axis in 24 hours. He speculated that the moon might also be a magnet caused to orbit by its magnetic attraction to the Earth. This was perhaps the first proposal that a force might cause a heavenly orbit.

Gilbert did not, however, express an opinion as to whether this rotating Earth was at the centre of the universe or in orbit around the Sun. In traditional cosmology the Earth was fixed and it was the sphere of the fixed stars, carrying the other heavens with it, which rotated in 24 hours. Since the Copernican cosmology needed a new physics to undergird it, Copernicans such as Johannes Kepler and Galileo were very interested in Gilbert's magnetic researches. Galileo's efforts to make a truly powerful armed lodestone for his patrons probably date from his reading of Gilbert's book.

As the first major scientific work produced in England, Gilbert's *De Magnete* reflected a new attitude toward scientific investigation. Until then, scientific experiments were not in fashion; instead, books relied on quotes of ancient authorities and that is where the myth about garlic interfering with the compass started. Unlike most medieval thinkers, Gilbert was willing to rely on sense experience and his own observations and experiments rather than the authoritative opinion or deductive philosophy of others. In the treatise he not only collected and reviewed critically older knowledge on the behaviour of the magnet and electrified bodies but described his own researches, which he had been conducting for 17 years. It was because of this scientific attitude, together with his contribution to our knowledge of magnetism, that a unit of magneto motive force, also known as magnetic potential, was named the Gilbert in his honour.

Questions 1–10

Do the following statements agree with the information given in the Reading Passage?

In boxes 1–10 on your answer sheet, write.

      TRUE   *if the statement agrees with the information*

      FALSE   *if the statement contradicts the information*

      NOT GIVEN   *if there is no information on this*

1   It was Gilbert who first discovered some substances with magnetic properties.

2   Arabs invented the magnetic compass in which an iron magnet always pointed south.

3   Odyssey noted that people believed the magnetic mountain would wreck the ship.

4   Gilbert explained the phenomenon of the magnetic compass in his book *De Magnete*.

5   Gilbert's mistaken notion about the distinction between electricity and magnetism held back the development of science.

6   James Clerk Maxwell demonstrated that there was close relationship between electricity and magnetism.

7   Gilbert speculated that the moon orbited the Earth by magnetic force.

8   Copernicans such as Galileo favoured traditional cosmology which held that the Earth was the centre of the universe.

9   Gilbert's magnetic theories contradicted the traditional cosmology.

10   As a scientist, Gilbert set himself apart by favouring an intuitive approach and experiments rather than the deductive reason.

▶ 核心词汇

词汇	释义
magnetism	['mægnətɪzəm] *n.* 磁，磁力，磁学
accredit	[ə'kredɪt] *v.* 归功于
lodestone	['ləʊdstəʊn] *n.* 天然磁石，吸引人的东西
amber	['æmbə(r)] *n.* 琥珀
jet	[dʒet] *n.* 黑玉
rub	[rʌb] *v.* 擦，摩擦
treatise	['triːtɪs] *n.* 论文，论述
prominent	['prɒmɪnənt] *adj.* 卓越的，显著的，突出的
compass	['kʌmpəs] *n.* 罗盘，指南针；圆规
seafaring	['siːfeərɪŋ] *n.* 航海事业，水手工作
yank	[jæŋk] *v.* 猛拉（Yank 作名词还指"美国佬"，是单词Yankee的变形，中文一般译做"扬基佬"。这个美国人绰号的来历众说纷纭，据传与荷兰人有关）
garlic	['gɑːlɪk] *n.* 大蒜，蒜头
interfere	[ˌɪntə'fɪə(r)] *vi.* 干涉，干预，妨碍，打扰
ingenious	[ɪn'dʒiːnɪəs] *adj.* 机灵的；有独创性的；精制的
polarity	[pə'lærətɪ] *n.* 极性
permanent	['pɜːmənənt] *adj.* 永久的，持久的
parallel	['pærəlel] *adj.* 平行的，类似的
phenomena	[fə'nɒmɪnə] *n.* 现象
static	['stætɪk] *adj.* 静态的，静力的（反义词：dynamic）
maxwell	['mækswel] *n.*【物】麦克斯韦（磁通量单位）
electromagnetism	[ɪˌlektrəʊ'mægnətɪzəm] *n.* 电磁，电磁学
analogy	[ə'nælədʒɪ] *n.* 类似，类推（常用短语：be analogous to类似于……，与……相似）
animistic	[ˌænɪ'mɪstɪk] *adj.* 万物有灵论的(anim = breath 气息；soul 心灵。例如：animal有呼吸的东西→动物；animate使有呼吸→使有生气，活泼；inanimate使没有呼吸→无生命的；unanimous呼吸一致，一个鼻孔出气→意见一致的，无异议的。)
spherical	['sferɪkl] *adj.* 球的，球形的
align	[ə'laɪn] *v.* 排列；对准
sphere	[sfɪə(r)] *n.* 球，球体；范围，领域（atmosphere 大气层，大气圈）
undergird	[ʌndə'gɜːd] *v.* 加强，巩固……的底部
medieval	[ˌmedɪ'iːvl] *adj.* 中世纪的，老式的
deductive	[dɪ'dʌktɪv] *adj.* 推论的，推导的

▶ 雅思阅读真题同义词考点

accredit	—ascribe, attribute, assign
wreck	—demolish, destroy, devastate, dismantle, ruin
distinction	—difference, variation
permanent	—forever, always, eternal
parallel	—alike, analogical, like, similar, win

CHAPTER 3

Paragraph Heading
段落中心思想题

介绍：唯一出在文章之前的题型。要求阅读自然段，选出自然段中心思想。

概率：真实考试40个题目中平均6个题，通常只针对1篇出题。

难度：★★★★★

段落中心思想题

雅思机考 (IELTS Computer Based) 界面及说明:

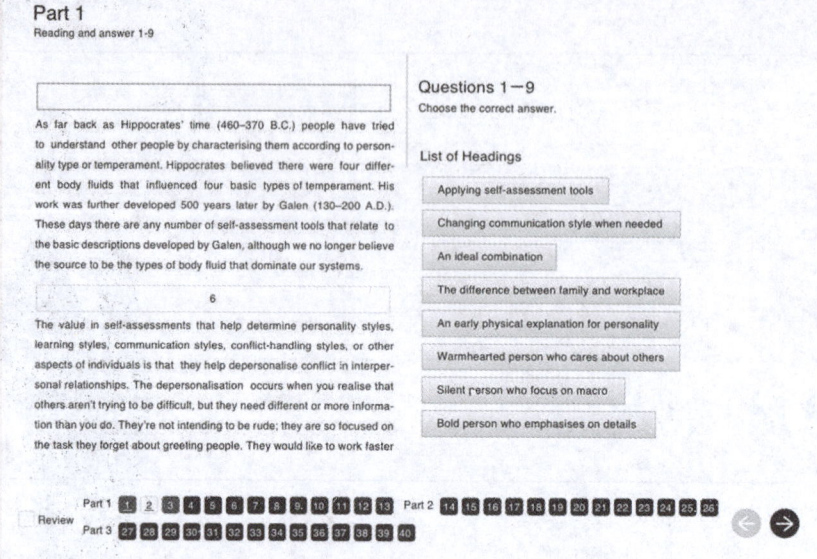

段落中心思想题一般为拖拽形式,左侧文章区有答题框,右侧是备选项。

如何答题:点击右侧标题并将其移至左侧文章段落中的答题框中。

修改答案:移动右侧新的标题覆盖在原答案上。

清除答案:把选择的标题拖动回原处。

www.ieltscb.com 提供免费机考练习。

下篇导读: 【珍珠】

考试时间: 2009-08-22,2014-02-15……

　　古代珍珠的价值;有人把它当药用。天然和养殖珍珠的介绍;珍珠价值的区别。世界上顶级珍珠的产地是巴林,后因发现了石油,污染了海域。😊

Reading Passage 27

Question 1–8

*Choose the most suitable headings for paragraphs **B–I** from the list of headings below.*

*Write appropriate numbers (**i–xii**) in boxes 1–8 on your answer sheet.*

NB   *There are more headings than paragraphs, so you will not use them all.*

List of Headings

i   The importance of pearls in ancient time

ii   The risk of pearl farming

iii   The mussels' life circle

iv   Different types of pearls

v   Irrelevance to water source

vi   How pearls form naturally

vii   Artificial pearls are not durable

viii The most expensive colour

ix   Freshwater pearls are more valuable

x   The difference between natural and cultured pearls

xi   Factors that determine the value

xii   Petroleum ruined pearl production

Example	*Answer*
Paragraph **A**	**i**

1   Paragraph **B**

2   Paragraph **C**

3   Paragraph **D**

4   Paragraph **E**

5   Paragraph **F**

6   Paragraph **G**

7   Paragraph **H**

8   Paragraph **I**

Pearls

A   Throughout history, pearls have held a unique presence within the wealthy and powerful. For instance, the pearl was the favoured gem of the wealthy during the Roman Empire. This gift from the sea had  been brought back from the orient by the Roman conquests. Roman women wore pearls to bed so they could be reminded of their wealth immediately upon waking up. Before jewelers learned to cut gems, the pearl was of greater value than the diamond. In the Orient, pearls were ground into powders to cure anything from heart disease to epilepsy, with possible aphrodisiac uses as well. Pearls were once considered an exclusive privilege for royalty. A law in 1612 drawn up by the Duke of Saxony prohibited the wearing of pearls by nobility, professors, doctors or their wives in an effort to further distinguish royal appearance. American Indians also used freshwater pearls from the Mississippi River as decorations and jewelry.

B   There are essentially three types of pearls: natural, cultured and imitation. A natural pearl (often called an Oriental pearl) forms when an irritant, such as a piece of sand, works its way into a particular species of oyster, mussel, or clam. As a defense mechanism, the mollusk secretes a fluid to coat the irritant. Layer upon layer of this coating is deposited on the irritant until a lustrous pearl is formed.

C   A cultured pearl undergoes the same process. The only difference is that the irritant is a surgically implanted bead or piece of shell called Mother of Pearl. Often, these shells are ground oyster shells that are worth significant amounts of money in their own right as irritant-catalysts for quality pearls.

The resulting core is, therefore, much larger than in a natural pearl. Yet, as long as there are enough layers of nacre (the secreted fluid covering the irritant) to result in a beautiful, gem-quality pearl, the size of the nucleus is of no consequence to beauty or durability.

D   Pearls can come from either salt or freshwater sources. Typically, saltwater pearls tend to be higher quality, although there are several types of freshwater pearls that are considered high in quality as well. Freshwater pearls tend to be very irregular in shape, with a puffed rice appearance the most prevalent. Nevertheless, it is each individual pearls merits that determines value more than the source of the pearl.

E   Regardless of the method used to acquire a pearl, the process usually takes several years. Mussels must reach a mature age, which can take up to 3 years, and then be implanted or naturally receive an irritant. Once the irritant is in place, it can take up to another 3 years for the pearl to reach its full size. Often, the irritant may be rejected, the pearl will be terrifically misshapen, or the oyster may simply die from disease or countless other complications. By the end of a 5 to 10 year cycle, only 50% of the oysters will have survived. And of the pearls produced, only approximately 5% are of substantial quality for top jewelry makers. From the outset, a pearl farmer can figure on spending over $100 for every oyster that is farmed, of which many will produce nothing or die.

F   Imitation pearls are a different story altogether. In most cases, a glass bead is dipped into a solution made from fish scales. This coating is thin and may eventually wear off. One can usually tell an imitation by biting on it. Fake pearls glide across your teeth, while the layers of nacre on real pearls feel gritty. The Island of Mallorca is known for its imitation pearl industry.

G   To an untrained eye, many pearls may look quite similar. There is, to the contrary, an intricate hierarchy to pearls and several factors exist that determine a pearl's worth. Luster and size are generally considered the two main factors to look for. Luster for instance, depends on the fineness and evenness of the layers. The deeper the glow, the more perfect the shape and surface, the more valuable they are. Moreover, if you can see a reflection of your face clearly by gazing into the pearl, that is a high quality luster. The foggier the reflection, the less valuable the pearl. Size on the other hand, has to do with the age of the oyster that created the pearl (the more mature oysters produce larger pearls) and the location in which the pearl was cultured. The South Sea waters of Australia tend to produce the larger pearls; probably because the water along the coast line is supplied with rich nutrients from the ocean floor. Also, the type of mussel common to the area seems to possess a predilection for producing comparatively large pearls.

H   Pearls also come in many colours. The most popular colours are whites, creams, and pinks. Silver, black, and gold are also gaining increasing interest. In fact, a deep lustrous black pearl is one of the rarest finds in the pearling industry, usually only being found in the South Sea near Australia. Thus, they can be one of the more costly items.

I   Historically, the world's best pearls came from the Persian Gulf, especially around what is now Bahrain. The pearls of the Persian Gulf were natural created and collected by breath-hold divers. The secret to the special luster of Gulf pearls probably derived from the unique mixture of sweet and salt water around the island. Unfortunately, the natural pearl industry of the Persian Gulf ended abruptly in the early 1930's with the discovery of large deposits of oil. Those who once dove for pearls sought prosperity in the economic boom ushered in by the oil industry. The water pollution resulting from spilled oil and indiscriminate over-fishing of oysters essentially ruined the once pristine pearl producing waters of the Gulf. Today, pearl diving is practiced only as a hobby. Still, Bahrain remains one of the foremost trading centres for high quality pearls. In fact, cultured pearls are banned from the Bahrain pearl market, in an effort to preserve the location's heritage.

J   Nowadays, pearls predominately come from Japan, Australia, Indonesia, Myanmar, China, India, Philippines, and Tahiti. Japan however, controls roughly 80% of the world pearl market, with Australia and China coming in second and third, respectively.

▶ 核心词汇

词汇	释义
pearl	[pɜːl] *n.* 珍珠
gem	[dʒem] *n.* 宝石（近义词：jewellery 珠宝。区别：germ 微生物，细菌）
exclusive	[ɪkˈskluːsɪv] *adj.* 排外的，唯一的（the exclusive news 独家新闻）
privilege	[ˈprɪvəlɪdʒ] *n.* 特权
prohibit	[prəˈhɪbɪt] *v.* 禁止，阻止
imitation	[ˌɪmɪˈteɪʃn] *n.* 仿制品
irritant	[ˈɪrɪtənt] *n.* 刺激（物）（动词形式：irritate）
oyster	[ˈɔɪstə(r)] *n.* 牡蛎
mussel	[ˈmʌsl] *n.* 贻贝，蚌类（区别：muscle 肌肉）
lustrous	[ˈlʌstrəs] *adj.* 光亮的，有光泽的 [名词形式：luster 光彩，光泽。luc/lux/lust =bright 明亮的。如：il(on) + lustr(bright) + -ate (*v.*) 使明亮，使清晰→图解说明；lucent *adj.* 光亮的，透明的；美国朗讯科技以此为名。力士香皂的品牌 Lux。撒旦的名字叫 Lucifer，字根也是"光明"，因为古人眼里最邪恶的恰恰就是那貌似光明的。]
catalyst	[ˈkætəlɪst] *n.* 刺激因素，催化剂
misshapen	[ˌmɪsˈʃeɪpən] *adj.* 畸形的
bead	[biːd] *n.* （空心）小珠子
solution	[səˈluːʃn] *n.* 溶液（另一常见词义为：解决方案。动词形式：solve）
hicrarchy	[ˈhaɪərɑːkɪ] *n.* 等级制度
predilection	[ˌpriːdɪˈlekʃn] *n.* 偏爱，偏好，嗜好（同义词：preference）
usher	[ˈʌʃə(r)] *v.* 引导（常用词组：usher in）
spill	[spɪl] *v.* 使溢出
indiscriminate	[ˌɪndɪˈskrɪmɪnət] *adj.* 不分皂白的，不加选择的（discriminate *v.* 歧视）
pristine	[ˈprɪstiːn] *adj.* 质朴的
foremost	[ˈfɔːməʊst] *adj.* 首要的

▶ 雅思阅读真题同义词考点

determine	—decide, judge, resolve, settle
exclusive	—only, barely, merely, unique
irritate	—spur, agitate, provoke, incite, stimulate, stir up
usher	—lead, guide, conduct
foremost	—chief, important, dominant, first, leading, main, primary, principal

下篇导读：【性格与人际关系】

考试时间：2010-04-10……

　　多血质、黏液质、抑郁质、胆汁质四种个性；它们有不同的交流方式；判断一下你是哪一种？高效的工作团队需要四种结合。

Reading Passage 28

Question 1–9

*Choose the most suitable headings for sections **A—I** from the list of headings below.*

*Write appropriate numbers (**i–xii**) in boxes 1–8 on your answer sheet.*

NB   *There are more headings than sections, so you will not use them all.*

List of Headings
i   Applying self-assessment tools
ii   Changing communication style when needed
iii   An ideal combination
iv   The difference between family and workplace
v   An early physical explanation for personality
vi   Warmhearted person who cares about others
vii   Silent person who focus on macro
viii Bold person who emphasises on details
ix   Factual and logic personality
x   The benefits of understanding communication styles
xi   Energetic person who encourages team
xii   Summary of personality types

1   Section **A**

2   Section **B**

3   Section **C**

4   Section **D**

5   Section **E**

6   Section **F**

7   Section **G**

8   Section **H**

9   Section **I**

Temperaments and Communication Styles

Knowing your communication style and having a mix of styles on your team can provide a positive force for resolving conflict.

Section A

As far back as Hippocrates' time (460–370 B.C.) people have tried to understand other people by characterising them according to personality type or temperament. Hippocrates believed there were four different body fluids that influenced four basic types of temperament. His work was further developed 500 years later by Galen (130–200 A.D.). These days there are any number of self-assessment tools that relate to the basic descriptions developed by Galen, although we no longer believe the source to be the types of body fluid that dominate our systems.

Section B

The value in self-assessments that help determine personality styles, learning styles, communication styles, conflict-handling styles, or other aspects of individuals is that they help depersonalise conflict in interpersonal relationships. The depersonalisation occurs when you realise that others aren't trying to be difficult, but they need different or more information than you do. They're not intending to be rude; they are so focused on the task they forget about greeting people. They would like to work faster but not at the risk of damaging the relationships needed to get the job done. They understand there is a job to do, but it can only be done right with the appropriate information, which takes time to collect. When used appropriately, understanding communication styles can help resolve conflict on teams. Very rarely are conflicts true personality issues. Usually they are issues of style, information needs, or focus.

Section C

Hippocrates and later Galen determined there were four basic temperaments: sanguine, phlegmatic, melancholic and choleric. These descriptions were developed centuries ago and are still somewhat apt, although you could update the wording. In today's world, they translate into the four fairly common communication styles described below.

Section D

The sanguine person would be the expressive or spirited style of communication. These people speak in pictures. They invest a lot of emotion and energy in their communication and often speak quickly, putting their whole body into it. They are easily sidetracked onto a story that may or may not illustrate the point they are trying to make. Because of their enthusiasm they are great team motivators. They are concerned about people and relationships. Their high levels of energy can come on strong at times and their focus is usually on the bigger picture, which means they sometimes miss the details or the proper order of things. These people find conflict or differences of opinion invigorating and love to engage in a spirited discussion. They love change and are constantly looking for new and exciting adventures.

Section E

The phlegmatic person—cool and persevering—translates into the technical or systematic communication style. This style of communication is focused on facts and technical details. Phlegmatic people have an orderly methodical way of approaching tasks, and their focus is very much on the task, not on the people, emotions, or concerns that the task may evoke. The focus is also more on the details necessary to accomplish a task. Sometimes the details overwhelm the big picture and focus needs to be brought back to the context of the task. People with this style think the facts should speak for themselves, and they are not as comfortable with conflict. They need time to adapt to change and need to understand both the logic of it and the steps involved.

Section F

The melancholic person who is softhearted and oriented toward doing things for others translates into the considerate or sympathetic communication style. A person with this communication style is focused on people and relationships. They are good listeners and do things for other people—sometimes to the detriment of getting things done for themselves. They want to solicit everyone's opinion and make sure everyone is comfortable with whatever is required to get the job done. At times this focus on others can distract from the task at hand. Because they are so concerned with the needs of others and smoothing over issues, they do not like conflict. They believe that change threatens the status quo and tends to make people feel uneasy, so people with this communication style, like phlegmatic people, need time to consider the changes in order to adapt to them.

Section G

The choleric temperament translates into the bold or direct style of communication. People with this style are brief in their communication—the fewer words the better. They are big picture thinkers and love to be involved in many things at once. They are focused on tasks and outcomes and often forget that the people involved in carrying out the tasks have needs. They don't do detail work easily and as a result can often underestimate how much time it takes to achieve the task. Because they are so direct, they often seem forceful and can be very intimidating to others. They usually would welcome someone challenging them, but most other styles are afraid to do so. They also thrive on change, the more the better.

Section H

A well-functioning team should have all of these communication styles for true effectiveness. All teams need to focus on the task, and they need to take care of relationships in order to achieve those tasks. They need the big picture perspective or the context of their work, and they need the details to be identified and taken care of for success.

Section I

We all have aspects of each style within us. Some of us can easily move from one style to another and adapt our style to the needs of the situation at hand—whether the focus is on tasks or relationships. For others, a dominant style is very evident, and it is more challenging to see the situation from the perspective of another style.

The work environment can influence communication styles either by the type of work that is required or by the predominance of one style reflected in that environment. Some people use one style at work and another at home. The good news about communication styles is that we all have the ability to develop flexibility in our styles.

The greater the flexibility we have, the more skilled we usually are at handling possible and actual conflicts. Usually it has to be relevant to us to do so, either because we think it is important or because there are incentives in our environment to encourage it. The key is that we have to become flexible with our communication style. As Henry Ford said, "Whether you think you can or you can't, you're right!"

▶ **核心词汇**

词汇	释义
conflict	['kɒnflɪkt] *n.* 冲突，矛盾
temperament	['temprəmənt] *n.* 气质，性情（temper *n.* 脾气）
self-assessment	[selfə'sesmənt] *n.* 自我评估
dominate	['dɒmɪneɪt] *v.* 控制，支配
depersonalise	[diː'pɜːsənəlaɪz] *v.* 使失去个性
appropriate	[ə'prəʊprɪət] *adj.* 适当的
update	[ˌʌp'deɪt] *v.* 更新，校正（区别：up-to-date *adj.* 最近的，新式的）
enthusiasm	[ɪn'θjuːzɪæzəm] *n.* 热情，热心（及其含义可追溯到希腊词enthoes，意为"心中有神灵，它由en-，表"在……里"，和theos-，意为"神"构成。显示了古人对宗教的狂热）"
motivator	['məʊtɪveɪtə(r)] *n.* 动力，激励因素（动词形式：motivate）
engage in	从事于（参加）
factual	['fæktʃəl] *adj.* 事实的，真实的
evoke	[ɪ'vəʊk] *v.* 引起，唤起
oriented	['ɔːrɪəntɪd] *adj.* 导向的，定向的（ori = to rise 升起，to begin 开始。oriental太阳升起的地方→东方的；origin升起的地方→起源；originator发起人；orientate使向东，引申为定方向；国外大学新学期开学前有一周叫O-week，即Orientation Week，给新生介绍大学的各种情况，让他们摸清方向，尽快适应。）
detriment	['detrɪmənt] *n.* 损害，伤害（形容词形式：detrimental）
solicit	[sə'lɪsɪt] *v.* 征求；招揽
choleric	['kɒlərɪk] *adj.* 易怒的，暴躁的
bold	[bəʊld] *adj.* 大胆的（同义词：brave；反义词：timid）
underestimate	[ˌʌndər'estɪmeɪt] *v.* 低估，看轻
perspective	[pə'spektɪv] *n.* 远景，透视图
at hand	在手边；即将到来
incentive	[ɪn'sentɪv] *n.* 动机，刺激（商业上指绩效工资）
flexible	['fleksəbl] *adj.* 灵活的，柔韧的
macro	['mækrəʊ] *adj.* 宏观的，巨大的（反义词：micro）
logical	['lɒdʒɪkl] *adj.* 合逻辑的（名词形式：logic 逻辑。该词为英语译音。近代著名启蒙思想家严复在《穆勒名学》中首次用逻辑二字作为英文logic的音译。）

▶ 雅思阅读真题同义词考点

understand	—appreciate, comprehend, know, realise, recognise, perceive
encourage	—inspire, promote, sponsor, support, urge, motivate
detrimental	—harmful, bad, deleterious
underestimate	—undervalue, overlook, ignore, neglect
logical	—reasonable, fair, sound, justifiable

下篇导读： 【电子书】

考试时间： 2009-04-04，2010-09-11······

　　从纸质书的历史到电子书概念的提出，最后到电子书的实现。人类文明传承的方式逐步改变。注意雅思阅读真题还有一篇讲网络资料的储存。

Reading Passage 29

Question 1–8

*Choose the most suitable headings for paragraphs **A–I** from the list of headings below.*

*Write appropriate numbers (**i–xi**) in boxes 1–8 on your answer sheet.*

NB   *There are more headings than paragraphs, so you will not use them all.*

List of Headings

i	"Virtual" libraries on the horizon
ii	The problem of lucid reading
iii	The success of electronic encyclopedias
iv	Early setbacks in electronic publishing
v	Problems solved with the advent of the World Wide Web
vi	Improved readability
vii	Unrestrained reading experience
viii	Easy delivery and mass storage capacities
ix	Milestones in reading "technology" evolution
x	Accessing Library of Congress made possible
xi	Initial imagination or prediction

---

1   Paragraph **A**

2   Paragraph **B**

3   Paragraph **C**

4   Paragraph **D**

5   Paragraph **E**

6   Paragraph **F**

7   Paragraph **G**

8   Paragraph **I**

E-book

A Reading on paper is so much a part of our lives that it is hard to imagine anything could ever replace inky marks on shredded trees. Since Johannes Gutenberg invented an economical way to make movable metal type in the 15th century, making it possible to produce reading matter quickly, comparatively cheaply and in large quantities, the printed word has proved amazingly resilient. So how could anyone believe that sales of electronic books will equal those of paper books within a decade or so? First, it is worth remembering that paper is only the latest in a long line of reading "technologies" that were made obsolete each time an improved solution emerged. Pictures drawn on rock gave way to clay tablets with cuneiform characters pressed into the clay before it dried. Clay gave way to animal skin scrolls marked with text, and then to papyrus scrolls. By 100 AD the codex had arrived, but it was not until the ninth century that the first real paper book was produced. In Europe, paper was rare until after Gutenberg's breakthrough.

B It took a few more centuries for e-books to emerge. They were first envisioned in 1945 by Vannevar Bush, director of the United States Office of Scientific Research and Development. In his classic essay, "As We May Think", Bush described a gadget he called a "Memex"—"a device in which an individual stores all his books, records, and communications. Most of the memex contents are purchased on microfilm ready for insertion. Books of all sorts, pictures, current periodicals, newspapers, are thus obtained and dropped into place. Wholly new forms of encyclopedias will appear, ready-made with a mesh of associative trails running through them."

C Although science-fiction writers eagerly adopted Bush's ideas notably on the television show "Star Trek", where portable electronic books featured regularly, the real world has remained loyal to paper. Only in the encyclopedia market, which was transformed by CD-roms in the mid-1980s, has the e-book made real progress. Far more encyclopedias, from Microsoft's Encarta to Encyclopedia Britannica, are sold on CD-rom than were ever sold on paper, because they cost a fraction of the price and are easier to search. But attempts to broaden the appeal of e-book technology to appeal to readers have been unsuccessful. Since the late 1980s the electronic publishing world has seen several failed e-book ventures. Why? Most of them used devices that were either too bulky to carry around, or forced users to "stock up" their electronic library in inconvenient ways. One even required visits to a "book bank", an ATM-like machine that was to be located in bookstores. Before widespread adoption of the Internet, there was no universal way to download new reading material.

D But the most fundamental problem was the lack of a display technology that could compete with paper when it came to lucid reading. For paper books, readability depends on many factors: typeface and size, line length and spacing, page and margin size, and the colour of print and paper. But for e-books there are even more factors, including resolution, flicker, luminance, contrast and glare. Most typefaces were not designed for screens and, thanks to a limited number of pixels, are just fuzzy reproductions of the originals. The result is that reading on-screen is hard on the eyes and takes a lot more effort. People do it only for short documents. The longer the read, the more irritating and distracting are all the faults in display, layout and rendering.

E Most of these problems are now being solved. The World Wide Web offers an amazingly flexible way to deliver books and as investments in broadband infrastructure increase, it will get even easier to stock an e-library. And dozens of companies established publishing firms such as R.R. Donnelly, Penguin Putnam, and Nokia. Barnes & Noble and Microsoft have joined to create an open e-book standard, so that book-lovers will be able to read any title on any e-book. There have also been some incredible technological breakthroughs that will make it much easier to read long texts on a screen. Microsoft has developed a font display technology called ClearType that, by manipulating the red, green and blue sub-pixels that make up the pixels on an LCD screen, improves resolution by up to a factor of three. Coupled with the latest e-book reading software and hardware, this provides an on-screen reading experience that begins to rival paper.

F But why would anyone prefer an e-book to a p-book, regardless of improved readability? Because e-books have many other advantages. You will get instant delivery from your web bookshop to your e-book, and be able to store hundreds of novels on a device the size of a paperback. E-book technology enables you to have an entire library in your pocket. Or you can keep it on your PCs—a modern laptop can hold more than 30,000 books. You won't have to wait for out-of-stock books to be ordered, and books will never go out of "print". Your children will be able to listen to unfamiliar words pronounced for them as they read. You will have unabridged audio synchronised to the text, so you can continue the story in situations where you are unable to read, for example, while driving.

G In addition, e-books promise to revolutionise the way the world reads. Whereas paper books are stand-alone entities, e-books can include hypertext links to additional content, whether it is in other books, databases or web sites. So e-books will not be restricted to a linear structure that is the same for every one. Every reader will be free to make use of the links, images and sounds differently. You will also be able to customise e-books by adding your own notes, links and images. In a paper book, content is fixed; with e-book technology it is flexible.

H The e-book will also revolutionise the economics of the industry. The cost of publishing books will fall dramatically, the result of savings on materials, labour, manufacturing and distribution. In the process, a lot of trees will also be saved and even the most obscure author will be able to self-publish, which means more choice for readers. The retail price of books will fall; sales will explode.

I It is hard to imagine today, but one of the greatest contributions of e-books may eventually be in improving literacy and education in less-developed countries. Today people in poor countries cannot afford to buy books and rarely have access to a library. But in a few years, as the cost of hardware continues to decline, it will be possible to set up "virtual" public libraries which will have access to the same content as the Library of Congress.

▶ 核心词汇

词汇	释义
obsolete	['ɒbsəliːt] *adj.* 荒废的；陈旧的
clay	[kleɪ] *n.* 黏土，泥土；肉体，人体
cuneiform	['kjuːnɪfɔːm] *adj.* 楔形的，楔形文字的
scroll	[skrəʊl] *n.* 卷轴，卷形物，名册（游戏玩家必备词汇：魔法卷轴Enchant Scroll）
papyrus	[pə'paɪrəs] *n.* 【植】纸草，草制成之纸
codex	['kəʊdeks] *n.* (*pl.* -dices [daɪsɪs]) *n.* （圣经等古籍的）抄本；古法典
envision	[ɪn'vɪʒn] *v.* 想象，预想
gadget	['gædʒɪt] *n.* 小器具，小配件，小玩意儿；诡计
portable	['pɔːtəbl] *adj.* 手提（式）的，便携式的
bulky	['bʌlkɪ] *adj.* 大的，容量大的，体积大的
lucid	['luːsɪd] *adj.* 明晰的
typeface	['taɪpfeɪs] *n.* 字体，字样，打字机字体
resolution	[ˌrezə'luːʃn] *n.* 分辨率
flicker	['flɪkə(r)] *n.* 扑动，闪烁，闪光，颤动
luminance	['luːmɪnəns] *n.* 发光，光亮亮度
glare	[gleə(r)] *n.* 刺目，刺眼
pixel	['pɪksl] *n.* （显示器或电视机图像的）像素
fuzzy	['fʌzɪ] *adj.* 模糊的，失真的
unabridged	[ˌʌnə'brɪdʒd] *adj.* 未经删节的，完整的
synchronise	['sɪŋkrənaɪz] *v.* 同步（chron=time 时间。希腊神话中宙斯Zeus的爸爸名叫克洛诺斯Cronus，是时间之神，和希腊语中的"时间"chronos拼写和读音上很相似。而该神害怕自己的子女反抗自己，曾吞食了自己的后代，就像时间的无情，正如谚语所说：时间吞噬一切。所以字根chron代表时间。如：chronic 耗费时间的，慢性的；chronology年代学，年表。syn-=same一致，所以synchronise指"使时间一致，同步"。）
hypertext	['haɪpətekst] *n.* 超文本
linear	['lɪnɪə(r)] *adj.* 线的，直线的，线性的
customise	['kʌstəmaɪz] *v.* 定制，用户个性化
literacy	['lɪtərəsɪ] *n.* 有文化，有教养，有读写能力
virtual	['vɜːtʃʊəl] *adj.* 虚拟的（Virtual Reality 虚拟现实）
setback	['setbæk] *n.* 挫折
milestone	['maɪlstəʊn] *n.* 里程碑（古罗马军团正步走一千步的距离。这一千步在拉丁语叫做milia passuum，常略作milia。从milia演变而来mile一词。）

▶ 雅思阅读真题同义词考点

portable	—conveyable, movable, transferable
envision	—imagine, foresee, predict
virtual	—fictitious, unreal
setback	—frustration, disappointment, failure
milestone	—turning point, landmark, benchmark, holy grail

下篇导读：【自我营销】

考试时间：……

  在一个人口日益增长的社会里，如何把自己从候选者的茫茫人海中推销出去，让面试官印象深刻。面试的各种心得技巧，对雅思口语面试同样有帮助。😊

Reading Passage 30

Question 1–7

*Choose the most suitable headings for paragraphs **B**, **D**, **E**, **H**, **I**, **K**, **M** from the list of headings below.*

*Write appropriate numbers (**i–x**) in boxes 1–7 on your answer sheet.*

NB *There are more headings than paragraphs, so you will not use them all.*

<table>
<tr><td colspan="2">List of Headings</td></tr>
<tr><td>i</td><td>Honesty: the highest principle</td></tr>
<tr><td>ii</td><td>Professional paper preparation</td></tr>
<tr><td>iii</td><td>Appropriate attire</td></tr>
<tr><td>iv</td><td>Benefit of rehearsal</td></tr>
<tr><td>v</td><td>Test of personality</td></tr>
<tr><td>vi</td><td>Do not badmouth your last boss</td></tr>
<tr><td>vii</td><td>Test specifics during a job interview</td></tr>
<tr><td>viii</td><td>Rejoicing in hope, patient in tribulation</td></tr>
<tr><td>ix</td><td>Psychometric testing: an essential part in some interviews</td></tr>
<tr><td>x</td><td>Be a joy angel</td></tr>
</table>

1 Paragraph **B**

2 Paragraph **D**

3 Paragraph **E**

4 Paragraph **H**

5 Paragraph **I**

6 Paragraph **K**

7 Paragraph **M**

Self-marketing

A Whether one is in a job looking to advance on the career ladder or unemployed looking for work, the only way to succeed is to market himself or herself. Any good marketer will confidently remark that the key to success is to have good campaign and to never give up. And to make it in the job market today one has to be aware of that and to do just that. Please consider the following points to get on the right track:

B Curriculum Vitae or Resumé, Business Cards, and References or Letters of Recommendation from previous employers must all be in impeccable condition before one takes any concrete action to engage oneself into another working environment. Employers' first point of contact with the applicant will be what they see on paper, so it must look proficient to create a good impression.

C Happiness is the ultimate principle whoever one is, a prince or a pauper. And undeniably smile and friendly approach will make one look upbeat and interesting, which will greatly enhance one's chances of winning the interviewer's favour and consequently market oneself successfully.

D Consider a variety of questions that one may be asked at interview then consider answers to the questions. Get a friend to pretend as the interviewer and then rehearse how to tackle them. This will let one brush up on interviewing skills, and make one appear more confident on the day.

E Even if the job applied for does not require professional attire, one should still wear a business suit, unless told otherwise. If in doubt, the safest option is to dress conservatively. Having the right look will not only help one present the right image; it will increase one's self-confidence, enabling one to concentrate all their energies into what they have to say, rather than worrying about how people respond to their looks. But what not to wear: One's role in the interview process is to convince the employer that he or she is the right person for the job. Thus, any clothes, which will distract the employer's attention from delivering that message, should be avoided. To this end avoid excessive jewellery and loud colours or bright patterns of clothing. This type of attire has the potential to engender a negative reaction from the employer.

F Always appear interested in the profession one is trying to get into. Show knowledge of the market and investigate the latest developments within the sector. Be positive. Keep all negative thoughts away from the interview and do not say anything derogatory about one's previous employer.

G If one wants to land a specific role within a company, find out exactly what experience, qualifications, and requirements are needed to secure the position. Then target sufficient energies into obtaining these things.

H Sometimes, the company one is applying for includes some form of psychometric testing as a routine part of their selection procedure. Do not worry and make oneself excessively nervous. The most widely used tests fall into two main categories: personality and ability/aptitude.

I An individual's personality plays an important part in how they perform in their job. Potential employers can gain an insight into a person's overall character, especially when these tests are used alongside other tests and methods of assessment. Candidates are usually presented with a series of multiple-choice questions to which there are no right or wrong answers—the employer obtains the information required by analysing the candidates' answers.

J Future performance is accurately indicated by aptitude and ability, hence tests which measure both ability and aptitude have become an important way for employers to make and confirm their recruitment selections. These tests can take many forms and can be administered in both printed and electronic formats.

K Commonly, candidates are presented with a number of different tests (with a break between each of them), namely, numerical tests, which will test a candidate's skills with numerical information which may be presented in tabular, textual or graphical format; abstract tests, which may involve studying groups of patterns to find similarities and differences, and verbal tests, which may test a candidate's comprehension of reports which may not be dependable in their objectivity or honesty, for instance.

L Make sure that one prepares himself or herself for taking the tests—have plenty of sleep; arrive in good time; remember to bring things like glasses/hearing-aids if one normally wears them and reads any literature one was given by testers. Ensure that one performs to the best of his or her ability in the tests—listen carefully and follow instructions but do not be afraid to ask questions if things are still unclear and try to work quickly and accurately as most tests are timed.

M Consider one's best attributes and bring these to the fore in one's marketing campaign. Never lie to employer about qualifications of which one is not in possession, because one will definitely get found out, and this will only ruin one's chances of further employment. Be honest with the employer and make them aware of the achievements and accomplishments previously made in one's career.

▶ 核心词汇

词汇	释义
confidently	['kɒnfɪdəntlɪ] *adv.* 自信地，肯定地（相应词形变化：confident *adj.*，confidence *n.*，confide *v.*）
remark	[rɪ'mɑːk] *v.* 说，评论
campaign	[kæm'peɪn] *n.* 运动；（包括一系列战斗的）战役
curriculum vitae/ resumé	（求职者写的）简历，履历（Curriculum Vitae简称CV）
reference	['refrəns] *n.* 推荐信，介绍信（与文中提到的Letter of Recommendation表达同一含义，英联邦国家喜欢用Reference，北美则倾向用Letter of Recommendation。）
previous	['priːvɪəs] *adj.* 以前的，先前的
concrete	['kɒŋkriːt] *adj.* 具体的，实际的
proficient	[prə'fɪʃnt] *adj.* 精通的，熟练的
ultimate	['ʌltɪmət] *adj.* 最终的，终极的
pauper	['pɔːpə(r)] *n.* 穷人，贫民（Mark Twain曾著Prince and Pauper《王子与贫民》）
undeniably	[ˌʌndɪ'naɪəblɪ] *adv.* 不可否认地，无可争辩地（相应词形变化：undeniable *adj.*，deniable *adj.*，deny *v.*）
upbeat	['ʌpbiːt] *adj.* 乐观的，活泼的，生机勃勃的
enhance	[ɪn'hɑːns] *v.* 提高，增大，增强
rehearse	[rɪ'hɜːs] *v.* 排练，排演，练习（名词形式：rehearsal）
attire	[ə'taɪə(r)] *n.* 服装，衣着
option	['ɒpʃn] *n.* 选择（相应词形变化：opt *v.*，option *n.*，optional *adj.*）[optimistic *adj.* 乐观的（"opt"表示"选择"，名词"乐观主义"——"optimism"，这里是它的形容词形式。一个人什么时候会很乐观，走到绝路的时候吗？不！当各种各样的"选择"都冲他打开大门的时候才觉得自己有价值，进而很乐观。）]
conservatively	[kən's3ːvətɪvlɪ] *adv.* 保守地，传统地（形容词形式：conservative，英国两大执政党之一保守党即为Conservative Party；很多人用conservative和reticent两个词语来形容英国人的个性，后者表示其很矜持，轻易不开口讲话，不像很多北美人给人留下的印象IBM——International Big Mouth，从早到晚都在blah。）
distract one's attention from	将注意力从……转移/分散
to this end	为此，为达到这一目的（"为达到那一目的"该怎么讲？"to that end"喽！）
excessive	[ɪk'sesɪv] *adj.* 过分的，过多的
potential	[pə'tenʃl] *n.* 潜能，可能性
engender	[ɪn'dʒendə(r)] *v.* 造成，引起，招致

negative	['negətɪv] *adj.* 负面的，消极的（与下文中的 "positive" 互为反义词；表示 "阴性—阳性、负数—正数、消极—积极"。）
sector	['sektə(r)] *n.* 部门
positive	['pɒzətɪv] *adj.* 积极的，有建设性的
specific	[spə'sɪfɪk] *adj.* 具体的，特定的（动词形式：specify）
secure	[sɪ'kjʊə(r)] *v.* 获得
routine	[ruː'tiːn] *n.* 惯例，固定项目
fall into	分成
category	['kætəgərɪ] *n.* 种类，类别
candidate	['kændɪdət] *n.* 候选人，投考者 ["cand-" 表示 "白"，例如 "candle" 最初指 "白色蜡烛"， "candid" 是形容词，表示 "坦白的"；而这里 "candidate" 的来历要说到古罗马，当时凡是要参加竞选公职的人要穿宽松的白色长袍（white toga），代表无论此人的性格还是名誉上都毫无瑕疵、洁白如玉，所以以上三个单词都来自这个表示 "白" 的字根。]
aptitude	['æptɪtjuːd] *n.* 倾向，才能（美国College Entrance Examination高中生毕业考试SAT全称为Scholastic Aptitude Test，意为 "学术倾向性测试"。）
insight	['ɪnsaɪt] *n.* 洞察力，深入了解
overall	[ˌəʊvər'ɔːl] *adj.* 总的，全面的
confirm	[kən'fɜːm] *v.* 证实，进一步确定（名词形式：confirmation）
recruitment	[rɪ'kruːtment] *n.* 招收，招聘（动词形式：recruit）
administer	[əd'mɪnɪstə(r)] *v.* 实施，执行
format	['fɔːmæt] *n.* 版式，样式
comprehension	[ˌkɒmprɪ'henʃn] *n.* 理解，理解力（动词形式：comprehend）
objectivity	[ˌɒbdʒek'tɪvətɪ] *n.* 客观（性）
literature	['lɪtrətʃə(r)] *n.* 文献，图书资料
attribute	[ə'trɪbjuːt] *n.* 特性，属性
to the fore	在前面，在显著的地位
ruin	['ruːɪn] *v.* 毁坏，毁灭

▶ 雅思阅读真题同义词考点

previous	—earlier, prior, former
engender	—produce, cause, bring about, generate
secure	—obtain, acquire, capture, procure
category	—class, sort, type, classification
recruitment	—staffing, employment, enlistment
comprehension	—understanding, conception, grasp

下篇导读： 【地图册】

考试时间： 2010-11-06，2012-04-14……

　　手绘地图的历史。在古代，地图是商业和战争必不可少的工具。地图绘制的发展，地图册的出现。现代电脑绘制代替了铜板雕刻。Google Earth代替了"北京市旅游交通图嘞，八毛！" ☺

Reading Passage 31

Question 1–8

*Choose the most suitable headings for paragraphs **A—H** from the list of headings below.*

*Write appropriate numbers (**i—xi**) in boxes 1–8 on your answer sheet.*

NB   *There are more headings than paragraphs, so you will not use them all.*

List of Headings

i	The effects of the great events on mapmaking
ii	Superior version with high quality and price
iii	From copper to computers
iv	From plaster to paper
v	The modern atlas was born
vi	A guide for Roman travellers
vii	Columbus' discovery of the New World
viii	Driven by trade and military
ix	Atlas of cities and seas
x	The best-seller in 1572
xi	The first use of the term

---

1   Paragraph **A**

2   Paragraph **B**

3   Paragraph **C**

4   Paragraph **D**

5   Paragraph **E**

6   Paragraph **F**

7   Paragraph **G**

8   Paragraph **H**

Maps
and
Atlas

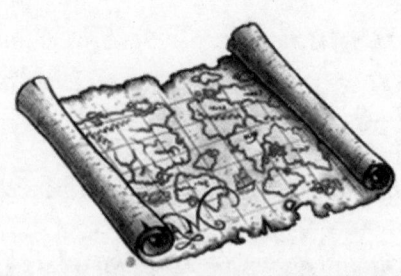

A No one knows when the first map was made. Perhaps it was some paleolithic hunter scratching lines in the earth to direct his comrades to where he had seen prey. The oldest surviving physical object which could be called a map is a wall painting of a town plan at the archeological site in Anatolia, Turkey. Radiocarbon examination dates it from about 6200 B.C. Maps are known from classical times—a clay tablet with a city plan from Mesopotamia; a world map on bronze supposedly shown to the King of Sparta circa 500 B.C.; an Egyptian papyrus showing a gold mine.

B Perhaps the most celebrated of ancient maps is the Peutinger Table which survives at the Royal Library of Vienna. It is a 12th or 13th century manuscript copy of a road map of the Roman Empire which was probably created in the 5th century A.D. During the Middle Ages most maps were either of small local areas or were cosmic maps of the world. The former were for land ownership purposes, and the latter were cosmological—providing inspiration about the place of this world in relation to the next. It is possible the world maps could also have been helpful to travelers, though only the largest contained enough detail to be of much use.

C All the above maps were manuscript, i.e., made by hand. In the 15th century European map-making was influenced by several events. One was the invention of movable type by Gutenberg circa 1555, which led to the extensive production of printed books. Some books, such as geographies needed maps, creating a demand for printed maps. Another great event was the rediscovery of Ptolemy in the West. Ptolemy (circa 150 A.D.) was a scholar of Alexandria, Egypt whose *Geographia* explained his system of coordinates for locating places on the map. It included coordinates for several thousand places. This great work was lost to the West for over a thousand years, but was retained in the East. As the Byzantine Empire came under pressure from the Turks, refugees fled west taking their possessions with them, including texts of the *Geographia*.

D Then came a third great event, Columbus' discovery of the New World. The discovery effectively stopped creation of printed world maps for more than a decade as the information was absorbed and interpreted. By the early 1500's mapmakers were getting lots of new data to put on their maps; not just of the New World, but also of Africa and Asia. Some of the best early mapmakers were in Italy. The Italian city-states were leading centres of trade and had great interest in anything that might affect their commerce. This was part of a pattern which was repeated over the centuries—leadership in mapmaking went along with commercial and military prominence. Maps were essential tools of both commerce and war.

E   As the century went on trade shifted to western Europe and the major ports of the Low Countries became important commercial centres, as well as places of map production. It was there that on May 20, 1570 Abraham Ortelius produced what is generally regarded as the first modern atlas. It was titled *Theatrum Orbis Terrarum* and contained 53 maps, all uniform in size and style. The maps were entirely modern, as Ortelius had sought the best available maps and then redesigned them to a standard format to fit his atlas. The *Theatrum* was an immediate success, going through four printings in its first year. It continued through more than 40 editions over the next generation.

F   In 1572 Georg Braun and Frans Hogenberg published the *Civitates Orbis Terrarum*, the first atlas of city views and plans. It too became a best-seller of its time. A third important work soon emerged. Lucas Jansz Waghenaer created the *Speighel der Zeevaerdt*, the first atlas of sea charts. The charts were engraved by the van Deutecom brothers and are as artistic as they are functional.

G   At the same time Gerard Mercator was busily creating maps. He and Ortelius were friends as well as colleagues. Mercator was of a more scholarly temperament and his productions came forth more slowly. Before creating a modern atlas he wanted to produce a definitive edition of Ptolemy, which was published in 1578. He was the first to use the term "atlas" as the name of a book of maps. Sections of his modern atlas began to appear in the 1580's, and the complete work was issued by his heirs in 1595, the year after his death.

H   In 1662 an extraordinary atlas was published. It was Joan Blaeu's *Grand Atlas* or *Atlas Major* with approximately 600 beautifully-engraved maps on thick paper in ten to twelve volumes depending on the edition. Lavish versions were issued with sumptuous bindings and brilliant colouring; sometimes they were purchased by the Dutch Republic as gifts for royalty and other notable personages. The *Grand Atlas* was to normal atlases as a Rolls Royce is to an ordinary sedan.

I   The 17th- and 18th-century maps were printed by copper engraving, a process introduced in Europe in the 16th century. Various specialists associated with the print shop worked to produce a map: the mapmaker, the engraver, the printer, the papermaker, the colourist. Since map dealers and printers were usually licensed separately, a dealer would sell the maps from his own shop, either separately or bound together in an atlas. Maps and atlases were also sold at publishers' book and map fairs across Europe. This basic process of map and atlas production and distribution continues to this day around the world, although computer graphics have replaced copper engraving.

▶ 核心词汇

词汇	释义
paleolithic	[ˌpælɪəʊˈlɪθɪk] *adj.* 旧石器时代的
scratch	[skrætʃ] *v.* 划
Turkey	[ˈtɜːkɪ] *n.* 土耳其
radiocarbon	[ˌreɪdɪəʊˈkɑːbən] *n.* 放射性碳，碳的一种放射性同位素，尤指碳14
classical	[ˈklæsɪkl] *adj.* 古典的，经典的
tablet	[ˈtæblət] *n.* 碑，牌匾，小块
Mesopotamia	[ˌmesəpəˈteɪmɪə] *n.* 美索不达米亚（西南亚地区）
bronze	[brɒnz] *n.* 青铜，青铜器
Sparta	[ˈspɑːtə] *n.* 斯巴达（古希腊军事重镇）
circa	[ˈsɜːkə] *prep.* 大约
papyrus	[pəˈpaɪrəs] *n.* 【植】纸草，草制成之纸（埃及人用纸草这种植物所制成的纤维上书写文字。纸paper这个词便是源于此。）
celebrated	[ˈselɪbreɪtɪd] *adj.* 著名的
Vienna	[vɪˈenə] *n.* 维也纳（奥地利首都）
cosmic	[ˈkɒzmɪk] *adj.* 宇宙的，广大无边的（名词形式：cosmos宇宙）
inspiration	[ˌɪnspəˈreɪʃn] *n.* 感召；启示，灵感
movable type	活字印刷术
extensive	[ɪkˈstensɪv] *adj.* 广泛的
coordinate	[kəʊˈɔːdɪneɪt] *v.* （使）互相配合（使）协调，调整
Alexandria	[ˌælɪgˈzɑːndrɪə] *n.* 亚历山大大帝
Byzantine Empire	拜占庭帝国，东罗马帝国
refugee	[ˌrefjʊˈdʒiː] *n.* 难民，流亡者
possession	[pəˈzeʃn] *n.* 拥有；所有，（私人）财产
atlas	[ˈætləs] *n.* 地图，地图集（Atlas是希腊神话中泰坦Titans巨神之一，因背叛宙斯Zeus被罚在世界的西边尽头以双肩扛天。位于北非的阿特拉斯山脉the Atlas Mountains就是因为这一传说而得名。16世纪地理学家麦卡脱把Atlas擎天图作为一本地图册的卷首插图。后人争相效仿，该神最终成为"地图册"的形象代言人。）
format	[ˈfɔːmæt] *n.* 开本，版式，形式，格式
best-seller	[ˌbestˈselə(r)] *n.* 畅销书，畅销货
chart	[tʃɑːt] *n.* 图，图表，示意图，航线图，海图图表
engrave	[ɪnˈgreɪv] *v.* 刻上，雕上
artistic	[ɑːˈtɪstɪk] *adj.* 艺术的，有美感的，精美的

scholarly	['skɒlərlɪ] *adj.* 学者气质的，学者风度的（名词形式：scholar）
heir	[eə(r)] *n.* 继承人，后嗣
extraordinary	[ɪk'strɔːdnrɪ] *adj.* 别的，非凡的，突出的，奇特的
approximately	[ə'prɒksɪmətlɪ] *adv.* 近似地，大约
volume	['vɒljuːm] *n.* 卷，册
lavish	['lævɪʃ] *adj.* 过分丰富的，浪费的，奢侈的
binding	['baɪndɪŋ] *n.* 装订
personage	['pɜːsənɪdʒ] *n.* 要人，名流（同义词：celebrity）
superior	[suː'pɪərɪə(r)] *adj.* 高级的，出众的
military	['mɪlətrɪ] *adj.* 军事的

▶ 雅思阅读真题同义词考点

military	—army, force, arms, war, battle, weapon, foe
format	—model, mold, pattern, type
extraordinary	—exceptional, marvelous, noteworthy, remarkable, special, unusual
approximately	—about, around, almost, nearly
lavish	—sumptuous, extravagant, generous

下篇导读：　【染料和颜料】

考试时间：　……

　　古代天然染料介绍。中文说"大红大紫，紫气东来"，西方说：Born to the purple. 紫色的高贵特性，东西皆然。颜料的使用，染料和颜料的区别。☺

Reading Passage 32

Question 1–7

*Choose the most suitable headings for paragraphs **A—G** from the list of headings below.*

*Write appropriate numbers (**i–xi**) in boxes 1–7 on your answer sheet.*

NB   There are more headings than paragraphs, so you will not use them all.

List of Headings

i	Clothing symbolising status
ii	The factors determining the dye's quality
iii	The invaluable colour
iv	The importance of plants in ancient times
v	From family to industry
vi	The value of colours
vii	Dyestuff sources in the past
viii	Availability and durability of a dye
ix	The competitive and secret industry
x	Pigments, insoluble colouring materials
xi	The definition of dyeing

---

1   Paragraph **A**

2   Paragraph **B**

3   Paragraph **C**

4   Paragraph **D**

5   Paragraph **E**

6   Paragraph **F**

7   Paragraph **G**

Dyes and Pigments

A

Dyeing is a process of colouring materials, or cloth fibers, whereby the colour becomes part of the fiber. The fastness of the colour, or its permanency, depends upon the dye and the process used. True dyeing is a permanent colour change, and the dye is absorbed by, or chemically combined with, the fiber.

B

In ancient times all the dyes used were natural; actually, this was true up until mid-1800. The dyestuffs came from a variety of natural sources, some commonly available, others rare or difficult to produce. Some of the common dyes included logwood or quercitron, fustic, woad, and indigo. An example of the rare dyes would be cochineal and Tyrian purple. Collectively, these substances are called dyestuffs, and were occasionally traded as a commodity. The dyestuffs were extracts from plants, mollusks, insects, woods, or naturally occurring minerals. There are many plants which produce dye suitable in the dyeing process, and many were heavily cultivated. Madder and woad were grown in Europe specifically for their dyeing properties. Saffron was also extensively grown in Anatolia for its yellow dye. Probably one of the most famous dyes was Tyrian purple, from a Mediterranean shellfish. The Phoenicians of Tyre, in Lebanon, produced this very expensive dye long before written history began. Many other areas had special dyes which were famous in antiquity.

C

The value of a dye is not just its availability, but also its fastness or durability against daily use. It must withstand washing, wearing, sunlight, perspiration, without losing an appreciable amount of its colour. The colour, and its brightness, also helped determine the dye's value. Premium colours were purple, blue, and bright shades of red.

D

There are two classifications of dyeing, the home craft and the trade, or industrial, dyeing. The manufacturing of clothing, the spinning, weaving and embroidery, tended to stay within the family unit. An exception to this would be the carpets made in

Anatolia and Persia, for example, or the very fine, sheer linen woven in Egypt. But the manufacture of dyes and their use in dyeing yarn and cloth soon became an industry, supporting large numbers of people, even entire cities. The art of dyeing was one of the earliest arts known to man after he became civilised. Trade dyeing was, however, a highly competitive business. These were the professionals of the ancient world when it came to dyed cloth. Many of the processes were closely guarded secrets, and many of the special skills were handed down over generations. The ingredients may come from far away; the tools may be specialised and the process often was steeped in superstition.

E

As far back as man can historically see, rulers have set themselves apart from everyone else by wearing exotic and rare items, and dyed clothing was very early a part of this status proclamation. Still today the important and the wealthy prefer to wear items not available to all. In Egypt, the pharaohs wore specially made clothing, dyed with colours difficult to obtain. Dyed fabrics from tombs of early Egyptian attest to the antiquity of the dyers art.

F

In the ancient Greek and Roman world, Tyrian purple became the colour of choice for rulers and emperors. The dye was extremely expensive, therefore, available to only a few. When in later times merchants, considered unimportant, became wealthy enough to buy purple-dyed cloth. Laws were passed to prevent their diluting the impressiveness of the colour. Only rulers, or emperors, were allowed to wear purple. Later, however, the law was changed to include the rulers' family; then senators; and so on, eventually losing its status. This is where the phrase "born to the purple" came from.

G

The word pigment comes from the Latin "pigmentum" meaning coloured material. Pigments are generally distinguished from dyes as colouring materials on the basis of their soluble ability (solubility) characteristics. Pigments are used mainly in the colouration of paints, printing inks and plastics, although they are used to a certain extent in a much wider range of applications including textiles, ceramics, paper, and cosmetics. In contrast to dyes, pigments are highly insoluble colouring materials, which are incorporated into an applications medium by dispersion, and they remain as discrete solid particles held mechanically within a polymeric matrix. Pigments are thus required to resist dissolving in solvents, which they may contact in application to minimise problems such as "bleeding" and migration. In addition to solvent resistance, pigments are required to be fast to light, weathering, heat and chemicals such as acids and alkalis to a degree dependent on the demands of particular application.

H

Natural inorganic pigments, derived mainly from mineral sources, have been used as colourants since pre-historic times and a few, notably iron oxides, remain of some significance today. The origins of the synthetic inorganic pigment industry may be traced to the introduction of Prussian blue in the early 18th century, pre-dating the synthetic organic colourant industry by some 150 years. The organic pigments are the oxides, sulfides, hydroxides, silicates, sulfates and carbonates of metals. The colour of a pigment is due to its interactions with light by scattering and absorption.

I

The synthetic organic pigment industry emerged towards the end of the 19th century out of the established synthetic textile dyestuffs industry. Many of the earliest organic pigment were known as "lakes". These products were prepared from established water soluble dyes by precipitation on to an insoluble inorganic substrate. A further significant early development in organic pigments was the introduction of a range of azo pigments. One of the most critical events in the development of the organic pigment industry was the discovery, in 1928, of copper phthalocyanine blue. This was the first pigment to offer the outstanding intensity and brightness of colour typical of organic pigments, combined with an excellence range of fastness properties, comparable with many inorganic pigments. Organic pigments generally provide higher intensity and brightness of colour than inorganic pigments. However, organic pigments are unable to provide the degree of opacity offered by most inorganic pigments which have the lower reflectance.

▶ 核心词汇

词汇	释义
pigment	['pɪgmənt] *n.* 色素，颜料
fiber	['faɪbə(r)] *n.* 纤维
dyestuff	['daɪstʌf] *n.* 染料
property	['prɒpətɪ] *n.* 性质，特性（某人占有的 "property" 是他或她的财产，某事物占有的 "property" 是该物质的特性、性质。）
Mediterranean	[ˌmedɪtə'reɪnɪən] *n.* 地中海的（简单地理解为 "medi-terra-nean" —— "中间 + 地、土地 + 形容词词尾"，由此得来 "地中海的" 这个含义。那么单词 "Medieval" 又表示什么呢？"Medi-ev-al" —— "中间 + 时代 + 形容词词尾"，指 "中世纪的"。）
antiquity	[æn'tɪkwətɪ] *n.* 古代
durability	[ˌdjʊərə'bɪlətɪ] *n.* 耐久性，耐用性（形容词形式：durable。字根 "dur" 表示 "持续，持久"，加上表示 "可……的" 这个形容词词尾 "-able" 之后，基本含义为 "可持续很久时间的"，这里是名词形式，引申为上义。）
perspiration	[ˌpɜːspə'reɪʃn] *n.* 汗（水）（动词形式：perspire）
premium	['priːmɪəm] *adj.* 特佳的，特级的
shade	[ʃe] *n.* 阴暗部分，暗影
craft	[krɑːft] *n.* 工艺，手艺（单词 "craftsman" 表示 "工匠，手艺精巧的人"。）
superstition	[ˌsuːpə'stɪʃn] *n.* 迷信（形容词形式：superstitious）
proclamation	[ˌprɒklə'meɪʃ] *n.* 宣告，宣布（动词形式：proclaim。注意动词和名词之间的词形转化，类似exclaim与它的名词形式exclamation。）
fabric	['fæbrɪk] *n.* 织品，织物
dilute	[daɪ'luːt] *v.* 冲淡，稀释（名词形式：dilution。美国前总统尼克松Richard M. Nixon在著名的《在竞技场上》In the Arena一书中曾评论 "一次会晤或谈话的质量与参与谈话人的数量之间的关系—— 'Every person you add to a meeting dilutes the quality of the conversation.' " 显然，他的意思是参加谈话的人越多，谈话质量越低。）
senator	['senətə(r)] *n.* （古罗马）元老院议员，参议员（现在也用来指美国、澳大利亚参议院Senate的成员。）
soluble	['sɒljəbl] *adj.* 可溶解的（名词形式：solution 溶液；解决方案）
discrete	[dɪ'skriːt] *adj.* 不连续的，分立的，离散的（区别：discreet *adj.*小心的，慎重的）
solvent	['sɒlvənt] *n.* 溶媒，溶剂
minimise	['mɪnɪmaɪz] *v.* 将……减到最少（前文提到过它的形容词兼名词形式 "minimum"。）
synthetic	[sɪn'θetɪk] *adj.* 人造的，合成的

textile	['tekstaɪl] *adj.* 纺织的（"textile industry"表示"纺织业"。）
precipitation	[prɪˌsɪpɪ'teɪʃn] *n.* 沉淀（动词形式："precipitate"）
substrate	['sʌbstreɪt] *n.*（等于substratum）底层（"substratum"的复数形式比较特殊，写作"substrata"，类似与"datum"与"data"之间的变化。）
opacity	[əʊ'pæsətɪ] *n.* 不反光，不透光（形容词形式："opaque"）

▶ 雅思阅读真题同义词考点

antiquity	—ancient past, the distant past, time immemorial, bygone days
shade	—cover, shelter, shadow, obscurity, subtle
durability	—permanence, endurance, indestructibility
discrete	—separate, disconnected, detached
minimise	—abate, reduce, lessen, minimalise

下篇导读：【电视瘾】

考试时间：2009-04-25，2010-09-25……

　　关于看电视上瘾的研究。为什么有人下班回家之后会自动打开电视？看电视太久会有内疚感？有人睡着了都不让关电视。 ☺

Reading Passage 33

Question 1–7

*Choose the most suitable headings for paragraphs **A–G** from the list of headings below.*

*Write appropriate numbers (**i–xi**) in boxes 1–7 on your answer sheet.*

NB There are more headings than paragraphs, so you will not use them all.

List of Headings

i   Televisions and family battles

ii   Comparisons made among heavy viewers and nonviewers

iii   Psychological expertise helps to interpret television addiction

iv   Television addiction being proved by tragedies

v   Resist the power of television addiction

vi   Children got no affections

vii   Similarities of using televisions and alcohols

viii Findings from the campus

ix   Conception of television addition being proposed

x   Empirical search for DSM-IV

xi   Applying methods from television addiction studies to other platforms

---

1   Paragraph **A**

2   Paragraph **B**

3   Paragraph **C**

4   Paragraph **D**

5   Paragraph **E**

6   Paragraph **F**

7   Paragraph **G**

TV Addiction

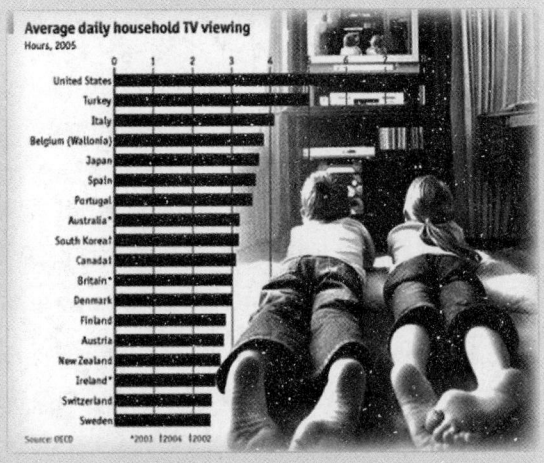

Average daily household TV viewing
Hours, 2005

A In 1977, Winn argued in The Plug-in Drug that television has properties of addiction. Researchers have been intrigued by this idea, but few have tried to study it systematically. Anecdotal accounts and speculation comprise most of the research on television addiction. Furthermore, similar to the alcohol and drug abuse literature, a conceptual haze between the concepts of heavy exposure, reliance, dependence, and addiction to television remains problematic. A clear distinction needs to be made between these concepts to determine the difference between normal and problem viewing.

B Foss and Alexander had researched on objects that contain both self-defined heavy viewers (6 hours per day) and nonviewers. They found that many nonviewers called television a drug or a religion and believed that it caused less interaction with friends and family, less time spent doing more productive or healthier things, and less critical thought. Nonviewers reported that television was simply too seductive to have around. Heavy viewers saw addiction to television as a likely outcome, but not for themselves. For them, it was simply a means for escape and relaxation. People who avoid television tend to cite its addictive properties as the reason. Nonviewers in Australia wouldn't watch because they couldn't "resist its power." They regarded it as a depressant drug that dulls the senses. Mander collected around 2,000 anecdotal responses to television that made it sound like "a machine that invades, controls and deadens the people who view it." Common statements resulted, such as "I feel hypnotised" and "I just can't keep my eyes off it." In talking about their television behaviour, people compared themselves to mesmerised, drugged-out, and spaced-out vegetables. Similarly, Singer asked, "why do we turn the set on almost automatically on awakening in the morning or on returning home from school or work?" Singer, though, said that addiction to television is an extreme position, and speculated that television's magnetism can be explained by a human "orienting reflex." That is, we are programmed to respond to new or unexpected stimuli, and because novel and sudden images are key features of television, it draws our attention. Singer said that the addictive power of television is probably to minimise problems by putting other thoughts in your mind.

C In an empirical search for this seemingly pervasive psychological phenomenon, Smith used popular literature to generate items for a measure of television addiction. Although the resultant scale was not directly based on the DSM-IV (Diagnostic and Statistical Manual of Mental Disorders), it included some of the concepts such as loss of control, time spent using, withdrawal, attempts to quit, and guilt. Her study via mail of 491 adults living in some mountain areas found that very few of the participants identified with the concepts in her measure; only 11 out of 491 respondents admitted television addiction, although 64% of the respondents reported that television was addictive. Smith found a strong relationship between the amount of time spent viewing and the tendency to call oneself an addict.

D Noting that there have been almost no empirical studies of television addiction, McIlwraith, Jacobvitz, Kubey, and Alexander cited an earlier version of the DSM-IV to discuss a possible relationship to television viewing. Using Smith's measure, they found that only 17 out of 136 college students were self-designated addicts. They reported twice as much television viewing as non-addicts, more mind wandering, distractibility, boredom, and unfocused daydreaming, and tended to score higher on scales measuring introversion and neuroticism. They also reported significantly more dysphoric mood watching, and watching to fill time.

E Also using Smith's measure of television addiction, Anderson, Collins, Schmitt, and Jacobvitz found that, for women, stressful life events predicted television addiction-like behaviour and guilt about television watching. They argued that women used television in a way that was "analogous to alcohol," and wondered if television watching served to delay more healthy and appropriate coping strategies. Also using Smith's measure, McIlwraith found only 10% of the 237 participants sampled while visiting a museum identified themselves as television addicts. McIlwraith found that those who admitted addiction to television watched significantly more hours of television than others, and watched more to escape unpleasant moods and to fill time. McIlwraith's sample echoed Smith's, who found that participants most often responded never on all the items about television addiction.

F According to Smith, the phenomenon of television addiction is unsubstantiated in empirical research, but is robust in anecdotal evidence. For example, like other addictions, television watching is thought to contribute to conflict and breakdowns in family relationships. One woman explained how her husband's addiction to television contributed to their separation: "There was absolutely no way of spending an evening alone with my husband without television. He was most resentful if I stuck out for my choice of program and most resentful if I turned it off while he slept in front of it." There are worse stories. Fowles related tragic newspaper accounts due to quarrels about television: "Charles Green of East Palo Alto, California stabbed his sister to death with a hunting knife after she took out the electrical fuses so he would stop viewing. In Latwell, Louisiana, John Gallien shot his sister-in-law because she kept turning down the volume." Studies of television deprivation also indicate profound and real withdrawal-like symptoms, supporting the notion of addiction.

G A handful of studies have attempted to study other types of media addiction directly using APA criteria. For example, Fisher found that children could be classified as addicted to video games. The children's pathological video game playing was based on model criteria such as frequency and duration of play, supernormal expenditures, borrowing and selling of possessions to play, and self-awareness of a problem. Phillips, Rolls, Rouse, and Griffiths studied the video game habits of 868 children, aged 11 to 16. They found that 50 could be classified as addicts. The addicted children played nearly every day, for longer time periods than intended, often to the neglect of homework. They reported feeling better after play, and using play to avoid other things. Also based on APA criteria, a case study in the United Kingdom effectively diagnosed a young man as addicted to pinball machines. Consistent with third-person effect literature, the young man thought that he played too much, but that he was not "addicted."

▶ 核心词汇

词汇	释义
addiction	[əˈdɪkʃn] *n.* 沉溺，上瘾
property	[ˈprɒpəti] *n.* 性质，特性，性能
intrigue	[ɪnˈtriːg] *v.* 激起……的好奇心
depressant	[dɪˈpresnt] *adj.* 有镇静作用的（动词形式：depress）
invade	[ɪnˈveɪd] *v.* 侵入，侵略
hypnotise	[ˈhɪpnətaɪz] *v.* 对……施催眠术；使着迷（hypno=sleep睡眠。希腊神话中夜之女神Nyx有两个双胞胎twin儿子，一个是睡神Hypnos，罗马神话中称之为Somnus，另一个是死神Thanatos。Hypnos衍生出单词hypnosis 催眠；hypnotist 催眠师；Somnus衍生出单词insomnia 失眠；hypersomnia嗜睡；somnambulist 梦游者；而死神则衍生出 thanatology死亡学；euthanasia安乐死等单词。睡神有个儿子很出名，叫梦神Morpheus，衍生出单词morphine吗啡。）
mesmerise	[ˈmezməraɪz] *v.* 使入迷
stimuli	[ˈstɪmjəlaɪ] *n.* 刺激，刺激物（该词的单数形式为：stimulus）
empirical	[ɪmˈpɪrɪkl] *adj.* 以实验为依据的；经验的
pervasive	[pəˈveɪsɪv] *adj.* 普遍的，普及的
respondent	[rɪˈspɒndənt] *n.* 调查对象（动词形式：respond）
analogous	[əˈnæləgəs] *adj.* 相似的，可比拟的
robust	[rəʊˈbʌst] *adj.* 强壮的，健全的（乐百氏商标：Robust）
stab	[stæb] *v.* 刺，扎，刺伤
fuse	[fjuːz] *n.* 保险丝
diagnose	[ˈdaɪəgnəʊz] *v.* 诊断
criteria	[kraɪˈtɪərɪə] *n.* 标准（该词的单数形式为：criterion）
frequency	[ˈfriːkwənsɪ] *n.* 频率
possession	[pəˈzeʃn] *n.* 拥有；着迷（动词形式：possess）
classify	[ˈklæsɪfaɪ] *v.* 分类
intend	[ɪnˈtend] *v.* 想要，打算
avoid	[əˈvɒɪd] *v.* 避免

▶ 雅思阅读真题同义词考点

intrigue	—evoke, spark, encourage
depress	—discourage, lessen, lower, reduce
pervasive	—prevalent, universal, popular
criteria	—standard, benchmark, specification
possess	—have, hold, maintain, occupy, own

下篇导读：【中世纪玩具】

考试时间： ……

　　考古发现中世纪时期的玩具相当精美。驳斥了观点："中世纪战乱频繁，儿童生存率低，父母对子女没有感情依恋。" 每读此文，心怀激荡。父母的爱从来没有改变。☺

Reading Passage 34

Question 1–7

*Choose the most suitable headings for paragraphs **A–G** from the list of headings below.*

*Write appropriate numbers (**i–x**) in boxes 1–7 on your answer sheet.*

NB   There are more headings than paragraphs, so you will not use them all.

<table>
<tr><td colspan="2">List of Headings</td></tr>
<tr><td>i</td><td>Toys challenging the early conceptions</td></tr>
<tr><td>ii</td><td>Parental love never changes</td></tr>
<tr><td>iii</td><td>Toy Representing Medieval Art</td></tr>
<tr><td>iv</td><td>The first archaeological evidence</td></tr>
<tr><td>v</td><td>Various sources of medieval toys</td></tr>
<tr><td>vi</td><td>Development of toy industry and trade</td></tr>
<tr><td>vii</td><td>Written evidence of toys</td></tr>
<tr><td>viii</td><td>Window to the Middle Ages childhood</td></tr>
<tr><td>ix</td><td>Tangible proof of toys</td></tr>
<tr><td>x</td><td>Exceptionally rare toys</td></tr>
</table>

1   Paragraph **A**

2   Paragraph **B**

3   Paragraph **C**

4   Paragraph **D**

5   Paragraph **E**

6   Paragraph **F**

7   Paragraph **G**

Medieval Toys and Childhood

A This toy knight comes from a rich harvest of archaeological finds, made in the mud banks of the River Thames in London during the last 30 years. It was manufactured in about 1300, and illustrates several facets of medieval childhood. Then as now, children liked playing with toys. Then as now, they had a culture of their own, encompassing slang, toys, and games. Then as now, adults cared for children and encouraged their play. An adult made this toy and another adult bought it for a child, or gave a child money to buy it. The toy knight was made from a mould, and produced in large numbers. It probably circulated among the families of merchants, shopkeepers, and craft workers, as well as those of the nobility and gentry. The finds also include toys that girls might have liked: little cups, plates, and jugs, some sturdy enough to heat up water by a fireside. There is even a self-assembly kit: a cupboard cut out of a sheet of soft metal, instead of the plastic that would be used today. Toys give us a positive view of medieval childhood.

B Medieval toys might be home-made by adults with time on their hands, fashioned by the children themselves, or bought from wandering peddlers or merchants at fairs—even ordered specially from the most prestigious makers. Some of the dolls appear to have been given to children once their usefulness as fashion models was past. Naturally, the types and magnificence of the toys varied with the status of the recipient.

C Many of the dolls sold in England came from abroad, chiefly from Germany and Holland, although very fancy dolls were sold in the Palais du Justice, alongside other expensive luxuries. However, the industry was slow to develop into a guild, hampered partly by its own rules—toys had to be finished by the appropriate masters, and thus could not be made all in one workshop, for instance. There was also the hindrance that toy making was for a long time considered an addition to a "real" trade, and to a great extent left to the local craftsmen in their spare time, rather than quickly becoming an industry of its own, as was the case in many other fields. However, dolls among other toys appear to have been traded on a small but constant—and gradually increasing—level throughout the Middle Ages and Renaissance. Dockenmacher ("doll-makers") are recorded in Nuremberg from 1413, and their very existence indicates the rising importance of the toy trade on both the local and the international scene.

D Written sources for the existence of toys, and to some extent of their type and manufacture, are fairly plentiful, from legal records, to poetry describing the age of innocence, and sermons on the immature behaviour of the socialites of the day. Most pictorial sources are generally later, but one drawing survives from around 1200, which shows two youths playing with a pair of foot soldiers. The warriors appear to be on strings, enabling them to be pulled back and forth in semblance of battle. Boys are often shown in illustrations playing with such warrior dolls, and various jousting figures survive which show the perfection of articulated armour and fine horse-trappings which could be achieved in a boy's plaything. In portraiture of the sixteenth century, noble girls are often pictured holding exquisitely dressed dolls, possibly bought new for the sitting as they seem fresh from the box and neither grubby nor worn down with use. These dolls are likely to be accurately painted rather than idealised, as the sitters themselves often were, so it must be assumed that such dolls were indeed artistically finished, beautifully attired and painted with the most delicate of features. In contrast, the seventeenth-century painting of a peasant family, by Adriane van Ostade, offers proof that children of more humble origins also played with dolls.

E Archaeological evidence is more widely available than might at first be thought. Naturally, more survives, the closer we get to modern times, and the material of which dolls were made doubtless influences our picture of their history. From Viking settlements in the far north a few dolls have been separated from the multitude of figures identified by the experts as idols and funerary figures. Some heads and limbs have been found, which may once have had cloth bodies, although it is uncertain whether these were designed as toys or votive offerings. Although no surviving pieces have thus far been uncovered, wealthy Anglo-Saxon children in England may have entertained themselves with carved alabaster dolls, a substance which had been used for doll-making since the Roman occupation, while poorer children of this age would have owned wooden or cloth dolls.

F Dating from as early as the 13th century, items unearthed from the mud banks of the River Thames include tiny cannons and guns, metal figurines, and miniaturised household objects such as stools, jugs, cauldrons, and even frying pans complete with little fish. Made mainly from pewter (a tin-lead alloy), these medieval toys are exceptionally rare and have helped transform perceptions of childhood during the Middle Ages, says Hazel Forsyth, curator of post-medieval collections at the Museum of London. "In the 1960s French historian Philippe Aries claimed that there wasn't really such a thing as childhood in the Middle Ages and that parents didn't form emotional attachments with their offspring, regarding them as economic providers or producers for the household," Forsyth said. Aries pioneered ways of looking beyond kings, politics, and war to everyday medieval life. He argued that parents invested little emotional capital in their children because they had lots of offspring, many of them died in infancy, and that surviving children were sent to work at the ages of six or seven.

G Aries's views had a lot of currency. And for very many years, people took it for granted. It has only been recently, with discovery of ancient childhood items by contemporary treasure hunters, that we've challenged this received wisdom. "Surprise, surprise, human nature doesn't change," Forsyth said, "Some parents from the Middle Ages were very devoted to their children and gave them every luxury and pleasure they could afford."

▶ 核心词汇

词汇	释义
mudbank	[mʌdbæŋk] *n.*（河、湖或海边的）泥滩
encompass	[ɪnˈkʌmpəs] *v.* 包围，环绕，包含或包括某事物（compass 罗盘，包围）
slang	[slæŋ] *n.* 俚语，行话
mould	[məʊld] *n.* 肥土，壤土
circulate	[ˈsɜːkjəleɪt] *v.* 使流通，循环，传播
merchant	[ˈmɜːtʃənt] *n.* 商人，批发商，贸易商，店主（merchandise商品）
craft	[krɑːft] *n.* 工艺，手艺
gentry	[ˈdʒentrɪ] *n.* 贵族们（同义词：noble）
sturdy	[ˈstɜːdɪ] *adj.* 强健的；坚定的，毫不含糊的
kit	[kɪt] *n.* 成套工具，用具包，工具箱，成套用具
plastic	[ˈplæstɪk] *n.* 塑胶，可塑体，塑料制品（plastic bag塑料袋）
wander	[ˈwɒndə(r)] *v.* 漫步，徘徊，迷路
peddler	[ˈpedlə(r)] *n.* 小贩，传播者
prestigious	[preˈstɪdʒəs] *adj.* 享有声望的，声望很高的（名词形式：prestige）
recipient	[rɪˈsɪpɪənt] *adj.* 容易接受的，感受性强的（动词形式：receive）
hamper	[ˈhæmpə(r)] *v.* 妨碍，牵制（区别：hammer锤子）
hindrance	[ˈhɪndrəns] *n.* 妨碍，障碍
renaissance	[rɪˈneɪsns] *n.* 复兴，复活，新生，文艺复兴（指13世纪末在意大利各城市兴起，以后扩展到西欧各国，于16世纪在欧洲盛行的一场思想文化运动，带来一段科学与艺术革命时期，揭开了近代欧洲历史的序幕，被认为是中古时代和近代的分界）
sermon	[ˈsɜːmən] *n.* 训诫，说教，布道（同义词：preach）
socialite	[ˈsəʊʃəlaɪt] *n.* 社交名流
pictorial	[pɪkˈtɔːrɪəl] *adj.* 图示的
semblance	[ˈsembləns] *n.* 外表；伪装
portraiture	[ˈpɔːtrətʃə(r)] *n.* 肖像画法
humble	[ˈhʌmbl] *adj.* 卑下的，微贱的，谦逊的（hum= ground 土地。《圣经》说上帝在地上抓了一把土，按照自己的形象捏了一人儿，吹了口气，泥人活了。《淮南子》说女娲娘娘用黄土和水造人。所以呢，我们都是泥人儿hum-man→human。humble就是地面的，地位低下的→谦卑的；谦虚的。泥人儿human都应humble一点。别忘了，天使之所以会飞，不是因为有翅膀，而是因为她们把自己看得很轻。）
votive	[ˈvəʊtɪv] *adj.* 奉献的

carve	[kɑːv] *v.* 雕刻，切开
cannon	['kænən] *n.* 大炮，加农炮
miniaturise	['mɪnətʃəraɪz] *v.* 使小型化（同义词：downsize）
challenging	['tʃælɪndʒɪŋ] *adj.* 有挑战性的
archaeological	[ˌɑːkɪə'lɒdʒɪkl] *adj.* 考古学的（名词形式：archaeology）
tangible	['tændʒəbl] *adj.* 切实的；可触摸的

▶ 雅思阅读真题同义词考点

encompass	—encircle, enclose, include, surround
slang	—jargon, term
hamper	—hinder, impede, block, limit
challenge	—confront, defy, dispute, doubt, question
semblance	—appearance, look, camouflage

CHAPTER 4

Matching
信息匹配题

介绍：可细分为1.句子信息与段落匹配；2.关系型匹配。

概率：真实考试40个题目中平均8个题。

难度：1.句子信息与段落匹配：★★★★★

2.关系型匹配：★★★☆☆

信息匹配题

雅思机考 (IELTS Computer Based) 界面及说明：

Part 1
reading and answer 1-5

A

Most of the effort applied to understanding how birds make a migratory flight has been directed toward environmental cues that birds use to maintain a particular flight direction. These cues are landmarks on the Earths surface, the magnetic lines of flux that longitudinally encircle the Earth, both the sun and the stars in the celestial sphere arching over the Earth, and perhaps prevailing wind direction and odors.

B

Landmarks are useful as a primary navigation reference only if the bird has been there before. For cranes, swans, and geese that migrate in family groups, young of the year could learn the geographic map for their migratory journey from their parents. But most birds do not migrate in family flocks, and on their initial flight south to the wintering range or back north in the spring must use other cues. Yet birds are aware of the landscape over which they are crossing and appear to use landmarks for orientation purposes. Radar images of migrating birds subject to a strong crosswind were seen to drift off course, except for flocks migrating parallel to a major river. These birds used the river as a reference to shift their orientation and correct for drift in order to maintain the proper ground track.

Questions 1－5

	A	B	C	D	E	F	G
Wind might play a role.							
The secretions from birds' brain respond to the sun.		✓					
The birds count on a combination of clues to cope with the versatile environment.							
After some nerves were cut off, the birds cannot orient as usual.							
Birds might use magnetic field to find their way.							

信息匹配题一般为综合图表式。左侧是用ABCD标出段落的文章，右侧是问题清单。

如何答题：查看左侧的文章，然后在右侧图表中勾选出与问题匹配的段落。

修改答案：点击所选择的新答案。

清除答案：再次点击答案。

www.ieltscb.com 提供免费机考练习。

下篇导读：【鸟类定向】

考试时间： 2010-07-31，2012-05-10……

　　鸟儿是怎样迁徙的，为什么它们长途迁徙几千千米都不会迷失方向？它们通过地标地位，磁场定位，太阳星辰定位，还是GPS定位？ ☺

Reading Passage 35

Orientation of Birds

A Most of the effort applied to understanding how birds make a migratory flight has been directed toward environmental cues that birds use to maintain a particular flight direction. These cues are landmarks on the Earths surface, the magnetic lines of flux that longitudinally encircle the Earth, both the sun and the stars in the celestial sphere arching over the Earth, and perhaps prevailing wind direction and odors.

B Landmarks are useful as a primary navigation reference only if the bird has been there before. For cranes, swans, and geese that migrate in family groups, young of the year could learn the geographic map for their migratory journey from their parents. But most birds do not migrate in family flocks, and on their initial flight south to the wintering range or back north in the spring must use other cues. Yet birds are aware of the landscape over which they are crossing and appear to use landmarks for orientation purposes. Radar images of migrating birds subject to a strong crosswind were seen to drift off course, except for flocks migrating parallel to a major river. These birds used the river as a reference to shift their orientation and correct for drift in order to maintain the proper ground track. That major geographic features like Point Pelee jutting into Lake Erie or Cape May at the tip of New Jersey are meccas for bird-watchers only reflects the fact that migrating birds recognise these peninsulas during their migration. Migrating hawks seeking updrafts along the north shore of Lake Superior or the ridges of the Appalachians must pay attention to the terrain below them in order to take advantage of the energetic savings afforded by these topographic structures.

C Since humans learned to use celestial cues, it was only natural that studies were undertaken to demonstrate that birds could use them as well. Soon after the end of the Second World War, Gustav Kramer showed that migratory European Starlings oriented to the azimuth of the sun when he used mirrors to shift the sun's image by ninety degrees in the laboratory and obtained a corresponding shift in the birds' orientation. Furthermore, since the birds would maintain a constant direction even though the sun traversed from east to west during the day, the compensation for this movement demonstrated that the birds were keeping time. They knew what orientation to the sun was appropriate at 9 a.m. They knew what different angle was appropriate at noon, and again at 4 p.m. It has been recently shown that melatonin secretions from the light-sensitive pineal gland on the top of the bird's brain are involved in this response. Not only starlings but homing pigeons, penguins, waterfowl, and many species of perching birds have been shown to use solar orientation. Even nocturnal migrants take directional information from the sun. European Robins and Savannah Sparrows that were prevented from seeing the setting sun did not orient under the stars as well as birds that were allowed to see the sun set. Birds can detect polarised light from sunlight's penetration through the atmosphere, and it has been hypothesised that the pattern of polarised light in the evening sky is the primary cue that provides a reference for their orientation.

D   Using the artificial night sky provided by planetariums demonstrated that nocturnal migrants respond to star patterns. (quite analogous to Kramer's work on solar orientation, Franz Sauer demonstrated that if the planetarium sky is shifted, the birds make a corresponding shift in their orientation azimuth). Steve Emlen was able to show that the orientation was not dependent upon a single star, like Polaris, but to the general sky pattern. As he would turn off more and more stars so that they were no longer being projected in the planetarium, the bird's orientation became poorer and poorer. While the proper direction for orientation at a given time is probably innate, Emlen was able to show that knowing the location of "north" must be learned. When young birds were raised under a planetarium sky in which Betelgeuse, a star in Orion of the southern sky, was projected to the celestial north pole, the birds oriented as if Betelgeuse was "north" when they were later placed under the normally orientated night sky, even though in reality it was south!

E   Radar studies have shown that birds do migrate above cloud decks where landmarks are not visible, under overcast skies where celestial cues are not visible, and even within cloud layers where neither set of cues is available. The nomadic horsemen of the steppes of Asia used the response of lodestones to the Earth's magnetic field to find their way, and the hypothesis that migrating birds might do the same was suggested as early as the middle of the nineteenth century. Yet it was not until the mid-twentieth century that Merkel and Wiltschko demonstrated in a laboratory environment devoid of any other cues that European Robins would change their orientation in response to shifts in an artificial magnetic field that was as weak as the Earth's natural field. Although iron-containing magnetite crystals are associated with the nervous system in homing pigeons, Northern Bobwhite, and several species of perching birds, it is unknown whether they are associated with the sensory receptor for the geomagnetic cue. An alternate hypothesis for the sensory receptor suggests that response of visual pigments in the eye to electromagnetic energy is the basis for geomagnetic orientation. It has been shown, however, that previous exposure to celestial orientation cues enhances the ability of a bird to respond more appropriately when only geomagnetic cues are available.

F   Radar observations indicate that birds will decrease their air speed when their ground speed is augmented by a strong tail wind. We also know that birds can sense wind direction as gusts ruffling the feathers stimulate sensory receptors located in the skin around the base of the feather. Since there are characteristic patterns of wind circulation around high and low pressure centres at the altitude most birds migrate, it has been hypothesised that birds could use these prevailing wind directions as an orientation cue. However, there presently is no experimental support for this hypothesis.

G   The sense of smell in birds was considered for a long time to be poorly developed, but more recent evidence suggests that some species can discriminate odors quite well. If the olfactory nerves of homing pigeons are cut, the birds do not return to their home loft as well as birds whose olfactory nerves were left intact. A similar experiment has demonstrated that European Starlings with severed olfactory nerves returned less often than unaffected control birds even at distances as great as 240 km from their home roosts. And even more interesting, when these starlings returned to the nesting area the following spring, the starlings with nonfunctioning olfactory nerves returned at a significantly lower frequency than the other starlings.

H   Considering the array of demonstrated and suggested cues that birds might use in their orientation, it is clear that they rely upon a suite of cues rather than a single cue. For a migrating bird this redundancy is critical, since not all sources of orientation information are equally available at a given time, nor are all sources of information equally useful in a given situation.

Questions 1–7

Reading Passage has 8 paragraphs A—H.

Which paragraphs state the following information?

Write the appropriate letters A—H in boxes 1—7 on your answer sheet.

1   Wind might play a role.

2   The secretions from birds' brain respond to the sun.

3   The birds count on a combination of clues to cope with the versatile environment.

4   After some nerves were cut off, the birds cannot orient as usual.

5   Birds might use magnetic field to find their way.

6   Disoriented cues were made in the experiments.

7   The birds that always migrate alone could not use this clue.

▶ 核心词汇

词汇	释义
cue	[kjuː] *n.* 暗示，提示
landmark	['lændmɑːk] *n.* 地标
flux	[flʌks] *n.* 【物】流量；磁通量
celestial	[sə'lestɪəl] *adj.* 天的，天空的，天体的
arch over	拱悬于……之上，把……拱盖起来
odor	['əʊdə(r)] *n.* 气味
crane	[kreɪn] *n.* 鹤
swan	[swɒn] *n.* 天鹅
geese	[dʒiːs] *n.* 鹅肉，雌鹅
crosswind	['krɒswɪnd] *n.* 横风，侧风
jut	[dʒʌt] *v.* （使）突出，（使）伸出，突击
mecca	['mekə] *n.* 众人渴望去的地方（源自地名Mecca麦加。沙特阿拉伯西部城市，它是伊斯兰教创始人穆罕默德的诞生地，是伊斯兰教最神圣之地，也是笃信伊斯兰教的虔诚教徒的朝拜中心。）
peninsula	[pə'nɪnsjələ] *n.* 半岛
Appalachians	[ˌæpə'leɪtʃənz] *n.* [the Appalachians 阿巴拉契亚山脉（北美洲）]
topographic	[ˌtɒpə'græfɪk] *adj.* 地志的，地形学上的
starling	['stɑːlɪŋ] *n.* 八哥
corresponding	[ˌkɒrə'spɒndɪŋ] *adj.* 相当的，对应的，适合的，一致的
traverse	[trə'vɜːs] *vt.* 横过，穿过，经过，在……来回移动
secretion	[sɪ'kriːʃn] *n.* （动植物的）分泌，分泌液（动词形式：secrete）
pineal	[paɪ'niːəl] *adj.* 【解】（脑部的）松果腺的，松果体的
gland	[glænd] *n.* 【解】腺
penguin	['peŋgwɪn] *n.* 企鹅
waterfowl	['wɔːtəfaʊl] *n.* 水鸟，水禽
perch	[pɜːtʃ] *v.* （鸟）栖息，栖止
planetarium	[ˌplænɪ'teərɪəm] *n.* 行星仪，天文馆
analogous	[ə'næləgəs] *adj.* 相似的；类似的
Polaris	[pəʊ'leərɪs] *n.* 【天】北极星
Orion	[ə'raɪən] *n.* 【天】猎户座
overcast	[ˌəʊvə'kɑːst] *adj.* 多云的；阴暗的
steppe	[step] *n.* 干草原；疏树大平原

devoid	[dɪ'vɒɪd] *adj.* 全无的，缺乏的
sensory	['sensərɪ] *adj.* 感官的；感觉器官的
receptor	[rɪ'septə(r)] *n.* 接收器，感受器
augmented	[ɔːg'mentɪd] *adj.* 增音的，扩张的
gust	[gʌst] *n.* 阵风；一阵狂风（雨、火、烟、雹、声音等）
olfactory	[ɒl'fæktərɪ] *adj.* 嗅觉的
loft	[lɒft] *n.* 阁楼
intact	[ɪn'tækt] *adj.* 完整的；未动过的

▶ 雅思阅读真题同义词考点

cue	—clue, hint, key, signal
secrete	—discharge, excrete, exude, release
devoid	—blank, empty, vacant, lack
olfactory	—odor, smell
intact	—complete, unchanged, uninjured, untouched, whole

下篇导读：【测谎仪】

考试时间：2009-03-21, 2010-01-30, 2012-01-12, 2013-08-29, 2014-01-25……

　　想不想一眼就能看出她在对你说谎？哪些表情最难假装？动物也会说谎？读读这篇文章，告诉你每人每天平均说谎200次。😊

Reading Passage 36

Liar Detector

A However much we may abhor it, deception comes naturally to all living things. Birds do it by feigning injury to lead hungry predators away from nesting young. Spider crabs do it by disguise: adorning themselves with strips of kelp and other debris, they pretend to be something they are not—and so escape their enemies. Nature amply rewards successful deceivers by allowing them to survive long enough to mate and reproduce. So it may come as no surprise to learn that human beings—who, according to psychologist Gerald Jellison of the University of South California, are lied to about 200 times a day, roughly one untruth every five minutes—often deceive for exactly the same reasons: to save their own skins or to get something they can't get by other means.

B But knowing how to catch deceit can be just as important a survival skill as knowing how to tell a lie and get away with it. A person able to spot falsehood quickly is unlikely to be swindled by an unscrupulous business associate or hoodwinked by a devious spouse. Luckily, nature provides more than enough clues to trap dissemblers in their own tangled webs—if you know where to look. By closely observing facial expressions, body language and tone of voice, practically anyone can recognise the telltale signs of lying. Researchers are even programming computers—like those used on Lie Detector—to get at the truth by analysing the same physical cues available to the naked eye and ear. "With the proper training, many people can learn to reliably detect lies," says Paul Ekman, professor of psychology at the University of California, San Francisco, who has spent the past 15 years studying the secret art of deception.

C In order to know what kind of lies work best, successful liars need to accurately assess other people's emotional states. Ekman's research shows that this same emotional intelligence is essential for good lie detectors, too. The emotional state to watch out for is stress, the conflict most liars feel between the truth and what they actually say and do.

D Even high-tech lie detectors don't detect lies as such; they merely detect the physical cues of emotions, which may or may not correspond to what the person being tested is saying. Polygraphs, for instance, measure respiration, heart rate and skin conductivity, which tend to increase when people are nervous—as they usually are when lying. Nervous people typically perspire, and the salts contained in perspiration conduct electricity. That's why a sudden leap in skin conductivity indicates nervousness—about getting caught, perhaps?—which might, in turn, suggest that someone is being economical with the truth. On the other hand, it might also mean that the lights in the television studio are too hot—which is one reason polygraph tests are inadmissible in court. "Good lie detectors don't rely on a single sign," Ekman says, "but interpret clusters of verbal and nonverbal clues that suggest someone might be lying."

E Those clues are written all over the face.

Because the musculature of the face is directly connected to the areas of the brain that process emotion, the countenance can be a window to the soul. Neurological studies even suggest that genuine emotions travel different pathways through the brain than insincere ones. If a patient paralysed by stroke on one side of the face, for example, is asked to smile deliberately, only the mobile side of the mouth is raised. But tell that same person a funny joke, and the patient breaks into a full and spontaneous smile. Very few people—most notably, actors and politicians—are able to consciously control all of their facial expressions. Lies can often be caught when the liar's true feelings briefly leak through the mask of deception. "We don't think before we feel," Ekman says. "Expressions tend to show up on the face before we're even conscious of experiencing an emotion."

F One of the most difficult facial expressions to fake—or conceal, if it is genuinely felt—is sadness. When someone is truly sad, the forehead wrinkles with grief and the inner corners of the eyebrows are pulled up. Fewer than 15% of the people Ekman tested were able to produce this eyebrow movement voluntarily. By contrast, the lowering of the eyebrows associated with an angry scowl can be replicated at will by almost everybody. "If someone claims they are sad and the inner corners of their eyebrows don't go up," Ekman says, "the sadness is probably false."

G The smile, on the other hand, is one of the easiest facial expressions to counterfeit. It takes just two muscles—the zygomaticus major muscles that extend from the cheekbones to the corners of the lips—to produce a grin. But there's a catch. A genuine smile affects not only the corners of the lips but also the orbicularis oculi, the muscle around the eye that produces the distinctive "crow's—feet" associated with people who laugh a lot. A counterfeit grin can be unmasked if the lip corners go up, the eyes crinkle but the inner corners of the eyebrows are not lowered, a movement controlled by the orbicularis oculi that is difficult to fake. The absence of lowered eyebrows is one reason why false smiles look so strained and stiff.

H Ekman and his colleagues have classified all the muscle movements—ranging from the thin, taut lips of fury to the arched eyebrows of surprise—that underlie the complete repertoire of human facial expressions. In addition to the nervous tics and jitters that can give liars away, Ekman discovered that fibbers often allow the truth to slip through in brief, unguarded facial expressions. Lasting no more than a quarter of a second, these fleeting glimpses of a person's true emotional state—or "microexpressions," as Ekman calls them—are reliable guides to veracity.

I In moderation, lying is a normal—even necessary—part of life. "It would be an impossible world if no one lied," Ekman says. But by the same token, it would be an intolerable world if we could never tell when someone was lying. For those lies that are morally wrong and potentially harmful, would-be lie detectors can learn a lot from looking and listening very carefully. Cheating partners, snake oil salesmen and scheming politicians, beware! The truth is out there.

Questions 1–9

*Reading Passage has nine paragraphs, **A–I**.*

Which paragraph contains the following information?

*Write the correct letter, **A–I**, in boxes 1–9 on your answer sheet.*

NB *You may use any letter more than once.*

1 Hard to judge whether a movie star tells a lie

2 Building a databank of human facial expressions

3 Why sweating might be a clue

4 The easiest facial expressions by which people can identify a lie

5 The importance of differentiating lie from truth

6 Why this faked facial expression looks so unnatural

7 Technical equipment far from enough

8 The role of evaluating emotional states

9 Examples of wildlife which cheat in order to avoid dying out

▶ 核心词汇

词汇	释义
abhor	[əb'hɔ:(r)] *v.* 痛恨，憎恶
deception	[dɪ'sepʃn] *n.* 欺骗，欺诈，骗术
disguise	[dɪs'gaɪz] *n.* 伪装，假装
debris	['debri:] *n.* 碎片，残骸
pretend	[prɪ'tend] *v.* 假装，伪装
escape	[ɪ'skeɪp] *v.* 逃避，逃脱
amply	['æmplɪ] *adv.* 充足地，广大地
swindle	['swɪndl] *v.* 诈取，被骗
unscrupulous	[ʌn'skru:pjələs] *adj.* 肆无忌惮的，不讲道德的
hoodwink	['hʊdwɪŋk] *v.* 蒙蔽，欺骗
spouse	[spaʊs] *n.* 配偶
dissembler	[dɪ'semblə] *n.* 伪善者，伪君子
tangled	['tæŋgld] *adj.* 紊乱的；纠缠的，缠结的；复杂的
tone	[təʊn] *n.* 语气；色调；音调，音色
naked	['neɪkɪd] *adj.* 裸体的；无装饰的
polygraph	['pɒlɪgræf] *n.* 测谎仪（poly-多；graph写。polygraph指多种波动描记器：一种能同时记录诸如心跳、血压和汗液分泌等生理变化的仪器，常被用作测谎器。还记得单词polymath吗？）
respiration	[ˌrespə'reɪʃn] *n.* 呼吸
perspire	[pə'spaɪə(r)] *v.* 流汗，分泌
economical	[ˌi:kə'nɒmɪkl] *adj.* 经济的，节约的，合算的
musculature	['mʌskjələtʃə(r)] *n.* 肌肉组织
neurological	[ˌnjʊərə'lɒdʒɪkl] *adj.* 神经病学的，神经学上的
paralyzed	['pærəlaɪzd] *adj.* 瘫痪的，麻痹的
deliberately	[dɪ'lɪbərətlɪ] *adv.* 故意地；谨慎地，慎重地
spontaneous	[spɒn'teɪnɪəs] *adj.* 自发的，自然的，无意识的
leak	[li:k] *n.* 泄露
conceal	[kən'si:l] *v.* 隐藏，隐瞒
wrinkle	['rɪŋkl] *n.* 皱纹，皱褶
grief	[gri:f] *n.* 悲痛，忧伤，不幸
eyebrow	['aɪbraʊ] *n.* 眉毛

scowl	[skaʊl] *n.* 愁容，怒容，阴沉沉的样子
counterfeit	['kaʊntəfit] *v.* 伪造，仿造，假装，伪装
lip	[lɪp] *n.* 嘴唇（还记得口红怎么说吗？lipstick）
grin	[grɪn] *n.* 露齿笑
strained	[streɪnd] *adj.* 紧张的；勉强的
stiff	[stɪf] *adj.* 呆板的，坚硬的
repertoire	['repətwɑː(r)] *n.* 全部本领，全部节目（区别：reservoir水库）
fibber	['fibə(r)] *n.* 撒小谎者，惯撒小谎的人
glimpses	[glɪmps] *n.* 一瞥，一看（同义词：glance）
veracity	[və'ræsətɪ] *n.* 诚实；精确性
intolerable	[ɪn'tɒlərəbl] *adj.* 无法忍受的，难耐的
morally	['mɒrəlɪ] *adv.* 道德上，有道德地（名词和形容词形式：moral）
potentially	[pə'tenʃlɪ] *adv.* 可能地，潜在地（名词和形容词形式：potential）
would-be	['wʊd'bɪ] *adj.* 想要成为的；自称的；冒充的

▶ 雅思阅读真题同义词考点

pretend	—disguise, deceive, conceal, lie
escape	—evade, flee, get away
spouse	— husband, wife, mate
identify	— distinguish, differentiate, recognise, know
potential	— hidden, likely, possible, promising

下篇导读： 【左撇子】

考试时间： 2010-01-30，2011-09-17……

　　为什么世界上右撇子居多？大多数动物也是右撇子吗？左撇子强于艺术，右撇子强于逻辑？为什么左脑控制语言？雅思学不好是左脑的问题？ ☺

Reading Passage 37

Left-handed
The world is designed for right-handed people. Why does a tenth of the population prefer the left?

Paragraph A

The probability that two right-handed people would have a left-handed child is only about 9.5 percent. The chance rises to 19.5 percent if one parent is a lefty and 26 percent if both parents are left-handed: The preference, however, could also stem from an infant's imitation of his parents. To test genetic influence, starting in the 1970s British biologist Marian Annett of the University of Leicester hypothesised that no single gene determines handedness. Rather, during fetal development, a certain molecular factor helps to strengthen the brain's left hemisphere, which increases the probability that the right hand will be dominant, because the left side of the brain controls the right side of the body, and vice versa. Among the minority of people who lack this factor, handedness develops entirely by chance. Research conducted on twins complicates the theory, however, one in five sets of identical twins involves one right-handed and one left-handed person, despite the fact that their genetic material is the same. Genes, therefore, are not solely responsible for handedness.

Paragraph B

Genetic theory is also undermined by results from Peter Hepper and his team at Queen's University in Belfast, Ireland. In 2004 the psychologists used ultrasound to show that by the 15th week of pregnancy, fetuses already have a preference as to which thumb they suck. In most cases, the preference continued after birth. At 15 weeks, though, the brain does not yet have control over the body's limbs. Hepper speculates that fetuses tend to prefer whichever side of the body is developing quicker and that their movements, in turn, influence the brain's development. Whether this early preference is temporary or holds up throughout development and infancy is unknown. Genetic predetermination is also contradicted by the widespread observation that children do not settle on either their right or left hand until they are two or three years old.

Paragraph C

But even if these correlations were true, they did not explain what actually causes left-handedness. Furthermore, specialisation on either side of the body is common among animals. Cats will favour one paw over another when fishing toys out from under the couch. Horses stomp more frequently with one hoof than the other. Certain crabs motion predominantly with the left or right claw. In evolutionary terms, focusing power and dexterity in one limb is more efficient than having to train two, four or even eight limbs equally. Yet for most animals, the preference for one side or the other is seemingly random. The overwhelming dominance of the right hand is associated only with humans. That fact directs attention toward the brain's two hemi-spheres and perhaps toward language.

Paragraph D

Interest in hemispheres dates back to at least 1836. That year, at a medical conference, French physician Marc Dax reported on an unusual commonality among his patients. During his many years as a country doctor, Dax had encountered more than 40 men and women for whom speech was difficult, the result of some kind of brain damage. What was unique was that every individual suffered damage to the left side of the brain. At the conference, Dax elaborated on his theory, stating that each half of the brain was responsible for certain functions and that the left hemisphere controlled speech. Other experts showed little interest in the Frenchman's ideas.

Paragraph E

Over time, however, scientists found more and more evidence of people experiencing speech difficulties following injury to the left brain. Patients with damage to the right hemisphere most often displayed disruptions in perception or concentration. Major advancements in understanding the brain's asymmetry were made in the1960s as a result of so-called split-brain surgery, developed to help patients with epilepsy. During this operation, doctors severed the corpus callosum—the nerve bundle that connects the two hemispheres. The surgical cut also stopped almost all normal communication between the two hemispheres, which offered researchers the opportunity to investigate each side's activity.

Paragraph F

In 1949 neurosurgeon Juhn Wada devised the first test to provide access to the brain's functional organisation of language. By injecting an anesthetic into the right or left carotid artery, Wada temporarily paralysed one side of a healthy brain, enabling him to more closely study the other side's capabilities. Based on this approach, Brenda Milner and the late Theodore Rasmussen of the Montreal Neurological Institute published a major study in 1975 that confirmed the theory that country doctor Dax had formulated nearly 140 years earlier:

in 96 percent of right-handed people, language is processed much more intensely in the left hemisphere. The correlation is not as clear in lefties, however. For two thirds of them, the left hemisphere is still the most active language processor. But for the remaining third, either the right side is dominant or both sides work equally, controlling different language functions.

Paragraph G

That last statistic has slowed acceptance of the notion that the predominance of right-handedness is driven by left-hemisphere dominance in language processing. It is not at all clear why language control should somehow have dragged the control of body movement with it. Some experts think one reason the left hemisphere reigns over language is because the organs of speech processing—the larynx and tongue—are positioned on the body's symmetry axis. Because these structures were centreed, it may have been unclear, in evolutionary terms, which side of the brain should control them, and it seems unlikely that shared operation would result in smooth motor activity.

Paragraph H

Language and handedness could have developed preferentially for very different reasons as well. For example, some researchers, including evolutionary psychologist Michael C. Corballis of the University of Auckland in New Zealand, think that the origin of human speech lies in gestures. Gestures predated words and helped language emerge. If the left hemisphere began to dominate speech, it would have dominated gestures, too, and because the left brain controls the right side of the body, the right hand developed more strongly.

Paragraph I

Perhaps we will know more soon. In the meantime, we can revel in what, if any, different handedness brings to our human talents. Popular wisdom says right-handed, left-brained people excel at logical, analytical thinking. Left-handed, right-brained individuals are thought to possess more creative skills and may be better at combining the functional features emergent in both sides of the brain. Yet some neuroscientists see such claims as pure speculation. Fewer scientists are ready to claim that left-handedness means greater creative potential. Yet lefties are prevalent among artists, composers and the generally acknowledged great political thinkers. Possibly if these individuals are among the lefties whose language abilities are evenly distributed between hemispheres, the intense interplay required could lead to unusual mental capabilities. Or perhaps some lefties become highly creative simply because they must be cleverer to get by in our right-handed world. This battle, which begins during the very early stages of childhood, may lay the groundwork for exceptional achievements.

Questions 1–9

*The Reading Passage has nine paragraphs, **A–I**.*

Which paragraph contains the following information?

*Write the correct letter, **A–I**, in boxes 1–9 on your answer sheet.*

NB   *You may use any letter more than once.*

1   The first study into the functions of each brain side

2   How the relation between left brain and language was first observed

3   The likelihood that one-handedness is born

4   A discovery that people's concentration is controlled by the right hemisphere

5   Why animals prefer to using one side of the body

6   A common belief that left-handed people are good at arts

7   The age when the preference of using one hand is confirmed

8   Same genetic material which developed different handedness

9   How body language contributed to right handedness

▶ 核心词汇

词汇	释义
preference	['prefrəns] *n.* 偏好（动词形式：prefer）
fetal	['fiːt(ə)l] *adj.* 胎的，胎儿的
molecular	[mə'lekjələ(r)] *adj.* 【化学】分子的
identical	[aɪ'dentɪkl] *adj.* 同一的，完全相同的
undermine	[ˌʌndə'maɪn] *v.* 破坏，渐渐破坏（under-下方；mine挖矿）
ultrasound	['ʌltrəsaʊnd] *n.* 超声，超音波
pregnancy	['pregnənsɪ] *n.* 怀孕（形容词形式：pregnant）
limb	[lɪm] *n.* 肢，臂（同义表达：arms and legs）
contradict	[ˌkɒntrə'dɪkt] *v.* 反驳，否认
correlation	[ˌkɒrə'leɪʃn] *n.* 相关，关联，相互关系
predominantly	[prɪ'dɒmɪnəntlɪ] *adv.* 主要地，显著地
dexterity	[dek'sterətɪ] *n.* 灵巧，敏捷，机敏
conference	['kɒnfərəns] *n.* 会议；协商（同义词：meeting）
patient	['peɪʃnt] *n.* 病人，患者（形容词词义：耐心的。想象一下病人安静地在病床上躺了一天，多么有耐心啊）
asymmetry	[ˌeɪ'sɪmətrɪ] *n.* 不对称
epilepsy	['epɪlepsɪ] *n.* 癫痫，癫痫症
bundle	['bʌndl] *n.* 束，捆
anesthetic	[ˌænəs'θetɪk] *n.* 麻醉剂，麻药（区别：aesthetic *adj.* 美学的；审美的；有审美感的。aesthetic源自希腊文，原意为"可感知的"。该词后来逐渐用于对事物美丑的感知能力或评价，即审美。anesthesia，an-否定 + aesthesia感觉→没有感觉，即"麻醉"。）
formulate	['fɔːmjʊleɪt] *v.* 明确地表达
reign	[reɪn] *v.* 统治，支配（区别：regime 政权）
larynx	['lærɪŋks] *n.* 喉，喉头（同义词：throat）
predate	[priː'deɪt] *v.* 时间上先于……（显然是由"pre-date"两部分构成的，字面意思"在日期上先于……"，引申而来上义。）
emergent	[ɪ'mɜːdʒənt] *adj.* 浮现的
exceptional	[ɪk'sepʃənl] *adj.* 异常的，例外的
likelihood	['laɪklɪhʊd] *n.* 可能性（后缀-hood表示"状态"。如：childhood, adulthood, neighbourhood）
hemisphere	['hemɪsfɪə(r)] *n.* 半球
concentrate	['kɒnsntreɪt] *v.* 集中

prevalent	['prevələnt] *adj*. 普遍的，流行的

▶ 雅思阅读真题同义词考点

identical	—same, alike, duplicate
undermine	—damage, destroy, weaken
likelihood	—possibility, feasibility, presumption, probability
concentrate	—focus, emphasise, intensify
exceptional	—special, extraordinary, notable, outstanding, remarkable, unusual
predate	—precede, antedate, preexist, antecede

下篇导读： 【选择与幸福】

考试时间： 2008-08-13，2011-07-30，2013-05-18……

　　"你幸福吗？""是，我姓福。""你满足吗？""我满族。"为什么我们面临的选择越多却越不容易感到幸福？这和机会成本有关。买半价票的人比买全价票的人更容易缺席演出。买衣服只逛两家店会增强幸福感。☺

Reading Passage 38

Choice and Happiness

A Americans today choose among more options in more parts of life than has ever been possible before. To an extent, the opportunity to choose enhances our lives. It is only logical to think that if some choice is good, more is better; people who care about having infinite options will benefit from them, and those who do not can always just ignore the 273 versions of cereal they have never tried. Yet recent research strongly suggests that, psychologically, this assumption is wrong. Although some choice is undoubtedly better than none, more is not always better than less.

B Recent research offers insight into why many people end up unhappy rather than pleased when their options expand. We began by making a distinction between "maximisers" (those who always aim to make the best possible choice) and "satisficers" (those who aim for "good enough," whether or not better selections might be out there).

C In particular, we composed a set of statements—the Maximisation Scale—to diagnose people's propensity to maximise. Then we had several thousand people rate themselves from 1 to 7 (from "completely disagree" to "completely agree") on such statements as "I never settle for second best." We also evaluated their sense of satisfaction with their decisions. We did not define a sharp cutoff to separate maximisers from satisficers, but in general, we think of individuals whose average scores are higher than 4 (the scale's midpoint) as maximisers and those whose scores are lower than the midpoint as satisficers. People who score highest on the test—the greatest maximisers—engage in more product comparisons than the lowest scorers, both before and after they make purchasing decisions, and they take longer to decide what to buy. When satisficers find an item that meets their standards, they stop looking. But maximisers exert enormous effort reading labels, checking out consumer magazines and trying new products. They also spend more time comparing their purchasing decisions with those of others.

D We found that the greatest maximisers are the least happy with the fruits of their efforts. When they compare themselves with others, they get little pleasure from finding out that they did better and substantial dissatisfaction from finding out that they did worse. They are more prone to experiencing regret after a purchase, and if their acquisition disappoints them, their sense of well-being takes longer to recover. They also tend to brood or ruminate more than satisficers do.

E Does it follow that maximisers are less happy in general than satisficers? We tested this by having people fill out a variety of questionnaires known to be reliable indicators of well-being. As might be expected, individuals with high maximisation scores experienced less satisfaction with life and were less happy, less optimistic and more depressed than people with low maximisation scores. Indeed, those with extreme maximisation ratings had depression scores that placed them in the borderline clinical range.

F Several factors explain why more choice is not always better than less, especially for maximisers. High among these are "opportunity costs." The quality of any given option cannot be assessed in isolation from its alternatives. One of the "costs" of making a selection is losing the opportunities that a different option would have afforded. Thus an opportunity cost of vacationing on the beach in Cape Cod might be missing the fabulous restaurants in the Napa Valley. If we assume that opportunity costs reduce the overall desirability of the most preferred choice, then the more alternatives there are, the deeper our sense of loss will be and the less satisfaction we will derive from our ultimate decision.

G The problem of opportunity costs will be worse for a maximiser than for a satisficer. The latter's "good enough" philosophy can survive thoughts about opportunity costs. In addition, the "good enough" standard leads to much less searching and inspection of alternatives than the maximiser's "best" standard. With fewer choices under consideration, a person will have fewer opportunity costs to subtract.

H Just as people feel sorrow about the opportunities they have forgone, they may also suffer regret about the option they settle on. My colleagues and I devised a scale to measure proneness to feeling regret, and we found that people with high sensitivity to regret are less happy, less satisfied with life, less optimistic and more depressed than those with low sensitivity. Not surprisingly, we also found that people with high regret sensitivity tend to be maximisers. Indeed, we think that worry over future regret is a major reason that individuals become maximisers. The only way to be sure you will not regret a decision is by making the best possible one. Unfortunately, the more options you have and the more opportunity costs you incur, the more likely you are to experience regret.

I   In a classic demonstration of the power of sunk costs, people were offered season subscriptions to a local theater company. Some were offered the tickets at full price and others at a discount. Then the researchers simply kept track of how often the ticket purchasers actually attended the plays over the course of the season. Full-price payers were more likely to show up at performances than discount payers. The reason for this, the investigators argued, was that the full-price payers would experience more regret if they did not use the tickets because not using the more costly tickets would constitute a bigger loss.

J   LESSONS

Choose when to choose.

We can decide to restrict our options when the decision is not crucial. For example, make a rule to visit no more than two stores when shopping for clothing.

Learn to accept "good enough."

Settle for a choice that meets your core requirements rather than searching for the elusive "best." Then stop thinking about it.

Don't worry about what you're missing.

Consciously limit how much you ponder the seemingly attractive features of options you reject. Teach yourself to focus on the positive parts of the selection you make.

Control expectations.

"Don't expect too much, and you won't be disappointed" is a cliché. But that advice is sensible if you want to be more satisfied with life.

Questions 1–8

The Reading Passage contains 10 paragraphs A–J.

Which paragraph contains the following information?

Write the appropriate letters A–J in boxes 1–8 on your answer sheet.

NB *You may use any letter more than once.*

1 Do not spend lots of energy shopping for clothing.

2 A method was taken to identify maximisers and satisficers.

3 A survey proved that satisficers are much happier.

4 People don't feel happy even though they did better than others.

5 The greatest maximisers are in danger of psychological disease.

6 A term indicates that various options are not isolated.

7 The key factor contributes to less satisfaction experienced by maximisers.

8 A study showed that payment affected people's choice.

▶ 核心词汇

词汇	释义
option	['ɒpʃn] *n.* 可选择的办法
psychologically	[ˌsaɪkə'lɒdʒɪklɪ] *adv.* 心理上地，心理学地
cereal	['sɪərɪəl] *n.* 谷物；谷类（古罗马遭受大旱，教士们求助女巫占卜，占卜的结果是要立一位新的女神Ceres，向她供奉，这样她就会给大地带来雨水。此后，Ceres就变成了庄稼的保护神。cereal是从拉丁语变化而来，意即"of Ceres"属于谷物女神的。cereals早餐麦片。）
distinction	[dɪ'stɪŋkʃn] *n.* 区别，明显差别
maximise	['mæksɪmaɪz] *v.* 使（某事物）增至最大限度
satisfy	['sætɪsfaɪ] *v.* 满足，使满意
acquisition	[ˌækwɪ'zɪʃn] *n.* 获得物
well-being	[wel'biːɪŋ] *n.* 幸福
optimistic	[ˌɒptɪ'mɪstɪk] *adj.* 乐观的，乐观主义的（反义词：pessimistic）
subtract	[səb'trækt] *v.* 减去
clinical	['klɪnɪkl] *adj.* 临床的
opportunity costs	机会成本
questionnaire	[ˌkwestʃə'neə(r)] *n.* 调查问卷（同义词：survey）
alternative	[ɔːl'tɜːnətɪv] *adj. & n.* 取舍，抉择，可供选择的事物
uitimate	['ʌltɪmət] *adj.* 最后的，最终的（ultim=last 最后的。如：ultimo=in the last month 上个月的。）
crucial	['kruːʃl] *adj.* 决定性的，紧要关头的
consciously	['kɒnʃəslɪ] *adv.* 有意识地，自觉地
sunk cost	滞留成本，沉入成本
subscription	[səb'skrɪpʃn] *n.* 订阅（动词形式：subscribe）
elusive	[ɪ'luːsɪv] *adj.* 难懂的，难捉摸的
isolate	['aɪsəleɪt] *v.* 使隔离，使孤立

▶ 雅思阅读真题同义词考点

satisfy　—appease, content, gratify

option　—choice, alternative, selection

crucial　—critical, important, key, essential, pivotal

ultimate　—eventual, final, last, terminal

elusive　—ambiguous, unclear, blur, obscure

下篇导读：　【管理学之父】

考试时间：　2010-02-20，2012-01-07，2013-03-09……

　　彼得·德鲁克——现代管理学之父；提出了知识型员工、目标管理；率先倡导商业的社会责任；一生做出许多精准的经济预测；记住他的名言：While we may not be able to predict the future, we could create it.

Reading Passage 39

The Father of

Modern Management

A Peter Drucker, "The Father of Modern Management" was a genius whose interests and contributions extended into many areas of economics and social endeavor as well as both business and nonprofit management. His many contributions and amazingly effective advice and accurate predictions became legendary.

B Forty years ago Drucker predicted nearly every major change in management that has occurred since. He saw the need for a new name for workers and so he coined one himself that is in common usage today. The word is "knowledge worker" and he predicted that this new class of worker would dominant the workplace of the future. He invented management by objectives (MBO) and showed executives how to approach problems with their ignorance and questions rather than relying on their knowledge and experience. He predicted the tremendous rise in the health care market, yet taught us that while we may not be able to predict the future, we could create it.

C All of his predictions, theories, and exhortations to managers had an important fact at their root. Drucker really cared about people and the society in which they work and live. He spent considerable effort in exploring, analysing, writing, and teaching ways not only of making workers more effective in the workplace, but also showing how businesses and other organisations could improve the lot of workers as individuals and for society as a whole. Moreover, Drucker recognised that accomplishing this depended on competent, maybe even extraordinary, leadership by managers. He integrated the requirements of leadership which the requirements of fulfilling social responsibilities would demand.

D Peter Drucker recognised and preached that people were not a cost; they were a resource. He was one of the first to do so as an aspect of management. He concluded that considerations for workers in and out of the workplace were the responsibility of the corporate leader just as much as the profits, survival, and growth of the business or organisation. Therefore, it should come as no surprise that Drucker wrote and taught us about the social responsibilities of business and how these responsibilities could best be satisfied.

E As a result, Drucker, "the Father of Modern Management" was also called a pioneer of business social responsibility. In his first book *The End of Economic Man* written in the early to late 1930's and published in 1939, Drucker had already documented and began to develop his theories of social responsibility. As Drucker saw it, the age of mercantilism in which economics was the only force that to need to be considered was dead. Although *The End of Economic Man* was primarily an attack on fascism and Nazism, its very title predicted the end of a society based solely on the economic objective. Drucker even stated that impoverishment, a clear and critical economic issue, was "a far lesser evil" than the complete collapse of freedom and liberties. Drucker went on to write that it was no good pretending that just any policy of social benefits might be "good for business" and could be judged on this criterion and weighed against the economic sacrifice they might involve. He argued that a destruction of economic assets might be socially beneficial and necessary, but it could still be harmful economically. Therefore, we shouldn't deceive ourselves with "purchasing power" or "spending" theories. Meeting social needs might cost something, but it should be done anyway.

F Of course at this point Drucker was analysing economic and social responsibility at the macro level and there are differences from those elements which became a part of Drucker's concepts of social responsibility for individual organisations. This early theme of the fading of economics as the sole consideration was continued in 1942 with the publishing of his second book, *The Future of Industrial Man*. "We have already abandoned the belief that economic progress is always and by necessity the highest goal," he wrote. While these early writings on the subject seemed to favour the universal importance of social issues over economic ones, Drucker made clear that the first responsibility of management was to produce satisfactory economic results since without this, the organisation could not fulfill its social responsibilities.

G However, Drucker drew an unusual distinction between two differing categories of social responsibility. This was represented by two American businessmen. Drucker considered both of them revolutionary in their concern with the public welfare. One was Andrew Carnegie. Carnegie was a poor Scottish immigrant to the United States who had made millions in the steel industry and had become the richest man in America by the late 19th century. He was the Bill Gates of his day. Carnegie believed that the sole purpose of being rich was to be a philanthropist, to give the money away in worthwhile causes. He was retired at the time he started his major philanthropy and began a crusade of his philosophy to the American public. The money he gave to public causes was from his personal fortune. It had nothing to do with his company. No one can deny that his acts of philanthropy were socially responsible.

H The other man was Julius Rosenwald. In the late 19th century as Carnegie began to give away his money, Rosenwald took over a failing business, Sears Roebuck and Company, and built it into one of the largest retailers in the world. Previous to these two individuals, wealthy men had basically spent money building monuments to their achievements. Both differed from their predecessors in spending their money in the public interest and practiced social responsibility. However, there was difference between the two. Whereas, Carnegie responsibly gave his money away from his private fortune for social good, Rosenwald practiced social responsibility as a part of his business, Sears Roebuck and Company. No one else had ever done this previously. The largest part of Sears Roebuck's market in those days was in agriculture, and Rosenwald spent millions to bring scientific knowledge of this field to his customers, most of whom were farmers. This also benefited the business as Rosenwald knew that his business depended on the welfare of his customers. One famous case was the 4-H Club movement in the U.S. which taught competency and promoted the prosperity of various aspects of agriculture. Sears Roebuck founded the movement and funded it totally and independently for ten years. Eventually it grew to teach more, focused on youth, was funded by many corporations, integrated locally in more than 3000 local counties across the U.S., and connected to more than a hundred universities for research. Today, the organisation serves over 6.5 million members in the United States from ages 5 to 19 in approximately 90,000 clubs. This was the kind of social responsibility that Drucker saw as the responsibility of organisations in the community to initiate.

I Both Carnegie and Rosenwald were good men and both practiced social responsibility. However, Drucker made this distinction: Carnegie believed in the social responsibility of wealth. Rosenwald believed in the social responsibility of business. The social responsibility of business was something truly something different and a notion that was totally new and different even from philanthropy. Drucker firmly embraced it.

Questions 1–9

*The Reading Passage has nine paragraphs, **A–I**.*

Which paragraph contains the following information?

*Write the correct letter, **A–I**, in boxes 1–9 on your answer sheet.*

***NB** You may use any letter more than once.*

1 A notion that workers are not financial expenses, but important assets

2 A term Drucker first used to represent future workers

3 A choice between poverty and liberty

4 Drucker' preference about two types of social responsibility

5 A successful example of the social responsibility of business

6 Somebody's goal of being rich

7 The uniform and underlying consideration of Drucker's theories

8 A method of the goal-oriented management

9 The book which confirms that economic success is a priority of management

▶ 核心词汇

词汇	释义
endeavor	[ɪnˈdevə(r)] *n.* 努力，尽力
legendary	[ˈledʒəndrɪ] *adj.* 传说中的，传奇
coin	[kɒɪn] *v.* 创造（名词含义为"硬币"，动词含义"铸造、创造"为学术阅读考点）
objective	[əbˈdʒektɪv] *n.* 目标
executive	[ɪgˈzekjətɪv] *n.* 总经理（CEO，Chief Executive Officer）
exhortation	[ˌegzɔːˈteɪʃn] *n.* 敦促，极力推荐
explore	[ɪkˈsplɔː(r)] *v.* 探索，探究，仔细查看
integrate	[ˈɪntɪgreɪt] *v.* 使整合，使完整
preach	[priːtʃ] *v.* 宣扬，说教
document	[ˈdɒkjʊmənt] *v.* 证明，为……提供证明；记录
mercantilism	[mɜːˈkæntɪlɪzəm] *n.* 商业主义，重商主义
fascism	[ˈfæʃɪzəm] *n.* 法西斯主义
Nazism	[ˈnɑːtsɪzəm] *n.* 纳粹主义
impoverishment	[ɪmˈpɒvərɪʃmənt] *n.* 贫穷，穷困，贫化
criterion	[kraɪˈtɪərɪən] *n.* （批评、判断等的）标准，准则，规范（复数为criteria）
destruction	[dɪˈstrʌkʃn] *n.* 破坏，毁灭，消灭
element	[ˈelɪmənt] *n.* 原理，基础；要素
distinction	[dɪˈstɪŋkʃn] *n.* 区别
philanthropist	[fɪˈlænθrəpɪst] *n.* 慈善家（先学anthropology人类学。源自希腊语anthropo人，人类 + logy学。再学phil爱 + anthrop人类 + -ist的人，构成：爱人类的人，慈善家）
crusade	[kruːˈseɪd] *v.* 从事改革运动
monument	[ˈmɒnjʊmənt] *n.* 纪念碑
competency	[ˈkɒmpɪtənsɪ] *n.* 资格，能力
embrace	[ɪmˈbreɪs] *v.* 接受；信奉
uniform	[ˈjuːnɪfɔːm] *adj.* 统一的（名词含义：制服。比如：school uniform）
priority	[praɪˈɒrətɪ] *n.* 优先（动词形式：prioritise）

▶ 雅思阅读真题同义词考点

coin	—devise, invent, make up, first use, originate
integrate	—combine, unite, mix, cooperate, coordinate
poverty	—poor, impoverishment, destitution
uniform	—consistent, constant, symmetrical, unvaried, same, even
priority	—highest, first, precedence

下篇导读：【龙涎香】

考试时间： 2010-07-10……

昂贵的龙涎香，水中的软黄金。龙涎香的来历、用途。第一次听说龙涎香是在电脑游戏《仙剑奇侠传》里，第二次就是在雅思考试里了。😊

Reading Passage 40

Ambergris

The name ambergris is derived from the Spanish "ambar gris", ambar meaning amber and gris meaning grey, thus the name signifies grey amber. The use of ambergris in Europe is now entirely confined to perfumery—as a material of perfumery. Its high price varies from $15 to $25 an ounce, though it formerly occupied on inconsiderable place in medicine. Ambergris was also decorated and worn as jewelry, particularly during the Renaissance. It occupies a very important place in the perfumery of the East, and there it is also used in pharmacy, and as a flavouring material in cookery.

Amber, however, is quite a different substance from ambergris and this discrepancy has puzzled some people. Amber is the fossilised resin from trees that was quite familiar to Europeans long before the discovery of the New World, and prized for jewelry. Although considered a gem, amber is a hard, transparent, wholly-organic material derived from the resin of extinct species of trees. In the dense forests of the Middle Cretaceous and Tertiary periods, between 10 and 100 million years ago, these resin-bearing trees fell and were carried by rivers to coastal regions. There, the trees and their resins became covered with sediment, and over millions of years the resin hardened into amber.

Ambergris and amber are related by the fact that both wash up on beaches. Ambergris is a solid, waxy, flammable substance of a dull grey or blackish colour, with the shades being variegated like marble. It possesses a peculiar sweet, earthy odour not unlike isopropyl alcohol. It is now known to be a morbid secretion formed in the intestines of the sperm whale, found in the Atlantic and Pacific oceans. Being a very lightweight material, ambergris is found floating upon the sea, on the sea-coast, or in the sand near the sea-coast. It is met with in the Atlantic Ocean, on the coasts of Brazil and Madagascar; also on the coast of Africa, of the East Indies, China, Japan, and the Molucca Islands; but most of the ambergris which is brought to England comes from the Bahama Islands. It is also sometimes found in the abdomen of whales, always in lumps in various shapes and sizes, weighing from 1/2 oz. to 100 or more lb. A piece which the Dutch East India Company bought from the King of Tydore weighed 182 lb. An American fisherman from Antigua found, inside a whale, about 52 leagues south-east from the Windward Islands, a piece of ambergris which weighed about 130 lb, and sold for 500 sterling.

Like many other substances regarding the origin of which there existed some obscurity or mystery, ambergris in former times possessed a value, and had properties attributed to it, more on account of the source from which it was drawn than from its inherent qualities. Many ridiculous hypotheses were started to account for its origin, and among others it was conjectured to be the solidified foam of the sea, a fungous growth in the ocean similar to the fungi which form on trees.

The true source and character of ambergris was first satisfactorily established by Dr. Swediaur in a communication to the Royal Society. It was found by Dr Swediaur that ambergris very frequently contained the horny mandibles or beaks of the squid, on which the sperm whales are known to feed. That observation, in connection with the fact of ambergris being frequently taken from the intestines of the sperm whale, sufficiently proved that the substance is produced by the whale's intestine as a means of facilitating the passage of undigested hard, sharp beaks of squid that the whale has eaten.

It was further observed that the whales in which ambergris was found were either dead or much wasted and evidently in a sickly condition. From this it was inferred that ambergris is in some way connected with a morbid condition of the sperm whale. Often expelled by vomiting, ambergris floats in chunks on the water and is of a deep grey colour, soft consistence, and an offensive, disagreeable smell. Following months to years of photo-degradation and oxidation in the ocean, this precursor gradually hardens, developing a dark grey or black colour, a crusty and waxy texture, and a peculiar odour that is at once sweet, earthy, marine, and animalist. Its smell has been described by many as a vastly richer and smoother version of isopropanol without its stinging harshness.

In that condition its specific gravity ranges from 0.780 to 0.926. It melts at a temperature of about 145 F into a fatty yellow resin-like liquid. It is soluble in ether, volatile and fixed oils, but only feebly acted on by acids. By digesting in hot alcohol, a peculiar substance termed ambrein is obtained. In chemical constitution ambrein very closely resembles cholesterin, a principle found abundantly in biliary calculi. It is therefore more than probable that ambergris, from the position in which it is found and its chemical constitution, is a biliary concretion analogous to what is formed in other mammals.

The industries founded on ambergris resulted in the slaughter of sperm whales almost to extinction. Sperm whales were killed in two massive hunts, the Moby Dick whalers who worked mainly between 1740-1880, and the modern whalers whose operations peaked in 1964, when 29,255 were killed. Most recent estimates suggest a global population of about 360,000 animals down from about 1,100,000 before whaling. In the 20th century, 90% of ambergris was derived in the processing of killing sperm whales. To this day, ambergris is still the most expensive product in the whole body of sperm whale. Depending on its quality, raw ambergris fetches approximately 20 USD per gram. In the United States, possession of any part of an endangered species—including ambergris that has washed ashore—is a violation of the Endangered Species Act of 1978.

Historically, the primary commercial use of ambergris has been in fragrance chemistry. However, it is difficult to get a consistent and reliable supply of high quality ambergris. Due to demand for ambergris and its high price, replacement compounds have been sought out by the fragrance industry and chemically synthesised. The most important of these is Ambrox, which has taken its place as the most widely used amber odorant in perfume manufacture. Procedures for the microbial production of Ambrox have also been devised.

Questions 1–8

Classify the following statements as applying to

> **A**   *Ambergris only*
>
> **B**   *Amber only*
>
> **C**   *Both amber and ambergris*
>
> **D**   *Neither amber nor ambergris*

*Write the correct letter, **A**, **B**, **C** or **D**, in boxes 1–8 on your answer sheet.*

1   from plant

2   from animal

3   much lighter

4   very costly

5   used in medicine

6   used as currency

7   wash up on beaches

8   could be seen through

▶ 核心词汇

词汇	释义
ambergris	['æmbəgriːs] *n.* 龙涎香
perfumery	[pə'fjuːməri] *n.* 香料店（perfume 香水）
substance	['sʌbstəns] *n.* 物质，实质，主旨
discrepancy	[dɪs'krepənsɪ] *n.* 相差，差异，矛盾（同义词：contradiction）
fossilise	['fɒsəlaɪz] *v.* 使成化石，使陈腐（名词形式：fossil）
transparent	[træns'pærənt] *adj.* 透明的（名词形式：transparency）
organic	[ɔː'gænɪk] *adj.* 有机的（反义词：inorganic）
sediment	['sedɪmənt] *n.* 沉淀物，沉积
waxy	['wæksɪ] *adj.* 像蜡的，蜡状的
flammable	['flæməbl] *adj.* 易燃的，可燃性的（单词 flame 指"火焰"；猜猜这个单词：flamingo）
variegate	['veərɪəgeɪt] *v.* 使成斑驳，使多样化
marble	['mɑːbl] *n.* 大理石
morbid	['mɔːbɪd] *adj.* 病的，由病引起的，病态的，恐怖的（谐音记忆："毛病的"）
sperm	[spɜːm] *n.* 精子（反义词：egg 卵子）
sperm whale	抹香鲸
float	[fləʊt] *n.* 漂流物
abdomen	['æbdəmən] *n.* 腹，腹部
lump	[lʌmp] *n.* 块（尤指小块），肿块
obscurity	[əb'skjʊərətɪ] *n.* 阴暗；朦胧，含糊；偏僻，隐匿
fungi	['fʌndʒaɪ] *n.* 真菌（单数形式为：fungus）
horny	['hɔːnɪ] *adj.* 角状的（名词形式：horn。猜猜单词 unihorn 是什么东西？独角兽？哈哈，英语中没这词儿。独角兽是：unicorn，字面意思是"一个玉米"，其实这里字母 c 是 h 的变形）
beak	[biːk] *n.* 鸟嘴，喙
squid	[skwɪd] *n.* 鱿鱼
vomit	['vɒmɪt] *n.* 呕吐，呕吐物，催吐剂　*vi.* 呕吐，大量喷出
chunk	[tʃʌŋk] *n.* 大块，矮胖的人或物
photo-degradation	['fəʊtəʊˌdegrə'deɪʃn] *n.* 光降解（作用）
oxidation	[ˌɒksɪ'deɪʃn] 氧化
crusty	['krʌstɪ] *adj.* 有硬壳的；顽固的；脾气暴躁的（名词形式：crust）
soluble	['sɒljəbl] *adj.* 可溶的，可溶解的
ether	['iːθə(r)] *n.* 乙醚

feebly	['fi:blɪ] *adj.* 无力的；虚弱的（形容词形式：feeble）
biliary	['bɪlɪərɪ] *adj.* 胆汁的，输送胆汁的，由于胆汁异状的
slaughter	['slɔːtə(r)] *n.* 屠宰，残杀，屠杀
synthesise	['sɪnθəsaɪz] *v.* 综合，合成
microbial	[maɪ'krəʊbɪəl] *adj.* 微生物的，由细菌引起的（名词形式：microbe）

▶ 雅思阅读真题同义词考点

transparent	—see through, crystal, translucent
discrepancy	—difference, confliction, contradiction
synthesise	—integrate, combine, mix
feeble	—frail, powerless, weak
microbe	—virus, microorganism, bacteria

下篇导读：【口译】

考试时间：2010-11-27，2011-03-19……

　　口译和翻译的定义。同声传译和交替传译的区别，对翻译者的要求，各自实用的场合。联合国大会和国务院答外国记者问时分别是哪种口译？ :)

Interpretation

Translation and interpretation are the ultimate jobs for people who love language. However, there are a lot of misunderstandings about these two fields, including the difference between them and what kind of skills and education they require.

For some reason, most laypeople refer to both translation and interpretation as "translation." Although translation and interpretation share the common goal of taking information that is available in one language and converting it to another, they are in fact two separate processes. So what is the difference between translation and interpretation? It's very simple. Translation is written—it involves taking a written text (such as a book or an article) and translating it in writing into the target language. Interpretation is oral—it refers to listening to something spoken (a speech or phone conversation) and interpreting it orally into the target language. Incidentally, those who facilitate communication between hearing persons and deaf/hard-of-hearing persons are also known as interpreters. This might seem like a subtle distinction, but if you consider your own language skills, the odds are that your ability to read/write and listen/speak are not identical—you are probably more skilled at one pair or the other. So translators are excellent writers, while interpreters have superior oral communication skills. In addition, spoken language is quite different from written, which adds a further dimension to the distinction. Then there's the fact that translators work alone to produce a translation, while interpreters work with two or more people/groups to provide an interpretation on the spot during negotiations, seminars, phone conversations, etc.

There are two types of interpretation: simultaneous and consecutive interpretation. The main difference between them lies in the time lag between the original speech and the interpretation into the foreign language. Simultaneous is "continuous flow" whereas consecutive has a "stop-and-go" rhythm. It is comparable to the difference between doing consecutive and concurrent time.

Simultaneous is real-time interpreting: speakers talk as they normally would, without pause, as the interpreter listens to one language and speaks in another, all at the same time (hence the term simultaneous), with the voices overlapping, though the speaker's voice is dominant and the interpreter whispers into a microphone. It is also known as U.N.-style interpreting. Simultaneous interpreting is the only way to provide a running rendition of everything said in the courtroom by judge, counsel, witnesses, etc., without requiring the original speaker to stop after every sentence. Few people can interpret simultaneously at a high level of accuracy (80% or better) , regardless of their ability to speak the two languages in question. Simultaneous interpretation calls for concentration, mental flexibility, and wide-ranging vocabulary in both languages. Research has shown that 23 cognitive skills are involved in simultaneous interpreting. Current neurological research reveals that interpreting draws heavily upon both left-brain and right-brain functions.

Consecutive interpreting involves a pause between language conversions: first the interpreter listens to the entire original phrase or passage, then interprets it into the other language. This mode is used for Q & A of non-English speaking witnesses, and requires more waiting time. It is important for the interpreter not to be seen whispering to the witness, for that would convey intimacy or collusion to the jury. It is equally important for anyone else in the courtroom to hear the interpreter's choice of words so that the transparency of the proceedings be evident. Consecutive interpreting calls for excellent short-term and long-term memory, note-taking skills, a grasp of subtle nuances in both languages, and a mastery of speaking styles so as to preserve the "flavour" of a witness.

Then, which is harder to do, simultaneous or consecutive? It is a matter of preference, skills and practice. Simultaneous involves more diverse brain functions and most people need special training and much practice to acquire the skill. However, consecutive, especially at the witness stand, is not easy, either, and is more stressful because everyone is watching and the interpretation is always open to criticism. In some situations, such as attorney-client interviews, interpreters may use a combination of both techniques so as not to lose the flow of natural conversation. However, it is difficult to interpret simultaneously without equipment, because at close quarters, both voices overlap, and it will be hard to hear either the original or the interpretation.

Interpreting, whether done simultaneously or consecutively, is mentally taxing and requires much more concentration than that required for ordinary speaking. Interpreters in a courtroom are under oath to be completely accurate as well as fair and impartial, which creates significant pressure. (One research panel likened the stress level to greater than that experienced by a neurosurgeon while operating.) Studies show that significant errors in meaning occur after 30–45 minutes on task in simultaneous interpretation. For this reason, all international agencies (U.N., European Commission, etc.) follow a policy of providing for rotation of interpreters every 30 minutes. The Southern District Interpreters Office follows this policy as well in providing a team of two interpreters for every trial or long proceeding.

Why do interpreters need remote equipment; why can't they just sit next to the person and whisper? Imagine if you had to whisper your entire opening statement to an agent at counsel table while at the same time listening to someone else speak. Remote equipment has many advantages: the interpreter has an unobstructed view of the speakers; the interpreter can move if there are audibility problems; the interpreter is free to concentrate on the message without interruption or distraction; and the team can function smoothly by relaying on the microphone at convenient times. Also, since the equipment can transmit on two channels, two different languages can be broadcast at once (with a separate interpreter in each language), and there can be more than one person listening.

Questions 1–8

Classify the following descriptions as referring to

    T   *Translation*

    I   *Interpretation*

    S   *Simultaneous interpretation*

    C   *Consecutive interpretation*

*Write the correct letter, **T**, **I**, **S** or **C**, in boxes 1–8 on your answer sheet.*

1   It requires more concentration than usual.

2   It requires good memory.

3   It requires flexible mind.

4   It is more likely to receive criticism.

5   It requires reading a text.

6   Voices overlap.

7   Remote equipment is needed.

8   People work alone to accomplish it.

▶ 核心词汇

词汇	释义
translation	[træns'leɪʃn] *n.* 翻译（动词形式：translate）
interpretation	[ɪnˌtɜːprɪ'teɪʃn] *n.* 口译（动词形式：interpret）
misunderstanding	[ˌmɪsʌndə'stændɪŋ] *n.* 误会，误解
laypeople	['leɪpiːpl] *n.* 外行，非专业人员
available	[ə'veɪləbl] *adj.* 可得到的，可利用的
converting	[kən'vɜːtɪŋ] *n.* 转换，变换（动词形式：convert）
target	['tɑːɡɪt] *n.* 目标，对象
oral	['ɔːrəl] *adj.* 口头的，口语的
incidentally	[ˌɪnsɪ'dentlɪ] *adv.* 附带地，顺便地
facilitate	[fə'sɪlɪteɪt] *v.* 使容易，促进
subtle distinction	微妙的差别
odds	[ɒdz] *n.* 可能性，可能的机会
identical	[aɪ'dentɪkl] *adj.* 同一的，同样的
dimension	[daɪ'menʃn] *n.* 尺寸，尺度，维度（3D是Three Dimensions的简称，分别指空间的长、宽、高，也就是立体啦。所以3D电影就是立体电影。但是我们生活在四维时空中，多一个time dimension。）
on the spot	马上，立刻；当场；在现场
negotiation	[nɪˌɡəʊʃɪ'eɪʃn] *n.* 谈判，协商，商谈（动词形式：negotiate）
seminar	['semɪnɑː(r)] *n.* 研究会，讨论发表会
simultaneous	[ˌsɪml'teɪnɪəs] *adj.* 同时的，同时发生的
consecutive	[kən'sekjətɪv] *adj.* 连续的，连贯的
rhythm	['rɪðəm] *n.* 节奏，韵律（区别：melody旋律；lyric歌词）
concurrent	[kən'kʌrənt] *adj.* 并发的，协作的，一致的
overlapping	[ˌəʊvə'læpɪŋ] *n.* 重叠，搭接（动词形式：overlap）
dominant	['dɒmɪnənt] *adj.* 占优势的，支配的
whisper	['wɪspə(r)] *v.* 低声说，耳语
running	['rʌnɪŋ] *adj.* 流动的，连续的
rendition	[ren'dɪʃn] *n.* 翻译
courtroom	['kɔːtruːm] *n.* 法庭，审判室
counsel	['kaʊnsl] *n.* 辩护律师
accuracy	['ækjərəsɪ] *n.* 准确性，精确性
regardless	[rɪ'ɡɑːdləs] *adj.* （与of连用）不管……的，不顾……的

concentration	[ˌkɒnsn'treɪʃn] *n.* 专心，集中（注意力）
mental	['mentl] *adj.* 心理的；智力的
neurological	[ˌnjʊərə'lɒdʒɪkl] *adj.* 神经学上的
conversion	[kən'vɜːʃn] *n.* 转变，变换
intimacy	['ɪntɪməsɪ] *n.* 亲密，隐私（形容词形式：intimate）
collusion	[kə'luːʒn] *n.* 共谋，勾结，串通
call for	要求
nuance	['njuːɑːns] *n.* 细微差别
quarter	['kwɔːtə(r)] *n.* 住处，岗位
taxing	['tæksɪŋ] *adj.* 繁重的，费力的（同义词：demanding）
impartial	[ɪm'pɑːʃl] *adj.* 公平的，不偏不倚的
trial	['traɪəl] *n.* 审讯，审判
unobstructed	[ˌʌnəb'strʌktɪd] *adj.* 无阻的，不受阻拦的
audibility	[ˌɔːdə'bɪlətɪ] *n.* 听得见，能听度
distraction	[dɪ'strækʃn] *n.* 分心，注意力转移，精力不集中

▶ 雅思阅读真题同义词考点

identical	—same, no difference, exact
target	—goal, aim, object
odds	—chance, opportunity, possibility, likelihood
call for	—require, demand, need, want
impartial	—fair, indifferent, neutral, unbiased, unprejudiced, even, equal

下篇导读：【法律顾问】
考试时间：……
　　英国律师行业介绍。出庭律师和法律顾问的区别，从事的业务各有哪些。一个人在海外生活求学，一定要善于用法律的武器保护自己。☺

Reading Passage 42

Barristers
and
Solicitors

Law firms from many different jurisdictions have long come to appreciate the expert and cost effective service offered by the Bar of England and Wales. In many jurisdictions there is one generic category of "lawyer", although some may specialise in advocacy and specialist legal advice whereas others do deals and rarely go to Court. In England, the legal profession is split between solicitors and barristers.

There are nearly 11,000 self-employed barristers in England and Wales. The role of barristers is to appear in Court and give specialist advice. By far the greatest part of higher level advocacy in English Courts and arbitral tribunals is undertaken by barristers. Leading advocates are designated "Queen's Counsel" or QC, a quality mark which allows one to identify those who are the most experienced in their particular field. There are about 1300 QC's. Cases are typically referred to barristers by solicitors, much in the way that a general practitioner in the medical field might refer someone to a consultant. However, foreign lawyers can also use the bar directly, as explained below. Recruitment to specialist barristers' chambers is highly competitive, and the largest sets take on as pupils (trainees) only three or four students out of many hundreds of applicants. They often accept as tenants only one or two of those. The hallmark of a successful pupil and a successful barrister is academic excellence and flair as an advocate.

Barristers specialise in legal argument and cross-examination, both in Court and in arbitration in England/Wales and abroad, advice on the strength and weaknesses of cases and on the evidence required to support them, and the giving of opinions on points of law even in a non-contentious context. Senior barristers are also frequently appointed as arbitrators, mediators and adjudicators, and to appear as expert witnesses abroad. In several important jurisdictions barristers can obtain temporary admission to argue cases in court. These include Australia, Malaysia, Singapore, Brunei, Bermuda, the Cayman Islands and parts of the Caribbean. All barristers have rights of audience in the European Court of Justice and the European Court of Human Rights. Specialist chambers are networked to legal research tools and web-linked, so that points can be raised and answered by email, and a barrister can readily be incorporated into a team.

Barristers can be approached directly by foreign lawyers including in-house counsel. The advantages are multifarious: The nature of barristers' work means that they develop current knowledge and courtroom instinct in their fields, so that their advice is particularly reliable.

The bar remains primarily a referral profession, so that there is no danger of barristers or their chambers taking away clients. On the contrary, the bar can work closely with foreign lawyers to improve efficiency and deliver an enhanced service. Often the overseas firm can do much of the preparation for litigation and collect the evidence identified as necessary by the barrister. If a solicitor's firm is needed to handle correspondence, filings and provide trial infrastructure, a barrister can usefully advise which firm to engage, which helps to keep costs under control. The firms of solicitors who do most litigation in the United Kingdom use the bar, rather than in-house advocates, for heavy cases. Accordingly, a specialist barrister in a particular field will know which solicitors are best for the job. Barristers often charge lower fees than solicitors for equivalent time. The reason is that barristers need to sustain a smaller office. They work for themselves with no need to keep associates employed, and, as specialists in their field, they often need to do less research to get the right answer. The self-employed status of barristers also contributes to real objectivity and independence.

A solicitor's role is to give specialist legal advice and help on all matters of the law to their clients, who may be members of the public, businesses or voluntary bodies etc. This can include representing them in court, but often in complex cases this role is given to a barrister and the role of the solicitor becomes one of research and advice to the client on their case.

There are over 60,000 solicitors practising in England and Wales and their work varies enormously. Most solicitors are employed by a private practice, which is a firm of solicitors run by the "partners" of the firm who regulate the flow of work to the solicitors. The size of the firm can vary from a huge international firm with many offices and hundreds of partners to a small practice with one or two partners. It is also possible for solicitors to work for Central and Local Government, the Crown Prosecution Service or the Magistrate's Courts Service, as well as "in-house" with a commercial or industrial organisation.

Firms can also vary in the type of work they offer to their clients. Private practice firms are usually general practice where work will involve matters such as conveyancing (the buying and selling of houses and land), personal injury claims, representing clients in court in divorce cases or making wills, as well as offering services to businesses such as advice on contracts and partnerships. Firms can also become specialists in a particular niche field such as shipping or aviation and tailor all their services to businesses in that industry. Alternatively they can concentrate on clients who are legally aided, where they will advise their clients who are unable to afford solicitor's fees.

A career as a solicitor offers the chance to combine intellectual challenges and diverse interesting work, with the opportunity to work closely with and for many different types of people. However, training is very competitive, and anyone intending to become a solicitor should be aware of the commitment which is required. Currently there are many more students with the Legal-Practice-Course qualification than there are training contracts and the big firms can take their pick from the very best candidates.

Questions 1–7

Categorise the following specialities as applying to

    A barrister

    B solicitor

1 appearing in court on behalf of a client, especially in rather complicated cases

2 assuming a majority of higher-level legal counseling in English courts

3 a general practitioner in the legal community

4 working for either a private practice or the central or local government, among many others

5 The most experienced could become QC.

6 wider rights of audience in courts

7 charging more money for the same amount of time

▶ **核心词汇**

词汇	释义
barrister	['bærɪstə(r)] *n.* 出庭律师
solicitor	[sə'lɪsɪtə(r)] *n.* 律师，法律顾问
bar	[bɑ:(r)] *n.* 律师职业，律师界（本文主要介绍了英国律师界的一些基本情况，除此之外，常用的缩写ABA指的是American Bar Association，即"美国律师协会"。）
specialise in	专门研究，专门从事（专门研究某一领域的人是specialist "专家"，和expert同义。）
self-employed	[selfɪm'plɔɪd] *adj.* 自雇的，非受雇于人的（简单讲就是"自己雇用自己"，接近自由职业者的生活模式。）
arbitral	['ɑ:bɪtrəl] *adj.* 仲裁的（下文出现了它的其他词形arbitration和arbitrator。）
tribunal	[traɪ'bju:nl] *n.* 法庭，（审理特别案件的特定）法庭
undertake	[ˌʌndə'teɪk] *v.* 着手做，承担，负责（什么是undertaker？现代社会里尤指"承办丧事的人"，不是一般意义的着手做某件事情的人。）
designate	['dezɪgneɪt] *v.* 把……定名为（英国女王在位时的）王室法律顾问（King's Counsel指的又是什么呢？当然就是"王室法律顾问"喽，这里不用强调是不是女王在位啦。）
identify	[aɪ'dentɪfaɪ] *v.* 识别，鉴别（名词形式：identification *n.*，ID Card 身份证 Identification Card）
consultant	[kən'sʌltənt] *n.* 会诊医师；顾问（相应词形变化consult *v.*，consulting *adj.*）
hallmark	['hɔ:lmɑ:k] *n.* 标志，特征
cross-examination	[krɒsɪgˌzæmɪ'neɪʃn] *n.* 盘问，反诘问（指诉讼当事人的一方向对方证人就其所提供的证词进行盘问，以便发现矛盾，推翻其证词）
senior	['si:nɪə(r)] *adj.* 地位较高的，年资较深的，高级的（"sen"表示"老"，"ior"表示形容词比较级，因此"senior"的基本含义表示"相对较老的"；依此类推，"jun"表示"年轻"，所以"相对年轻的，初级的"就是"junior"。那么"superior"和"inferior"又表示什么？首先，我们将下列两个单词列在一起：super-man，super-ior，"superman"大家都认识，"超人"吗！这个含义有助于理解"super-"这个前缀，表示"超，在……上方"，而前边我们提到"ior"预示该单词含有比较意味，因此，"superior"表示"优秀于……的"、"高于……的"，而"inferior"是它的反义词。）
incorporate	[ɪn'kɔ:pəreɪt] *v.* 使并入，吸收（可以这样理解这个单词in-corpor-ate，"corp"或"corpor"表示body，指人的身体，后来引申为"实体"，因此incorporate的基本含义就是"把……放入身体/实体当中"，进而引申为现在使用的含义；单词corporal表示"身体的，肉体的"这个含义也由此而来。）

multifarious	[ˌmʌltɪ'feərɪəs] *adj.* 各式各样的
litigation	[ˌlɪtɪ'geɪʃn] *n.* 诉讼，起诉（英语单词里lawsuit也表示"诉讼"，侧重指民事诉讼，prosecution侧重指刑事诉讼。）
correspondence	[ˌkɒrə'spɒndəns] *n.* 通信，信件（动词形式：correspond）
accordingly	[ə'kɔːdɪŋlɪ] *adv.* 因此，从而
associate	[ə'səʊʃɪeɪt] *n.* 同事，伙伴，合伙人
prosecution	[ˌprɒsɪ'kjuːʃn] *n.* 起诉，检举（和前边提到的lawsuit在一起记忆。）
tailor	['teɪlə(r)] *vt.* 针对特定对象作修改，使适应特定需要（这个单词在文章中用得很漂亮，当"tailor"作名词的时候，它表示"裁缝"，这里活用成动词，意为"量体裁衣，根据具体的对象制作合体的衣服"，进而引申为文中的含义。）
alternatively	[ɔːl'tɜːnətɪvlɪ] *adv.* 二者择一地，如其不然（相应词形变化：alternate *v.*，alternative *adj.*）

▶ **雅思阅读真题同义词考点**

undertake　　—take on, assume, carry out

designate　　—title, entitle, term, call

identify　　　—recognise, pinpoint, detect, ascertain

hallmark　　　—characteristic, trait, feature, token

senior　　　　—leading, chief, primary, superior, major

incorporate　—include, absorb, integrate, unite

multifarious　—diverse, diversified, varied, various, miscellaneous

下篇导读：【炼金术】

考试时间： ……

　　点石成金是古代中国神仙做的事，也是古代西方炼金术士想做的事。他们为了这个理想把不同的物质放进瓶瓶罐罐熬啊熬，没有熬成阿香婆也没有炼成金子，却搞出了烧杯烧瓶化合物。他们成了化学家的祖先。☺

An Exploration of Alchemy

A depiction of the four elements blending in universal creation.

Alchemy is one of the two oldest sciences known to the world. The other is astrology. The beginnings of both extend back into the obscurity of prehistoric times. According to the earliest records extant, both of them were considered as divinely revealed to man so that by their aid he might regain his lost estate.

In spite of what many people may believe, Alchemy is not dead. The practice of Alchemy has continued for more than two millennia, some say it is nearly as old as human civilisation itself. For a time in the Dark Ages, it was also thought to have been dead, but it re-emerged in Western Europe in the twelfth century. Alchemy and its underlying principles have evolved over time, much like the transformation of metals with which it is concerned; it too has transformed into something else.

In Alchemy, the primary aspiration was to change ordinary metals into gold. The secondary aim was to achieve spiritual perfection. The alchemists viewed their work as a melding of spirituality and science. Their belief was that matter has a common soul which alone is permanent, the body, or outward form, being merely a mode of manifestation of the soul and therefore transitory and transmutable into other forms.

The beginnings of Alchemy can be traced to the ancient Egyptian city of Alexandria, which was the acknowledged centre of the intellectual world about 300 BC. But to better understand Alchemy requires a step backward to the times of Aristotle and Plato, who lived about a century earlier. At that time, there were two opposing views concerning the nature of matter. Aristotle believed that matter is continuous and therefore capable of infinite subdivision, but Epicurus, elaborating the pre-Aristotelian views of Democritus, held it to have a grained or discontinuous structure, consisting of atoms of the same primordial material which differed in their size, shape and form. Aristotle held that the basis of the material world was something called "prime" or "first matter." The embodiment and realisation of the prime matter came through the first stage of form, found in the four elements of Earth, Air, Fire and Water. The elements are related by qualities of dry(cold), moist, hot and dry. Each basic element was characterised by an imbalance in proportion of the basic qualities, so fire was characterised by hot and dry, as water was by cold and wet. Thus, each element could be transformed in another by changing the quality which they share.

A depiction of the four elements blending in universal creation.

Plato ascribed to the theory of the four elements constituting all other substances. He had an idea that the constituting units (particles) of the four elements were based on the geometry of triangles. He considered gold as consisting of homogeneous particles (which today we know is true). Here is an explanation by Plato regarding these four elements:

...out of the elements of this kind, the body of the universe is created, being brought into concord through proportion; and from these it derived friendship, so that coming to unity with itself, it became dissoluble by any force, and save the will of him who joined it. Now the making of the earth took up the whole bulk of each of these four elements.

The alchemists adopted Aristotle's theories into their art. Early alchemical theories of the origin and changes of matter were based on their interpretation of the four elements as constituents of matter, principally as formulated by Plato and Aristotle. Their reasoning, in attempting to accomplish the feat (of transmutation to gold), was based on their belief in the unity of matter, and in the existence of a potent transmuting agent known as the Philosopher's Stone. The "Philosopher's Stone," which had many other names, was that mystic substance when combined with base metals would remove the impurities of those metals and result in the transmutation to (the pure metal of) gold or silver.

Closely connected to the symbolism of the Philosopher's Stone, was the concept of the Prima Materia, or primary material, which was thought to be a prime, chaotic matter, which might come into actual existence if impressed by "form." In time, the Alchemists came to modify the theory of the four elements, apparently to better suit the model of their pursuit.

The books and manuscripts explaining the chemicals and processes were obscure and subject to various interpretations. The symbolic language used was incomprehensible except to an initiated few. It is clear that a majority of these manuscripts are nothing more than cryptic recipes and processes conveyed through intricate drawings and diagrams which are awe-inspiring. Most of the earlier records contain recipes which would be used by the goldsmiths to make gold alloys harder, heavier or more brilliant (in colour). Some of the ingredients used by the alchemists include copper, lead, sulfur, arsenic, urine and bile. They would mix these ingredients together in the proper proportions, then try to remove the "impurities," to be left with gold or silver. Heat was the fundamental requirement of nearly every alchemical process, from distilling dew to smelting lead. Indeed it seems that they tried just about everything.

However, without the technical knowledge and understanding, the alchemists were in effect just "spinning their wheels." They possessed neither the knowledge of atomic structure nor a refined technical apparatus. Many rumours remain about how this alchemist or that one succeeded in creating or capturing some of this elusive substance, but they all seem to lack any credibility. All of these things and more contributed to its demise.

A sixteenth century physician and alchemist named Parcelsus changed the course of history by insisting that the true goal of Alchemy was finding medical cures. Some of his followers abandoned their search for the Philosopher's Stone and focused on more constructive experiments, resulting in many important discoveries. Then in 1645 the Royal Society of London, a national academy of science, was formed and began to hold weekly meetings. King Charles II inaugurated the group, and it was Robert Boyle, one of the groups' first members, whose published work "Skeptical Chemist" (1661) challenged the long accepted principles of Aristotle's four elements, and the alchemists three. It was the final blow to Alchemy, which came to be replaced by more rigid (and productive) sciences—namely chemistry and physics.

Questions 1–6

Classify the following statements with A, B, C, D, E and F.

    A   Aristotle

    B   Epicurus

    C   Plato

    D   Parcelsus

    E   Boyle

    F   King Charles II

1   Gold comprises homogeneous particles.

2   retargeting the goal of Alchemy to heal rather than change metals into gold

3   publication of "Skeptical Chemist"

4   principle of four elements

5   The universe (proper) was brought into harmony by proportion.

6   calling the basis of the material world "prime"

7   Matter has discontinuous structure.

Questions 8–9

According to the author, normally alchemists regard their work as a marriage of

8 .... and **9** .... (using one word to fill in each blank)

▶ 核心词汇

词汇	释义
alchemy	['ælkəmɪ] *n.* 炼金术
astrology	[ə'strɒlədʒɪ] *n.* 占星术（"astr" 表示"星星"，"-ology" 表示"科学、学问"。所以 "astrology" 表示"研究星星位置的科学"。类似的例子：disaster。可以分成两个部分看dis-aster，"否定含义＋星星"，古罗马人相信星位不正就代表不祥，必有灾祸发生，因此，这个单词表示"灾难"。）
obscurity	[əb'skjʊərətɪ] *n.* 蒙昧；昏暗（下文中出现了它的形容词形式obscure。）
prehistoric	[ˌpriːhɪ'stɒrɪk] *adj.* 史前的
extant	[ek'stænt] *adj.* 现存的，现有的
re-emerge	[reɪɪ'mɜːdʒ] *vi.* 重新浮现，重新出现（这里的 "re-" 表示"再一次"，"emerge" 表示"出现，浮现"。名词形式：re-emergence。）
evolve	[ɪ'vɒlv] *vi.* 进化，发展（名词形式：evolution）
aspiration	[ˌæspə'reɪʃn] *n.* 热望，渴望（动词形式：aspire）
manifestation	[ˌmænɪfe'steɪʃn] *n.* 表现（形式）（动词形式：manifest）
opposing	[ə'pəʊzɪŋ] *adj.* 相反的，对立的（相应词形变化：oppose *v.*，opposition *n.*）
infinite	['ɪnfɪnət] *adj.* 无限的，无穷的（英国著名诗人William Blake曾写下一段十分美丽的诗句：To see a World in a Grain of Sand, And a Heaven in a Wild Flower; Hold Infinity in the palm of your hand, And Eternity in an hour. 粗略地理解为"从一粒沙子看到一个世界，从一朵野花看到一个天堂，把握在你手心里的就是无限，永恒也就消融于一个时辰"。由小见大，可见其磅礴气势。国内有中文功底深厚者将其译为"一花一世界，一沙一天国；君掌盛无边，刹那含永劫"。）
elaborate	[ɪ'læbərət] *vt.* 详细阐述
primordial	[praɪ'mɔːdɪəl] *adj.* 原始的
embodiment	[ɪm'bɒdɪmənt] *n.* 具体化，具体体现（动词形式：embody）
substance	['sʌbstəns] *n.* 物质
triangle	['traɪæŋgl] *n.* 三角形
regarding	[rɪ'gɑːdɪŋ] *prep.* 关于
concord	['kɒnkɔːd] *n.* 和谐，一致，协调（Concorde从拼写上来看比concord多了一个字母 "e"，表示"协和式飞机"，英法合造的超音速客机）
constituent	[kən'stɪtjʊənt] *n.* 组分，成分
formulate	['fɔːmjʊleɪt] *v.* 阐述，明确地表达（名词形式：formulation）
feat	[fiːt] *n.* 功绩，壮举
agent	['eɪdʒənt] *n.* 【化】剂
mystic	['mɪstɪk] *adj.* 神秘的
impurity	[ɪm'pjʊərətɪ] *n.* 杂质，混杂物（相关单词：impure *adj.*，pure *adj.*，purity *n.*）

symbolism	['sɪmbəlɪzəm] *n.* 象征主义（相关单词：symbol *n.*，symbolise *vt.*）
chaotic	[keɪ'ɒtɪk] *adj.* 杂乱的，无秩序的（名词形式：chaos，这个单词比较有效的记忆方法是将它的拼写想象成汉语拼音"吵死"，能让人觉得很吵的环境一定是很乱的，这个名词的含义就是"混乱，混沌"。但是一定要注意发音，不要把汉语读音读出来哦！）
initiate	[ɪ'nɪʃieɪt] *v.* 开始，发起（形容词形式：initial）
recipe	['resəpɪ] *n.* 方法，诀窍；处方
awe-inspiring	[ɔːɪn'spaɪərɪŋ] *adj.* 使人产生敬畏之心的，令人惊叹的
ingredient	[ɪn'griːdɪənt] *n.* 成分
refined	[rɪ'faɪnd] *adj.* 精确的，精致的（动词形式：refine）
rumour	['ruːmə(r)] *n.* 传闻，谣言（还可以写成rumor，"散布流言飞语的人"叫做rumourmonger。）
elusive	[ɪ'luːsɪv] *adj.* 难以表述的，令人困惑的
credibility	[ˌkredə'bɪlətɪ] *n.* 可信性（形容词形式：credible，而"incredible"则表达"不可思议的，难以置信的"之意。一般作褒义词用，但也会听到英语国家的人见到一个腰围等于身高的人身着紧身连衣裙时的效果，发出"incredible"的感叹，想必是慨叹她的勇气！）
demise	[dɪ'maɪz] *n.* 中止，死亡

▶ 雅思阅读真题同义词考点

manifestation	—exhibition, expression, indication, demonstration
regarding	—concerning, about, as regards, on the topic of
concord	—harmony, accord, unity
formulate	—frame, verbalise, voice, articulate
demise	—death, decease, departure, termination

下篇导读： 【工程师布鲁内尔】

考试时间： 2010-06-05，2014-02-22……

    英国的詹天佑，工程师布鲁内尔。大西部铁路的总工程师，克里夫顿吊桥设计者，建造了当时最大的轮船横跨大西洋，放置了海底电缆，使越洋电报通信成为现实。☺

Reading Passage 44

Isambard Kingdom Brunel

Isambard Kingdom Brunel was born on 9 April 1806 in Portsmouth. His father Mark was a French engineer who had fled France during the Revolution. Brunel was educated both in England and in France. When he returned to England he went to work for his father. Brunel's first notable achievement was the part he played with his father in planning the Thames Tunnel from Rotherhithe to Wapping, completed in 1843. In 1831 Brunel's designs won the competition for the Clifton Suspension Bridge across the River Avon. Construction began the same year but it was not completed until 1864.

The work for which Brunel is probably best remembered is his construction of a network of tunnels, bridges and viaducts for the Great Western Railway. In 1833, he was appointed chief engineer of the Great Western Railway, one of the wonders of Victorian Britain, running from London to Bristol and later Exeter. At that time, Brunel made two controversial decisions: to use a broad gauge of 2,140 mm for the track, which he believed would offer superior running at high speeds; and to take a route that passed north of the Marlborough Downs, an area with no significant towns, though it offered potential connections to Oxford and Gloucester and then to follow the Thames Valley into London. His decision to use broad gauge for the line was controversial in that almost all British railways to date had used standard gauge. Brunel said that this was nothing more than a carry-over from the mine railways that George Stephenson had worked on prior to making the world's first passenger railway. Brunel worked out through mathematics and a series of trials that his broader gauge was the optimum railway size for providing stability and a comfortable ride to passengers, in addition to allowing for bigger carriages and more freight capacity. He surveyed the entire length of the route between London and Bristol himself. Drawing on his experience, the Great Western contained a series of impressive achievements—soaring viaducts, specially designed stations, and vast tunnels including the famous Box Tunnel, which was the longest railway tunnel in the world at that time.

Many difficulties were met with and overcome. The Brent Valley, the Thames at Maidenhead and the hill at Sonning between Twyford and Reading had to be crossed on the stretch of track that was to be laid from London to Reading. Brent Valley was crossed by a 960 ft. long viaduct, costing £40,000. Where the railway had to cross the Thames, Brunel built a brick bridge with two main spans of 128 ft. with a rise of only 24-1/2 ft., and the elliptical spans of Maidenhead Bridge are probably the most remarkable ever constructed in brickwork. The high ground between Twyford and Reading necessitated a two-miles cutting, sometimes of 60 ft. in depth.

Brunel's solo engineering feats also started with bridges. And he is perhaps best remembered for the Clifton Suspension Bridge in Bristol. Spanning over 700 ft (213 m), and nominally 200 ft (61 m) above the River Avon, it had the longest span of any bridge in the world at the time of construction. Brunel submitted four designs to a committee headed by Thomas Telford and gained approval to commence with the project. Afterwards, Brunel wrote to his brother-in-law, the politician Benjamin Hawes: "Of all the wonderful feats I have performed, since I have been in this part of the world, I think yesterday I performed the most wonderful. I produced unanimity among 15 men who were all quarrelling about that most ticklish subject—taste." He did not live to see it built, although his colleagues and admirers at the Institution of Civil Engineers felt the bridge would be a fitting memorial, and started to raise new funds and to amend the design. Work started in 1862 and was complete in 1864, five years after Brunel's death.

Even before the Great Western Railway was opened, Brunel was moving on to his next project: transatlantic shipping. He used his prestige to convince his railway company employers to build the Great Western, at the time by far the largest steamship in the world, and the much longer the Great Eastern, fitted out with the most luxurious appointments and capable of carrying over 4,000 passengers.

The Great Eastern was designed to be able to cruise under her own power non-stop from London to Sydney and back since engineers of the time were under the misapprehension that Australia had no coal reserves, and she remained the largest ship built until the turn of the century. Like many of Brunel's ambitious projects, the ship soon ran over budget and behind schedule in the face of a series of momentous technical problems. She has been portrayed as a white elephant, but it can be argued that in this case Brunel's failure was principally one of economics—his ships were simply years ahead of their time. His vision and engineering innovations made the building of large-scale, screw-driven, all-metal steamships a practical reality, but the prevailing economic and industrial conditions meant that it would be several decades before transoceanic steamship travel emerged as a viable industry. Great Eastern was built at John Scott Russell's Napier Yard in London, and after two trial trips in 1859, set forth on her maiden voyage from Southampton to New York on 17 June 1860.

Though a failure at her original purpose of passenger travel, she eventually found a role as an oceanic telegraph cable layer, and the Great Eastern remains one of the most important vessels in the history of shipbuilding—the Trans-Atlantic cable had been laid, which meant that Europe and America now had a telecommunications link.

Brunel died at the relatively early age of fifty-seven, had led a charmed life, for on several occasions his life was in danger. In 1838, while aboard the steamer Great Western, he fell down a ladder, and was found unconscious with his face in a pool of water. Twice he was nearly killed on the Great Western Railway; and he had yet another escape when he swallowed a half-sovereign which, after being six weeks in his windpipe, was at last extracted by means of an apparatus designed by the engineer himself. The patient was attached to an enlarged edition of a looking-glass frame and then the frame and the patient quickly inverted. After several attempts the coin fell into his mouth. While his life was in danger, public excitement was intense, so high was his place in public estimation.

Questions 1-7

Classify the following statements with corresponding project designed by Brunel.

C Clifton Suspension Bridge

E Great Eastern Steamship

W Great Western Railway

T Thames Tunnel

1 adopted broader gauge for tracks than normal.

2 had not been completed before the death of Brunel.

3 started a telecommunications link between European and America by laying an undersea cable.

4 contained the longest railway tunnel in the world at that time.

5 is believed as the first famous architectural project Brunel took part in.

6 was selected and modified from four of Brunel's original designs.

7 was compared to a white elephant.

▶ 核心词汇

词汇	释义
suspension bridge	吊桥
viaduct	['vaɪədʌkt] *n.* 高架桥
gauge	[geɪdʒ] *n.* 规格，尺度
superior	[suːˈpɪərɪə(r)] *adj.* 较高的，高级的（常用词组：be superior to；反义：be inferior to）
prior to	在前
a series of	一系列的
optimum	['ɒptɪməm] *adj.* 最适宜的；最有利的
freight	[freɪt] *n.* 货运，货物
vast	[vɑːst] *adj.* 巨大的
span	[spæn] *n.* 跨度（lifespan 寿命）
elliptical	[ɪˈlɪptɪkl] *adj.* 椭圆的
brickwork	['brɪkwɜːk] *n.* 砖结构（brick 砖）
commence	[kəˈmens] *v.* 开始
schedule	['ʃedjuːl] *n.* 时间表（拼音记忆"死车堵了"）
unanimity	[ˌjuːnəˈnɪmətɪ] *n.* 一致同意，全体一致
prestige	[preˈstiːʒ] *n.* 威信，威望，声望
cruise	[kruːz] *v.* 乘船巡游
momentous	[məˈmentəs] *adj.* 重大的，严重的
portray	[pɔːˈtreɪ] *v.* 描述，描绘，描写
prevailing	[prɪˈveɪlɪŋ] *adj.* 占优势的，主要的，流行的（动词形式：prevail）
vessel	['vesl] *n.* 船，舰
apparatus	[ˌæpəˈreɪtəs] *n.* 器具，仪器
invert	[ɪnˈvɜːt] *v.* 使倒置，使反转

▶ 雅思阅读真题同义词考点

superior	—better, greater, higher
schedule	—timetable, arrangement
apparatus	—equipment, device, outfit
invert	—reverse, turn around, upside down
modify	—adjust, alter, change, vary, shift, adapt, amend, revise

下篇导读：【艺术家指纹】

考试时间：2010-03-20，2011-11-26……

　　画家作画时会在画布上留下自己的指纹。这幅画是达·芬奇画的吗？用这幅画上的指纹和《蒙娜丽莎的微笑》上的指纹进行对比，答案就出现了。☺

Reading Passage 45

Artist　Fingerprints

A Works of art often bear the fingerprints of the artist who created them. Such crucial evidence usually goes unnoticed even by connoisseurs, art experts and conservators. If present, such evidence could be valuable in clarifying questions about authorship and dating.

B The use of the term forensic usually contains elements like crime, legal procedure or academic rhetoric. Our objective, however, is not to see who committed a crime but rather who committed the work of art in question and to put forward evidence sound enough to stand up to professional scrutiny. The value of such evidence is extremely high as the probability for the existence of two identical finger impressions from different individuals is nil and no such occurrence has ever been noticed in any part of the world at any time. The science of fingerprint identification is based on that accepted fact.

C The unique character of ridges on our hands has been recognised for thousands of years. The study of ancient pottery for example reveals the utilisation of fingerprint impressions in the clay as a maker's mark. In prehistoric times, we find examples of hand prints in cave painting. Only as recently as 1858 did Sir William Herschel establish its use for identification. In 1888, Sir Francis Galton undertook to refine and formulate Herschel's observations. Identification by fingerprint was first adopted in England in 1905 and received general acceptance worldwide in 1908.

D The combination of a number of characteristics in a given finger impression is specific to a particular print. The placing of implicit reliance on fingerprint evidence by our courts of law has always been on the assumption (now accepted as a fact) that no two fingers can have identical ridge characteristics. Galton's mathematical conclusions

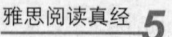

predicted the possible existence of some 64 billion different fingerprint patterns.

E Artists in the area of the visual arts use their hands for creation. Their tools, such as brushes often isolate them from the surface they are working on. Inaccurate deposits of paint are often corrected by modeling with the fingertip. Some artists used the fingertip to soften the marks left by the brush by gently tapping or stroking the still wet surface. In some instances, the fingertip was used for literally "stamping" the fine network of ridges onto the painting.

F The eventual authentication of a painting by J. M. W. Turner entitled *Landscape with Rainbow* in 1993 is a good illustration of the process. The painting was discovered in the early 1980's. Fingerprint evidence was discovered on the painting during restoration, appropriately documented and re-examined by a veteran expert. A match was found between the fingerprint on *Landscape with Rainbow* and one photographed on another painting by the same artist that hangs in the Tate Gallery, London. The evidence was duly disregarded by the puzzled scholars and art experts. But, the fingerprint on *Landscape with Rainbow* and a fingerprint from Turner's *Chichester Canal* clearly matched. In both instances the fingertip was used to model still wet paint. Turner's *Chichester Canal* picture has an unquestionable provenance all the way back to the artist. In addition, it is well known that Turner always worked alone and had no assistants. This reduces the chances of accidental contribution substantially. Some of the various experts who formerly rejected the attribution of the painting to Turner recanted under heavy media coverage. The painting was finally sold at auction at Phillips in London in 1995.

G In 1998, three envelopes containing old correspondence had been purchased in an antique shop. One of the envelopes postmarked April 2, 1915 was found to contain a drawing folded in half. The drawing depicts a woman's head. It is executed in red chalk with an inscription written in reverse with brown ink. The design is faded and worn. Some spots suggest foxing and subsequent discolouration. The paper is yellowed and contaminated.

H The newly discovered design bears great similarity to that of the *Head of St Anne* by Leonardo da Vinci, in the Windsor Collection since 1629. The medium is different, red chalk being used instead of black. The scale of the two images is different so offsetting (copying by contact transference) is not a satisfactory explanation for the new drawing. Differences also exist in the design itself, principally in the folds of the veil, in the presence of an additional strand of braid and in the angle of the head. The figure is softer, which may be due to fading, wear and contamination. In addition, the use of a damp brush is indicated in microscopic examination and is likely responsible in part for the softness of the image. When the paper was first examined, several fingerprints have been noticed on the verso. One of them was found clear and containing many ridges suitable for comparison, however, no analysis was done at the time due to the lack of reference material. Many of Leonardo's works are not easily accessible and fingerprint data either does not exist or is not published.

I   By chance, on March 30, 1999, several clear and useable fingerprints were found on an unusually good detail photo in a publication on Leonardo. The photograph of Leonardo's *St Jerome*, in the Vatican Museum, revealed no less than 16 partial fingertip marks. The importance of this is that the fingerprints are left in the still wet paint and without doubt the use of the fingertip served to model paint. Since the authorship of the painting of *St Jerome* is unquestioned by scholarship and has always been ascribed to Leonardo, the conclusion that these fingerprints are his would be hard to argue against.

J   The fingerprints on the *St Jerome* illustration were scanned and enlarged so comparisons could be made with the fingerprint on the newly discovered drawing. One of them proved to match. The result of the analyses was presented on March 31, 1999 to fingerprint examiner Staff Sergeant André Turcotte for an independent assessment. He agreed with the findings and confirmed the conclusion. The matching fingerprint is powerful circumstantial evidence. It dates the drawing to Leonardo's lifetime and it proves that Leonardo had to have physically handled the paper.

Questions 1–7

*Choose ONE phrase from the list of phrases **A–K** below to complete each of the sentences 1–7 below. Write the appropriate letters in boxes 1–7 on your answer sheet.*

1 The fingerprint in ancient pottery ....

2 The science of fingerprint identification ....

3 The authentication of a painting without signature ....

4 Landscape with Rainbow ....

5 Visual artists ....

6 The drawing depicting a woman's head ....

7 Leonardo's fingerprint data ....

A used fingers to remove unwanted paint left by the brush.

B revealed the utilisation of clay.

C was based on Galton's mathematical assumption.

D was left to identify the person who made it.

E was in poor condition.

F was sold in high price after its author had been identified.

G was widely accepted because of a reliable system available.

H was preserved in the Windsor Collection.

I could be done by comparing with fingerprints left from other sources.

J could be used to find out who committed a crime.

K was obtained from the painting of *St Jerome*.

▶ 核心词汇

词汇	释义
bear	[beə(r)] *v.* 带有，具有；承担
authorship	['ɔːθəʃɪp] *n.* 作者的身份
connoisseur	[ˌkɒnə'sɜː(r)] *n.* 鉴赏家，鉴定家，行家
rhetoric	['retərɪk] *n.* 修辞；辩术
clarify	['klærəfaɪ] *v.* 使清楚，澄清
scrutiny	['skruːtənɪ] *n.* 细看，细查；监视
ridge	[rɪdʒ] *n.* 皱褶，纹理
utilisation	[ˌjuːtəlaɪ'zeɪʃn] *n.* 利用（动词形式：utilise）
clay	[kleɪ] *n.* 黏土，泥土（区别：mud 泥）
implicit	[ɪm'plɪsɪt] *adj.* 暗示的（反义词：explicit）
undertake	[ˌʌndə'teɪk] *v.* 承担（区别：undergo 经历）
formulate	['fɔːmjʊleɪt] *vt.* 确切地阐述
stroke	[strəʊk] *n.* 一画，一笔
pattern	['pætn] *n.* 模式，式样
contaminate	[kən'tæmɪneɪt] *v.* 污染（名词形式：contamination）
authentication	[ɔːˌθentɪ'keɪʃn] *n.* 证明，鉴定（动词形式：authenticate）
illustration	[ˌɪlə'streɪʃn] *n.* 例证，实例
veteran	['vetərən] *n.* 经验丰富的人
depict	[dɪ'pɪkt] *vt.* 描绘，描画
damp	[dæmp] *adj.* 潮湿的
ascribe	[ə'skraɪb] *v.* 认为……属于
circumstantial	[ˌsɜːkəm'stænʃl] *adj.* 依照环境的，依照情况的（circumstantial evidence 旁证）

▶ 雅思阅读真题同义词考点

authenticate	—verify, distinguish, certify, prove
veteran	—experienced, practiced, sophisticated
damp	—wet, moist, humid
ascribe	—attribute, assign, contribute
circumstance	—condition, situation, case, scenario, environment, surrounding

下篇导读： 【大脑体操】

考试时间： 2005-06-25，2011-03-19……

　　经常去健身房的人身体健康身材好；经常做雅思阅读的人思维敏捷知识丰富。那么，你做过大脑体操吗？据说会提升你的创新力。☺

Reading Passage 46

Mental Gymnastics

A The working day has just started at the head office of Barclays Bank in London. Seventeen staff are helping themselves to a buffet breakfast as young psychologist Sebastian Bailey enters the room to begin the morning's training session. But this is no ordinary training session. He's not here to sharpen their finance or management skills. He's here to exercise their brains.

B Today's workout, organised by a company called the Mind Gym in London, entitled "having presence". What follows is an intense 90-minute session in which this rather abstract concept is gradually broken down into a concrete set of feelings, mental tricks and behaviours. At one point the bankers are instructed to shut their eyes and visualise themselves filling the room and then the building. They finish up by walking around the room acting out various levels of presence, from low-key to over the top.

C It's easy to poke fun. Yet similar mental workouts are happening in corporate seminar rooms around the globe. The Mind Gym alone offers some 70 different sessions, including ones on mental stamina, creativity for logical thinkers and "zoom learning". Other outfits draw more directly on the exercise analogy, offering "neurotics" courses with names like "brain sets" and "cerebral fitness". Then there are books with titles like *Pumping Ions*, full of brainteasers that claim to "flex your mind", and software packages offering memory and spatial-awareness games.

D But whatever the style, the companies' sales pitch is invariably the same—follow our routines to shape and sculpt your brain or mind, just as you might tone and train your body. And, of course, they nearly all claim that their mental workouts draw on serious scientific research and thinking into how the brain works.

E One outfit, Brainergy of Cambridge, Massachusetts (motto: "Because your grey matter matters") puts it like this: "Studies have shown that mental exercise can cause changes in brain anatomy and brain chemistry which promote increased mental efficiency and clarity. The neuroscience is cutting-edge." And on its website, Mind Gym trades on a quote from Susan Greenfield, one of Britain's best known neuroscientists: "It's a bit like going to the gym, if you exercise your brain it will grow."

F Indeed, the Mind Gym originally planned to hold its sessions in a local health club, until its founders realised where the real money was to be made. Modern companies need flexible, bright thinkers and will seize on anything that claims to create them, especially if it looks like a quick fix backed by science. But are neurotic workouts really backed by science? And do we need them?

G Nor is there anything remotely high-tech about what Lawrence Katz, co-author of *Keep Your Brain Alive*, recommends. Katz, a neurobiologist at Duke University Medical School in North Carolina, argues that just as many of us fail to get enough physical exercise, so we also lack sufficient mental stimulation to keep our brain in trim. Sure we are busy with jobs, family and housework. But most of this activity is repetitive routine. And any leisure time is spent slumped in front of the TV.

H So, read a book upside down. Write or brush your teeth with your wrong hand. Feel your way around the room with your eyes shut. Sniff vanilla essence while listening intently to orchestral music. Anything, says Katz, to break your normal mental routine. It will help invigorate your brain, encouraging its cells to make new connections and pump out neurotrophins, substances that feed and sustain brain circuits.

I Well, up to a point it will. "What I'm really talking about is brain maintenance rather than bulking up your IQ," Katz adds. Neurotics, in other words, is about letting your brain fulfill its potential. It cannot create super-brains. Can it achieve even that much, though? Certainly the brain is an organ that can adapt to the demands placed on it. Tests on animal brain tissue, for example, have repeatedly shown that electrically stimulating the synapses that connect nerve cells thought to be crucial to learning and reasoning, makes them stronger and more responsive. Brain scans suggest we use a lot more of our grey matter when carrying out new or strange tasks than when we're doing well-rehearsed ones. Rats raised in bright cages with toys sprout more neural connections than rats raised in bare cages—suggesting perhaps that novelty and variety could be crucial to a developing brain. Katz and neurologists have proved time and again that people who lose brain cells suddenly during a stroke often sprout new connections to compensate for the loss especially if they undergo extensive therapy to overcome any paralysis.

J Guy Claxton，an educational psychologist at the University of Bristol, dismisses most of the neurological approaches as "neuron-babble". Nevertheless, there are specific mental skills we can loam, he contends. Desirable attributes such as creativity, mental flexibility, and even motivation, are not the fixed faculties that most of us think. They are thought habits that can be learned. The problem, says Claxton, is that most of us never get proper training in these skills. We develop our own private set of mental strategies for tackling tasks and never learn anything explicitly. Worse still, because any learned skill—even driving a car or brushing our teeth—quickly sinks out of consciousness, we can no longer see the very thought habits we're relying upon. Our mental tools become invisible to us.

K Claxton is the academic adviser to the Mind Gym. So not surprisingly, the company espouses his solution—that we must return our thought patterns to a conscious level, becoming aware of the details of how we usually think. Only then can we start to practise better thought patterns, until eventually these become our new habits. Switching metaphors, picture not gym classes, but tennis or football coaching.

L In practice, the training can seem quite mundane. For example, in one of the eight different creativity workouts offered by the Mind Gym—entitled "creativity for logical thinkers"—one of the mental strategies taught is to make a sensible suggestion, then immediately pose its opposite. So, asked to spend five minutes inventing a new pizza, a group soon comes up with no topping, sweet topping, cold topping, price based on time of day, flat-rate prices and so on.

M Bailey agrees that the trick is simple. But it is surprising how few such tricks people have to call upon when they are suddenly asked to be creative: "They tend to just label themselves as uncreative, not realising that there are techniques that every creative person employs." Bailey says the aim is to introduce people to half a dozen or so such strategies in a session so that what at first seems like a dauntingly abstract mental task becomes a set of concrete, leasable behaviours. He admits this is not a short cut to genius. Neurologically, some people do start with quicker circuits or greater handling capacity. However, with the right kind of training he thinks we can dramatically increase how efficiently we use it.

N It is hard to prove that the training itself is effective. How do you measure a change in an employee's creativity levels, or memory skills? But staff certainly report feeling that such classes have opened their eyes. So, neurological boosting or psychological training? At the moment you can pay your money and take your choice. Claxton for one believes there is no reason why schools and universities shouldn't spend more time teaching basic thinking skills, rather than trying to stuff heads with facts and hoping that effective thought habits are somehow absorbed by osmosis.

Question 1–8

*Use the information in the passage to match the people (listed **A–D**) with opinions or deeds below.*

*Write the appropriate letters, **A–D**, in boxes **1–8** on your answer sheet.*

NB   You may use any letter more than once

> **A**   Guy Claxton
>
> **B**   Sebastian Bailey
>
> **C**   Susan Greenfield
>
> **D**   Lawrence Katz

1   We do not have enough inspiration to keep our brains fit.

2   The more you exercise your brain like exercise in the gym, the more your brain will grow.

3   Exercise can keep your brain healthy instead of improving someone's IQ.

4   It is valuable for schools to teach students about creative skills besides basic known knowledge.

5   We can develop new neuron connections when we lose old connections via certain treatment.

6   People usually mark themselves as not creative before figuring out there are approaches for each person.

7   An instructor in Mind Gym who guided the employees to exercise.

8   Majority of people don't have appropriate skills-training for brain.

► 核心词汇

词汇	释义
buffet	['bʊfeɪ] *n.* 自助餐（拼写很好记，只要注意和bullet的区别就行了）
psychologist	[saɪ'kɒlədʒɪst] *n.* 心理学家，心理学者
session	['seʃn] *n.* 学期；（会议、课程的）一段时间（training session 培训课程，训练项目）
mental	['mentl] *adj.* 精神的；心理的
low-key	['ləʊkiː] *adj.* 低调的
stamina	['stæmɪnə] *n.* 毅力，精力，持久力（sta站，stamina 是stamen 的复数，该词指直立的织布机上的经线，经纱。根据希腊神话，命运女神（the Fates）根据上天的旨意，纺织每个人的命运之线→人的生命线，生命力）
neurotic	[njʊə'rɒtɪk] *adj.* 神经的，神经刺激的
shape	[ʃeɪp] *v.* 形成，塑造
sculpt	[skʌlpt] *v.* 塑造
anatomy	[ə'nætəmɪ] *n.* 解剖
chemistry	['kemɪstrɪ] *n.* 化学
flexible	['fleksəbl] *adj.* 灵活的
high-tech	[haɪtek] *adj.* 高科技的，高技术的
physical	['fɪzɪkl] *adj.* 身体的
stimulation	[ˌstɪmjʊ'leɪʃn] *n.* 刺激，激励
leisure	['leʒə(r)] *adj.* 休闲的，空闲的
essence	['esns] *n.* 精华；本质，内涵
orchestral	[ɔː'kestrəl] *adj.* 管弦乐的，管弦乐队的
invigorate	[ɪn'vɪgəreɪt] *v.* 鼓舞
circuit	['sɜːkɪt] *n.* 回路
sprout	[spraʊt] *v.* 出现，涌现出
novelty	['nɒvltɪ] *n.* 新奇，新奇的事物
neurologist	[njʊə'rɒlədʒɪst] *n.* 神经病学家，神经专家
therapy	['θerəpɪ] *n.* 治疗
paralysis	[pə'ræləsɪs] *n.* 瘫痪，停顿
motivation	[ˌməʊtɪ'veɪʃn] *n.* 动机，动力
strategy	['strætədʒɪ] *n.* 战略，策略
explicitly	[ɪk'splɪsɪtlɪ] *adv.* 明确地，明白地
consciousness	['kɒnʃəsnɪs] *n.* 意识，知觉
invisible	[ɪn'vɪzəbl] *adj.* 无形的，看不见的，隐形的

pattern	['pætn] *n.* 模式
metaphor	['metəfə(r)] *n.* 暗喻，隐喻，比喻（源于希腊语 "metapherein"，"meta" 意为 "从一边到另一边"；"pherein" 的意思是 "传达、传送"，二者合一意指用一个事物的某些特征认识另一事物）
sensible	['sensəbl] *adj.* 明智的
technique	[tek'niːk] *n.* 技巧，技术，手法
osmosis	[ɒz'məʊsɪs] *n.* 潜移默化，耳濡目染

▶ 雅思阅读真题同义词考点

therapy	—treatment, medical care
label	—mark, tag, classify
symbol	—sign, icon, representation
refresh	—renew, restore, rejuvenate, recover
sponsor	—back up, fund, promote, support
exotic	—foreign, strange, colourful

CHAPTER 5

Multiple Choice
选择题

介绍：可细分为1.单选题（4选1）；2.多选题；3.选标题（全文中心）。

概率：不是每次考试都出现。

难度：★★★☆☆

选择题

雅思机考（IELTS Computer Based）界面及说明：

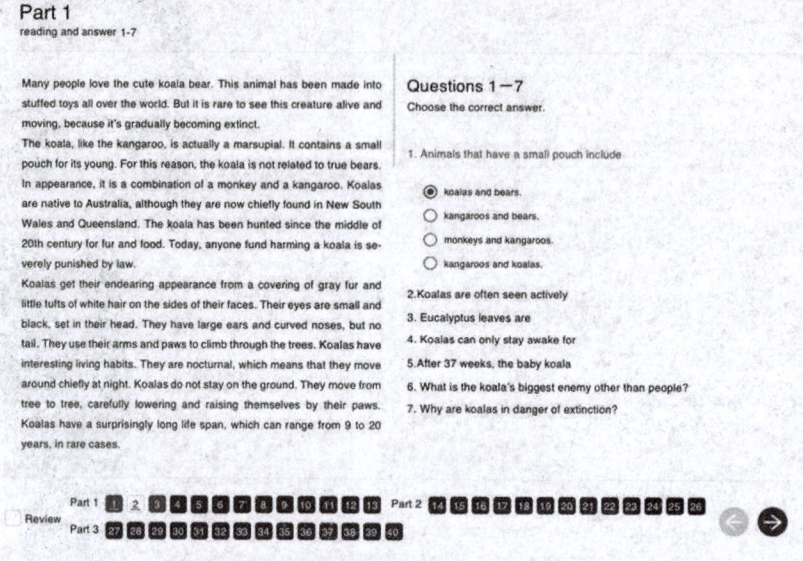

选择题又分为两类：单选题和多选题，两者都是左侧显示文章，右侧显示题目。

如何答题：点击正确答案。

修改答案：点击新答案。

清除答案：再次点击该答案。

修改多选题中任意一个答案：先点击想要消除的答案，再点击新答案。

www.ieltscb.com 提供免费机考练习。

下篇导读：【考拉】

考试时间：2010-06-26，2013-04-13……

　　澳大利亚国宝。多么可爱的动物啊，好温柔，一动不动。原来它是中毒了。什么导致它们濒临灭绝？还有，考拉暴走愤怒的表现很可爱，打嗝！hiccup？ ☺

Reading Passage 47

Koala

Many people love the cute koala bear. This animal has been made into stuffed toys all over the world. But it is rare to see this creature alive and moving, because it's gradually becoming extinct.

The koala, like the kangaroo, is actually a marsupial. It contains a small pouch for its young. For this reason, the koala is not related to true bears. In appearance, it is a combination of a monkey and a kangaroo. Koalas are native to Australia, although they are now chiefly found in New South Wales and Queensland. The koala has been hunted since the middle of 20th century for fur and food. Today, anyone fund harming a koala is severely punished by law.

Koalas get their endearing appearance from a covering of gray fur and little tufts of white hair on the sides of their faces. Their eyes are small and black, set in their head. They have large ears and curved noses, but no tail. They use their arms and paws to climb through the trees. Koalas have interesting living habits. They are nocturnal, which means that they move around chiefly at night. Koalas do not stay on the ground. They move from tree to tree, carefully lowering and raising themselves by their paws. Koalas have a surprisingly long life span, which can range from 9 to 20 years, in rare cases.

The Koala is the only mammal, other than the Greater Glider and Ringtail Possum, which can survive on a diet of eucalytus leaves. Eucalyptus leaves are very fibrous and low in nutrition, and to most animals are extremely poisonous. To cope with such a diet, nature has equipped koalas with specialised adaptations. A very slow metabolic rate allows koalas to retain food within their digestive system for a relatively long period of time, maximising the amount of energy able to be extracted. At the same time, this slow metabolic rate minimises energy requirements. Koalas also sleep somewhere between 18 and 22 hours each day in order to conserve energy. Koalas eat only the leaves of the eucalyptus, which is another reason that they are now becoming extinct. The eucalyptus tree is disappearing from their natural habitats, fighting a battle against extinction all its own.

Koalas raise their young in a special way. A cub is usually about one inch at birth, where it lays in the mother's pouch. It will stay in the pouch for a little over half a year, during which time the mother carries and feeds the baby. At seven weeks, a tiny koala has a head larger than its body, of about 26 millimetres. By 22 weeks, the baby begins to turn in the pouch and kick, occasionally looking out into the natural world. By 24 weeks, the cub is fully covered with fur, and brain development is complete. Teeth are fully formed. At thirty weeks, the cub climbs in and out of the pouch, clinging to the mother's belly in agreeable weather. From 37 weeks onward, the baby is independent of the mother, although it will rarely move more than a metre away from her in its first few weeks. Baby koalas are strongly protected by their mothers, and the familial bond is very strong in the koala world. One can tell if a baby is separated from its mother by tiny squeaks of panic.

Because koala bears are so cute and rare, they are often found in zoos, where their natural environment can be maintained. Although they only wake at night, sometimes it is possible to see them moving around at twilight and early morning. During the day, they mainly sleep in trees, but they are fun to watch, nonetheless.

The largest force to contribute to koala extinction has been hunting. Koala furs are luxurious and warm, and at one point they were in demand all over the world. In 1924, at least 2.1 million skins were exported from Australia alone! The koala's worst enemy, besides hunters, is fire. When a tree is inflamed, often they cannot run fast enough to save themselves. Baby koalas are in danger around certain kinds of lizards and eagles, although they are protected today by natural habitats set up for them. It is interesting to note that many koalas die from being hit by cars, and some are even attacked by dogs! Their main form of defense is climbing, but they sometimes try to use their paws.

Koalas are in grave danger also because of other threats. Their source of food is depleting, because the eucalyptus is susceptible to loggers, pharmacists and changing weather. The koala's body chemistry is also delicate, and it is extremely susceptible to diseases and bacteria not native to its environment. Finally, a certain strain of venereal disease is killing off many Australian koalas, causing deformity at birth and short life spans.

The war to save koalas has been effective. Their numbers have increased slightly, and actions have been taken to curb contact that will spread venereal deformity. In the next few years, their numbers may rise again, bringing them safely out of the danger zone.

Questions 1–6

Choose the appropriate letters A–D and write them in boxes 1–6 on your answer sheet.

1　Animals that have a small pouch include

　A　koalas and bears.

　B　kangaroos and bears.

　C　monkeys and kangaroos.

　D　kangaroos and koalas.

2　Koalas are often seen actively

　A　climbing trees.

　B　on the ground.

　C　during the day.

　D　at night.

3　Eucalyptus leaves are

　A　extremely toxic to all mammals.

　B　only eaten by koalas.

　C　getting rarer and rarer.

　D　low in fibre.

4　Koalas can only stay awake for

　A　18 hours a day.

　B　between 18 and 22 hours a week.

　C　between 2 and 6 hours a week.

　D　between 2 and 6 hours a day.

5　After 37 weeks, the baby koala

　A　lives alone but not far from its mother.

　B　can protect its mother.

C   is isolated from its mother.

D   does not need its mother.

6   What is the koala's biggest enemy other than people?

A   Cars.

B   Lizards and eagles.

C   Dogs.

D   Forest fire.

Questions 7–9

*Choose **THREE** letters A–F.*

Why are koalas in danger of extinction?

A   They are vulnerable to foreign disease.

B   Their life span is short.

C   They are hunted by people.

D   Eucalytus leaves are poisonous.

E   Their birth rate is low.

F   Their food source is decreasing.

▶ 核心词汇

词汇	释义
koala	[kəʊ'ɑːlə] *n.*【动】(=koala bear, coala) 考拉
stuff	[stʌf] *v.* 填充，塞
kangaroo	[ˌkæŋgə'ruː] *n.*【动】袋鼠
pouch	[paʊtʃ] *n.* 小袋，育儿袋
chiefly	['tʃiːflɪ] *adv.* 首要，主要地（同义词：primarily）
endearing	[ɪn'dɪərɪŋ] *adj.* 惹人喜爱的
curve	[kɜːv] *v.* 弯，使弯曲（作名词指"曲线，曲线图"。雅思A类小作文常见）
ringtail	['rɪŋteɪl] *n.*【动】浣熊
eucalyptus	[ˌjuːkə'lɪptəs] *n.* 桉树
fibrous	['faɪbrəs] *adj.* 含纤维的，纤维性的（名词形式：fiber）
extremely	[ɪk'striːmlɪ] *adv.* 极端地，非常地
adaptation	[ˌædæp'teɪʃn] *n.* 适应性的改变，感官适应性调节
metabolic	[ˌmetə'bɒlɪk] *adj.* 代谢作用的，新陈代谢的（名词形式：metabolism）
relatively	['relətɪvlɪ] *adv.* 相对地；比较地
inflame	[ɪn'fleɪm] *v.* 燃烧
lizard	['lɪzəd] *n.*【动】蜥蜴
habitat	['hæbɪtæt] *n.*（动、植物的）产地，栖息地
cub	[kʌb] *n.* 幼兽
millimetre	['mɪlɪmiːtə(r)] *n.* 毫米（centimetre厘米）
agreeable weather	宜人的天气
onward	['ɒnwəd] *adj.* 向前的
squeak	[skwiːk] *n.* 尖叫声，吱吱声
twilight	['twaɪlaɪt] *n.* 黎明（吸血鬼Vampire主题经典电影《暮光之城》Twilight）
susceptible	[sə'septəbl] *adj.*（与to连用）易受影响的
logger	['lɒgə(r)] *n.* 伐木工
pharmacist	['fɑːməsɪst] *n.* 制药者，药商；药剂师
venereal	[və'nɪərɪəl] *adj.* 性交的，性病的
deformity	[dɪ'fɔːmətɪ] *n.* 残缺，畸形，残废，畸形的人或物
demand	[dɪ'mɑːnd] *n.* 要求，请求
clearance	['klɪərəns] *n.* 清除
transmit	[træns'mɪt] *v.* 传播，传递；传染
slightly	['slaɪtlɪ] *adv.* 轻微地，有一点儿，略

curb	[kɜːb] *v.* 控制，约束（该词源于curve，指弯曲的勒马链，勒马索，用于控制马匹。）

▶ 雅思阅读真题同义词考点

curve	—bend, curl, turn, twist
demand	—want, require, need
susceptible	—vulnerable, fragile, subject
transmit	—send, deliver, transfer
curb	—control, restrain, check

下篇导读：　【小提琴制作】

考试时间：　2010-02-27，2012-05-19，2014-06-28……

　　独奏之王小提琴的历史；古代小提琴工匠和现代大规模生产的比较；著名的意大利制琴师阿玛蒂及其两位巨匠学徒；为什么古董小提琴价值千万？ :)

Reading Passage 48

Violin Making

With many stringed instruments (by "stringed" we refer to instruments played with a bow) in existence, all over the world and throughout history, the violin may be the most iconic stringed instrument—at least with regard to soloing. The most expensive instruments in existence today are particular violins, with makers studying the art all over the world.

The idea of bowed stringed instruments may have come to Europe from Asia, either from the Far East or from the Indian subcontinent. It is also possible that the origin of bowed strings is found in the Middle East, or, most likely of all, it may be that the idea of producing music by applying an ordinary hunting bow to a taut string was discovered independently in many parts of the world.

Amazingly, no one knows who exactly invented the violin. All we know for sure is that it first came to light in the north of Italy in the late 15th century or so, the product of a long line of experimentation by stringed-instrument makers. (The name luthier, as applied to stringed instrument makers reflects their earlier role as lute makers and repairers.) Cultural developments of the Renaissance take credit for the inception of the violin. Makers added a fingerboard to the medieval instrument, allowing the instrument to be bowed and strings shortened with fingers, rather than only plucked. The viola da braccio was the direct predecessor of the violin, eventually being made with four strings tuned in fifths (the violin's string intervals), the f-holes, and a peg-box for tuning. Compared to most other string-family instruments, the violin makes a higher, "soprano" sound, with short strings making a clear tonal sound lending itself for soloing. Production of sound comes from horse hair attached to a wooden bow, coated with "rosin" made from the resin of tree sap.

Violin making reached its apogee sometime in the seventeenth century in the town of Cremona, near the Po River. The Modern violin differs from the Baroque era (of the 17th and 18th centuries) in a few aspects: the neck of the modern violin slopes downward where the Baroque's extents straight, and the modern fingerboard goes much farther toward the bridge of the violin. The Baroque bow differs from the modern bow also, with the wood parallel to the hair until curving toward downward at the tip, while the modern bow curves downward and then back up in a very slight concave shape.

If you are a violinist, you would love to have an antique violin in your hands right now. Antique violins, just like other antiques, are priced objects that have a long history behind them. And they are probably very rare today, and valued at high prices, and sometimes reach millions of dollars.

Why can antique violins command such high prices in auctions? The first ever violin made was in 1555 by famous violin maker Andrea Amati. He was the most well-known violin maker in the 16th century. However, into the 17th century, Amati's disciples, Antonio Stradivari and Guarneri del Gesu rose to the stage. Stradivari and Guarneri improved and refine the violin models, which also become the definite model for violins today. While they are both rivals in violin-making, Stradivari and Guarneri went to on become famous violin makers in the 17th and 18th century, and also probably the best violin makers in history of violin. Though numerous violin makers come after them, they were no where near the top quality workmanship of the violin making masters. Stradivari and Guarneri together had just over a thousand violins that are still in existence today. Hence, the rarity, along with the creator of the violin, give the antique violins reasons to command million-dollar prices at public auctions.

The quality of the materials used to make the antique violins does determine the price of the violins too. You may notice that famous violins were made in the period between 1700 and 1725. Many termed this Stradivari's "golden period". Many experts discussed that the violins made during the period were considered the best due to the presence of a special quality of wood which only exist during that period.

For the violinmaker, wood is the most important material; it is only natural that the correct choice of wood is vital in order to achieve the best quality of sound. Wood that is too heavy because of its specific weight cannot be used—although it looks perhaps marvelous. It is also because of this aspect that mass-production of violins has to fail: these days even with modern, computer-controlled machines; the works is too mechanical, without any consideration for materials used. Mass-production will never fulfill the fundamental aspect, because each piece of wood needs to be treated differently, even when the wood is chopped out of the same trunk, the single pieces are very different of each other. At the lower end of the trunk, the wood is generally harder than at the top, also, parts which grew in the sunshine obviously differ from parts that grew in the shadow.

However, some experts believe that despite a widespread belief in the old violins' superiority and the millions of dollars it now costs to buy a Stradivarius, the fiddles made by the old masters do not in fact sound better than high-quality modern instruments, according to a blindfolded hearing test. The modern instruments are very easy to play and sound good to ears, but what made the old instruments great was their power in a hall.

Questions 1–6

Choose the appropriate letters A–D and write them in boxes 1–5 on your answer sheet.

1 Bowed stringed instruments were invented most possibly by

   A hunters who used a bow and string to produce sound.

   B people who lived in the Middle East.

   C Italian in the late 15th century.

   D luthier whose earlier job was to make and repair lutes.

2 The following statements describe the features of violin *EXCEPT*?

   A It has the f-holes and four strings.

   B It has a fingerboard and a peg-box.

   C Its strings can be shortened with fingers.

   D It can only be plucked.

3 One reason why antique violins are so valuable is that

   A they were made several centuries ago.

   B most of them were made by Andrea Amati.

   C their makers were students of Andrea Amati.

   D they were made by masters and remained fewer.

4 Large scale production may not make the best violin because

   A the best wood with special qualities no longer exists.

   B even computer-controlled machines cannot pick out the correct wood.

   C wood is too heavy to be applied to mass-production.

   D harder wood is better and has to be chopped out manually.

5 According to a blindfolded hearing experiment,

   A a modern violin sounds better than a Stradivarius.

   B a Stradivarius sounds better than a modern violin.

C a Stradivarius sounds better in a special place.

D audiences can distinguish a modern violin and a Stradivarius.

Questions 6–9

*Choose **FOUR** letters, A–G.*

According to the passage above, what are the difference between The Modern and the Baroque's violin?

A The coating rosin

B The shape of the bow

C The horse hair

D The length of the fingerboard

E The bridge of the violin

F The shape of the neck

G The sound in a hall

10 Which of the following is the most suitable heading for the Reading Passage?

A The factors in determining the price of violins

B The origin of the violin and violin making

C The process of how to make a violin

D The difference between ancient and modern violin makers

▶ 核心词汇

词汇	释义
string	[strɪŋ] *n.* 弦；线，细绳
bow	[baʊ] *n.* 弓（另一词义为"鞠躬"）
instrument	['ɪnstrəmənt] *n.* 乐器；工具
iconic	[aɪˈkɒnɪk] *adj.* 符号的；图标的（名词形式：icon）
solo	[ˈsəʊləʊ] *n.* 独奏（sol-指单独的。如：solely *adv.* 独自地，单独地。还有前面学过的solitude, isolation）
taut	[tɔːt] *adj.* 紧的，绷紧的
lute	[luːt] *n.* 琵琶（flute笛；drum 鼓；piano 钢琴；guitar 吉他；bass 贝斯；harmonica 口琴；harp竖琴）
luthier	[ˈluːtɪə] *n.* 拨弦乐器制作匠
inception	[ɪnˈsepʃn] *n.* 开始，开端
medieval	[ˌmediˈiːvl] *adj.* 中古的，中世纪的
soprano	[səˈprɑːnəʊ] *adj.* 最高音的
tonal	[ˈtəʊnl] *adj.* 声调的，调性的
rosin	[ˈrɒzɪn] *n.* 松香，树脂
sap	[sæp] *n.* 树液
apogee	[ˈæpədʒiː] *n.* 最高点
slope	[sləʊp] *v.* 倾斜
parallel	[ˈpærəlel] *v.* 使平行
concave	[kɒnˈkeɪv] *n.* 凹面，成凹形（反义词：convex）
antique	[ænˈtiːk] *adj.* 古老的，古代的
auction	[ˈɔːkʃn] *n.* 拍卖
rival	[ˈraɪvl] *n.* 对手，竞争者
fulfill	[fʊlˈfɪl] *v.* 履行，实现，完成
fundamental	[ˌfʌndəˈmentl] *adj.* 基础的
aspect	[ˈæspekt] *n.* 方面
marvelous	[ˈmɑːvələs] *adj.* 不可思议的，非凡的
hall	[hɔːl] *n.* 礼堂，大厅
pluck	[plʌk] *v.* 拨（弦）

▶ 雅思阅读真题同义词考点

rival	—competitor, opponent
fulfill	—carry out, complete, perform, execute
fundamental	—basic, elementary, primary, underlying, preliminary
marvelous	—exceptional, extraordinary, glorious, magnificent, miraculous
pick out	—choose, select, sort out

下篇导读：【厄尔尼诺】

考试时间：2010-02-06，2012-08-11，2013-04-06······

　　厄尔尼诺又叫圣婴现象。形成的原因；如何破坏整个海洋生物的食物链；对全球气候的影响；它的妹子叫拉尼娜，老是跟它反着来。其实考拉的数量减少也和厄尔尼诺有关系，你能从下文找到蛛丝马迹吗？ ☺

Reading Passage 49

El Niño

A Fishermen who ply the waters of the Pacific off the coast of Peru and Ecuador have known for centuries about the El Niño. Every three to seven years during the months of December and January, fish in the coastal waters of these countries virtually vanish, causing the fishing business to come to a standstill. South American fishermen have given this phenomenon the name El Niño, which is Spanish for "the Boy Child," because it comes about the time of the celebration of the birth of the Christ Child. During an El Niño, the physical relationships between wind, ocean currents, oceanic and atmospheric temperature, and biosphere break down into destructive patterns that are second only to the march of the seasons in their impacts to weather conditions around the world.

B The vast tropical Pacific Ocean receives more sunlight than any other region on Earth. Much of this sunlight is stored in the ocean in the form of heat. Typically, the Pacific trade winds blow from east to west, dragging the warm surface waters westward, where they accumulate into a large, deep pool just east of Indonesia, and northeast of Australia. Meanwhile, the deeper, colder waters in the eastern Pacific are allowed to rise to the surface, creating an east-west temperature gradient along the equator known as the thermocline tilt.

C The trade winds tend to lose strength with the onset of springtime in the northern hemisphere. Less water is pushed westward and, consequently, waters in the central and eastern Pacific begin to heat up (usually several degrees Fahrenheit) and the thermocline tilt diminishes. But the trade winds are usually replenished by the Asian summer monsoon, and the delicate balance of the thermocline tilt is again maintained.

D Sometimes, and for reasons not fully understood, the trade winds do not replenish, or even reverse direction to blow from west to east. When this happens, the ocean responds in several ways. Warm surface waters from the large, warm pool east of Indonesia begin to move eastward. Moreover, the natural spring warming in the central

Pacific is allowed to continue and also spread eastward through the summer and fall. Beneath the surface, the thermocline along the equator flattens as the warm waters at the surface effectively act as a 300-foot-deep cap preventing the colder, deeper waters from upwelling. As a result, the large central and eastern Pacific regions warm up (over a period of about 6 months) into an El Niño. On average, these waters warm by 3°F to 5°F, but in some places the waters can peak at more than 10°F higher than normal.

E In the east, as temperatures increase, the water expands, causing sea levels to rise anywhere from inches to as much as a foot. But in the western Pacific, sea level drops as much of the warm surface water flows eastward. During the 1982-83 El Niño, this drop in sea level exposed and destroyed upper layers of coral reefs surrounding many western Pacific islands.

F During normal years, when there is a steep thermocline tilt, the cold, deep currents flowing from Antarctica up the west coast of South America are allowed to upwell, bringing essential nutrients that would otherwise lie at the bottom. Phytoplankton living near the surface depend upon these nutrients for survival. In turn, fish and mammals depend upon phytoplankton as the very foundation of the marine food chain. As previously explained, the warm surface waters of an El Niño prevent this upwelling, effectively starving the phytoplankton population there and those animals higher up the food chain that depend upon it. Fishermen in Peru and Ecuador generally suffer heavy losses in their anchovy and sardine industries.

G At Christmas Island, as a result of the sea level rise during the 1982-83 El Niño, sea birds abandoned their young and flew out over a wide expanse of ocean in a desperate search for food. Along the coast of Peru during that same time period, 25 percent of the adult fur seal and sea lion populations starved to death, and all of the pups in both populations died. Similar losses were experienced in many fish populations.

H Meanwhile, over a six-month period about 100 inches of rainfall fell in Ecuador and northern Peru—ordinarily a desert region. Vegetation thrived and the region grew lush with grasslands and lakes, attracting swarms of grasshoppers and, subsequently, birds and frogs that fed on the grasshoppers. Many fish that had migrated upstream during the coastal flooding became trapped in the drying lakes and were harvested by local residents. Shrimp harvests were also very high in some of the coastal flood regions, but so too was the incidence of malaria cases due to thriving mosquito populations.

I El Niño's effects are not limited to the tropical regions off the western coasts of Peru and Ecuador. Its effects are felt all over the world, where the disruption of normal local weather patterns can have tragic and/or profound economic consequences. As warm water migrates eastward, increased heat and moisture rises into the atmosphere, altering the weather patterns in neighbouring regions, which in turn can ripple out to affect still other region weather patterns around the globe. For instance, a severe El Niño will enhance the jet stream over the western Pacific and shift it eastward, leading to stronger winter storms over California and the southern United States, with accompanying floods and landslides. In contrast, El Niño can also cause severe droughts over Australia, Indonesia, and parts of southern Asia.

J While El Niño is known to lower the probability of hurricanes in the Atlantic, it increases the chances of cyclones and typhoons in the Pacific. The 1982-83 El Niño is estimated by NOAA to have caused some $8 billion in damages due to floods, severe storms, droughts and fires around the world.

K And that's not the end of it. It is not uncommon for an El Niño winter to be followed by a La Niña one—where climate patterns and worldwide effects are, for the most part, the opposite of those produced by El Niño. Where there was flooding there is drought, where winter weather was abnormally mild, it turns abnormally harsh. La Niñas have followed El Niños three times in the past 15 years—after the 1982-83 event and after those of 1986-87 and 1995.

Questions 1–5

Choose the appropriate letters A–D and write them in boxes 1–5 on your answer sheet.

1 Why do people call this natural phenomenon El Niño?

    A Fishermen use this name to celebrate the birth of their children.

    B It is the name of a Spanish.

    C It happens around the time of Christmas.

    D It has negative impacts on weather.

2 According to paragraph B, surface waters in the eastern Pacific along the equator

    A are lower than those in the west.

    B are higher than those in the west.

    C have the same temperature as those in the west.

    D create a temperature gradient.

3 What is the writer doing in paragraph B, C, and D?

    A Explain how the thermocline tilt is created.

    B Propose a hypothesis about El Niño.

    C Describe the features of trade winds.

    D Illustrate the process of how El Niño forms.

4 How does El Niño affect coral reefs?

    A They are ruined by warm water.

    B They are destroyed due to rising sea level.

    C They are exposed to the air due to declining sea level.

    D They surround many islands.

5 Which of the following describes the marine food chain from bottom to top sequence?

    A Phytoplankton, nutrients, fish, sea birds

    B Nutrients, phytoplankton, fish, sea birds

C Fish, phytoplankton, nutrients, sea birds

D Sea birds, fish, nutrients, phytoplankton

Questions 6–9

*Choose **FOUR** letters, A–H.*

What are the impacts of El Niño mentioned by the passage?

A Change of landscape

B Many hurricanes

C Preventing La Niña

D Short of food source for mammals

E Causing world financial crisis

F Epidemic disease among people

G Global weather abnormality

H Long winter

10 What does this passage mainly discuss?

A The relation between El Niño and La Niña

B How El Niño emerges and how to predict it

C The formation and effects of El Niño

D How to prevent El Niño

E El Niño and natural disasters

▶ 核心词汇

词汇	释义
ply	[plaɪ] *v.* 使用（工具）；经营生意
virtually	['vɜːtʃʊəlɪ] *adv.* 事实上
standstill	['stændstɪl] *n.* 停顿，停止，停滞
biosphere	['baɪəʊsfɪə(r)] *n.* 生物圈，生物界
destructive	[dɪ'strʌktɪv] *adj.* 破坏性的，毁灭性的
tropical	['trɒpɪkl] *adj.* 热带的
gradient	['greɪdɪənt] *n.* 【物】梯度，（温度、气压等）变化率
thermocline	['θɜːməˌklaɪn] *n.* 温跃层，温度突变层
onset	['ɒnset] *n.* 攻击，袭击
diminish	[dɪ'mɪnɪʃ] *v.* （使）减少，缩小
replenish	[rɪ'plenɪʃ] *v.* 补充
flatten	['flætn] *v.* 变平，使（某物）变平
expose	[ɪk'spəʊz] *v.* 使暴露；使遭受
steep	[stiːp] *adj.* 陡峭的；极高的
nutrient	['njuːtrɪənt] *n.* 营养物，营养品，养分
phytoplankton	[ˌfaɪtəʊ'plæŋktən] *n.* 浮游植物
coral	['kɒrəl] *n.* 珊瑚
reef	[riːf] *n.* 礁石
anchovy	['æntʃəvɪ] *n.* 凤尾鱼，鳀鱼
starve	[stɑːv] *v.* 饿死（famine *n.* 饥荒）
pup	[pʌp] *n.* 幼崽，幼畜
grasshopper	['grɑːshɒpə(r)] *n.* 蚱蜢（区别：locust 蝗虫；cockroach 蟑螂）
disruption	[dɪs'rʌpʃn] *n.* 分裂，瓦解
moisture	['mɒɪstʃə(r)] *n.* 水分，湿气
enhance	[ɪn'hɑːns] *v.* 提高，增加，加强
cyclone	['saɪkləʊn] *n.* 气旋
hurricane	['hʌrɪkən] *n.* 飓风（一起记忆各种natural disaster相关单词：earthquake 地震；volcano 火山；tornado 龙卷风；typhoon 台风；tsunami 海啸；avalanche 雪崩；mudslide 泥石流；flood 洪水；drought 干旱；famine 饥荒；plague 瘟疫；glacier 冰川；iceberg 冰山）
harsh	[hɑːʃ] *adj.* 粗糙的；刺耳的；残酷的

▶ 雅思阅读真题同义词考点

replenish	—complement, furnish, provide, supply
flatten	—level, smooth
steep	—sharp, dramatic, noticeable
enhance	—better, enrich, improve, uplift
harsh	—coarse, rough, tough, rude

下篇导读：【麻鸦回归】

考试时间：2010-01-09，2012-03-08，2013-03-09……

　　麻鸦，一种在英国已绝迹百年的小鸟又回来了！全国人民陶醉在雄鸟高亢嘹亮的叫声中。来吧，一起保护麻鸦。 ☺

Reading Passage 50

Booming Bittern

The boom of the bittern is being heard across Britain once again, after more than a century in which the bird has hovered on the edge of extinction.

Noted for its foghorn-like call or "boom", the bittern has made a recovery in numbers that the Royal Society for the Protection of Birds (RSPB) described last year as "a phenomenal success".

However, experts warn that the bird, one of Britain's rarest, still faces severe threats posed by climate change. "Bitterns are not out of danger yet," said Grahame Madge of the RSPB. "On the other hand, this is a very encouraging trend."

Bitterns are a member of the heron family and have the long legs, long neck, dagger-like beak and broad rounded wings. They are smaller than a grey heron at 70 -80 cms long. Their plumage is a mixture of browns and buffs with lots of dark brown and black streaks and bars giving it a mottled appearance. In flight the rounded wings curve downwards giving them an almost owl-like appearance. Depending on the light they can appear warm orange-brown to dark brown or even black.

The bittern is a secretive bird and its subtle colouring makes it hard to spot in its wetland surroundings—although its mating call testifies to its presence. As yet, scientists do yet fully understand how the male bittern makes its deep "booming" call. It is thought that the bird gulps in air, before expelling it again to produce its loud "boom," which can be heard up to 4.5km (2.8 miles) away. Males are thought to "boom" to alert female bitterns to their presence. Usually the birds "boom" in the twilight at dusk, hidden among the darkness and reeds. Even seeing a bittern in daylight is rare, let alone seeing one produce its mating call.

It was once common across the UK, but numbers began to fall in the Middle Ages—the bird was considered a delicacy and was eaten at banquets up to Tudor times. In the 18th and 19th centuries, the bird became a popular target for taxidermists. The drainage of England's wetlands devastated the surviving population and by 1886 the bird had disappeared from Britain.

Early in the 20th century the population slowly began to return and by the 1950s there were 60 bitterns in the UK, but water pollution then destroyed its habitat. By 1997, the bird's numbers had fallen back to 11.

"We created a research programme to save the bittern and discovered the major threat was not the loss of their habitat, but a degradation of it," said Madge. "Bitterns prefer living in particularly wet reed beds, where they can fish easily. But mud often builds up and the reed beds dry up. In large wetlands, small patches will always dry up and new ones form. However, nature reserves are hemmed in today and there is little opportunity for new reed beds to form when the old ones die out." Litter only makes the problem worse, he added.

The bittern has been classified by the EU as a "priority species". With European funding, the RSPB lowered reed beds at several reserves and pumped out mud, creating improved habitats. A new site was set up at Lakenheath in Suffolk. Today there are at least 100 bitterns, most of them in southern England.

However, climate change means some habitats are vulnerable to rising sea levels, particularly the important RSPB site at Minsmere in Suffolk, where tides could flood freshwater areas with salt water, ruining them for the bittern. Droughts also endanger the species by drying out wetlands.

The RSPB is now working to create new inland nesting areas. "We no longer have a landscape where natural processes can take place on a large scale, so conservationists must work within the areas that are available," said Madge.

"Creating bigger wetlands not only houses a larger diversity of species but also buffers against climate change. If the RSPB's legacy of habitat creation and preservation is maintained, the unique and dynamic bittern's boom can continue to sound out across our wetlands."

Conservationists are particularly excited that Kingfisher's Bridge—a privately-owned newly-created site in Cambridgeshire—has been the centre for recolonisation of the Fens. The 150-acre wetland site—which in 1995 was Grade 1 arable land—has been partially converted to reed bed by the landowner Andrew Green, with help from wildlife consultant Roger Beecroft.

Andrew Green, the landowner, said: "After all our hard work, we are delighted that bitterns are nesting again in the Fens. We think the key to the project's success is dependent upon a number of factors: good evidence-based habitat management; pure water and control of water levels; the creation of a rich fishery, providing excellent feeding opportunities for bitterns; and the rigorous control of foxes and mink. We are grateful to the RSPB for its research into bitterns, which has helped design an ideal site, and for the supply of reed seeds."

Dr Mark Avery added: "If we thought about it, the RSPB might just be a little envious that Andrew Green has been the first landowner since 1938 to have nesting bitterns in the Fens. We congratulate Andrew on his fantastic achievement and look forward to the spread of this fantastic bird to its rightful home in the heart of East Anglia and, hopefully, to our fenland recreation sites too!"

Questions 1–6

Choose the appropriate letters A–D and write them in boxes 1–5 on your answer sheet.

1 Experts believe that the bittern

   A is still on the edge of dying out.

   B is a successful species.

   C can fight climate change.

   D is disappearing.

2 It is difficult to find a bittern in its habitat because

   A it is smaller than a grey heron.

   B it hides among the darkness.

   C its appearance is colourful.

   D it is adept at camouflage.

3 The bittern produces loud booming call to

   A alert its natural enemy.

   B attract the female.

   C gulp in air.

   D communicate with other birds.

4 In the Middle Ages the number declined because

   A bitterns vanished from Britain.

   B bitterns were eaten by eagles.

   C bitterns became a target of hunters.

   D bitterns became a popular food.

5 Grahame Madge of the RSPB said the main threat to bitterns is that

   A nature reserves are few.

   B they had no where to live.

C   their habitat deteriorates.

D   waste pollutes their habitat.

6   Climate change poses a danger to bitterns because

A   sea water could flood wetlands.

B   they prefer the colder weather.

C   reed beds become lower.

D   their breeding season is changed.

Questions 7–10

*Choose **FOUR** letters, A–H.*

According to Andrew Green, what are the essential factors when protecting bitterns?

A   Control of other birds

B   Amply food provision

C   Providing reed seeds

D   Limiting predators

E   Encouraging breeding

F   Protecting freshwater

G   Well-managed habitat

H   Increasing sea level

▶ 核心词汇

词汇	释义
boom	[buːm] *v.* 繁荣；发隆隆声（该文标题含义双关）
bittern	['bɪtən] *n.* 麻鸦
heron	['herən] *n.* 鹭，苍鹭
streak	[striːk] *n.* 条纹，线条
secretive	['siːkrətɪv] *adj.* 秘密的（名词形式：secret 秘密。区别：secrete *v.* 分泌）
expel	[ɪk'spel] *v.* 驱逐，开除
dusk	[dʌsk] *n.* 黄昏（区别：dust 灰尘）
let alone	更别提（同义表达：not to mention）
delicacy	['delɪkəsɪ] *n.* 美味，佳肴（形容词形式：delicious）
banquet	['bæŋkwɪt] *n.* 宴会，盛宴
legacy	['legəsɪ] *n.* 遗产
habitat	['hæbɪtæt] *n.*【生态】栖息地，产地
reserve	[rɪ'zɜːv] *n.* 保留地（动词词义为：预订；保存）
wetland	['wetlənd] *n.* 湿地
degradation	[ˌdegrə'deɪʃn] *n.* 退化
reed	[riːd] *n.* 芦苇
landscape	['lændskeɪp] *n.* 风景，景色
diversity	[daɪ'vɜːsətɪ] *n.* 多样性，差异
consultant	[kən'sʌltənt] *n.* 顾问，咨询者
evidence-based	['evɪdənsbeɪst] *adj.* 基于证据的
fishery	['fɪʃərɪ] *n.* 渔业，渔场
rigorous	['rɪgərəs] *adj.* 严格的，严厉的
mink	[mɪŋk] *n.* 水貂
adept	[ə'dept] *adj.* 熟练的，拿手的（be adept at 擅长于）
camouflage	['kæməflɑːʒ] *n.* 伪装
gulp	[gʌlp] *v.* 吞咽

▶ 雅思阅读真题同义词考点

boom	—flourish, prosper, thrive
legacy	—heritage, heredity
rigorous	—hard, harsh, relentless, rigid, severe, strict
adept	—apt, expert, proficient, skillful, good at
camouflage	—disguise, masquerade, mask, pretence

CHAPTER 6

Diagram
图表题

介绍：可细分为1. 填表格；2. 填示意图；3. 填流程图；4. 选图。

概率：不是每次考试都出现。

难度：★☆☆☆☆

图表题

雅思机考 (IELTS Computer Based) 界面及说明:

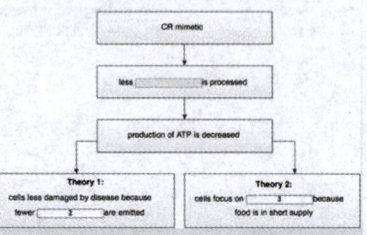

图表题有两种答题形式，填空题和选择题。右侧是文章，左侧是图标答题区。

填空题：将答案直接填入输入框内。

选择题：查看右侧文章，在左侧选择相应的答案。一般为单选题。

www.ieltscb.com 提供免费机考练习。

下篇导读：【播种机的发明】

考试时间：2012-05-19……

　　还记得历史教科书上说英国工业革命推动了人类生产力的进步。比如大家都知道瓦特发明了蒸汽机。对于大家还不熟悉的，英国人就通过雅思阅读考试来给全球考生普及并炫耀一下：Jethro Tull发明了播种机，拉开了农业机械化的序幕。☺

Reading Passage 51

Jethro Tull
and Seed Drill

While a British rock band made his name famous nearly 300 years after his birth, Jethro Tull (1664—1741) was renowned in his own right as an agricultural pioneer and the inventor of the seed drill, the horse drawn hoe, and an improved plough, all major developments in the 18th century agricultural revolution, a period marked by rapid advancements in agricultural productivity and developments in farming technology.

Tull was born in Basildon, Berskhire, England in 1664. He studied law and graduated from Oxford University in 1699. Although he was admitted to the bar in the same year, he never practiced law. Tull began farming on his father's land in 1700 and took great interest in agricultural processes.

At the time, farmers typically planted crop seeds by carrying the seeds in a bag and walking up and down the field while randomly throwing or broadcasting the seed by hand on to the ploughed and harrowed ground. Tull deemed the method inefficient as the seed was not distributed evenly and much of it was wasted and did not take root.

In 1701, Tull solved this problem with an invention called the seed drill. A seed drill is a machine for sowing seeds that exactly positions the seeds in the soil and then covers them. It would sow seeds in uniform rows repeatedly instead of the wasteful method of scattering seeds by hand. The seed is stored in a hopper (seed box) and delivered by a tube into furrows in the ground. The furrows are made by a set of blades, or coulters, attached to the front of the drill. A harrow is drawn behind the drill to cover up the seeds. The seed drill allows farmers to sow seeds in well-spaced rows at specific depths at a specific seed rate; each tube creates a hole of a specific depth, drops in one or more seeds, and covers it over. This invention gave farmers much greater control over the depth that the seed was planted and the ability to cover the seeds without back-tracking. This greater control meant that seeds germinated consistently and in good soil. The result was an increased rate of germination, and a much-improved crop yield. According to Royal Berkshire History, Tull said of his invention, "It was named a drill because when farmers used to sow their beans and peas into channels or furrows by hand, they called that action drilling." Tull's improved drilling method allowed farmers to sow three rows of seeds simultaneously.

Improved Seed Drill

Tull took further scientific interest in plant nourishment. He correctly theorised that plants should be more widely spaced and the soil around them thoroughly broken down during growth. He further theorised that plants surrounded by loose soil would grow better not only during sowing, but in the early stages of growth as well.

Tull's theory, however, was based upon a fundamental error. He believed that the nourishment which the plant took from the earth was in the form of minute particles of soil. He did not believe that animal manure, which was commonly used as fertiliser, provided the plant with nourishment, but rather it provided a fermentative action in breaking up the soil particles. He saw no additional value in manure. He was highly criticised for this belief.

In 1709, he moved to a parcel of inherited land in Hungerford, called Prosperous Farm, where he continued his novel farming methods. In 1711, a pulmonary disorder sent him to Europe in search of treatment and a cure. While traveling, he noted the cultivation methods employed in the vineyards in the Languedoc area of France and in Italy, where it was usual practice to hoe the ground between the vines rather than manuring. On returning to Prosperous in 1714, he applied the same practice on his fields of grain and root crops.

Tull's crops were sown in widely spaced rows to allow the horse, drawing the hoe, to walk without damaging the plants, while enabling tillage to the soil during most of the period of growth. This ongoing cultivation of the soil while the plant was growing was the central point of Tull's theory and the practice continues today. He believed that the cultivation of the soil released nutrients and reduced the need for manure. While apparently successful—he grew wheat in the same field for 13 successive years without manuring—some believe that is more likely that the technique succeeded because it simply prevented weeds from overcrowding and competing with the seed.

At the time, there was much skepticism toward Tull's ideas. His seed drill was not immediately popular in England, although it was quickly adopted by the colonists in New England. In 1731, Jethro Tull published "An Essay on the Principles of Tillage and Vegetation." The book caused great controversy and his theories fell into disrepute, particularly his opinion on the value of manure for plant growth.

Although Tull laid the foundations for modern techniques of sowing and cultivation, a hundred years passed before his seed-drill displaced the ancient method of hand broadcasting the seed. While several other mechanical seed drills had also been invented, Tull's rotary system was a major influence on the agricultural revolution and its impact can still be seen in today's methods and machinery. His seed drill was improved in 1782 by adding gears to the distribution mechanism.

Tull died in the village where he was born in Shalbourne, Berkshire, England, on February 21, 1741, at the age of 67.

Questions 1–4

Label the diagram below.

*Choose **ONE WORD ONLY** from the passage for each answer.*

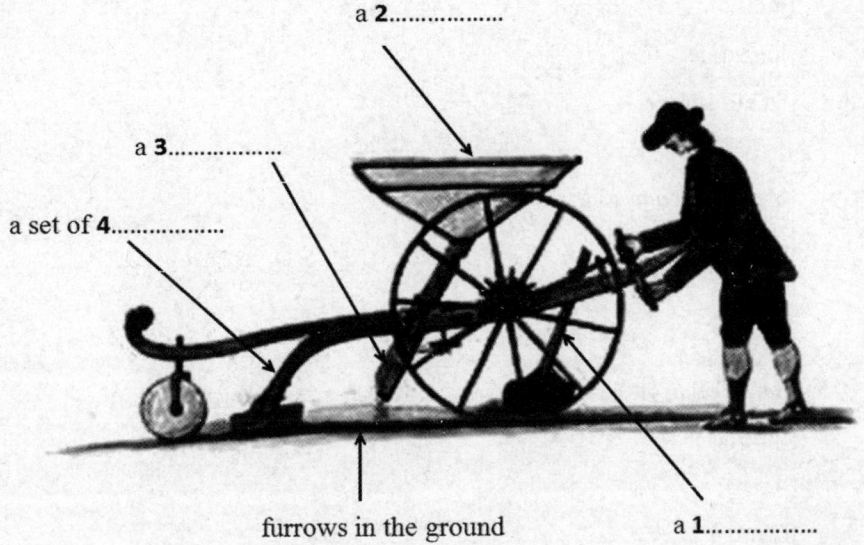

a **2**.................

a **3**.................

a set of **4**.................

furrows in the ground

a **1**.................

▶ **核心词汇**

词汇	释义
renown	[rɪˈnaʊn] *v.* 使有声望（作名词指：声望。同义词：fame, reputation, prestige）
drill	[drɪl] *n.* 钻孔机；播种机
hoe	[həʊ] *n.* 锄头
plough	[plaʊ] *n.* 犁
mark	[mɑːk] *v.* 标志（remark *n.* & *v.* 评论，备注）
rapid	[ˈræpɪd] *adj.* 迅速的
advancement	[ədˈvɑːnsmənt] *n.* 进步
the bar	律师界
randomly	[ˈrændəmlɪ] *adv.* 随便地，随机地
harrow	[ˈhærəʊ] *v.* 耙（地）
deem	[diːm] *v.* 认为，相信
scatter	[ˈskætə(r)] *v.* 分散，散开
hopper	[ˈhɒpə(r)] *n.* 储料器
tube	[tjuːb] *n.* 管子，管道
furrow	[ˈfʌrəʊ] *n.* 犁沟
blade	[bleɪd] *n.* 刀刃，刀片
coulter	[ˈkəʊltə] *n.* 犁刀
germinate	[ˈdʒɜːmɪneɪt] *v.* 发芽，发育，使生长（同义词：sprout萌芽）
sow	[səʊ] *v.* 播种
manure	[məˈnjʊə(r)] *n.* 肥料
fertiliser	[ˈfɜːtəlaɪzə(r)] *n.* 肥料（尤指化学肥料）（形容词形式：fertile）
fermentative	[fɜːˈmentətɪv] *adj.* 引起发酵的
inherited	[ɪnˈherɪtɪd] *adj.* 通过继承得到的（动词形式：inherit 继承，遗传）
pulmonary	[ˈpʌlmənərɪ] *adj.* 肺部的（lung *n.* 肺）
cultivation	[ˌkʌltɪˈveɪʃn] *n.* 耕作；培养，教养
vineyard	[ˈvɪnjəd] *n.* 葡萄园（yard指"院子"，而vin源自拉丁语，指"酒"。后来演化出wine，葡萄酒。vine就是和酒相关的，指葡萄树、葡萄藤啦。所以vineyard就是葡萄园。还有vinegar醋，vine葡萄的 + gar来自拉丁语指sour酸=vinegar像葡萄一样酸的东西。）
tillage	[ˈtɪlɪdʒ] *n.* 耕耘，耕地
ongoing	[ˈɒngəʊɪŋ] *adj.* 进行中的，正在进行的

▶ 雅思阅读真题同义词考点

rapid	—quick, swift, speedy, fast
mark	—manifest, indicate, sign
agriculture	—farming, cultivation, husbandry
deem	—believe, consider, judge, regard, suppose, think
distribute	—scatter, dispense, disperse, spread, allot, allocate
cultivate	—develop, improve, prepare, train, nurture

下篇导读：【深海奇船】

考试时间： 2010-10-14······

　　海洋学家的梦想：穿着牛仔裤和T恤衫坐着电梯到海底做研究，不用穿潜水服，不用担心潜水病。一种会翻跟斗的船实现了这个梦想。 ☺

Reading Passage 52

The Oceanographer's Dream Ship

It is every oceanographer's dream start to the day. Get out of bed, slip on a pair of jeans and a T-shirt, then take a lift to the bottom of the sea. No wetsuits, no submersibles, no decompression tanks, just a permanent trapdoor to the ocean floor.

Nobody's throwing away their wetsuit just yet, but a non-profit group of maritime engineers called the Ocean Technology Foundation reckon they can make the dream come true within ten years. They're planning to build a vessel that will take scientists, divers, tourists or anyone else who'll pay, to the bottom of the sea with the minimum of fuss.

One plan is for a vessel called the Deep Water Flip Ship. On paper at least, this is a huge, tubular boat that measures 330 metres from bow to stern, longer than the Eiffel Tower. To get access to the seabed, the ship first sails to wherever it's needed and then performs an astounding manoeuvre. Three huge ballast tanks on the stern flood with water and the rear part of the ship plunges beneath the waves, pulling the vessel through a 90° flip. Once vertical, more than three-quarters of the ship is submerged while the front end, with its cabins, control rooms and helicopter landing pad, sits up above the water. Most of the equipment on board is designed to rotate so it stays the right way up throughout the flip.

The idea may sound preposterous, but a smaller craft that performs similar maritime gymnastics has been around for nearly 30 years. Dubbed FLIP, or Floating Instrument Platform, it's operated by the Scripps Institution of Oceanography in San Diego, California. FLIP looks like a regular ship with the stern chopped off and a 100-metre pipe welded in its place. The pipe is basically one big ballast tank that floods to make the ship tip over. Once submerged, the tank provides stability so that scientists can park the craft and get on with their experiments.

Besides being able to perform the same manoeuvre, the ship designed by the Ocean Technology Foundation would bear little resemblance to FLIP. For one thing, it's more than three times as long. What's more, its rear portion isn't just a ballast tank but is designed to deposit the researchers as close to the seabed as possible while keeping them at atmospheric pressure. To do this, the hull is a sealed tube which, once flipped, turns into a lift shaft. Along the length of the shaft are laboratories linked to the surface by the lift and stairs.

The flipped ship could stay in one place for weeks or months at a stretch, stabilised by the submerged stern and the ship's propellers. And by varying the amount of water in its ballast tanks, the crew could control how much of the ship is submerged. The basic design has a depth range of 225 to 275 metres, enough to visit the deepest parts of the continental shelf. A wider range would be made possible by removing or adding segments to the hull, because this plan calls for the segments to be bolted together rather than welded. This would also mean specialised labs could be slotted in if need be. At first this would have to be done in dock, but it is hoped that it would eventually be possible at sea.

Pumping the water back out of the ballast tanks would right the craft. The experts estimate the manoeuvre would take around 12 hours, as would flipping from horizontal, but in an emergency the tanks could be blasted out with compressed air and the ship flipped in about a minute.

The flip ship, however, has its drawbacks. While cheaper than the previous type, it would still cost an estimated $200 million. And its depth range is limited. With these problems in mind, Clifford Ness, a retired Electric Boat submarine designer and a member of the Ocean Technology Foundation, came up with an alternative plan. Why not build a massive hinged arm with labs at the end that could be lowered like a penknife blade from the bottom of a ship?

Ness has been working on a plan to attach a 200-metre arm to a disused oil tanker. The appendage would be bolted to one end of the ship and housed in a hollowed-out compartment on the bottom. As with the flip design, the labs at the end of the arm would be designed to rotate, meaning they could be used at any angle. That would give the hinge ship more versatility than the flipper: the arm could be lowered to any depth down to 200 metres.

Economically, the arm also has the edge. While the flip ship would have to be built from scratch, the arm could be added to a converted oil tanker. Thanks to new regulations requiring the phasing out of single-hulled tankers in favour of stronger double-hulled ships, second-hand tankers are two a penny. Ness thinks one could be purchased and converted for around $60 million.

Details remain sketchy, but Ness envisages a lift running up and down the arm to ferry people and equipment to the labs. Extending the arm would take several hours, but the design allows for a 10-minute emergency retraction. The arm would also act as a massive keel, giving the ship tremendous stability. This, of course, would put enormous strain on the hinge. Ness says he's solved the problem but his tricks are under wraps until he can file a patent.

The Ocean Technology Foundation still has some way to go before it has enough money to build a ship. It's prepared to rope in anyone with an interest in the deep sea, from the oil and gas industry to the Navy. But the overall aim is to open up a new era of ocean exploration. Bizarre they may be, but ships that flip or have giant hinged arms might just be the breakthrough oceanography has been waiting for.

Questions 1–3

*Complete the picture below. Choose **NO MORE THAN THREE WORDS** from the passage for each answer.*

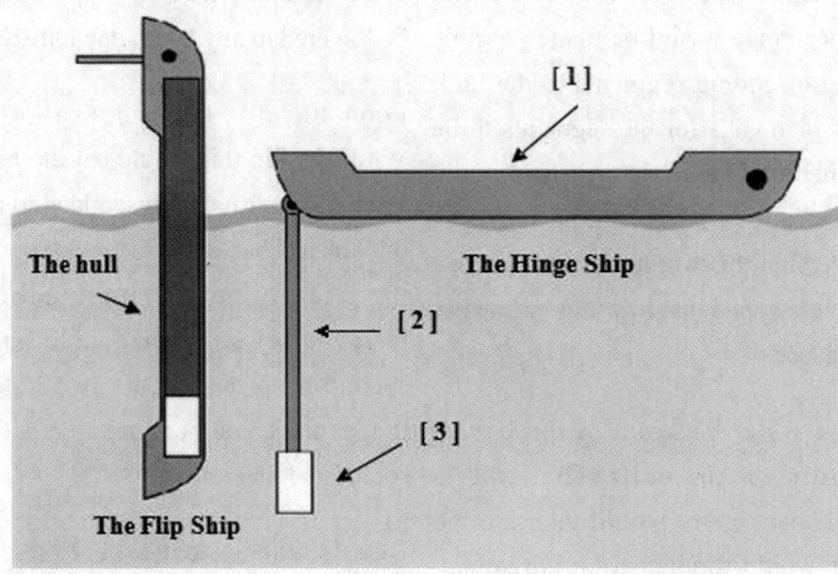

▶ 核心词汇

词汇	释义
flip	[flɪp] *n.* 轻弹，轻抛；（跳水或体操动作中的）空翻
submersible	[səb'mɜːsəbl] *n.* 潜水艇，可在水下作业的船只（动词形式submerse，相当于submerge，名词形式分别对应submersion和submergence。）
trapdoor	['træpdɔː(r)] *n.* 活板门（"trap"是"圈套，陷阱"的意思，因此"trapdoor"的基本含义是"陷阱门"，门板背后是与前边迥然不同的另一番天地，这片天地很可能含有很多危险！）
fuss	[fʌs] *n.* 忙乱，无谓纷扰（这个单词还可以作动词，其形容词形式是"fussy"。）
astounding	[ə'staʊndɪŋ] *adj.* 令人惊骇的，使人大吃一惊的（动词形式"astound"）
manoeuvre	[mə'nuːvə(r)] *n.* （敏捷的）操纵，演习（还可以拼写作"maneuver"。）
rear	[rɪə(r)] *adj.* 后面的，后方的
plunge	[plʌndʒ] *vi.* 投入，插入
vertical	['vɜːtɪkl] *adj.* 垂直的（反义词为前文提到过的"horizontal"。）
submerge	[səb'mɜːdʒ] *v.* 潜水；淹没，沉没（理解为两部分"sub-merge""在……下 + 浸，沾"，"沾入水中"进一步引申为上义。）
rotate	[rəʊ'teɪt] *vi.* 绕轴或中心转动，自转（"公转"对应的动词是"revolve"，其名词形式是"revolution"。）
preposterous	[prɪ'pɒstərəs] *adj.* 荒谬的（简单理解为"pre-post-erous""在……之前 + 在……之后 + 形容词词尾"，基本意思是"把应放在首位的事情放在了末位"，本末倒置，现代英语中引申为"颠倒的，不合情理的"，进一步得到上义。单词"prewar"表示"战前的"，而"postwar"则表示"战后的"。）
gymnastics	[dʒɪm'næstɪks] *n.* 体操训练，体操技巧
weld	[weld] *v.* 焊接
resemblance	[rɪ'zembləns] *n.* 相似（点）（动词形式：resemble）
deposit	[dɪ'pɒzɪt] *v.* 存放，放下
propeller	[prə'pelə(r)] *n.* 船上的螺旋推进器（相关单词：propel *v.*，propellant *n./adj.*）
drawback	['drɔːbæk] *n.* 缺点，不便之处
hinge	[hɪndʒ] *v.* 装上铰链，用铰链接合；*n.* 合叶，铰链
blade	[bleɪd] *n.* 刀刃，刀锋
appendage	[ə'pendɪdʒ] *n.* 附加物，附属物（它的动词形式是"append"，可理解为"ap-pend"，表示"加强意义 + 悬挂"，基本意思为"挂在……上"，表示"悬挂，附加"，这里在动词后加上"-age"变为名词。关于字根"pend"，还可以了解单词"pendant"这个名词，表示"悬挂的饰物"，即"垂饰"，古人腰间佩带的玉佩就是典型的例子，当然它还可以指"很长、通常也很漂亮的耳环"。）
compartment	[kəm'pɑːtmənt] *n.* 舱，室，隔间

versatility	[ˌvɜːsə'tɪlətɪ] *n.* 多功能（性）（形容词形式：versatile）
edge	[edʒ] *n.* 优势
convert	[kən'vɜːt] *v.* 使转变，转换（理解为 "con-vert"，表示 "加强意义 + 旋转、转变"，进而得到上义。该单词的名词形式为 "conversion"。）
retraction	[rɪ'trækʃn] *n.* 缩进，缩回，撤回（动词形式：retract，它的前两个字母与后边五个字母将其含义组合起来，前者表示 "往回的作用力"，后者表示 "拉" 这个动作，因此这个动词的基本含义是 "往回拉"，引申为 "撤回，缩回"，关于字根 "tract" 表示 "拉" 这个含义，记忆相关单词 "tractor" "拖拉机，牵引车"。）
breakthrough	['breɪkθruː] *n.* 突破（性的发现）（来自动词短语 "break through"。）

▶ 雅思阅读真题同义词考点

astounding	—amazing, astonishing, surprising, shocking
rotate	—revolve, spin, swivel, turn
resemblance	—semblance, similarity, likeness, sameness
drawback	—disadvantage, downside, weakness, minus
convert	—change, adapt, transform, transfer
breakthrough	—advance, step forward, revolution, development

下篇导读：【旅行游记】

考试时间：2011-01-08……

　　古今中外的徐霞客们的游记不仅提供了异国他乡的宝贵信息，还促进了人类文化文明的交流发展，对新知的探索。😊

Reading Passage 53

Travelers' Accounts

There are many reasons why individuals have traveled beyond their own societies. Some travelers may have simply desired to satisfy curiosity about the larger world. Until recent times, however, did travelers start their journey for reasons other than mere curiosity. While the travelers' accounts give much valuable information on these foreign lands and provide a window for the understanding of the local cultures and histories, they are also a mirror to the travelers themselves, for these accounts help them to have a better understanding of themselves.

Records of foreign travel appeared soon after the invention of writing, and fragmentary travel accounts appeared in both Mesopotamia and Egypt in ancient times. After the formation of large, imperial states in the classical world, travel accounts emerged as a prominent literary genre in many lands, and they held especially strong appeal for rulers desiring useful knowledge about their realms. The Greek historian Herodotus reported on his travels in Egypt and Anatolia in researching the history of the Persian wars. The Chinese envoy Zhang Qian described much of central Asia as far west as Bactria (modern-day Afghanistan) on the basis of travels undertaken in the first century BCE* while searching for allies for the Han dynasty. Hellenistic and Roman geographers such as Ptolemy, Strabo, and Pliny the Elder relied on their own travels through much of the Mediterranean world as well as reports of other travelers to compile vast compendia of geographical knowledge.

During the postclassical era (about 500 t0 1500 CE), trade and pilgrimage emerged as major incentives for travel to foreign lands. Muslim merchants sought trading opportunities throughout much of the eastern hemisphere. They described lands, peoples, and commercial products of the Indian Ocean basin from east Africa to Indonesia, and they supplied the first written accounts of societies in Sub-Saharan West Africa. While merchants set out in search of trade and profit, devout Muslims traveled as pilgrims to Mecca to make their hajj and visit the holy sites of Islam. Since the

*BCE: Before the common Era

prophet Muhammad's original pilgrimage to Mecca, untold millions of Muslims have followed his example, and thousands of hajj accounts have related their experiences. East Asian travelers were not quite so prominent as Muslims during the postclassical era, but they too followed many of the highways and sea lanes of the eastern hemisphere. Chinese merchants frequently visited southeast Asia and India, occasionally venturing even to east Africa, and devout East Asian Buddhists undertook distant pilgrimages. Between the 5th and 9th centuries CE, hundreds and possibly even thousands of Chinese Buddhists traveled to India to study with Buddhist teachers, collect sacred texts, and visit holy sites. Written accounts recorded the experiences of many pilgrims, such as Faxian, Xuanzang, and Yijing. Though not so numerous as the Chinese pilgrims, Buddhists from Japan, Korea, and other lands also ventured abroad in the interests of spiritual enlightenment.

Medieval Europeans did not hit the roads in such large numbers as their Muslim and East Asian counterparts during the early part of the postclassical era, although gradually increasing crowds of Christian pilgrims flowed to Jerusalem, Rome, Santiago de Compostela (in northern Spain), and other sites. After the 12th century, however, merchants, pilgrims, and missionaries from medieval Europe traveled widely and left numerous travel accounts, of which Marco Polo's description of his travels and sojourn in China is the best known. As they became familiar with the larger world of the eastern hemisphere and the profitable commercial opportunities that it offered-European peoples worked to find new and more direct routes to Asian and African markets. Their efforts took them not only to all parts of the eastern hemisphere, but eventually to the Americas and Oceania as well.

If Muslim and Chinese peoples dominated travel and travel writing in postclassical times, European explorers, conquerors, merchants, and missionaries took centre stage during the early modern era (about 1500 to 1800 CE). By no means did Muslim and Chinese travel come to a halt in early modern times. But European peoples ventured to the distant corners of the globe, and European printing presses churned out thousands of travel accounts that described foreign lands and peoples for a reading public with an apparently insatiable appetite for news about the larger world. The travel literature was so great that several editors, including Giambattista Ramusio, Richard Hakluyt, Theodore de Bry, and Samuel Purchas, assembled numerous travel accounts and made them available in enormous published collections.

During the 19th century, European travelers made their way to the interior regions of Africa and the Americas, generating a fresh round of travel writing as they did so. Meanwhile, European colonial administrators devoted numerous writings to the societies of their colonial subjects, particularly in Asian and African colonies they established. By mid-century, attention was flowing also in the other direction. Painfully aware of the military and technological prowess of European and Euro-American societies, Asian travelers in particular visited Europe and the United States in hopes of discovering principles useful for the reorganisation of their own societies. Among the most prominent of these travelers who made extensive use of their overseas observations and experiences in their own writings were the Japanese reformer Fukuzawa Yukichi and the Chinese revolutionary Sun Yat-sen.

With the development of inexpensive and reliable means of mass transport, the 20th century witnessed explosions both in the frequency of long-distance travel and in the volume of travel writing. While a great deal of travel took place for reasons of business, administration, diplomacy, pilgrimage, and missionary work, as in ages past, increasingly effective modes of mass transport made it possible for new kinds of travel to flourish. The most distinctive of them was mass tourism, which emerged as a major form of consumption for individuals living in the world's wealthy societies. Tourism enabled consumers to get away from home to see the sights in Rome, take a cruise through the Caribbean, walk the Great Wall of China, visit some wineries in Bordeaux, or go on safari in Kenya. A peculiar variant of the travel account arose to meet the needs of these tourists: the guidebook, which offered advice on food, lodging, shopping, local customs, and all the sights that visitors should not miss seeing. Tourism has had a massive economic impact throughout the world, but other new forms of travel have also had considerable influence in contemporary times.

Questions 1–8

Complete the table below.

Write no more than two words from the Reading Passage for each answer.

Time	Traveler	Destination	Purpose
Ancient Greece	Herodotus	Egypt and Anatolia	To study the history of 1 _____
Han Dynasty	Zhang Qian	Central Asia	To seek 2 _____
Roman Empire	Ptolemy, Strabo, Pliny the Elder	Mediterranean	To obtain 3 _____
Post-classical Era (about 500 to 1500CE)	4 _____	From east Africa to Indonesia Mecca	Trading and Pilgrimage
5th to 9th centuries CE	Chinese Buddhists	5 _____	To collect Buddhist texts and for spiritual enlightenment
During 19th century	Colonial administrator	Asia, Africa	To understand the 6 _____ they set up
By the mid-century of the 1900s	Sun Yat-sen Fukuzawa Yukichi	Europe and United States	To study the practical 7 _____ to reshuffle their societies
20th century	People from 8 _____ countries	Mass tourism	Entertainment and pleasure

▶ 核心词汇

词汇	释义
account	[ə'kaʊnt] *n.* 记录，记述（雅思听力中常指：账户）
fragmentary	['frægməntrɪ] *adj.* 碎片的，片断的
imperial	[ɪm'pɪərɪəl] *adj.* 帝国的，皇帝的
emerge	[ɪ'mɜːdʒ] *v.* 出现，浮现
realm	[relm] *n.* 领域，范围
envoy	['envɒɪ] *n.* 使节，外交官
compile	[kəm'paɪl] *v.* 汇编，编辑
compendia	[kəm'pendɪə] *n.* 概略，摘要
pilgrimage	['pɪlgrɪmɪdʒ] *n.* 朝圣之旅，参拜圣地
incentive	[ɪn'sentɪv] *n.* 动机，诱因
basin	['beɪsn] *n.* 盆地；盆
devout	[dɪ'vaʊt] *adj.* 虔诚的，真诚的
hajj	[hædʒ] *n.* 麦加朝圣
prophet	['prɒfɪt] *n.* 预言家，先知
lane	[leɪn] *n.* 航线
sacred	['seɪkrɪd] *adj.* 宗教的，神圣的
enlightenment	[ɪn'laɪtnmənt] *n.* 启迪，启发，教化
counterpart	['kaʊntəpɑːt] *n.* 与对方地位相当的人
genre	['ʒɑːnrə] *n.* 类型，流派
missionary	['mɪʃənrɪ] *n.* 传教士
sojourn	['sɒdʒən] *n.* 逗留，旅居
conqueror	['kɒŋkərə(r)] *n.* 征服者，占领者（古罗马帝国恺撒大帝传留下千古名言：I came, I saw, I conquered.我来了，我看见了，我就征服了。）
halt	[hɔːlt] *n.* 停止，中止
churn out	艰苦地做出
insatiable	[ɪn'seɪʃəbl] *adj.* 无法满足的
appetite	['æpɪtaɪt] *n.* 胃口，欲望（appetiser *n.*开胃菜）
prowess	['praʊəs] *n.* 英勇；高超技艺
diplomacy	[dɪ'pləʊməsɪ] *n.* 外交
winery	['waɪnərɪ] *n.* 葡萄酒酿造厂
safari	[sə'fɑːrɪ] *n.* 探险

| reshuffle | [ˌriːˈʃʌfl] *v.* 改组（shuffle指"洗牌"，是象声词哟。自己读三遍听听，像不像？那么reshuffle指"重新洗牌"，同义词：reform 改革） |

▶ **雅思阅读真题同义词考点**

account — story, record, statement, description

search — seek, find, look for, explore, hunt

enlighten — educate, explain, illuminate, inform, instruct, teach

practical — useful, functional, helpful, feasible

genre — type, sort, kind, classification, group

reshuffle — reorganise, reconstruct, reform

下篇导读： 【香水制造】

考试时间： 2009-05-16 ……

　　香水的历史，香水的各种制造方法，香水的各种作用。为什么马达加斯加的香薰油那么优质和受欢迎？女生必读。😊

Reading Passage 54

Perfume comes from the Latin "per" meaning "through" and "fumum," or "smoke."

Perfume

Many ancient perfumes were made by extracting natural oils from plants through pressing and steaming. The oil was then burned to scent the air. Since the beginning of recorded history, humans have attempted to mask or enhance their own odour by using perfume, which emulates nature's pleasant smells. Many natural and man-made materials have been used to make perfume to apply to the skin and clothing, to put in cleaners and cosmetics, or to scent the air. Because of differences in body chemistry, temperature, and body odours, no perfume will smell exactly the same on any two people.

Before perfumes can be composed, the odourants used in various perfume compositions must first be obtained. Synthetic odourants are produced through organic synthesis and purified. Odourants from natural sources require the use of various methods to extract the aromatics from the raw materials. Enfleurage, a process that uses odourless fats that are solid at room temperature to capture the fragrant compounds exuded by plants, is the oldest of fragrance extraction techniques. The process can be "cold" enfleurage or "hot" enfleurage.

In cold enfleurage, a large framed plate of glass, called a chassis, is smeared with a layer of animal fat, usually from pork or beef, and allowed to set. Botanical matter, usually petals or whole flowers, is then placed on the fat and its scent is allowed to diffuse into the fat over the course of 1-3 days. The process is then repeated by replacing the spent botanicals with fresh ones until the fat has reached a desired degree of fragrance saturation. In hot enfleurage, solid fats are heated and botanical matter is stirred into the fat. Spent botanicals are repeatedly strained from the fat and replaced with fresh material until the fat is saturated with fragrance. In both instances, the fragrance-saturated fat is now called the "enfleurage pomade". The enfleurage pomade is washed or soaked in ethyl alcohol to draw the fragrant molecules into the alcohol. The alcohol is then separated from the fat and allowed to evaporate, leaving behind the essential oil of the botanical matter. The spent fat is usually used to make soaps since it is still relatively fragrant.

This method of fragrance extraction is by far one of the oldest. It is also highly inefficient and costly but was the sole method of extracting the fragrant compounds in delicate floral botanical such as jasmine and tuberose, which would be destroyed or denatured by the high temperatures required by methods of fragrance extraction such as steam distillation. The method is now superseded by more efficient techniques such as solvent extraction or supercritical fluid extraction using liquid carbon dioxide (CO_2) or similar compressed gases.

The results of the extraction are either essential oils, absolutes, concretes, or butters, depending on the amount of waxes in the extracted product. All these techniques will, to a certain extent, distort the odour of the aromatic compounds obtained from the raw materials. This is due to the use of heat, harsh solvents, or through exposure to oxygen in the extraction process which will denature the aromatic compounds, which either change their odour character or renders them odourless.

The country-island Madagascar—known for its extremely unique biodiversity—is recognised as holding tremendous potential for the development of new products in the essential oils, cosmetic and body care, due to the fact that 80% of its flora and fauna is endemic—meaning so unique that they are found no where else in the world.

For 85 million years, the flora and fauna of Madagascar evolved in isolation from the rest of the world. Examples of the totally unique essential oils and botanicals from Madagascar include the Ravinsara leaf known for its aroma, spice and therapeutic applications. Aroma-therapists believe that the oil can travel deep into muscle tissues and joints. Some have suggested that the oil has antiviral properties, and it is thought to relieve rheumatism and joint inflammation. Another totally unique essential oil from Madagascar to relieve rheumatic pains is Katrafay, which is also used in Madagascar by women after giving birth as a fortifier and tonic. It is also believed to have anti-inflammatory properties.

Cinnamosma fragrance is used traditionally as a decoction for treatment of malarial symptoms. The essential oil is used for tired and aching muscles.

According to suppliers, there are quite a few other high quality aromatherapy oils produced in Madagascar. These include niaouli used for clearing, cleansing and mental stimulation; lantana camara used for flu, colds, coughs, fevers, yellow fever, dysentery and jaundice; ylang ylang used as an aphrodisiac; cinnamon (bark and leaf) used to destroy microbes and bacteria, and holding promise for people with diabetes; tamanu (Calophyllum inophyllum) used to treat skin ailments; wild orange petit grains, used as a lively and soothing fragrance and to relieve dry skin; a unique ginger (fresh) oil used for circulation, aching muscles and nausea; and clove bud oil, which has been utilised as a local anesthetic in dentistry, as a food preservative and as an alternative to Deet.

Because perfumes and essential oils depend heavily on harvests of plant substances and the availability of animal products, perfumery can often turn risky. Thousands of flowers are needed to obtain just one pound of essential oils, and if the season's crop is destroyed by disease or adverse weather, perfumeries could be in jeopardy. In addition, consistency is hard to maintain in natural oils. The same species of plant raised in several different areas with slightly different growing conditions may not yield oils with exactly the same scent.

Problems are also encountered in collecting natural animal oils. Many animals once killed for the value of their oils are on the endangered species list and now cannot be hunted. For example, sperm whale products like ambergris have been outlawed since 1977. Also, most animal oils in general are difficult and expensive to extract. Deer musk must come from deer found in Tibet and China; civet cats, bred in Ethiopia, are kept for their fatty gland secretions; beavers from Canada and the former Soviet Union are harvested for their castor.

Synthetic perfumes have allowed perfumers more freedom and stability in their craft, even though natural ingredients are considered more desirable in the very finest perfumes. The use of synthetic perfumes and oils eliminates the need to extract oils from animals and removes the risk of a bad plant harvest, saving much expense and the lives of many animals.

Questions 1–5

The flowchart below demonstrates the cold enfleurage method of fragrance extraction.
Complete the flowchart with **NO MORE THAN THREE WORDS** from the passage.

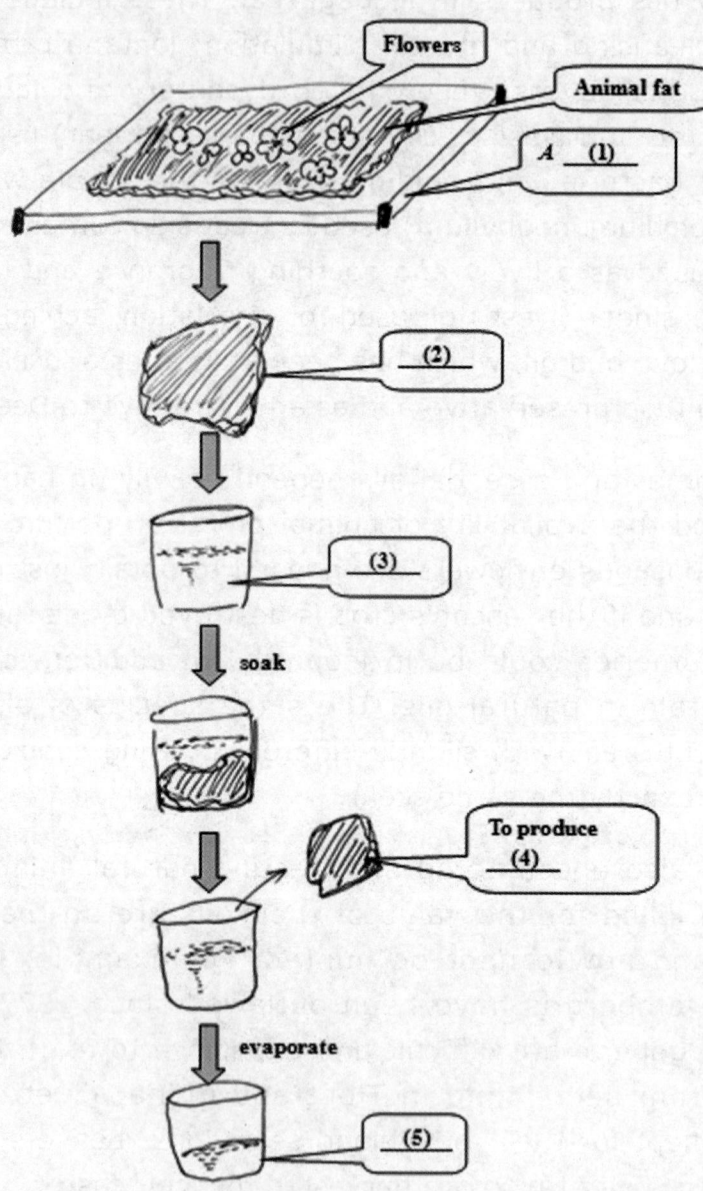

▶ 核心词汇

词汇	释义
perfume	['pɜːfjuːm] *n.* 香水
steam	[stiːm] *v.* 蒸
scent	[sent] *n.* 气味　*v.* 闻出，嗅，发觉
emulate	['emjʊleɪt] *n.* 仿效
odourant	['əʊdə(r)ænt] *n.* 有气味的东西
aromatic	[ˌærə'mætɪk] *adj.* 芬芳的
fragrant	['freɪɡrənt] *adj.* 芬芳的，香的（名词形式：fragrance）
exude	[ɪɡ'zjuːd] *v.* （使）流出，（使）渗出，发散开来
smear	[smɪə(r)] *v.* 涂上，抹掉，涂污；诽谤
diffuse	[dɪ'fjuːs] *v.* 散播，传播，漫射，扩散
saturated	['sætʃəreɪtɪd] *adj.* 渗透的；饱和的；深颜色的
soak	[səʊk] *v.* 浸，泡，浸透　*n.* 浸透
evaporate	[ɪ'væpəreɪt] *v.* （使）蒸发，消失
denature	[di'neɪtʃə(r)] *v.* 使改变本性
distillation	[ˌdɪstɪ'leɪʃn] *n.* 蒸馏，蒸馏法，蒸馏物；精华，精髓
solvent	['sɒlvənt] *adj.* 溶解的，有溶解力的；有偿付能力的
concrete	['kɒŋkriːt] *adj.* 具体的，有形的（名词含义：混领土）
biodiversity	[ˌbaɪəʊdaɪ'vɜːsətɪ] *n.* 生物剂量学
fauna	['fɔːnə] *n.* 动物群，动物志（反义词：flora 植物群。flora源自古罗马神话中的花神Flora芙洛拉。她嫁给了西风之神Zephyr，丈夫送给她一座满是奇花异草的园子。春天时，Flora和丈夫Zephyr会手挽手在园子里漫步，他们一路上走过的地方百花齐放。英文单词flower, flour, flourish, floral, florist和美国的Florida州都和她有关系。）
endemic	[en'demɪk] *n.* 地方病 *adj.* 风土的，地方的
aroma	[ə'rəʊmə] *n.* 芳香，香气，香味
spice	[spaɪs] *n.* 香料，调味品；情趣
therapeutic	[ˌθerə'pjuːtɪk] *adj.* 治疗的，治疗学的
antiviral	[ˌænti'vaɪrəl] *adj.* 抗滤过性病原体的
rheumatism	['ruːmətɪzəm] *n.* 风湿，风湿病
fortifier	['fɔːtɪfaɪə(r)] *n.* 使坚固的东西，筑城者
tonic	['tɒnɪk] *adj.* 激励的，滋补的
aromatherapy	[əˌrəʊmə'θerəpɪ] *n.* 用香料按摩
ailment	['eɪlmənt] *n.* 疾病（尤指微恙），不宁，不安

nausea	['nɔːzɪə] *n.* 晕船，恶心，作呕（nau，nav=ship船。如：navy船队，海军；naval 海军的；navigate 航行；nausea 船在海上航行→晕船；astronaut 星际航行者→太空人）

▶ 雅思阅读真题同义词考点

soak	—saturate, sop, steep, wet
evaporate	—disappear, fade away, vanish
concrete	—cement, solid, substantial, tangible
flora	—plant, foliage, vegetable, botany
spice	—flavour, season, taste

下篇导读：【从新手到专家】

考试时间： 2009-02-28，2010-10-23，2013-02-16……

　　一个人在某个领域从新手到专家要经历哪些学习过程，专家应该具备什么样的能力。其实硕士研究生的培养就是一个从新手到专家的过程。😊

From Novices to Experts

Expertise is commitment coupled with creativity. Specifically, it is the commitment of time, energy, and resources to a relatively narrow field of study and the creative energy necessary to generate new knowledge in that field. It takes a considerable amount of time and regular exposure to a large number of cases to become an expert.

An individual enters a field of study as a novice. The novice needs to learn the guiding principles and rules—the heuristics and constraints—of a given task in order to perform that task. Concurrently, the novice needs to be exposed to specific cases, or instances, that test the boundaries of such heuristics. Generally, a novice will find a mentor to guide her through the process of acquiring new knowledge. A fairly simple example would be someone learning to play chess. The novice chess player seeks a mentor to teach her the object of the game, the number of spaces, the names of the pieces, the function of each piece, how each piece is moved, and the necessary conditions for winning or losing the game.

In time, and with much practice, the novice begins to recognise patterns of behaviour within cases and, thus, becomes a journeyman. With more practice and exposure to increasingly complex cases, the journeyman finds patterns not only within cases but also between cases. More importantly, the journeyman learns that these patterns often repeat themselves over time. The journeyman still maintains regular contact with a mentor to solve specific problems and learn more complex strategies. Returning to the example of the chess player, the individual begins to learn patterns of opening moves, offensive and defensive game-playing strategies, and patterns of victory and defeat.

When a journeyman starts to make and test hypotheses about future behaviour based on past experiences, she begins the next transition. Once she creatively generates knowledge, rather than simply matching superficial patterns, she becomes an expert. At this point, she is confident in her knowledge and no longer needs a mentor as a guide—she becomes responsible for her own knowledge. In the chess example, once a journeyman begins competing against experts, makes predictions based on patterns, and tests those predictions against actual behaviour, she is generating new knowledge and a deeper understanding of the game. She is creating her own cases rather than relying on the cases of others.

The chess example is a rather short description of an apprenticeship model. Apprenticeship may seem like a restrictive 18th century mode of education, but it is still a standard method of training for many complex tasks. Academic doctoral programs are based on an apprenticeship model, as are fields like law, music, engineering, and medicine. Graduate students enter fields of study, find mentors, and begin the long process of becoming independent experts and generating new knowledge in their respective domains.

To some, playing chess may appear rather trivial when compared, for example, with making medical diagnoses, but both are highly complex tasks. Chess has a well-defined set of heuristics, whereas medical diagnoses seem more open ended and variable. In both instances, however, there are tens, if not hundreds, of thousands of potential patterns. A research study discovered that chess masters had spent between 10,000 and 20,000 hours, or more than ten years, studying and playing chess. On average, a chess master stores 50,000 different chess patterns in long-term memory.

Similarly, a diagnostic radiologist spends eight years in full time medical training—four years of medical school and four years of residency—before she is qualified to take a national board exam and begin independent practice. According to a 1988 study, the average diagnostic radiology resident sees forty cases per day, or around 12,000 cases per year. At the end of a residency, a diagnostic radiologist has stored, on average, 48,000 cases in long-term memory.

Psychologists and cognitive scientists agree that the time it takes to become an expert depends on the complexity of the task and the number of cases, or patterns, to which an individual is exposed. The more complex the task, the longer it takes to build expertise, or, more accurately, the longer it takes to experience and store a large number of cases or patterns.

Experts are individuals with specialised knowledge suited to perform the specific tasks for which they are trained, but that expertise does not necessarily transfer to other domains. A master chess player cannot apply chess expertise in a game of poker—although both chess and poker are games, a chess master who has never played poker is a novice poker player. Similarly, a biochemist is not qualified to perform neurosurgery, even though both biochemists and neurosurgeons study human physiology. In other words, the more complex a task is the more specialised and exclusive is the knowledge required to perform that task.

An expert perceives meaningful patterns in her domain better than non-experts. Where a novice perceives random or disconnected data points, an expert connects regular patterns within and between cases. This ability to identify patterns is not an innate perceptual skill; rather it reflects the organisation of knowledge after exposure to and experience with thousands of cases.

Experts have a deeper understanding of their domains than novices do, and utilise higher-order principles to solve problems. A novice, for example, might group objects together by colour or size, whereas an expert would group the same objects according to their function or utility. Experts comprehend the meaning of data and weigh variables with different criteria within their domains better than novices. Experts recognise variables that have the largest influence on a particular problem and focus their attention on those variables.

Experts have better domain-specific short-term and long-term memory than novices do. Moreover, experts perform tasks in their domains faster than novices and commit fewer errors while problem solving. Interestingly, experts go about solving problems differently than novices. Experts spend more time thinking about a problem to fully understand it at the beginning of a task than do novices, who immediately seek to find a solution. Experts use their knowledge of previous cases as context for creating mental models to solve given problems.

Better at self-monitoring than novices, experts are more aware of instances where they have committed errors or failed to understand a problem. Experts check their solutions more often than novices and recognise when they are missing information necessary for solving a problem. Experts are aware of the limits of their domain knowledge and apply their domain's heuristics to solve problems that fall outside of their experience base.

Questions 1–5

Complete the flowchart below.

*Use **NO MORE THAN THREE WORDS** from the passage for each answer.*

From a novice chess player to an expert

A novice
learns
● the ......1......of the game
● the number of spaces
● the name and function of each piece
● how each piece is moved
● the necessary conditions for win or lose

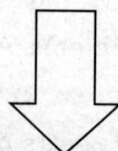

A ......2......
learns
● patterns of opening moves
● ......3...... game-playing strategies
● patterns of victory and ......4......

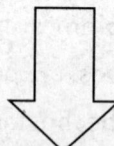

An expert
learns
● to make predictions based on patterns
● to test those predictions against actual behaviour
● to generate new knowledge
● to create ......5......

▶ 核心词汇

词汇	释义
novice	['nɒvɪs] *n.* 新手，初学者
commitment	[kə'mɪtmənt] *n.* 信奉，献身
principle	['prɪnsəpl] *n.* 法则，原则（区别：principal 负责人；校长）
heuristics	[hjʊ'rɪstɪks] *n.* 启发式教学法
constraint	[kən'streɪnt] *n.* 限制，约束
chess	[tʃes] *n.* 象棋
piece	[piːs] *n.* 棋子（同义词：chess figure）
mentor	['mentɔː(r)] *n.* 导师；有经验可信赖的顾问（来源于荷马史诗《奥德赛》*Odyssey*，盂托Mentor是奥德修斯Odysseus的忠实朋友，奥德赛出征时将其留下以掌管家事。智慧女神雅典娜都曾经将自己装扮成盂托Mentor而引导奥德赛之子忒勒马科斯Telemachus去寻找他的父亲。一个希腊人名经拉丁文演化而来的词 mentor 在法语和英语中成了一个意为"贤明的顾问"的普通名词。而且字根 ment 本身也有"思考"之意。如：mental）
radiologist	[ˌreɪdɪ'ɒlədʒɪst] *n.* 放射线学者
pattern	['pætn] *n.* 方式，形式
cognitive	['kɒgnətɪv] *adj.* 认知的
journeyman	['dʒɜːnɪmən] *n.* 熟手，熟练工人
strategy	['strætədʒɪ] *n.* 策略（形容词形式：strategic）
hypothesis	[haɪ'pɒθəsɪs] *n.* 假说，假设，前提
prediction	[prɪ'dɪkʃn] *n.* 预言，预言的事物
apprenticeship	[ə'prentɪʃɪp] *n.* 学徒的身份
respective	[rɪ'spektɪv] *adj.* 分别的，各自的
domain	[də'meɪn] *n.* 范围，领域（domain name 互联网域名）
perceive	[pə'siːv] *v.* 感觉，察觉，理解
utility	[juː'tɪlətɪ] *n.* 功用，效用
criteria	[kraɪ'ɪərɪən] *n.* 标准

▶ 雅思阅读真题同义词考点

novice	—beginner, freshman, greenhorn
principle	—doctrine, dogma, law, rule
pattern	—design, example, illustration, model
victory	—success, triumph, win
complex	—complicated, confused, sophisticated

下篇导读： 【乌鸦制造工具】

考试时间： 2009-02-07，2009-05-09……

　　剑桥雅思官方宠物。剑桥大学用乌鸦做了很多实验，结论是它很聪明。乌鸦喝水的寓言来自现实观察。乌鸦还会制造工具。

Reading Passage 56

Two Wings and *a Kit-box*

A Many animals use tools, but tool manufacture is rare. Rarer still is cumulative change in tool manufacture. Chimpanzee and orangutan tool manufacture, for example, is often haphazard, and their tools show no evidence of incremental improvements over time. In contrast, current human technology is the result of a long series of cumulative changes. The "ratchet-like" nature of this technological evolution means that design changes are retained at the population level until new, improved designs arise. This ratchet effect is possible because tool manufacture methods are socially transmitted with sufficient fidelity that individuals do not need to reinvent or recapitulate past inefficient designs. The skills required for the development of this cumulative technology are claimed to include high-fidelity social learning, an understanding of physical relationships and functional properties of objects, and the ability for fine object manipulation. Animals other than humans are generally presumed to lack the necessary neural hardware and cognitive sophistication for cumulative technological evolution.

B The New Caledonian crow, Corvus moneduloides, is an ideal model species to examine the links between tool manufacture, social learning and cognition. These crows make tools out of the twigs and the long, prickly **edges** of the leaves of the tropical pandanus tree to facilitate the capture of invertebrates, says New Zealander Gavin Hunt. He studies these crows, which live on islands between Australia and Fiji. Dr. Hunt has discovered that New Caledonian crows have three different designs for tools. They also make two kinds of stick tools—hooked and not hooked. The manufacture of pandanus tools provides a unique opportunity for study because a record of tool manufacture is faithfully recorded in "counterparts" or outlines remaining on the leaf edges. In the wild, adult New Caledonian crows sever long narrow pandanus (a stilt-rooted palm native to Southeast Asia) leaves and split them to keep the sharply serrated outside edge intact. The split leaves are cut again in roughly 8 lengths for bill-controlled tools to hook small insects from cracks or to swish rapidly through leaf litter to impale other prey.

C Recent work has revealed that these tools have four features previously thought to be unique to primitive humans: a high degree of standardisation, the use of hooks, "handedness," and cumulative changes in tool design. Evidence has been discovered of cumulative changes in a field survey documenting the shapes of 5,550 tools from 21 sites throughout the range of pandanus tools. Three distinct tool designs are found: wide tools, narrow tools, and stepped tools. The lack of ecological correlates of the different tool designs and their geographic overlap make it unlikely that they evolved independently. Similarities in the method of manufacture for each design suggest that pandanus tools have gone through a process of cumulative change from a common historical origin.

D Evidence is accumulating quickly on the inherent talent of crow's tool-making ability which indicates that this ability is at least partly inherited and not dependent on learning through social contacts. To date there is only circumstantial evidence that New Caledonian crows transmit tool-making knowledge via social learning. These crows live in small family units where juveniles have ample opportunity to learn foraging techniques. The social learning and reasoning abilities of other Corvus species are well documented. The high fidelity in the shape of tool design at sites makes individual trial-and-error learning unlikely. Similarly, the evidence that crows might have some grasp of the functional properties of their tools is also only inferential.

E Researchers have also found that crows use different sides of their beaks to make and use tools. This suggests that different parts of the brain may control making and using tools, and that the biology of handedness—or beakedness—may be more complex than we thought. Just like humans, New Caledonian crows are usually right "handed" when it comes to tasks such as making tools.

But it turns out the birds use their tools with left and right sides equally, although individual crows prefer one side or the other. "This has opened up Pandora's box," says William McGrew, who studies chimpanzees' tool use at Miami University. "People always assumed handedness would be the same for using and making tools." Scientists will now be more wary of making this assumption, he adds.

F A major breakthrough in these studies occurred when it became evident that traditional theory of brain evolution as espoused by Ludwig Edinger, a neurobiologist and the leading comparative anatomist of a hundred years ago, was wrong. He believed that brains evolved in a straight line with invertebrates at the low end and progressed upwards through fish, reptiles, birds, to mammals, with humans at the top. Neurobiologists now understand that bird brains, although constructed differently from that of mammals, nonetheless function as elegantly as any mammals' brain. In fact, in proportion to body size, a crow's brain is as large as a chimpanzee's.

G In mammals, the lower third of our brains consists of groups of neurons, whereas the upper two thirds there exists neo-cortexes made up of flat cells, six cell layers thick. The top part generates our rational or intellectual activity, whereas the bottom third controls our instinctive reactions such as extending an arm to soften a fall or jerking away a hand when touching something hot. In human evolution the six cell-layered sheet on the top of the brain spread to such an extent that the only way the scull-confined brain could contain its increased area was for it to become convoluted, i.e. with many folds and crevices. The tops of bird brains are smooth, not folded, and until recently were thought to consist of cells grouped in clusters similar to the lower part of mammal brains, and thus would make all bird behaviour merely instinctive. We know now this is not the case, but the exact neural pathways are still unclear. What seems to have happened is an example of convergent evolution of intelligence where two differing forms of brain structure eventually lead to almost equivalent brain power. "New Caledonian crows teach us that in many ways other animals are not so different from us, and we should respect them for their differences and similarities," says Hunt.

Questions 1–3

Look at the following diagrams A–F.

Match the correct diagram to each tool manufactured by the New Caledonian crow.

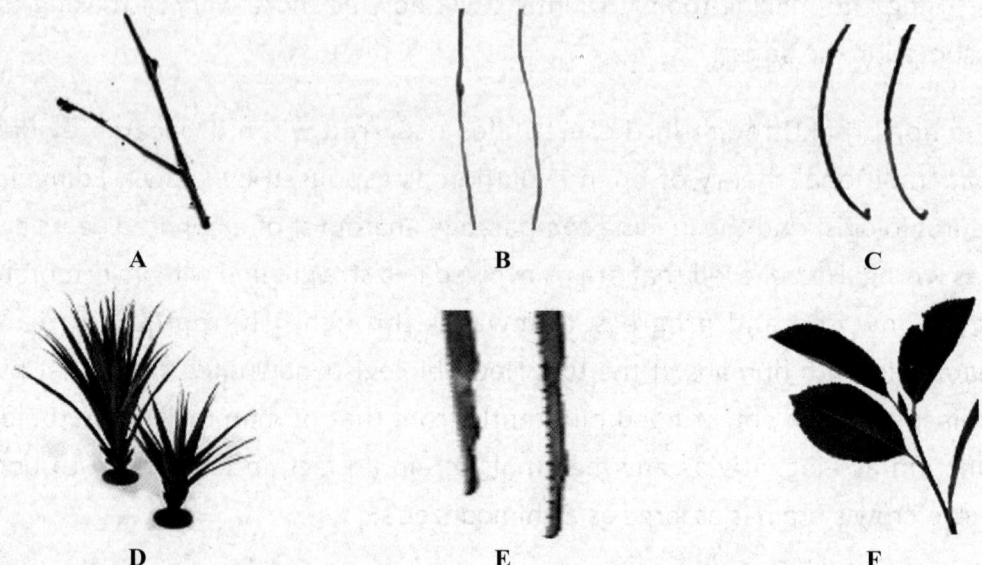

1 Hooked stick

2 Not hooked stick

3 Pandanus tool

► 核心词汇

词汇	释义
manufacture	[ˌmænjʊˈfæktʃə(r)] v. 制造，加工
cumulative	[ˈkjuːmjələtɪv] adj. 累积的
ratchet	[ˈrætʃɪt] n. （防倒转的）棘齿
fidelity	[fɪˈdeləti] n. 忠实，诚实，忠诚（fid=to trust信任。翻译界有一个著名的比喻，法语为Belles infideles。Belle指美女（名牌女鞋百丽）；infideles中的fid就是信任，前面的in表否定，infideles即为不值得信任，不忠诚。说翻译作品就是美丽而不忠实的女人：如果她美丽，她就不忠实；如果她忠实，那她就不美丽。）
manipulation	[məˌnɪpjʊˈleɪʃn] n. 操纵，操作（动词形式：manipulate）
neural	[ˈnjʊərəl] adj. 神经系统的，神经中枢的；背的
crow	[krəʊ] n. 乌鸦
prickly	[ˈprɪkli] adj. 多刺的
edge	[edʒ] n. 刀口，边缘；优势
hooked	[hʊkt] adj. 钩状的（名词形式：hook）
counterpart	[ˈkaʊntəpɑːt] n. 副本，极相似的人或物，配对物
sever	[ˈsevə(r)] v. 切断
split	[splɪt] v. 劈开
serrated	[səˈreɪtɪd] adj. 锯齿状的，有锯齿的
crack	[kræk] n. 裂缝；噼啪声
impale	[ɪmˈpeɪl] v. 刺穿，（作为刑罚）把……钉在尖桩上；使陷于苦境
ecological	[ˌiːkəˈlɒdʒɪkl] adj. 生态学的，社会生态学的
correlate	[ˈkɒrəleɪt] v. 使相互关联（名词形式：correlation）
trial-and-error	[ˈtraɪələndˈerə(r)] n. 反复试验
beak	[biːk] n. 鸟嘴，喙（同义词：bill）
wary	[ˈweəri] adj. 机警的
neurobiologist	[ˌnjʊərəʊbaɪˈɒlədʒɪst] n. 神经生物学
reptile	[ˈreptaɪl] n. 爬虫动物；卑鄙的人
convoluted	[ˈkɒnvəluːtɪd] adj. 盘绕的；费解的
crevice	[ˈkrevɪs] n. （墙壁，岩石等的）裂缝
convergent	[kənˈvɜːdʒənt] adj. 会集于一点的，会聚性的，收敛的

▶ 雅思阅读真题同义词考点

manufacture	—make, build, construct, create, devise
edge	—fringe, border, advantage
split	—bisect, separate, halve, divide
crack	—crevice, gap, rift
wary	—careful, cautious, guarded, suspicious

CHAPTER 7

Real Test
真题模考

介绍：真实的雅思阅读考试是周六上午10点至11点之间，在听力和写作之间。

雅思阅读考试时间为1小时，读3篇文章，回答共40道题。平均每篇文章13道题、20分钟完成。通常每篇文章由2至3种不同题型构成。

现在，让我们把前面各种题型的学习心得融合起来，征服雅思阅读考试。

Test 1

▶ **Reading Passage 1**

*You should spend about 20 minutes on **Questions 1–11** which are based on Reading Passage 1.*

The Spectacular Eruption of Mount St. Helens

A The eruption in May 1980 of Mount St. Helens, Washington State, astounded the world with its violence. A gigantic explosion tore much of the volcano's summit to fragments; the energy released was equal to that of 500 of the nuclear bombs that destroyed Hiroshima in 1945.

B The event occurred along the boundary of two of the moving plates that make up the Earth's crust. They meet at the junction of the North American continent and the Pacific Ocean. One edge of the continental North American plate over-rides the oceanic Juan de Fuca micro-plate, producing the volcanic Cascade range that includes Mounts Baker, Rainier and Hood, and Lassen Peak as well as Mount St. Helens.

C Until Mount St. Helens began to stir, only Mount Baker and Lassen Peak had shown signs of life during the 20th century. According to geological evidence found by the United States Geological Survey, there had been two major eruptions of Mount St. Helens in the recent (geologically speaking) past: around 1900 B. C., and about 1500 A. D. . Since the arrival of Europeans in the region, it had experienced a single period of spasmodic activity, between 1831 and 1857. Then, for more than a century, Mount St. Helens lay dormant.

D By 1979, the Geological Survey, alerted by signs of renewed activity, had been monitoring the volcano for 18 months. It warned the local population against being deceived by the mountain's outward calm, and forecast that an eruption would take place before the end of the century. The inhabitants of the area did not have to wait that long. On March 27, 1980, a few clouds of smoke formed above the summit, and slight tremors were felt. On the 28th, larger and darker clouds, consisting of gas and ashes, emerged and climbed as high as 20,000 feet. In April a slight lull ensued, but the volcanologists remained pessimistic. Then, in early May, the northern flank of the mountain bulged, and the summit rose by 500 feet.

E Steps were taken to evacuate the population. Most-campers, hikers, timber-cutters left the slopes of the mountain. Eighty-four-year-old Harry Truman, a holiday lodge owner who had lived there for more than 50 years, refused to be evacuated, in spite of official and private urging. Many members of the public, including an entire class of school children, wrote to him, begging him to leave. He never did.

F On May 18, at 8.32 in the morning, Mount St. Helens blew its top, literally. Suddenly, it was 1300 feet shorter than it had been before its growth had begun. Over half a cubic mile of rock had disintegrated. At the same moment, an earthquake with an intensity of 5 on the Richter scale was recorded. It triggered an avalanche of snow and ice, mixed with hot rock—the entire north face of the mountain had fallen away. A wave of scorching volcanic gas and rock fragments shot horizontally from the volcano's riven flank, at an inescapable 200 miles per hour. As the sliding ice and snow melted, it touched off devastating torrents of mud and debris, which destroyed all life in their path. Pulverised rock climbed as a dust cloud into the atmosphere. Finally, viscous lava, accompanied by burning clouds of ash and gas, welled out of the volcano's new crater, and from lesser vents and cracks in its flanks.

G Afterwards, scientists were able to analyse the sequence of events. First, magma molten rock—at temperatures above 2000°F—had surged into the volcano from the Earth's mantle. The build-up was accompanied by an accumulation of gas, which increased as the mass of magma grew. It was the pressure inside the mountain that made it swell. Next, the rise in gas pressure caused a violent decompression, which ejected the shattered summit like a cork from a shaken soda bottle. With the summit gone, the molten rock within was released in a jet of gas and fragmented magma, and lava welled from the crater.

H The effects of the Mount St. Helens eruption were catastrophic. Almost all the trees of the surrounding forest, mainly Douglas firs, were flattened, and their branches and bark ripped off by the shock wave of the explosion. Ash and mud spread over nearly 200 square miles of country. All the towns and settlements in the area were smothered in an even coating of ash. Volcanic ash silted up the Columbia River 35 miles away, reducing the depth of its navigable channel from 40 feet to 14 feet, and trapping sea-going ships. The debris that accumulated at the foot of the volcano reached a depth, in places, of 200 feet.

I The eruption of Mount St. Helens was one of the most closely observed and analysed in history. Because geologists had been expecting the event, they were able to amass vast amounts of technical data when it happened. Study of atmospheric particles formed as a result of the explosion showed that droplets of sulphuric acid, acting as a screen between the Sun and the Earth's surface, caused a distinct drop in temperature. There is no doubt that the activity of Mount St. Helens and other volcanoes since 1980 has influenced our climate. Even so, it has been calculated that the quantity of dust ejected by Mount St. Helens—a quarter of a cubic mile—was negligible in comparison with that of Mount Katmai in Alaska in 1912 (three cubic miles). The volcano is still active. Lava domes have formed inside the new crater, and have periodically burst. The threat of Mount St. Helens lives on.

Questions 1 and 2

Reading Passage 1 has 9 paragraphs labeled A–I.

Answer questions 1 and 2 by writing the appropriate letters A–I in boxes 1 and 2 on your answer sheet.

Example	Answer
Which paragraph compares the eruption to the energy released by nuclear bombs?	A

1 Which paragraph describes the evacuation of the mountain?

2 Which paragraph describes the moment of the explosion of Mount St. Helens?

Questions 3 and 4

3 What are the dates of TWO major eruptions of Mount St. Helens before 1980?

*Write **TWO** dates in box 3 on your answer sheet. Use **NO MORE THAN THREE WORDS** for each blank.*

……………………… and ……………………

4 How do scientists know that the volcano exploded around the two dates above?

*Use **NO MORE THAN THREE WORDS**. Write your answer in box 4 on your answer sheet.*

Questions 5–8

Complete the summary of events below leading up to the eruption of Mount St. Helens.

*Choose **NO MORE THAN THREE WORDS** from the passage for each answer.*

Write your answers in boxes 5–8 on your answer sheet.

In 1979 the Geological Survey warned …**5**… to expect a violent eruption before the end of the century. The forecast was soon proved accurate. At the end of March there were tremors and clouds formed above the mountain. This was followed by a lull, but in early May the top of the mountain rose by …**6**… People were …**7**… from around the mountain. Finally, on May 18th at …**8**…, Mount St. Helens exploded.

Questions 9 and 10

Complete the table below giving evidence for the power of the Mount St. Helens eruption.

Write your answers in boxes 9 and 10 on your answer sheet.

*Choose **NO MORE THAN THREE WORDS** from the passage for each answer.*

Item	Equivalent to
Example The energy released by the explosion of Mount St. Helens	**Answer** 500 nuclear bombs
The area of land covered in mud or ash	about …9…
The quantity of dust ejected	…10…

Questions 11

*Choose the appropriate letter **A–D** and write it in box 11 on your answer sheet.*

11   According to the text the eruption of Mount St. Helens and other volcanoes has influenced our climate by

   A   increasing the amount of rainfall.

   B   heating the atmosphere.

   C   cooling the air temperature.

   D   causing atmospheric storms.

▶ **Reading Passage 2**

*You should spend about 20 minutes on **Questions 12–25** which are based on Reading Passage 2.*

Questions 12–16

Reading Passage 2 has seven paragraphs A–G.

*Choose the most suitable headings for paragraphs **B–E** and **G** from the list of headings below. Write the appropriate numbers (**i–x**) in boxes 12–16 on your answer sheet.*

NB *There are more headings than paragraphs so you will not use all of them.*

You may use any of the headings more than once.

List of Headings

i	The effect of changing demographics on organisations
ii	Future changes in the European workforce
iii	The unstructured interview and its validity
iv	The person/skills match approach to selection
v	The implications of a poor person-environment fit
vi	Some poor selection decisions
vii	The validity of selection procedures
viii	The person-environment fit
ix	Past and future demographic changes in Europe
x	Adequate and inadequate explanations of organisational failure

---

Example	Paragraph A	Answer (x)
12 Paragraph **B**		
13 Paragraph **C**		
14 Paragraph **D**		
15 Paragraph **E**		

Example	Paragraph F	Answer (ix)
16 Paragraph **G**		

People and Organisations: The Selection Issue

A In 2001, according to the Department of Trade and Industry, a record 36,000 British companies went out of business. When businesses fail, the post-mortem analysis is traditionally undertaken by accountants and market strategists. Unarguably organisations do fail because of undercapitalisation, poor financial management, adverse market conditions etc. Yet, conversely, organisations with sound financial backing, good product ideas and market acumen often underperform and fail to meet shareholders' expectations. The complexity, degree and sustainment of organisational performance requires an explanation which goes beyond the balance sheet and the "paper conversion" of financial inputs into profit making outputs. A more complete explanation of "what went wrong" necessarily must consider the essence of what an organisation actually is and that one of the financial inputs, the most important and often the most expensive, is people.

B An organisation is only as good as the people it employs. Selecting the right person for the job involves more than identifying the essential or desirable range of skills, educational and professional qualifications necessary to perform the job and then recruiting the candidate who is most likely to possess these skills or at least is perceived to have the ability and predisposition to acquire them. This is a purely person/skills match approach to selection.

C Work invariably takes place in the presence and/or under the direction of others, in a particular organisational setting. The individual has to "fit" in with the work environment, with other employees, with the organisational climate, style of work, organisation and culture of the organisation. Different organisations have different cultures. Working as an engineer at British Aerospace will not necessarily be a similar experience to working in the same capacity at GEC or Plessey.

D Poor selection decisions are expensive. For example, the costs of training a policeman are about £20,000 (approx. US $30,000). The costs of employing an unsuitable technician on an oil rig or in a nuclear plant could, in an emergency, result in millions of pounds of damage or loss of life. The disharmony of a poor person-environment fit (PE-fit) is likely to result in low job satisfaction, lack of organisational commitment and employee stress, which affect organisational outcomes i.e. productivity, high labour turnover and absenteeism, and individual outcomes i.e. physical, psychological and mental well-being.

E   However, despite the importance of the recruitment decision and the range of sophisticated and more objective selection techniques available, including the use of psychometric tests, assessment centres etc., many organisations are still prepared to make this decision on the basis of a single 30 to 45 minute unstructured interview. Indeed, research has demonstrated that a selection decision is often made within the first four minutes of the interview. In the remaining time, the interviewer then attends exclusively to information that reinforces the initial "accept" or "reject" decision. Research into the validity of selection methods has consistently demonstrated that the unstructured interview, where the interviewer asks any questions he or she likes, is a poor predictor of future job performance and fares little better than more controversial methods like graphology and astrology. In times of high unemployment, recruitment becomes a "buyer's market" and this was the case in Britain during the 1990s.

F   The future, we are told, is likely to be different. Detailed surveys of social and economic trends in the European Community show that Europe's population is falling and getting older, The birth rate in the Community is now only three-quarters of the level needed to ensure replacement of the existing population. By the year 2020, it is predicted that more than one in four Europeans will be aged 60 or more and barely one in five will be under 20. In a five-year period between 1993 and 1998 the Community's female workforce grew by almost six million. As a result, 51% of all women aged 14 to 64 are now economically active in the labour market compared with 78% of men.

G   The changing demographics will not only affect selection ratios. They will also make it increasingly important for organisations wishing to maintain in their competitive edge to be more responsive and accommodating to the changing needs of their workforce if they are to retain and develop their human resources. More flexible working hours, the opportunity of work from home of job share, the provision of childcare facilities etc., will play a major role in attracting and retaining staff in the future.

Questions 17–22

Do the following statements agree with the views of the writer in Reading Passage 2?

In boxes 17–22 on your answer sheet write

YES	*if the statement agrees with the writer*
NO	*if the statement does not agree with the writer*
NOT GIVEN	*if there is no information about this in the passage*

17 Organisations should recognise that their employees are a significant part of their financial assets.

18 Open-structured 45 minute interviews are the best method to identify suitable employees.

19 Graphology is a good predictor of future job performance.

20 In the future, the number of people in employable age groups will decline.

21 In 2020, the percentage of the population under 20 will be smaller than now.

22 The rise in the female workforce in the European Community is a positive trend.

Questions 23–25

*Complete the notes below with words taken from Reading Passage 2. Use **NO MORE THAN TWO WORDS** for each answer.*

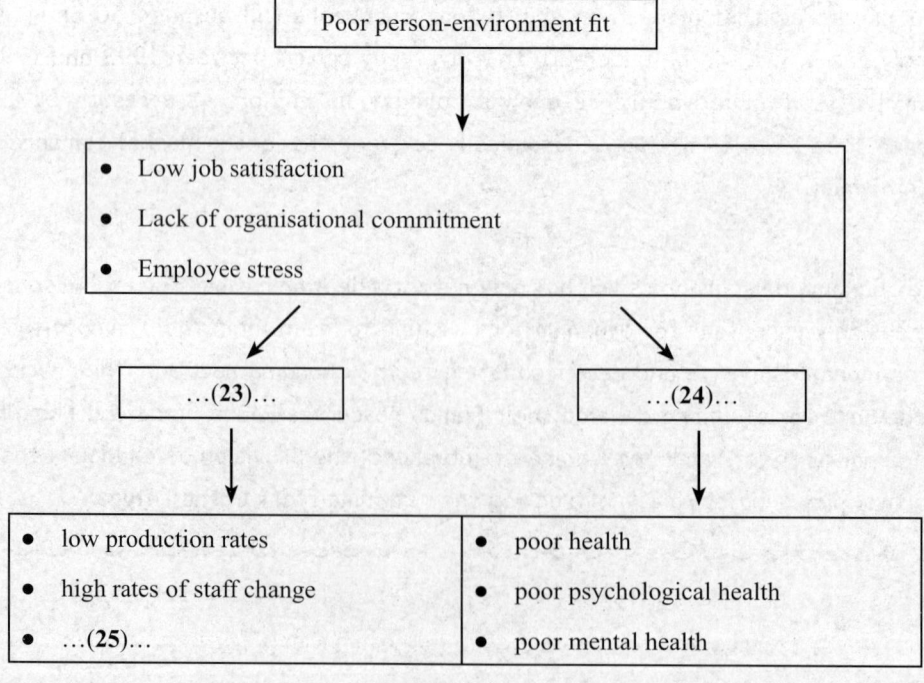

▶ **Reading Passage 3**

*You should spend about 20 minutes on **Questions 26–40** which are based on Reading Passage 3.*

The Roll Film Revolution

The introduction of the dry plate process brought with it many advantages. Not only was it much more convenient, so that the photographer no longer needed to prepare his material in advance, but its much greater sensitivity made possible a new generation of cameras. Instantaneous exposures had been possible before, but only with some difficulty and with special equipment and conditions. Now, exposures short enough to permit the camera to the held in the hand were easily achieved. As well as fitting shutters and viewfinders to their conventional stand cameras, manufacturers began to construct smaller cameras intended specifically for hand use.

One of the first designs to be published was Thomas Bolas's "Detective" camera of 1881. Externally a plain box, quite unlike the folding bellows camera typical of the period, it could be used unobtrusively. The name caught on, and for the next decade or so almost all hand cameras were called "Detectives". Many of the new designs in the 1880s were for magazine cameras, in which a number of dry plates could be pre-loaded and changed one after another following exposure. Although much more convenient than stand cameras, still used by most serious workers, magazine plate cameras were heavy, and required access to a darkroom for loading and processing the plates. This was all changed by a young American

bank clerk turned photographic manufacturer, George Eastman, from Rochester, New York.

Eastman had begun to manufacture gelatine dry plates in 1880, being one of the first to do so in America. He soon looked for ways of simplifying photography, believing that many people were put off by the complication and messiness. His first step was to develop, with the camera manufacturer William H. Walker, a holder for a long roll of paper negative "film." This could be fitted to a standard plate camera and up to forty-eight exposures made before reloading. The combined weight of the paper roll and the holder was far less than the same number of glass plates in their light-tight wooden holders. Although roll-holders had been made as early as the 1850s, none had been very successful because of the limitations of the photographic materials then available. Eastman's rollable paper film was sensitive and gave negatives of good quality; the Eastman-Walker roll-holder was a great success.

The next step was to combine the roll-holder with a small hand camera; Eastman's first design was patented with an employee, F. M. Cossitt, in 1886. It was not a success. Only fifty Eastman detective cameras were made, and they were sold as a lot to a dealer in 1887; the cost was too high and the design too complicated. Eastman set about developing a new model, which was launched in June 1888. It was a small box, containing a roll of paper based stripping film sufficient for 100 circular exposures 6 cm in diameter. Its operation was simple: set the shutter by pulling a wire string; aim the camera using the V line impression in the camera top; press the release button to activate the exposure; and turn a special key to wind the film. A hundred exposures had to be made, so it was important to record each picture in the memorandum book provided, since there was no exposure counter. Eastman gave his camera the invented name "Kodak"—which was easily pronounceable in most languages, and had two Ks which Eastman felt was a firm, uncompromising kind of letter.

The importance of Eastman's new roll-film camera was not that it was the first. There had been several earlier cameras, notably the Stirn "America", first demonstrated in the spring of 1887 and on sale from early 1888. This also used a roll of negative paper, and had such refinements as a reflecting viewfinder and an ingenious exposure marker. The real significance of the first Kodak camera was that it was backed up by a developing and printing service. Hitherto, virtually all photographers developed and printed their own pictures. This required the facilities of a darkroom and the time and inclination to handle the necessary chemicals, make the prints and so on. Eastman recognised that not everyone had the resources or the desire to do this. When a customer had made a hundred exposures in the Kodak camera, he sent it to Eastman's factory in Rochester (or later in Harrow in England) where the film was unloaded, processed and printed, the camera reloaded and returned to the owner. "You Press the Button, We Do the Rest" ran Eastman's classic marketing slogan; photography had been brought to everyone. Everyone, that is, who could afford $25 or five guineas for the camera and $10 or two guineas for the developing and printing. A guinea ($5) was a week's wages for many at the time, so this simple camera cost the equivalent of hundreds of dollars today.

In 1889 an improved model with a new shutter design was introduced, and it was called the No. 2 Kodak camera. The paper-based stripping film was complicated to manipulate, since the processed negative image had to be stripped from the paper base for printing. At the end of 1889 Eastman launched a new roll film on a celluloid base. Clear, tough, transparent and flexible, the new film not only made the roll film camera fully practical, but provided the raw material for the introduction of cinematography a few years later. Other, larger models were introduced, including several folding versions, one of which took pictures 21.6cm x 16.5cm in size. Other manufacturers in America and Europe introduced cameras to take the Kodak roll-films, and other firms began to offer developing and printing services for the benefit of the new breed of photographers.

By September 1889, over 5,000 Kodak cameras had been sold in the USA, and the company was daily printing 6-7,000 negatives. Holidays and special events created enormous surges in demand for processing: 900 Kodak users returned their cameras for processing and reloading in the week after the New York centennial celebration.

Questions 26–29

Do the following statements agree with the views of the writer in Reading Passage 3?

In boxes 26–29 on your answer sheet write

YES	*if the statement agrees with the writer*
NO	*if the statement does not agree with the writer*
NOT GIVEN	*if there is no information about this in the passage*

26 Before the dry plate process short exposures could only be achieved with cameras held in the hand.

27 Stirn's "America" camera lacked Kodak's developing service.

28 The first Kodak film cost the equivalent of a week's wages to develop.

29 Some of Eastman's 1891 range of cameras could be loaded in daylight.

Questions 30–34

*Complete the diagram below. Choose **NO MORE THAN THREE WORDS** from the passage for each answer.*

Writer your answers in boxes 30–34 on your answer sheet.

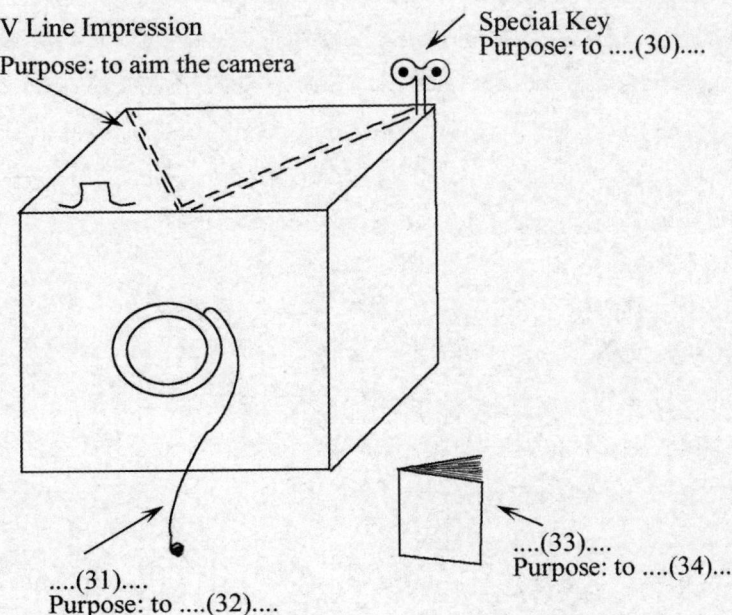

V Line Impression
Purpose: to aim the camera

Special Key
Purpose: to ....(30)....

....(31)....
Purpose: to ....(32)....

....(33)....
Purpose: to ....(34)....

Questions 35–40

*Complete the table below. Choose **NO MORE THAN THREE WORDS** from the passage for each answer.*

Write your answers in boxes 35–40 on your answer sheet.

Year	Developments	Name of Person/People
1880	Manufacture of gelatine dry plates	(35) ....
(36)	Release of "Detective" camera	Thomas Bolas
(37)	The roll-holder combined with (38)	Eastman and F. M. Cossitt
1889	Introduction of model with (39)	(40) ....

Test 2

▶ **Reading Passage 1**

*You should spend about 20 minutes on **Questions 1–13**, which are based on Reading Passage 1.*

The Origins of Laughter

While joking and wit are uniquely human inventions, laughter certainly is not. Other creatures, including chimpanzees, gorillas and even rats, laugh. The fact that they laugh suggests that laughter has been around for a lot longer than we have.

There is no doubt that laughing typical involves groups of people. "Laughter evolved as a signal to others—it almost disappears when we are alone," says Robert Provine, a neuroscientist at the University of Maryland. Provine found that most laughter comes as a polite reaction to everyday remarks such as "see you later," rather than anything particularly funny. And the way we laugh depends on the company we're keeping. Men tend to laugh longer and harder when they are with other men, perhaps as a way of bonding. Women tend to laugh more and at a higher pitch when men are present, possibly indicating flirtation or even submission.

To find the origins of laughter, Provine believes we need to look at play. He points out that the masters of laughing are children, and nowhere is their talent more obvious than in the boisterous antics, and the original context is play. Well-known primate watchers, including Dian Fossey and Jane Goodall, have long argued that chimps laugh while at play. The sound they produce is known as a pant laugh. It seems obvious when you watch their behavior—they even have the same ticklish spots as we do. But remove the context, and the parallel between human laughter and a chimp's characteristic pant laugh is not so clear. When Provine played a tape of the pant laughs to 119 of his students, for example, only two guessed correctly what it was.

These findings underline how chimp and human laughter vary. When we laugh the sound is usually produced by chopping up a single exhalation into a series of shorter with one sound produced on each inward and outward breath. The question is: does this pant laughter have the same source as our own laughter? New research lends weight to the idea that it does. The findings come from Elke Zimmerman, head of the Institute for Zoology in Germany, who compared the sounds made by babies and chimpanzees in response to tickling during the first year of their life. Using sound spectrographs to reveal the pitch and intensity of vocalisations, she discovered that chimp and human baby laughter follow broadly the same pattern. Zimmerman believes the closeness of baby laughter to chimp laughter supports the idea that laughter was around long before humans arrived on the scene. What started simply as a modification of breathing associated with enjoyable and playful interactions has acquired a symbolic meaning as an indicator of pleasure.

Pinpointing when laughter developed is another matter. Humans and chimps share a common ancestor that lived perhaps 8 million years ago, but animals might have been laughing long before that. More distantly related primates, including gorillas, laugh, and anecdotal evidence suggests that other social mammals nay do too. Scientists are currently testing such stories with a comparative analysis of just how common laughter is among animals. So far, though, the most compelling evidence for laughter beyond primates comes from research done by Jaak Panksepp from Bowling Green State University, Ohio, into the ultrasonic chirps produced by rats during play and in response to tickling.

All this still doesn't answer the question of why we laugh at all. One idea is that laughter and tickling originated as a way of sealing the relationship between mother and child. Another is that the reflex response to tickling is protective, alerting us to the presence of crawling creatures that might harm us or compelling us to defend the parts of our bodies that are most vulnerable in hand-to-hand combat. But the idea that has gained most popularity in recent years is that laughter in response to tickling is a way for two individuals to signal and test their trust in one another. This hypothesis starts from the observation that although a little tickle can be enjoyable, if it goes on too long it can be torture. By engaging in a bout of tickling, we put ourselves at the mercy of another individual, and laughing is a signal that we laughter is what makes it a reliable signal of trust according to Tom Flamson, a laughter researcher at the University of California, Los Angels. "Even in rats, laughter, tickle, play and trust are linked. Rats chirp a lot when they play," says Flamson. "These chirps can be aroused by tickling. And they get bonded to us as a result, which certainly seems like a show of trust."

We'll never know which animal laughed the first laugh, or why. But we can be sure it wasn't in response to a prehistoric joke. The funny thing is that while the origins of laughter are probably quite serious, we owe human laughter and our language-based humor to the same unique skill. While other animals pant, we alone can control our breath well enough to produce the sound of laughter. Without that control there would also be no speech—and no jokes to endure.

Questions 1–6

Look at the following research findings (questions 1–6) and the list of people below.

*Match each finding with the correct person, **A**, **B**, **C** or **D**.*

*Write the correct letter, **A**, **B**, **C** or **D**, in boxes 1–6 on your answer sheet.*

NB   You may use any letter more than once.

1   Babies and some animals produce laughter which sounds similar.

2   Primates are not the only animals who produce laughter.

3   Laughter can be used to show that we feel safe and secure with others.

4   Most human laughter is not a response to a humorous situation.

5   Animal laughter evolved before human laughter.

6   Laughter is a social activity.

List of People
A   Provine
B   Zimmerman
C   Panksepp
D   Flamson

Questions 7–10

*Complete the summary using the list of words, **A–K**, below.*

*Write the correct letter, **A–K**, in boxes 7–10 on your answer sheet.*

Some scientists believe that laughter first developed out of 7_____. Research has revealed that human and chimp laughter may have the same 8_____. Scientists have long been aware that 9_____ laugh, but it now appears that laughter might be more widespread than once thought. Although the reasons why humans started to laugh are still unknown, it seems that laughter may result from the 10_____ we feel with another person.

A	combat	B	chirps	C	pitch
D	origins	E	play	F	rats
G	primates	H	confidence	I	fear
J	babies	K	tickling		

Questions 11–13

Do the following statements agree with the information given in Reading Passage 1?

In boxes 11–13 on your answer sheet, write

TRUE	*if the statement agrees with the information*
FALSE	*if the statement contradicts the information*
NOT GIVEN	*if there is no information on this*

11 Both men and women laugh more when they are with members of the same sex.

12 Primates lack sufficient breath control to be able to produce laughs the way humans do.

13 Chimpanzees produce laughter in a wider range of situations than rats do.

▶ **Reading Passage 2**

*You should spend about 20 minutes on **Questions 14–26**, which are based on Reading Passage 2.*

The Lost City

Thanks to modern remote-sensing techniques, a ruined city in Turkey is slowly revealing itself as one of the greatest and most mysterious cities of the ancient world.

Sally Palmer uncovers more.

A The low granite mountain known as Kerkenes Dag juts from the northern edge of the Cappadocian plain in Turkey. Spawaled over the mountainside are the ruins of an enormous city, contained by crumbling defensive walls seven kilometres long. Many respected archaeologists believe these are the remains of the fabled city of Pteria, the sixth-century BC stronghold of the Medes that the Greek historian Herodotus described in his famous work *The Histories*. The short-lived city came under Median control and only fifty years later was sacked, burned and its strong stone walls destroyed.

B British archeologist Dr Geoffrey Summers has spent ten years studying the site. Excavating the ruins is a challenge because of the vast area they cover. The 7 km perimeter walls run around a site covering 271 hectares. Dr Summers quickly realised it would take far too long to excavate the site using traditional techniques alone. So the decided to use modern technology as well to map the entire site, both above and beneath the surface, to locate the most interesting areas and priorities where to start digging.

C In 1993, Dr Summers hired a special hand-held balloon with a remote-controlled camera attached. He walked over the entire site holding the balloon and taking photos. Then one afternoon, he rented a hot-air balloon and floated over the site, taking yet more pictures. By the end of the 1994 season, Dr Summers and his team had a jigsaw of aerial photographs of the whole site. The next stage was to use remote sensing, which would let them work out what lay below the intriguing outlines and ruined walls. "Archaeology is a discipline that lends itself very well to remote sensing because it revolves around space," says Scott Branting, an associated director of the project. He started working with Dr Summers in 1995.

D The project used two main remote-sensing techniques. The first is magnetometry, which works on the principle that magnetic fields at the surface of the Earth are influenced by what is buried beneath. It measures localised variations in the direction and intensity of this magnetic field. "The Earth's magnetic field can vary from place to place, depending on what happened there in the past," says Branting. "if something containing iron oxide was heavily burnt, by natural or human actions, the iron particles in it can be permanently reoriented, like a compass needle, to align with the Earth's magnetic field present at that point in time and space." The magnetometer detects differences in the orientations and intensities of these iron particles from the present-day magnetic field and uses them to produce an image of what lies below ground.

E Kerkenes Dag lends itself particularly well to magnetometry because it was all burnt at once in a savage fire. In places the heat was sufficient to turn sandstone to glass and to melt granite. The fire was so hot that there were strong magnetic signatures set to the Earth's magnetic field from the time—around 547 BC—resulting in extremely clear pictures. Furthermore, the city was never rebuilt. "if you have multiple layers confusing picture, because you have different walls from different periods giving signatures that all go in different directions," says Branting. "We only have on going down about 1.5 metres, so we can get a good picture of this fairly short-lived city."

F The other main sub-surface mapping technique, which is still being used at the site, is resistivity. This measures the way electrical pulses are conducted through sub-surface soil. It's done by shooting pulses into the ground through a thin metal probe. Different materials have different electrical conductivity. For example, stone and mudbrick are poor conductors, but looser, damp soil conducts very well. By walking around the site and taking about four readings per metre, it is possible to get a detailed idea of what is where beneath the surface. The teams then build up pictures of walls, hearths and other remains. "It helps a lot if it has rained, because the electrical pulse can get through more easily," says Branting. "Then if something is more resistant, it really shows up." This is one of the reasons that the project has a spring season, when most of the resistivity work is done. Unfortunately, testing resistivity is a lot slower than magnetometry. "If we did resistivity over the whole site it would take about 100 years," says Branting. Consequently, the team is concentrating on areas where they want to clarity pictures from the magnetometry.

G Remote sensing does not reveal everything about Kerkenes Dag, but it shows the most interesting sub-surface areas of the site. The archaeologists can then excavate these using traditional techniques. One surprise came when they dug out one of the fates in the defensive walls. "Our observations in early seasons led us to assume that we were looking at a stone base from a mudbrick city wall, such as would be found at most other cities in the Ancient Near East," says Dr Summers. "When we started to excavate we were staggered to discover that the walls were made entirely from stone and that the gate would have stood at least ten metres high. After ten years of study, Pteria is gradually giving up its secrets."

Questions 14–17

Reading Passage 2 has seven paragraphs, A–G.

Which paragraph contains the following information?

Write the correct letter, A–G, in boxes 14–17 on your answer sheet.

14　the reason for the deployment of a variety of investigative methods

15　an example of an unexpected finding

16　how the surface of the site was surveyed from above

17　the reason why experts are interested in the site

Questions 18–25

Complete the summary below.

*Choose **NO MORE THAN THREE WORDS** from the passage for each answer.*

Write your answers in boxes 18–25 on your answer sheet.

Exploring the ancient city of Pteria

Archaeologists began to work ten years ago. They started by taking photographs of the site from the ground and then from a distance in a **18** _____. They focused on what lay below the surface using a magnetometer, which identifies variations in the magnetic field. These occur when the **19** _____ in buried structures have changed direction as a result of great heat. They line up with the surrounding magnetic field just as a **20** _____ would do.

The other remote-sensing technique employed is resistivity. This uses a **21** _____ to fire electrical pulses into the earth. The principle is that building materials like **22** _____ and stone do not conduct electricity well, while **23** _____ does this much more effectively. This technique is mainly employed during the **24** _____, then conditions are more favourable. Resistivity is mainly being used to **25** _____ some images generated by the magnetometer.

Questions 26

Choose the correct letter, A, B, C or D.

Write the correct letter in box 26 on your answer sheet.

26 How do modern remote-sensing techniques help at the Pteria site?

    A   They detect minute buried objects for the archaeologists to dig up.

    B   They pinpoint key areas which would be worth investigating closely.

    C   They remove the need for archaeologists to excavate any part of the site.

    D   They extend the research period as they can be used at any time of the year.

▶ **Reading Passage 3**

*You should spend about 20 minutes on **Questions 27–40**, which are based on Reading Passage 3.*

Designed to Last

Could better design cure our throwaway culture?

Jonathan Chapman, a senior lecture at the University of Brighton, UK, is one of a new breed of "sustainable designers." Like many of us, they are concerned about the huge waste associated with Western consumer culture and the damage this does to the environment. Some, like Chapman, aim to create objects we will want to keep rather than discard. Others are working to create more efficient or durable consumer goods, or goods designed with recycling in mind. The waste entailed in our fleeting relationships with consumer durables is colossal.

Domestic power tools, such as electric drills, are a typical example of such waste. However much DIY the purchaser plans to do, the truth is that these things are thrown away having been used, on average, for just ten minutes. Most will serve "conscience time" gathering dust on a shelf in the garage; people are reluctant to admin that they have wasted their money. However, the end is inevitable; thousands of years in landfill waste sites. In its design, manufacture, packaging, transportation and disposal, a power tool consumes many times its own weight in resources, all for a shorter active lifespan than that of the average small insect.

To understand why we have become so wasteful, we should look to the underlying motivation of consumers. "People own things to give expression to who they are, and to show what group of people they feel they belong to," Chapman says. In a world of mass production, however, that symbolism has lost much of its potency. For most of human history, people had an intimate relationship with objects they used or treasured. Often they made the objects themselves, or family members passed them on. For more specialist objects, people relied on expert manufacturers living close by, whom they probably knew personally. Chapman points out that all these factors gave objects a history—a narrative—and an emotional connection that today's mass-produced goods cannot possibly match. Without these personal connections, consumerist culture idolises novelty instead. People know that they cannot buy happiness, but the chance to remake themselves with glossy, box-fresh products seems irresistible. When the novelty fades, they simply renew the excitement by buying more.

Chapman's solution is what he calls "emotionally durable design." He says the challenge for designers is to create things we want to keep. This may sound like a tall order, but it can be surprisingly straightforward. A favourite pair of old jeans, for example, just do not have the right feel until they have been worn and washed a hundred times. It is as if they are sharing the wearer's life story. The look can be faked, but it is simply not the same. Walter Stahel, visiting professor at the University of Surrery, UK, calls this "the teddy bear factor." No matter how ragged and worn a favourite teddy becomes, we don't abandon ours and buy another one. As adults, our teddy bear connects us to our childhood and this protects it from obsolescence. Stahel argues that this is what sustainable design needs to do with more products.

The information age was supposed to lighten our economies and recued our impact on the environment, but, in fact, the reverse seems to be happening. We have simply added information technology to the industrial era and speeded up the developed world's metabolism. The cure is hardly rocket science; minimise waste, stop moving things around so much and use people more. So what will post-throwaway consumerism look like? It might be as simple as installing energy-saving light bulbs, more efficient washing machines or choosing locally produced groceries with less packaging. In general, we will spend less on goods and more on services. Instead of buying a second car, for example, we might buy into a car-sharing network. Rather than following our current wasteful practices, we will buy less and rent a lot more; why own things such as tools that you use infrequently, especially things are likely to be updated all the time?

Consumer durables will increasingly be sold with plans for their disposal. Electronic goods such as mobile phones will be designed to be recyclable, with the extra cost added into the retail price. Following Chapman's notion of emotionally durable design, there will be a move away from mass production and towards tailor-made articles and products designed and manufactured with greater craftsmanship, products which will be repaired rather than replaced, in the same way as was done in our grandparents' time. Companies will replace profit from bulk sales by servicing and repairing producers chosen because we want them to last. Chapman acknowledges that it will be a challenge to persuade people to buy fewer goods, and ones that they intend to keep. At the moment, price competition between retailers makes it cheaper for consumers to replace rather than repair.

Products designed to be durable and emotionally satisfying are likely to be more expensive, so how will we be persuaded to choose sustainability? Tim Cooper, from Sheffield Hallam University in the UK, points our that many people are already happy to pay a premium for quality, and that they also tend to value and care more for expensive goods. Chapman is also positive:"People are ready to keep things for longer," he says, "The problem is that a lot of industries don't know how to do that." Chapman believes that sustainable design is here to stay. "The days when large corporations were in a position to choose whether to jump on the sustainability bandwagon or not are coming to an end," he says. Whether this is also the beginning of the end of the throwaway society remains to be seen.

Questions 27–31

*Choose the correct letter, **A**, **B**, **C** or **D**.*

Write the correct letter in boxes 27–31 on your answer sheet.

27 In the second paragraph, the expression "conscience time" refers to the fact that the owners

   A wish they had not bought the power tool

   B want to make sure the tool is stored safely

   C feel that the tool will increase in value in the future

   D would feel guilty if they threw the tool away immediately

28 Jonathan Chapman uses the word "narrative" in the third paragraph to refer to the fact that the owner

   A told a story about how the item was bought

   B was aware of how the item had come into being

   C felt that the item became more useful over time

   D was told that the item had been used for a long time

29 In the third paragraph, the writer suggests that mass-produced goods are

   A inferior in quality

   B less likely to be kept for a long time

   C attractive because of their lower prices

   D less tempting than goods which are traditionally produced

30 Lack of personal connection to goods is described as producing

   A a belief that older goods are superior

   B an attraction to well-designed packaging

   C a desire to demonstrate status through belongings

   D a desire to purchase a constant stream of new items

31 Jeans and teddy bears are given as examples of goods which

   A have been very well designed

B   take a long time to show wear

C   are valued more as they grow older

D   are used by the majority of the population

Questions 32–35

Do the following statements agree with the views of the writer in Reading Passage 3?

In boxes 32–35 on your answer sheet, write

>   **YES**   *if the statement agrees with the views of the writer*
>
>   **NO**   *if the statement contradicts the views of the writer*
>
>   **NOT GIVEN**   *if it is impossible to say what the writer thinks about this*

32   People often buy goods that they make little use of.

33   Understanding the reasons for buying goods will help to explain why waste occurs.

34   People already rent more goods than they buy.

35   Companies will charge less to repair goods in the future.

Questions 36–40

Complete the summary using the list of words, A–I below.

Write the correct letter, A–I, in boxes 36–40 on your answer sheet.

A cure for our wasteful habits

The writer believes that the recipe for reducing our impact on the environment is a simple one. He states that we should use less energy for things such as lighting or **36**____, and buy **37**____ that will not need to be moved across long distances. Some expensive items such as **38**____ could be shared, and others which may be less expensive but which are not needed often, such as **39**____ could be rented instead of being purchased. He believes that manufacturers will need to design high-technology items such as **40**____ so that they can be recycled more easily.

A	mobile phones	B	clothing	C	tools
D	laundry	E	computers	F	food
G	heating	H	cars	I	teddy bears

APPENDIX 附录

附录2　2004—2014真题一览表

2004年全年中国考区雅思考试阅读文章目录

考试日期	Passage 1	Passage 2	Passage 3
01.10	海底火山	英国绿色农业	语言变迁
01.17	社会行为	日本塔	语言变迁
01.31	自然韵律	钱币发展	数字起源
02.14	摩天大楼	澳洲疗法	运动员
02.21	阿斯旺水坝	校园暴力	医疗保健
02.28	老龄职工	国际贸易	眼镜蛇毒
03.13	钢化玻璃	公共交通	地图发展
03.20	工作家庭	公共交通	医疗保健
03.27	蚂蚁智商	澳洲疗法	欧洲森林保护
04.03	海底火山	校园暴力	运动员
04.17	儿童热带雨林	汽车发展	数字起源
04.24	校园暴力	运动员	海底火山
05.15	计时器	汽车发展	医疗保健
05.22	钢化玻璃	纸币发展	运动员
05.29	药品推销	钱币发展	欧洲森林保护
06.12	儿童热带雨林	激励实验	运动员
06.19	微波桥梁	公共交通	欧洲森林保护
06.26	外星生物	阿斯旺水坝	地图发展
07.10	面试技巧	眼镜蛇毒	公司营销
07.17	公共交通	澳洲疗法	语言变迁
07.24	老龄职工	公司营销	医疗保健
08.14	蚂蚁智商	校园暴力	数字起源
08.21	蝴蝶农场	澳洲疗法	盲人符号
08.28	日本塔	公共交通	语言变化
09.11	道路建设	钢化玻璃	拯救鲑鱼
09.18	阿斯旺水坝	汽车发展	动物思维
10.16	风筝建造金字塔	公司营销	农田生态管理
10.23	儿童多动症	拯救鲑鱼	科技英语
10.30	老龄职工	学生惩罚	青少年学习语言
11.13	人类与动物绝种	运输的发展	潮流消费
11.20	蝴蝶农场	钱币发展	海底探测船
11.27	日本数学教育	纸币发展	海底探测船

2005年全年中国考区雅思考试阅读文章目录

考试日期	Passage 1	Passage 2	Passage 3
01.08	蝴蝶农场	电压对人体的心理实验	莫尔斯电码
01.15	强化玻璃	纸币发展史	科技英语
01.22	澳洲考拉	俄罗斯考古	海底探测船
02.05	蚂蚁智力	运动与英国青少年健康	公路建设

02.19	修建城堡	未来汽车发展	妇女文盲婴儿死亡
02.26	儿童多动症	运动与英国青少年健康	气候影响因纽特人
03.05	老龄职工对公司作用	国际贸易与运输业	妇女文盲婴儿死亡
03.12	日本教育	伦敦大雾	消费心理
03.19	公共交通工具发展史	运动与英国青少年健康	自然韵律
04.02	风筝建金字塔	伦敦大雾	动物的思考与直觉
04.09	先天后天	电影发展史	科技英语
04.16	先天后天	管理职位	海底探测船
05.14	旅游业与经济	水资源短缺	飞机历史
05.21	同声翻译	电子书	欧洲森林保育
05.28	英国的一种草	电影发展史	老年人疾病和原因
06.11	蝙蝠	艺术随时间的变化	语言的变化
06.18	世界粮食	圆顶建筑	昆虫翅膀
06.25	大脑训练	伦敦大雾	蚂蚁智力
07.09	男女分校	各国古代钱币	莫尔斯电码
07.16	蝴蝶农场	美国移民史	英国战后农业发展
07.23	日本的塔	美国垃圾处理	儿童语言能力
08.06	计时器发展史	外语对商业的影响	老年人疾病和原因
08.13	人对自然进化的影响	地图发展史	消费心理
08.20	生物韵律	俄罗斯考古	海底探测船
09.03	一种要灭绝的植物	各国古代钱币	飞机移动电话
09.10	口译	孩子缺乏锻炼	鸟的定位方式
09.17	日本塔	照相机的使用	如何收集蚂蚁
10.15	人群的聚集	语言在各领域的要求	宠物
10.22	大脑训练	鲑鱼繁殖	噪音对人的影响
11.12	考拉	美国废物回收	盲人问题研究
11.19	一种植物	美国移民史	中世纪的玩具
11.26	风筝金字塔	亚洲移民去欧洲	公路建造
12.03	旅游的发展和影响	科学作弊	欧洲森林保护
12.10	世界旅游业的发展	伦敦大雾	记忆方法
12.17	蝙蝠和雷达	厄尔尼诺现象	动物的思考

2006年全年中国考区雅思考试阅读文章目录

考试日期	Passage 1	Passage 2	Passage 3
01.07	老龄职工	水利发展	因纽特人
01.14	旅游业的发展史	节能建筑	抓蚂蚁
01.21	蝙蝠和回声定位	语言与商业	生物杀虫
02.11	澳洲运动	英国绿色农业	妇女文盲和婴儿死亡率
02.18	农药和产量	关于艺术	非洲修建公路
02.25	拥挤与密度	美国垃圾回收	昆虫飞行进化
03.11	大脑训练	英国儿童缺乏运动	欧洲森林保护
03.18	育儿观念的改变	伦敦大雾	保存网络资料
03.25	口译	空间和权利	天才
04.08	男女合校	地图发展史	因纽特人
04.22	蚂蚁智力	古代钱币	电子书
04.29	化肥土壤	纸币的发展	小班教学研究

05.13	法国城堡建筑	科学中的欺骗行为	燃料电池
05.20	大脑训练	乌鸦制造工具	英语拼写与改革
05.27	香蕉	艺术变化	视觉盲点
06.10	蝴蝶保护色	美国航空管制	沉船保护
06.17	龙涎香和琥珀	英国儿童缺乏锻炼	英语发音的演变
07.08	水獭	生物杀虫	燃料电池
07.22	交通的发展	气候与国家富裕	抓蚂蚁
07.29	交通堵塞	阿拉斯加鲑鱼保护	面部表情
08.05	海底研究	电子书	氢能源动力
08.12	交通拥堵	空间和权利	短信互动电视
08.12	香蕉	摄影与绘画	味觉和嗅觉
09.02	日本宝塔	伦敦烟雾	动物灭绝
09.16	儿童后天教育	水污染处理	法国工业时代电影
09.23	美国肥胖症	地图制作	沙漠植物
10.14	城市公共交通	新陈代谢与寿命	美国港湾环境污染
10.21	农作物的发展	小提琴	30年代科幻片
10.28	磁场研究	俄罗斯考古	保存网络资料
11.04	日本儿童教育	业余科学家的数据价值	部落基因研究
11.18	手势的发展	电脑控制汽车	教学方法实验
11.25	生物钟	香水	阅读法
12.02	恐龙灭绝	英国农业	拯救濒危语言
12.09	龙涎香和琥珀	美国垃圾处理	生物杀虫剂
12.16	乐观与人类健康	澳大利亚更新能源	雪崩的研究

2007年全年中国考区雅思考试阅读文章目录

考试日期	Passage 1	Passage 2	Passage 3
01.06	玻璃制造	小冰期	昆虫翅膀进化
01.13	交通堵塞	广告	扑翼飞机
01.20	地球磁场	寻找外星人	旅游业发展
02.03	计时器发展史	语言与商业	手机短信与电视互动
02.10	蝴蝶颜色	英国绿色农业	英国建筑
03.03	风筝修建金字塔	手势	鸟类定向
03.10	恐龙足迹	气候与经济	中世纪儿童玩具
03.31	南美蔬菜引入欧洲	世界水资源	特技摄影
04.14	蚂蚁智力	汽车发展	虚拟现实技术
04.21	乐观与健康	彗星撞木星	语言发展
04.28	水獭	天才儿童	公路环保
05.12	珍稀植物	金星凌日	营销策略
05.19	大脑训练	生物多样性	大航海家
06.02	收音机发展	土壤学推广	智商测试
06.09	香蕉	定量研究	企业效率
06.16	美国肥胖	关于嗅觉	处理海上石油泄露
07.07	蝴蝶颜色	遥感机器帮助废墟探测	文化对国际贸易的影响
07.14	橡胶发展	开发冰山	远程教育
07.21	玻璃制造	双胞胎的研究	关于海龟

08.11	水獭	家长教育	卫星技术
08.18	龙涎香	航海	数码打印
08.25	计时器	传统技术建设房屋的优越性	科学进步与风险承担
09.01	撒谎者心理	蚂蚁防治农作物病虫害	音乐的影响
09.08	从初学者成为专家	地图的发展	企业发展
09.22	心理实验	幼鸟孵化和抚养	火星
10.13	文字记载的历史	小冰期	欧洲的公路运输
10.20	声音探测海洋	手势	企业发展
11.03	磁疗发展	植物净水	人类语言发展和大脑之间的关系
11.17	动物行为	美国电影发展历史	人的长相和性格关系
11.24	市场管理	香水	婴儿的模仿能力
12.01	茶叶和工业革命的关系	考古学发展	口译
12.08	恐龙足迹	英国利用潮汐发电	心理实验
12.15	远程教育	乌鸦制造工具	火星

2008年全年中国考区雅思考试阅读文章目录

考试日期	Passage 1	Passage 2	Passage 3
01.10	搔痒和笑	美国联邦航空管理局	纸张和电子文档
01.12	人口拥挤和稠密	湖底沉积物的研究分析	公司革新
01.19	海牛	美国的垃圾回收利用	美国人应减少工作时间
01.26	工程师布鲁内尔	苏梅克一列维彗星撞木星	鲸鱼文化及语言
02.02	种子的收集和用途	空间和权力	两种睡眠模式的比较
02.14	沙漠化的影响	儿童教育	听力理解
02.16	伦敦地铁	虚拟替身	商业革新
02.23	乐观与长寿的关系	植物的化学分泌物	人类语言的分类讨论
03.01	澳大利亚考拉生活习惯	伦敦的吊桥	思考机制
03.08	深海热沟	语言的分化和传播	人工智能
03.13	城市拥堵	儿童读物	明星作用
03.29	电视成瘾的消极影响	新型交通系统	北极的生物与环境
04.05	珍珠	学术造假	体育节目与大脑活动
04.12	家庭与工作的平衡	南极对气候和农业的影响	战后英国农业政策
04.19	口译	人的感官	厄尔尼诺现象
04.24	日本数学教育	过山车	农业发展
05.10	收音机制造过程	沙漠化	数字电影
05.22	香蕉	智力测验	争论
05.31	美国人肥胖	麋鹿的灭绝	植物战争
06.05	澳洲土著	净化水资源	N/A
06.14	恐龙专家	指纹	飓风
06.21	机器人	金星凌日	研究大猩猩
06.28	二氧化碳的危害	新的生产方式	人和猴子的恐惧程度
07.05	松树	计时器的发展	个人与团队合作
07.12	搔痒和笑	交易	动物保护
07.24	茶与工业革命	潜意识	英国的植被历史
07.26	青春期	加拿大移民	电视成瘾的消极影响

08.09	新西兰海藻	运动员研究	教学方式的不同
08.16	人的选择方式与满意度	电话过滤	阅读法
08.21	磁疗	澳洲的鹦鹉	竞争与结果
08.30	生物进化和人类活动	古代钱币	新型交通系统
09.06	商业革新	语言的分化和传播	VEP技术
09.13	口译	种子的传播	阿拉斯加的捕鱼
09.18	教学方式的不同	乘飞机旅行	有关花的实验
09.27	儿童教育	潮汐发电	英语的发展
10.11	种子的收集和用途	南极对气候和农业的影响	原始人的生存状况
10.23	交通堵塞	儿童文学在英国的发展	动物分布和大陆板块形成
10.25	生态旅游	双胞胎研究	语言的起源
11.08	植物的化学分泌物	气候和国家经济发展	手势
11.15	茶与工业革命	考古勘测	潮汐发电
11.20	博物馆	冰山	电视对学习的影响
11.29	智力测验	英国古遗址勘测	新的生产方式
12.04	交通拥堵	电子书	潜意识
12.06	航海计时	蜜蜂	语言的变迁
12.13	工程师布鲁内尔	人体彩绘	VR技术
12.20	计时器的发展	深海热沟	信息论

2009年全年中国考区雅思考试阅读文章目录

考试日期	Passage 1	Passage 2	Passage 3
01.10	象形文字	欧洲高温	英国父母谁来照看孩子
01.15	人脸识别技术	折射定律	物种多元化
01.17	笑的研究	管理学之父	海龟回陆地
02.07	乌鸦喝水	小冰河世纪	苏联工作时间变化
02.12	海洋探测和全球气候	英国农业结构和村落	学校对孩子影响
02.21	非洲传统农业	摄影对艺术的影响	从众心理
02.28	新手到专家	金星凌日	绘画和艺术效果
03.05	电脑对教育的影响	桥的共振	自尊的研究
03.07	奥运火炬的演变	海湾的污染问题	博物馆与主题公园
03.14	莫扎特音乐效果研究	关于考古	小语种的消失
03.21	辨别说谎	公司挖墙脚的影响	雪崩
04.04	市场营销	电子书	水下运动
04.18	可饮用水	气味与记忆	天体形成
04.25	竹子	电视上瘾	葡萄柚苦味的好处
04.30	听力障碍儿童教育	航海日志与气候变迁	弹性工作制
05.09	公园	乌鸦和工具	巧克力
05.16	澳洲生态旅游	香水制造	电子学习
05.21	澳洲甘蔗制糖	加拿大西部拓荒	美国地质学家
05.30	交通工具	香味和嗅觉	简明英语
06.11	建造城堡	过山车	获胜的决心
06.13	澳洲古尸	合成纤维	记忆竞赛
06.20	玻璃制造	海底古城发掘	梦的解析
06.27	欧洲交通系统	澳洲鹦鹉	伏尼契手稿

07.04	恐龙研究	树冠研究	广告
07.11	二氧化碳与能源	两种蚂蚁	读心术
07.23	计时的历史	珊瑚礁	性格与长相
07.25	英国工业革命	管理学发展	化学发展
08.08	新西兰海藻	蚂蚁教学	大航海家
08.13	选择与幸福感	汽车发展	蚂蚁自然队列
08.22	珍珠分类研究	记忆与年龄	大象交流方式
08.29	磁铁医疗	哺乳动物灭绝	婴儿理解能力研究
09.05	儿童教育发展	意大利疟疾	海滩石油污染
09.12	动物自疗	古代贸易	小班教学
09.17	飞机与环境	松树	广告始祖
09.26	学习历史作用	小冰期	神经美容
10.08	植物气味	图书馆	医药包装
10.10	生态旅游业	种植净水	冰川融化
10.24	大海能源	父母参与学校教育	声音制造业发展
10.31	蓝脚鲣鸟	复杂计算	英国电影院
11.07	桥梁诊断	人类的感官	运动和兴奋
11.14	茶的历史和发展	叶绿素	老年痴呆症研究
11.19	好莱坞大片展览馆	冰川时期	营销信息系统
11.21	实用行动	美国航空管制	物种进化的可逆性
12.03	水过滤	连锁超市	莫尔斯电码
12.05	航海计时器的发明	公司人才	创造性思维研究
12.12	海洋声波探测	鳄鱼	电报发明
12.19	经理角色	寻找外星人	幸福来源

2010年全年中国考区雅思考试阅读文章目录

考试日期	Passage 1	Passage 2	Passage 3
01.09	提炼饮用水	麻鸦回归	如何面对危机
01.14	人脸识别	壮观的土星	销售环保车辆
01.23	森林破坏与猩猩生存	全球变暖与动物影响	人类语言的发展
01.30	测谎仪	左右手和语言的关系	沙丘
02.06	噪音的影响	厄尔尼诺现象	远程作业
02.11	智力测试	手势	海洋密度
02.20	南非种族发展史	管理学之父	符号与图案的研究
02.27	奥运火炬的发展	小提琴制作	儿童顺从与成长
03.06	竹子	儿童读物的发展史	滑石粉
03.18	生态旅游	文化与猩猩	科技与发展
03.20	幸福的来源	指纹与名画	走路与健康
03.27	广告与儿童食品	苏梅克—列维彗星撞木星	天赋
04.10	清洁剂背后的公司发展	虚假广告与法律纠纷	性格与人际关系
04.15	市场的新概念	符号与性格研究	洞穴艺术
04.17	豌豆的研发	影响儿童成长的因素	嗅觉
04.24	噪音对孩子的影响	郁金香的货币作用	科学中的偶然性
05.08	孩子童年的今昔对比	气候变化与经济差异	语言研究
05.15	老龄员工	英国村庄的变迁	澳洲动物的灭绝

05.20	新植物能源	动物的冬眠	科技发展的负面影响
05.29	水獭	人类的识路机能	英国建筑风格的变迁
06.05	工程师布鲁内尔	海湾污染	科幻小说
06.17	气候与旅游业	汽车生产	北极地区的生态
06.19	人口密度与人口拥挤	抗干扰电子系统	早期人类航海迁徙
06.26	考拉	桥的共振	科学交流
07.10	龙涎香	食物对学生的影响	药物治疗
07.15	印度深井	立体农业	短信互动
07.17	非洲农业	讲故事	石油资源的前景
07.31	乐观与健康	鸟类迁徙	科学不均衡发展
08.05	吉尔伯特与磁学	量化研究	科幻电影
08.14	有机农业与传统农业	化石数据库	解密记忆力
08.21	午休对工作的益处	小鸟孵化	网上学习
08.28	一种"死灰复燃"的草	研究大猩猩	多任务对大脑的影响
09.04	笑的起源	迷失之城	环保设计
09.11	恐龙足迹	电子书	星体间的吸引力
09.16	植物命名	冰川	音乐
09.25	一种鸟的研究	看电视对人的影响	电脑对纸张的冲击
10.09	电脑与教学	面部复原	打哈欠
10.14	顺势疗法	海底探测船	语言研究
10.23	新手与老手	南极洲与全球气候	现代科技与历史教学
10.30	文身	欧洲高温	亚洲的卫星技术
11.04	不同国家的主食	原始社会的灭绝	潮汐发电
11.06	人工抗旱设施	电子书与传统书	儿童的学习能力
11.20	托马斯·杨	儿童意识的形成	消费现象的分析
11.27	同声传译	生物多样性	面部表情
12.04	海牛	双胞胎研究	电子产品对飞机的干扰
12.11	青春期研究	洪水治理	昆虫与科技
12.16	机器人	智力研究	恐龙研究
12.18	交通阻塞	企业与社会的关系	温室大棚效应

2011年全年中国考区雅思考试阅读文章目录

考试日期	Passage 1	Passage 2	Passage 3
01.08	香蕉	英国海岸线考古	旅行游记
01.15	收音机制作	动物自疗	生物钟
01.22	珊瑚鱼	语言的传播	火星探险
01.27	欧洲印刷术	嗅觉	儿童的性格
02.12	新交通系统	新西兰水产养殖业	研制新型药物的危险
02.17	古人记事	日本陶艺	合作
02.19	澳大利亚海滨	欧洲女子教育	欧洲交通
02.26	农村旅游	摄影与艺术家	盐碱化
03.05	生化产品	塔斯马尼亚虎	营销劝导
03.10	美国肥胖	航海发展史	如何教育儿童
03.12	农业杀虫剂	太阳能	做决定的研究
03.19	大脑体操（稍难）	数字认知	口译

04.02	工作与家庭	民间环境气候观察	解密记忆力
04.16	反刍动物	绘画与铸造	新能源汽车
04.30	诺贝尔	蜜蜂	公司营销策略
05.07	种子采集	工作压力	教育方法的研究
05.14	提炼饮用水	权利与空间	太空探索先驱号
05.19	无标题	石碳酸球	声音与数字的色彩
05.28	新概念市场	肥胖成因	火星
06.04	噪音对儿童的影响	图书馆	早期人类航海迁徙
06.11	茶的历史与发展	水过滤	多任务执行
06.23	声波测定海洋及其作用	蚂蚁生物防虫	国际公司的外语策略
07.09	竹子	儿童文学	科技对学术的重要性
07.16	生态旅行	垃圾回收	博物馆主题公园
07.28	城堡建设	加拿大移民历史	新西兰海平面上升
07.30	幸福感和选择	荷兰郁金香	葡萄柚苦味的好处
08.13	澳大利亚甘蔗业	猛犸象的灭绝	英国农村政策
08.20	邦戴海滩	澳大利亚能源和环保	大陆板块漂移说
09.03	模仿和设计	松树	镜子心理现象
09.15	动物行为心理学	气候变化对动物的影响	涂鸦争议
9.17	鹦鹉学舌	左撇子研究	语言起源
09.24	博物馆展览	欧洲家庭教育	音乐天赋
10.08	噪音	机器人	符号语言
10.20	大脑训练	大马哈鱼	噪音和工作表现之间的关系
10.26	创新研究	过山车历史	儿童文学
11.05	航空与环境	意大利疟疾	错误与商业创新
11.17	示例学习法	动画片发展	脸部识别
11.26	加州森林大火	艺术家指纹	创新与市场
12.01	澳大利亚羊	叶子变色	预言家
12.03	桥梁建设	语言发展	市场管理系统
12.10	历史研究的意义	鸟类的智力	海洋潮汐发电
12.17	国家的发展文化	涂鸦争议	对天才的看法

2012年全年中国考区雅思考试阅读文章目录

考试日期	Passage 1	Passage 2	Passage 3
01.07	动物自疗	管理学之父	网络信息存储
01.12	测谎仪	学术道德	雪崩
01.14	管理者的角色与功能	远古电脑	旅游拍照的影响
02.04	奥运火炬演变发展	深海采矿	阅读方式探讨
02.09	戏剧的发展	澳大利亚鹦鹉	感知与大脑
02.18	植物气味对生物的影响	气候变暖	交流与文化
02.25	超市起源	植物水净化系统	电视游戏的好处
03.08	麻鸦回归	商业广告	飓风研究
03.10	航海导航器材发展史	美国境内野狗	油画与电影的联系
03.17	人脸识别和记忆	节能的房屋	环保材料PLA
03.31	磁疗	亚历山大城考古	生物进化论
04.12	恐龙足迹	纸币发展	年轻人当父母

04.14	澳洲古人	地图册	读写技能
04.21	乡村小型交通工具	肌肉萎缩	英国森林破坏
04.28	商业广告	蚂蚁和真菌	金星凌日
05.10	古代钱币	鸟类定向	美国人工作强度
05.12	维京航海	动物冬眠	语言研究
05.19	Tull发明犁地机	小提琴制作	伏尼契手稿
05.26	夏威夷海岛考古	企业社会责任	双语儿童
06.09	珊瑚鱼	减肥研究	莫尔斯电码
06.14	动物交流	古头骨重建	体育运动发展
06.16	撒哈拉沙漠历史	摄影与艺术家	现代心理进化
06.30	中国古代战车	猩猩研究	莱斯特的新剧院
07.07	媒体影响儿童交流	日本陶器	福特混合动力车
07.12	电报发明	手势研究	动物感知自然灾害
07.21	天才学者	儿童课堂行为	苏联工作制
07.28	新西兰渔业	人类贸易天性	幸福来源
08.04	诺贝尔奖	猛犸象	雇员激励
08.11	厄尔尼诺现象	汽车发展	失乐症（Amusia）
08.25	洪水	涂鸦争议	巧克力的历史
09.01	机器人发展	化石数据库	儿童错误认知
09.06	吉尔伯特和磁场	儿童教育	艺术培训
09.15	农业肥料改革	科学与游戏	英国电影业
09.22	冰箱的历史	哈欠研究	简明英语
10.11	美国肥胖症	猴子研究	远程工作
10.13	农村旅游	生物钟	英语发音变化

2013年全年中国考区雅思考试阅读文章目录

考试日期	Passage 1	Passage 2	Passage3
01.05	儿童食品广告	海岸雕塑	滑石粉
01.10	关于豌豆和其他豆子繁殖的研究	Play和Game的区别	舌头味蕾感知味道
01.12	火对森林的好处	故事描述	Musicophilia书评
01.19	欧洲印刷术的历史	绘画艺术与工程铸造	水中加氢
02.02	猩猩研究	非洲农业	职员创新力
02.16	从新手到专家	鳄鱼的进化	音乐的起源和影响
02.23	青春期	博物馆	医学知识的来源
03.02	美国新能源	食物对非洲学生的影响	澳大利亚博物馆的改建
03.09	种种群落的发展	塔斯马尼亚虎	实验中的不确定性
03.14	大脑训练	新西兰男女生学习成绩分析	麋鹿灭绝
03.23	水獭	桥梁共振	营销劝导
04.06	收音机	厄尔尼诺和海鸟	流浪汉
04.13	考拉	南极气候	营销劝导
04.18	雨水回收系统	生物科技对人类发展的作用	化学的发展
04.27	橡胶简史	快乐的来源	古代钱币
05.11	一个企业产品分析	嗅觉和回忆	翻译口译
05.16	一个建筑	仿生机器人	气味的记忆研究

05.18	驾驶中接电话的影响	蚂蚁和真菌	选择与幸福
05.25	问卷调查	动物智力	药品包装
06.06	欧洲人开发新大陆	管理学之父	恐惧研究
06.08	鸟类迁徙	消费者对新产品不感冒的各种研究	室内做饭产生的污染
06.15	女性在工程科技上的研究	语言家族的发展和传播	运动员和普通人的成功
06.22	动物外貌皮毛的变异	18世纪女性学术贡献	Facebook等对社会的影响
07.06	网购	保护麻鸦	人类语言进化
07.13	海底鱼类与红光	美国电影和电影院发展史	科技带来的弊端
07.18	关于美国西部土地沙漠	鸟蛋的孵化	一些社会和文明的衰落原因
07.27	澳洲的岛屿	卖家分析买家的方法	网络虚拟教育
08.03	海底热源	广告与儿童	药物风险控制
08.17	仿生机器人	美国的三个图书馆	儿童对图像与实物的感知
08.24	黄蜂	有机农业和传统农业	恒星和行星
08.29	测谎仪	迷失之城	石油资源的衰落
09.07	海洋研究	广告对孩子的影响	记忆力研究
09.12	竹子	电视上瘾	一个部落的特殊语言体系
09.21	昆虫自我保护	伦敦雾霾	揭穿谎言的研究
09.28	全球变暖	水源进化	香港教育竞争培训计划
10.10	澳洲制粮业	遗迹考古	新西兰蜥蜴
10.12	香蕉	新西兰青蛙	欧洲陆路运输
10.19	文学批判	午休	纳米技术
10.26	动物学习机制	英格兰村庄布局特点	人文学科在医学中的运用
11.09	公园的发展	英国高温	对美的认知
11.16	霸王龙	英国话剧的发展	小班教学
11.21	理者角色和功能	蜘蛛丝做衣服	揭秘记忆力
11.30	人口密度和拥挤	生物多样性	镜子对任何动物的影响
12.07	印度深井	出生顺序导致孩子差异	文学和作者所处环境的关系
12.12	保护大猩猩	音乐对大脑的影响	大学排名与学术研究
12.14	磁疗的发展	明星员工	如何防止燃料燃烧污染
12.21	蓝脚鸟	古埃及运河	能量和时间管理

2014年全年中国考区雅思考试阅读文章目录

考试日期	Passage 1	Passage 2	Passage 3
01.09	社会市场学	英国儿童缺乏锻炼	火星地貌
01.11	埋藏在地下的答案	药物官司	联觉
01.18	美国人的工作时间	古希腊钱币	鸟类迁徙
01.25	测谎技术的使用	气候与财富	洞穴艺术
02.01	原始人的文字	日本陶艺	N/A
02.13	新型交通系统	科学家北极探险	画像与性格
02.15	珍珠的种类、制作和历史	人类五感	福尔摩斯
02.22	工程师——布鲁内尔	海湾污染	新西兰少年文学家
03.01	硬蹄草食动物——牛科动物	解决洪都拉斯农业问题的新方法	团队合作心理
03.08	它们自己的思维	制造业的创新——精益生产	科学的传授
03.13	动物自疗	自然爱好者	格林童话

03.15	中国古代战车	黑猩猩的研究	莱斯特的新剧院
04.05	海水净化系统	植物的抗争	20世纪30年代至50年代新西兰纺织
04.12	欧洲草药的发展	冰川解决淡水问题	音乐——我们共同的语言
04.24	试验项目与农业旅游	摄影	海水变化与盐分
04.26	脚踏水泵灌溉	自由玩耍	澳大利亚博物馆的改造：博物馆自身形象与艺术
05.10	猛犸象之死	公共管理理论的发展	音乐的力量
05.15	如何应对大自然的不确定性	企业社会责任	文化与交流
05.17	了不起的Waltkin Tench	处理太空图片	天赋与练习
05.24	亚马逊热带雨林里被掩埋的城市	体重那些事儿	有关多任务处理能力的讨论
06.07	菲什本宫殿	猛犸象之死	商业中的意外之喜
06.19	珍妮纺纱机	坚持	艺术
06.21	新西兰林业	面部复原术	大脑与年龄
06.28	土豆在欧洲的历史	小提琴的制作	北极的地理现象
07.10	食品进口	战胜意大利的疟疾	澳大利亚动物的灭绝
07.12	食品的味道	海边雕塑	新西兰的气候变暖问题
07.19	游戏与儿童	蚂蚁的领导者	氟对牙齿的好处
07.26	塑料	智力与天赋	会跑的植物
08.02	铅笔的历史	澳大利亚的鹦鹉	儿童文学
08.09	新西兰的路	艺术影响	听觉和视觉
08.16	新材料	年龄与记忆力的关系	科技对发达和发展中国家的影响
08.21	咖啡馆	全球变暖对动物的影响	员工激励
09.04	超市起源	植物净水	拯救濒危动植物
09.06	仿生工程	马戏团重生	互动合作
09.20	历史的益处	语言对商业的影响	社交媒体对人孤独的影响
09.27	骨头鉴定	纸币	超市顾客研究
10.02	广告设计	机器人与儿童	复活岛上的雕塑
10.11	新西兰珊瑚鱼	聪明的孩子	亚斯兰蒂斯考古
10.18	本科生戏剧学习	饮食的重要性	大蜥蜴——过去与未来
10.25	英国北极科考船	左撇子与右撇子	农业环保用品
11.01	古希腊硬币	西非	科幻小说
11.08	野马的保护和重归自然	南极对全球气候的影响	达尔文进化论在企业管理中的应用
11.13	新西兰本土鱼类	加拿大西部扩张历史	人们对工作时间的态度
11.22	收音机发展过程	传统建筑与现代建筑	留学对于创造力的影响
12.04	南非部落的演变	艺术和工程	新西兰对儿童进行的健康检查
12.06	墙纸	双胞胎基因	涂鸦争议
12.13	笑的起源	松树	文学批判
12.20	澳洲史前人	冬眠	集体智慧

附录3　答疑录

Student：老师，我有《真经1–4》。我想知道《真经5》跟前面的几本真经有什么不同？

Harvey：有很大不同。《真经5》其实不是《真经4》的续集，而是包含了《真经1—4》的精华总结、近年常考新文章、有典型价值的雅思阅读真题和真题考点词汇。它其实是《雅思阅读真经》系列的大成终极版本，这本书的背后融汇了全部真题题库及真题考点、考试机经和我们多年的雅思培训经验。

Student：我最关心《真经5》中的题目是真题吗？

Harvey：敏感话题。你很有可能在考场上碰到完全一样的题目。也有可能碰到题目有区别，但考点词和答案是一样的。比如：《真经5》中"印度深井"一文有一道题，考点是resemble一词。在《剑桥4》、《剑桥7》和《剑桥8》的阅读中都考到这个词。真题的考法是：原文中出现be similar to, look like, like，题目中出现resemble，或让考生选出这个词。《真经5》里所有题目考点都和真题考点完全一致。我认为这也是《真经5》最大的价值之一。

Student：《真经5》中的文章是考试原文吗？

Harvey：敏感话题。你很有可能在考场上碰到完全一样的文章。

Student：《雅思阅读真经》从什么时候使用？

Harvey：我希望能伴随你备考和考试之后的很长一段时间。真经其实是一种教学理念和体系，不仅能够提高你的雅思成绩，而且可以改善你的学习效率和质量。《真经5》的设计既适合刚开始备考的考生，循序渐进地熟练各种题型、各种题材和剑桥习惯的文章表述形式；也适合做完《剑桥雅思》系列后考前冲刺，强化自己的薄弱题型和熟悉题库机经，考前预测用。清华大学、北京理工大学、中央财经大学、北京师范大学的HND和SQA等国际项目我已经把《真经5》作为雅思基础阅读课程的指定教材。

Student：Harvey，三神器和《剑桥雅思》系列如何配合使用，现在我阅读5分。

Harvey：对于基础薄弱的学员，建议先学习《真经5》，然后学习《雅思阅读真经总纲》，掌握题型技巧和命题思路。最后再用《剑桥雅思》系列做模考，每做完一套《剑桥雅思》的题目要配合《剑桥雅思词汇真经》去背单词，并检查自己是否完全发现了命题者的考点词设计。

Student：Harvey，《真经5》咋个用，做题就行吗？

Harvey：先做题并纠错，再精读文章，结合文章背核心词汇，最后要熟记同义考点词。

Student：雅思阅读要背的单词太多了，我似乎时间不够了，有什么好办法吗？

Harvey：没时间了就直接背真题考点词。请参考《真经5》每篇文章后面的同义词考点。还推荐背《剑桥雅思词汇真经》中题目和原文对应的同义考点词列表。

Student：雅思阅读题量太大了，别的考试阅读似乎没有这么费劲？

Harvey：那肯定是阅读方法错了，或对雅思阅读的考试设计目的不理解。我们现在生活在信息时代，生存能力是需要在信息的海洋里短时间内找到自己想要的信息，并准确理解想要的信息。无关信息要忽视。建议学习《雅思阅读真经总纲》中的雅思阅读正确方法——文章一遍读完，所有题目做完。

Student：Harvey呀，我还有3个月考试，阅读想提高2分，有可能吗？

Harvey：不用质疑。阅读真题、题型技巧、考点词汇三名剑结合，加上《剑桥雅思》系列模考学习，从4分到7分要3个月；从6分到8分两个月以内就可以，其实6分学员的词汇量足够支持他考到7分以上，省下了许多背单词的时间。

Student：老师，我是二战，剑桥真题我都做过了，是不是只要做真经就可以了？

Harvey：是的。但仍然推荐去书店翻翻《雅思阅读真经总纲》，以确保你的阅读方法和解题思路是正确的。如果和你现在的做题方法一致，则不用购买。

Student：雅思阅读答案有书写要求吗？

Harvey：填单词的题除专有名词外无大小写要求。TRUE/FALSE/NOT GIVEN题答案可简写成T/F/NG。YES/NO/NOT GIVEN可写成Y/N/NG。但两者不可混淆，切记看清题目要求。

Student：老师，听说读写四门是同时复习么？

Harvey：听说并进，读写互通。听说是声音信号，读写是文字信号；听读是信息输入，说写是信息输出。就复习备考来说，一定先输入正确的信息，才能随后输出正确的。听力阅读是基础，写作口语是高级。所以，有效的复习不是今天我想练什么练什么，做完听力做阅读，练完口语练听力，这些安排都是低效的。建议每周一三五先练听力，下一个小时再练口语，把刚听到的短语和句型说出来；而二四六先阅读再写作，写作时你可以把刚才阅读文章中精彩的句型表达尝试运用起来。周日运动锻炼身体，以应对雅思考试的体力要求。

Student：真经中的同义词考点词汇和"说文解字"是怎么搭配的？

Harvey："说文解字"是我推广的一种背单词方法：说文化、讲文章、解记忆、解用法，其实是一种读写并进的概念，能够让考生充分利用剑桥本身题目内容提高自己的语言能力。同义词考点词汇是说文解字法的一种形式。考试时间紧张的考生直接背雅思真题同义词考点。

Student：背单词有什么好办法吗？

Harvey：正确的方法+足够的努力。请听我的雅思学习免费讲座（我微博里会有说明）。

Student：我的阅读时间不够，读不快怎么办？

Harvey：如果时间不够，需要有一些取舍；如果速度不快，需要熟悉词汇并且采用正确的阅读方法。所以要熟悉真经这种训练体系。

Student：我读不懂怎么办？

Harvey：这也就是真经的价值和训练意义。在你读完整个真题题库的精选版之后，还会有你读不懂的内容吗？

Student：雅思虐我已千遍，我待雅思如初恋。刘老师，我怎么办？

Harvey：请听我的雅思听说读写四大免费公开讲座。

Student：Harvey，听那讲座有用么？

Harvey：Francis-张:老师生日快乐啊。也就在听了你的阅读讲课后，我的阅读练习从6分直接稳定在7.5了，最好的一次就错两个，看来不是我单词不够，水平有限，而是方法有问题。最近又在早就您的15句，发现原来一直是错误的方法练习，难怪得了5.5。模板真是太有用了。太感谢了。(10月28日 11:01)
评论 我 的微博："在我37岁高龄之际，送给全国考生"

@戴钢盔的小熊猫:请把音频传给需要的人😁 //@戴钢盔的小熊猫:老师，我想说太太太感谢你了！！！我在9月底YY上听过你的一节阅读课，获益匪浅，阅读是6.5水平，考试有一篇没做完还考了7.5，总算可以跟雅思分手了，老师太感谢你了！！！ 🔟 (10月23日 22:07)
评论 我 的微博："回复@戴钢盔的小熊猫:请把音频传..."

柠檬纪香凯蒂宝:阅读真经那一课真心强大威武不解释啊～没有听的孩纸们一定要听！！！！绝对赛过其他机构啊...艾玛，强调一下，我不是水军。。。(10月16日 21:16)
评论 我 的微博："因为11月后会全国巡讲，近期我在..."

Student：哪里能上你的课？我不在北京。

Harvey：网上。贵学教育网校：http://school.guixue.com

附录4　剑桥大学雅思访问记

（该文获雅思官方剑桥雅思考察征文一等奖）

公元2011年9月25日，有幸参加由英国使馆文化教育处BC（British Council）主办的中国雅思教师英国访问之旅。同行者中国各大英语培训机构教师共十二人，BC领队二人，记者一人，风风火火，飞赴英伦。

次日首站，拜访BC伦敦总部。各官员粉墨登场亮相，重头戏为Sam McCarter的雅思演讲。他是雅思培训宗师级人物，资深雅思考官，毕生致力于英语教学研究，十几年精修拉丁语，代表BC周游世界各国培训雅思教师，至今仍屹立于英国雅思教学一线，面授、远程教学、出版专著。

老爷子红光满面，精神矍铄。讲起话来则春风化雨，绵绵泊泊，常作拈花微笑，俨然婉约派教学代表。我深知此类演讲者的可怕，信心强大，内功深厚，不疾不徐，仅靠内容的知识性、面目的生动和语调的抑扬顿挫，就使听者跌宕起伏、如痴如醉。比在讲台上声嘶力竭、挥汗如雨、上蹿下跳的激情派教师要持久，要可怕得多。果然，原定上午给他的时间不够，只讲完了雅思的听力和阅读，于是午餐后，继续写作和口语。

如是我闻：

"学习任何一门语言，最重要的是名词和动词的理解和运用。"

"雅思写作，最难的是写出总结；雅思口语，最难的是说出细节。"

诸如此类的如珠妙语是基于Sam的精深学术功底和丰富的全球教学经验，他对各行各业、世界各国雅思考生的不同问题如数家珍，鲜活的教学案例佐证信手拈来。Sam在演讲中诠释了一种高超的教学境界：重剑无锋，大巧不工。

当对一门技能通透理解后，就会做到庖丁解牛、举重若轻；眼花缭乱的剑招都是由刺、砍、点、架等简单的基本动作组成；纷繁复杂的雅思教学法其实也可以很简化。

Sam的演讲也留给我们一个忧虑。他认为：听说读写四项技能是互通的，是integrated完整的，不可separated分拆。每堂课应该按照技能逻辑或话题来组织（后来我们在观摩英国几所知名语言学校的雅思课程也印证了这一点）。其实英、美、澳等国的雅思培训课程都是如此。而我们中国的雅思培训课程却另辟蹊径，将听说读写四门课分拆开来，由四位不同的教师授课，创全球英语培训之先河。分拆的好处是对教师的要求不高，只需专研一门课程；学生则感觉针对性强，每门课的考试技巧翔实。但弊端是明显的：听力教师不会在课上花时间让学生把听到的对话进行角色扮演口语练习，阅读教师也只关心学员能否理解一个复杂句型，而不会要求或引导学员在写作中正确使用。长此以往，学员和教师都会孤立看待这四项技能，而非将英语看做一项综合的交流技能来培养。

两天后，这种担忧得到证实。BC通过全英学联邀请了伦敦周边各所大学在读的十几位中国学生和我们教师团进行了一次座谈。绝大多数学生参加过国内的雅思培训班，有的还在英国参加过雅思培训。这次座谈实为市场调研中的focus group，追踪国内雅思培训机构的客户（学员）的售后满意度。遗憾的是满意度不高，60%左右。在长达两小时的交流中，学员们表达了一个思想：在国内学雅思是为了通过考试，在英国学雅思是为了表达交流。

鉴于雅思考试题目完全取材于留学生的真实生活，结论就很明显而警醒：（1）中国雅思教师应该强调考题知识点在将来留学生活中的实际运用，而不仅仅是让学生用技巧将题做对；（2）国内的分拆式雅思课程体系需要改革。

这次座谈很可能成为中国英语培训模式升级的一个trigger，在此感谢BC和全英学联。

接下来的行程中，参观了两种风格迥异的语言培训机构，位于伦敦市中区的威斯敏斯特大学语言中心和IH（International House）语言学校，以及位于市郊的温布尔登英语学校WSE（Wimbledon School of English）。我们有幸走进了他们的教室，旁听雅思课程，与校长、教师、学生们座谈，受益匪浅，真心致谢！个人感觉在市中心的学校学习压力大，节奏快，喧嚣繁华，生活多彩；在郊区的WSE学习很放松，学校就像一个大家庭，课间教师学员一同采菊篱下，看那风景如画。要出国读语言的同学们可根据自己的性格喜好选择，但不论是现代派还是田园派学校，大家都要留意该语言学校是否取得了BC的授权认证。以上三所学校都获此认证，BC每年派inspector巡视，听课，打分，确保该学校的雅思教学质量。

最后一站，访问剑桥大学ESOL总部。ESOL考试中心是世界著名的教育测评机构和语言能力评估机构剑桥大学考试委员会（Cambridge Assessment）的直属部门，也是雅思考试的命题机构。雅思考试设计的最高学术团队由14位博士组成，其中一位Dr Andy Blackhurst热情接待了我们一行，并详尽介绍了雅思考试的设计流程，题目的测试原理。最后，我们被秘密带到了一个代号为DC10的地方，离ESOL大概15分钟车程，一栋不起眼的青灰色建筑，没有路牌指示，大门处没有标识。进入之后，手机相机随身小包等统统收缴，一人套一件黄色荧光安全背心，走过昏暗狭窄的通道，穿过厚重的安全门，放眼望去，一个巨型仓库，许多人忙忙碌碌。这里就是全球雅思考卷印刷、储存、派发的物流中心。当被告知我们是史上第一批进入此地参观的中国人时，不禁心潮激荡。

此次英国之旅的另一大所得，是收获了一群志同道合的朋友。中国天南海北各大英语培训机构的精英们藉此风云聚会，思想碰撞。商务考察之余，伦敦眼的远眺，康桥上的挥手，大英博物馆里的流连，温莎城堡中的赞叹，China Town 的欢聚，Bicester Village的血拼，这是属于我们共同的记忆。

衷心感谢主办方BC，James Shipton先生、鞠琳琳女士和邱爽女士。致谢一路同行的朋友们。

友情长青，作文记之。

附录5 口碑推荐："绝世好书"《雅思写作真经总纲》

@雅思教父刘洪波 我是来还愿的！@5月10那场，写作提了一分！！（请不要问我为什么口语掉了一分TT感冒鼻子堵了，脑子也堵了...)因为因为时间紧任务重只用了写作总纲，两个字评价：好书！四个字评价：绝世好书！从小到大一直很头疼作文，写作总纲简直就是救命稻草般的存在！仅一周的备考时间！但是距离我dream school的要求还是差一点TT 请问教主我这个成绩复议写作和口语成功的几率大不大？各提0.5就行TT...

听力	阅读	写作	口语	总成绩
8.5	8.5	6.5	6.5	7.5

听力	阅读	写作	口语	总成绩
8.5	8.5	5.5	7.5	7.5

真经派写作成绩单 (承诺完全真实)

//@计算机程序设计的艺术:http://weibo.com/1069290177/zu4zGr6gO 多亏看了刘老师的《最简化》全用上去了。我不是托哈，我不是做广告的

@计算机程序设计的艺术 ★
分享图片 用句数说话。4.27. 中国大陆出彩试卷，出彩分数。写作8.5口语8 @雅思教父刘洪波 @波比-孤哥 @颜炜 @程琳-贵学

↑ 收起 | 查看大图 | 向左转 | 向右转

8.5

总成绩	听力	阅读	写作	口语
8	7.5	7	8.5	8

5月13日 12:12 来自Weico Android   (1) | 转发(27) | 评论(20)

嗯，谢啦。//@猫村矿工: 回复@雅思教父刘洪波: 绝对要推荐的！这次准备了两周，就看了最简化写作，教主的书内容很精练，练了几篇积累了观点和句型，就拿到7.5。不像上次看了整一个月那个什么X天突破，却考了6。。。@雅思教父刘洪波:哇，感谢教主回复，受宠若惊。一直都是看您的教材复习，太棒了

@猫村矿工 ★
八年了，终于要说分手了！三次烤鸭终于拿到四个7。L/R/W/S: 05年10月A类7.5/7.5/7/6，总分7，拿到28。09年8月A类8/9/6/6，总分7.5，拿到29。13年3月23号G类8.5/7.5/7.5/7，总分7.5，拿到30.5。感谢@人人网雅思哥 和@墨尔本无忧雅思培训学校 的精彩口语预测！感谢刘桥雅思8和9，以及刘洪波最简化写作！

↑ 收起 | 查看大图 | 向左转 | 向右转

7.5

Test Centre Number: AU166
Test Date: 23/03/2013

Listening	Reading	Writing	Speaking	Overall
8.5	7.5	7.5	7.0	

weibo.com/feifa9999

第6图 06:03 来自   (1) | 转发 | 评论

写作最高。不错。明显本门阅读真经没有修炼。@贵学教育 奖书一本，写作上7。

@毛蕉出没
分享图片 @雅思教父刘洪波 老师，说好的super留学呢？一个周末看最简化，6到7的变化！

↑ 收起 | 查看大图 | 向左转 | 向右转

7

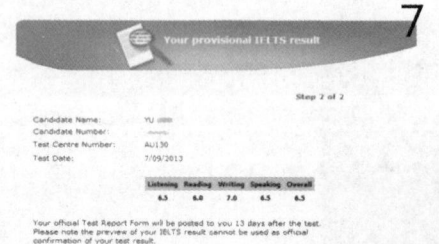

Your provisional IELTS result

Step 2 of 2

Candidate Name: YU
Candidate Number:
Test Centre Number: AU130
Test Date: 7/09/2013

Listening	Reading	Writing	Speaking	Overall
6.5	6.5	7	6.5	6.5

Your official Test Report Form will be posted to you 13 days after the test.
Please note the preview of your IELTS result cannot be used as official
confirmation of your test result.

二狗子雅思要冲7-_- ★
额= =成绩出来了。。有喜有悲，感谢@雅思教父刘洪波 教主的最简化写作，我是在去考试的路上看的书--说实话没看完，只是让自己理解了十五句的无敌句式，作文自己一篇也没有练过（抱头跑），作文就得到了6.5的好成绩，谢谢谢谢。PS。。。那什么来拯救我的听力！！！我的阅读怎么这个样子了--教主求助

↑ 收起 | 查看大图 | 向左转 | 向右转

5 ➚ 6.5

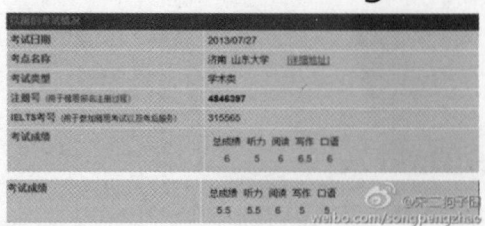

考试日期	2013/07/27
考点名称	济南 山东大学
考试类型	学术类
注册号	4846397
IELTS考试	315565
考试成绩	总成绩 听力 阅读 写作 口语 6 6.5
考试成绩	总成绩 听力 阅读 写作 口语 5.5 5 5 6

weibo.com/songpengtac

如果你写一个写作8.5分的学习心得呢，我就赠书一本。

@在大tse翻滚的疯子
#随手拍#@雅思教父刘洪波 雅思写作领进门老师！阅读高分老师！（第一次上了老师的课我阅读

↑ 收起 | 查看大图 | 向左转 | 向右转

8.5

Results

Listening: 7.5   Listening: 9.0
Reading: 7.0   Reading:
Writing: 7.0   Writing: 8.5
Speaking: 7.0   Speaking
Overall: 7.0   **Overall: 7.5**

@Mr乐乐乐不羊
@刘洪波-贵学 太感谢教主了！之前写作一直5.5，中断两年再考，提前一周翻了一遍《最简化》考出来7分!真是高兴疯了！移民澳洲前途光明啊!! 膜拜膜拜!!

↑ 收起 | 查看大图 | 向左转 | 向右转

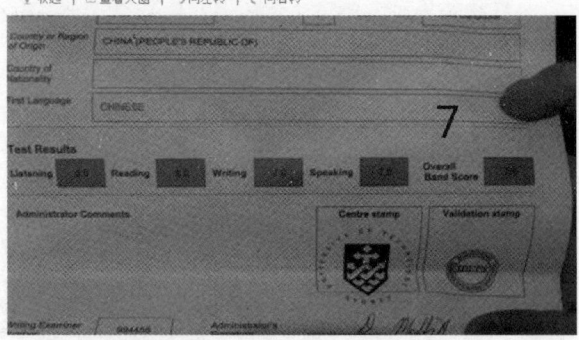

7

【寻人领奖】7.13日真经派状元终于在微信中现身了！写作从5.5到7，阅读从7.5到9，再说一次：本门主要靠众弟子高分口碑传播，严禁在我微信中自银自乐！这是谁？@贵学教育颁奖《留学Super之路》一本，留下心得，造福后人。

↑ 收起 | 查看大图 | 向左转 | 向右转

5.5 ➚ 7

papastudy ✎
刘老师，赞一个！我就是看了你的书写作从五点五到七，阅读七点五到九。

//@雅思教父刘洪波:希望你写个学习的方法，我推荐给其他4分的考生。因为我体会不到写不出来

@洛沫沙僧撒撒Darling ★
@雅思教父刘洪波 感谢最简化!! 考前背了好多书里的东西~~其他科目都是6分左右~这一门吓到我了~~~~大幅度大跨越~~~!! 感谢教主!!

↑ 收起 | 查看大图 | 向左转 | 向右转

4 ➚ 6.5

写作
6.5
2 2
4

图书在版编目 (CIP) 数据

雅思阅读真经5：机考笔试综合版 ／ 刘洪波编著.—3版.—北京：中国人民大学出版社，2016.9

ISBN 978-7-300-23346-8

Ⅰ．①雅…　Ⅱ．①刘…　Ⅲ．①IELTS-阅读教学-自学参考资料　Ⅳ．①H319.4

中国版本图书馆CIP数据核字（2016）第212824号

雅思阅读真经5（机考笔试综合版）

刘洪波　编著

Yasi Yuedu Zhenjing 5（Jikao Bishi Zongheban）

出版发行	中国人民大学出版社	
社　　址	北京中关村大街31号	邮政编码　100080
电　　话	010-62511242（总编室）	010-62511770（质管部）
	010-82501766（邮购部）	010-62514148（门市部）
	010-62515195（发行公司）	010-62515275（盗版举报）
网　　址	http://www.crup.com.cn	
	http://www.1kao.com.cn（中国1考网）	
经　　销	新华书店	
印　　刷	北京易丰印捷科技股份有限公司	
规　　格	185mm×260mm　16开本	版　次　2012年12月第1版
		2016年9月第3版
印　　张	26.25	印　次　2017年1月第4次印刷
字　　数	663 000	定　价　59.99元